# MODELS

# OF

# TEACHING

Bruce Joyce *and* Marsha Weil

*Columbia University Teachers College*

PRENTICE-HALL, INC., ENGLEWOOD CLIFFS, NEW JERSEY

*To Our Students and Colleagues at Teachers College*

ISBN: 13–586065–2

Library of Congress Catalog Card Number: 72–153987

Printed in the United States of America

10  9  8  7  6  5  4

PRENTICE-HALL INTERNATIONAL, INC., *London*
PRENTICE-HALL OF AUSTRALIA, PTY. LTD., *Sydney*
PRENTICE-HALL OF CANADA, LTD., *Toronto*
PRENTICE-HALL OF INDIA PRIVATE LIMITED, *New Delhi*
PRENTICE-HALL OF JAPAN, INC., *Tokyo*

# CONTENTS

## I

## Social Interaction

### as a

## Source of Models

### 27

# II
## Information Processing
### as a
## Source of Models
103

The noted Swiss psychologist, Jean Piaget, has
conducted extensive research for over 40 years
resulting in theories of intellectual development.
Several educators have developed models of teaching
built on Piaget's work, designed to increase the
rate and solidity of mental development, including
social relations and moral development. This chapter
analyzes several of these strategies.

# III

# The

# Personal Sources

## 205

From his studies of counseling and therapy,
Carl Rogers has developed a flexible model of
teaching emphasizing an environment which
encourages students to create their own environments
for learning.

Another therapist, Glasser, has also developed a
stance toward teaching—one which emphasizes
methods easily applicable in the classroom situation.

# IV

## Behavior Modification

### as a

### Source

267

# V

## Using Models

## of

## Teaching

295

Teaching is not just an "acting out" of life in
schools. School faculties and individual
teachers create life in school by models of teaching
they choose and create. The dialogue about the
alternatives is the fundamental business of
the educational profession.

# FOREWORD

*Models of Teaching* is an ambitious book. To some it will seem arrogantly and outrageously overreaching for it seeks the systematic exploration of interactions among educational purposes, pedagogical strategies, curricular designs and materials, and social and psychological theory. Even more ambitiously, it is not content to deal with particular and single exemplifications of such relationships, but designs, instead, to examine a diverse range of alternative patterns upon which teachers may model their behavior. To others, it will seem not at all overreaching, but a refreshing effort to describe teaching with the complexity and subtlety they intuitively know to be required. All will agree, however, that this book aims high.

*Models of Teaching* is a lively book written for the intellectually zestful and the temperamentally high-spirited. It is not likely to appeal to those who yearn for quick protection against classroom-induced anxieties and uncertainties. Indeed, it begins with the recognition that there is no royal freeway to pedagogical success, no painless solution to complex instructional problems, and no future in our persistent effort to describe "best teaching practice." Principles of teaching are not conceived as static tenets but as dynamically interactive with social and cognitive purpose, with the learning theory underlying procedures, with available support technology, and with the personal and intellectual characteristics of learning groups. What is emphasized is the wide range of options the teacher may adopt and adapt to his unique situation.

This is not at all to suggest that the reader is left with an inchoate maze of nebulously related variables which he is somehow expected to integrate in his own teaching practice. *Models of Teaching* indeed deals with models —structured, logically consistent, cohesive, and lucidly described alternative patterns of teaching. Furthermore, while each model is developed in its own theoretical terms, its attendant procedures are presented with all the specificity of detail the most practically-oriented teacher could desire.

*Models of Teaching* is a book for the present and for the future. Its authors suggest its major, but not exclusive, audience may be those preparing for initial teaching appointments, but I suspect that, unlike most textbooks, it won't quickly find its way into the second-hand book market. Inexperienced and experienced teachers will find it too valuable as a handbook, as a reference for frequent and continuing use, to part with it easily. Ordinary texts may be discarded after a summer or a semester; books which provide a framework and a stimulus for career-long learning are, unfortunately, rare. *Models of Teaching,* in my judgment, is a book for all seasons.

ROBERT J. SCHAEFER

# PREFACE

## *We Teach by Creating Environments for Children*

*Models of Teaching* was written from our conviction that, despite the fearsome troubles besetting education, there presently exists a really delightful and vigorous array of approaches to schooling which can be used to transform the world of childhood if only we will employ them. The purpose of this book is to identify for the teacher and curriculum-maker a range of models for teaching—approaches to creating environments for learning—and a way of thinking which can be used to analyze them, compare and contrast them, and decide what educational purposes they can serve.

Models for teaching can help a teacher build up his capacity to reach more children and create a richer and more diverse environment for them. They can help curriculum-makers plan learning centers and curriculums which offer to children a variety of educational alternatives. They can help materials makers create more interesting and effective instructional materials and learning sources. Most important, for the future, they may stimulate the development of new educational forms—the educational opportunities which will replace the schools of today.

In this book we describe models which represent four different "families" of approaches to teaching. Some of the models focus on the individual and the development of his unique personality. Some focus on the human group and represent ways of teaching which emphasize group energy, interpersonal skills, and social commitment. Others represent ways of teaching concepts, modes of inquiry from the disciplines, and methods for increasing intellectual capacity. Still others apply psychological models of operant conditioning to the teaching-learning process.

For the teacher we provide some advice on how to learn the various models based on our experiences in the Preservice Teacher Education Program at Teachers College, Columbia University. For curriculum and materials designers we include chapters on systematic planning using a variety of models of teaching. For both, we present a system for deciding what approaches to teaching are appropriate for what ends and how models can be selected to match the learning styles of children.

We believe that the world of education should be a pluralistic one—that children and adults alike should have a "cafeteria of alternatives" which stimulate their growth and nurture both their unique potential and their capacity to make common cause in the rejuvenation of our troubled society.

*New York*
*March, 1971*

BRUCE JOYCE
MARSHA WEIL

# AGAINST DOGMATISM

## *Alternative Sources of Reality*
## *In Teaching and Curriculum-Making*

We begin with some fairly typical teaching by three social studies teachers in three separate classrooms of a large metropolitan high school. All three teachers are working with sixteen-year-old students. Their classes are comparable, with a wide range of abilities and life experiences represented within each classroom. Their common task is to engage the students in the study of civil rights for black citizens in the United States. Emphasis is on voting rights and their exercise.

### THE GROUP INVESTIGATOR

As we observe the first classroom we find that the teacher has presented his class with the Civil Rights Commision's pamphlet, *Voting Rights in Mississippi*. The pamphlet contains a report by a federal commission which details, in cases and interviews, attempts to thwart black voting rights in Mississippi. The students are angered by what they are reading but their reactions vary, especially as they conjecture about the causes of the situation. The teacher is capitalizing on the differences in reaction and is organizing the students to explore their reactions, study how others feel, and engage in a cooperative inquiry into the whole area.

The teacher obviously enjoys teaching this way. He takes the discord among students seriously but is not bothered by it; rather, he seeks to use the involvement which is generated. "I teach through my relationship with the kids," he says. "We develop the relationship and then I confront them with puzzling situations that get them into significant study. The group interaction is the thing."

## THE STUDENT OF CASES

In the second classroom we find students studying a series of "cases" involving black voting rights. The teacher has purchased some of the case materials and assembled others himself. Altogether there are 12 cases, some focusing on constitutional provisions, amendments, and statutes, some centered on litigation, and some on drives to increase black participation through combinations of litigation, registration drives, and confrontation. For each case there is a set of original source documents. Working in groups, the students study the cases and report their findings, which are then discussed by the entire class.

This teacher is a good organizer. He likes history himself and has done a series of short studies on local political history. He feels that the methods of history are essential if students are to learn to dig out the truth of their heritage. "The facts will leave them," he says, "but if they can get the method they can use it all their lives."

Before undertaking the study, the students read a case study of a historian who had done a similar analysis of documents related to the development of the Massachusetts state government. The students are trying to employ some rigorous methodology used by the historian in his work.

## THE LECTURER

The third classroom is organized around a series of well-prepared, systematic lectures describing the subject from a social psychologist's point of view. The students are assigned readings correlated with the lectures. For example, when the teacher treats the reaction to deprivation of rights, students may read Eldridge Cleaver's *Soul on Ice,* although the lecture is not about the book as such, but includes a variety of responses. Excerpts from *Caste and Class in a Southern Town* are more directly tied in by the lectures.

"I really love to lecture," this teacher says. "Some people are against lecturing, but I believe that students need a good, strong intellectual structure to help them comprehend complex social problems. So I lay out the structure and tie it to critical social issues. I am good at this and they usually like it."

All three classes have the same objective and all three are studying what ostensibly is the same problem. Yet the three teachers are using very different approaches, even over common content. One is employing a group inquiry that emerges as the students identify issues and become involved in them. The teacher facilitates their study but the students, as a group, develop their own investigation into the social issue. The second teacher is employing historical methodology; his students are analyzing documents as a historian would. Through lectures, the third teacher helps his students consider social problems within the intellectual framework of the social psychologist. (Imagine the differences that could have resulted if the content had varied more!) What other approaches might have been tried? What would be their advantages? What kind of teacher and student behavior is essential to each? What kinds of instructional materials are necessary? What views of learning and teaching give rise to the alternative approaches which might be tried? How much is the approach related to the personality of the teacher? How much should teaching be varied to reach different students?

## APPROACHES TO TEACHING

In this book we will examine and compare a wide variety of approaches to teaching. In so doing, we suggest that there are many kinds of "good" teaching, and that the concept "good" when applied to teaching, is better stated "good for what?" and "good for whom?" Whether one is creating a curriculum (a plan for a long-term program of education), developing a course or a unit of study (components of a curriculum), developing instructional materials, or deciding what to do in response to a student's behavior, there are many possible courses of action. A model for teaching, as we use the term, is a pattern or plan, which can be used to shape a curriculum or course, to select instructional materials, and to guide a teacher's actions. As we describe models and discuss their uses, we will find that the task of selecting an appropriate model is complex and that the forms of "good" teaching are numerous, depending on our purposes.

We think of teaching as a process by which teacher and students create a shared environment including sets of values and beliefs (agreements about what is important) which in turn color their view of reality. The "models" of teaching which are chosen to pattern teaching activities have much to say about the kinds of realities which will be admitted to the classroom and the kinds of life-view which are likely to be generated as teacher and learner work together. Thus, it is not surprising that people care greatly about the models they use or that educators for millenia have sought the perfect model. We find it desirable to begin by challenging the idea that there is any such thing as a perfect model and by deprecating the idea that we should limit our personal search for a model of teaching to any single one, however attractive it may seem.

## THE SEARCH FOR GOOD TEACHING: "THE ONE RIGHT WAY" FALLACY

As in the case of art, good teaching is something many people feel they can recognize on sight, although they have difficulty expressing a reasoned basis for their judgment. Hence, implicit in many discussions about teaching is the notion that there is probably a certain kind of teaching which is really better than all the other kinds. We hear of "child-centered" teaching, "inductive" teaching, "inquiry," teachers who "really work the kids," others who "really make it interesting," curriculums which are "process-centered," and materials built on "behavior modification" principles. The usual implication is that there exists a certain definable way of working with students which helps them to grow more than any other way. Judging our three teachers of civil rights, many persons would vastly prefer one over the others and heated discussion of the question of which one is "best" would be easy to provoke.

The research evidence dealing with this question is remarkably ambiguous. There have been several hundred studies comparing one general teaching method to another, and the overwhelming portion of these studies, whether curriculums are compared, specific methods for teaching specific subjects are contrasted, or different approaches to counseling are analyzed, show few if any differences between approaches.[1] Although the results are very difficult to interpret, the evidence to date gives no encouragement to those who would hope that we have identified a single reliable, multipurpose teaching strategy that we can use with confidence that it is the best approach.

This conclusion annoys some people. Naturally, it bothers those people who feel that they *do* know such a single broad method. They are likely to say that the reason one particular approach to teaching (*their* approach) has not yet been proven superior is that our ability to measure learning outcomes is not yet sophisticated enough to detect the true power of *their* preferred strategy.

Unquestionably, their position may be correct. The art of measuring the outcomes of learning is still in its infancy, particularly with respect to the education of the emotions, the growth of personality, intellectual development, and creativity. It seems reasonable to suppose that as our technology for studying teaching and learning improves, people will discover regularities in the teaching-learning process that have not been apparent before. A few general methods *may* emerge as superior.

However, we can look at the problems of identifying and choosing teaching strategies from quite a different perspective if we hold in abeyance, pending better evidence, the search for a single right way and concentrate instead on the possibilities of the rich variety of models for teaching which our heritage has given us. Particularly, it behooves us to learn what approaches make contact with individual students and to learn to develop

---

1 A good example of evidence and opinion which gives pause to those who feel that the issues about how to teach are largely settled in favor of inductive teaching procedures is the fine collection of essays in: Lee S. Shulman and E. R. Karslar (eds.), *Learning By Discovery: A Critical Appraisal* (Skokie, Ill.: Rand McNally, 1966).

an environment in which the student is taught in ways that facilitate him and his development.

## THE SEARCH FOR MODELS OF TEACHING: "WHO FOCUSES ON WHAT?"

If we look at the work of those interested in teaching and learning, we find that most educators focus on certain aspects of teaching and give less emphasis to others. To be more explicit, educators tend to generate theories about learning that give the greatest prominence to particular kinds of learning goals and specific aspects of the learner's environment, while neglecting other goals and potentially useful aspects of learning situations. For example, some educators concentrate on improving the creativity of the student. When they enter a classroom and begin to make contact with the student, they find themselves thinking about whether he is creative, what *kind* of creativity he possesses, and what can be done either to awaken or to sustain its development. They try to determine the "state of creativity" of the student and they focus on certain ways of nurturing it.

Moreover, those who focus on creativity, or on some other aspect, vary among themselves in the approaches they take to nurturing it. Some who are interested in creativity feel that it is a spontaneous thing, which we can't do much to induce but should reward as it appears, fanning the natural spark of creativity in the student. Others feel that creativity is best promoted by developing activities causing the learner to engage in creative activity rather than waiting for it to arise. Still others feel that social influences are most critical, and they attempt to put the student into a social environment in which creativity is highly prized, and in which he will see many others being creative, and can imitate them.

In other words, educational procedures are generated from general views about human nature and about the kinds of goals and environments that enhance human beings. Because of their frames of reference—their views of man and what he should become, educators are likely to focus on specific kinds of learning outcomes and to favor certain ways of creating educational environments (which is another way of saying "teaching"). When an educator possesses identifiable focuses and a frame of reference which rationalizes them, we can then say that he has a model for teaching. He can tell us what aspects of the student interest him, what aspects of the environment he emphasizes, and *we* can, *if* we want to, "model" ourselves after his stance toward learning. (In this context, "model" does not mean to follow a pattern explicitly, but rather to guide one's behavior by the example of the model-builder.)

The workday lives of these model-builders represent a number of modes of activity.

1. Some educators who use characteristic models are practitioners. They teach in or organize schools to describe and demonstrate their models. For example, A. S. Neill, the well-known headmaster of Summerhill School, has written and lectured extensively on his model and of course directs the work at Summerhill.[2] His view of man emphasizes the importance of the uniqueness of each individual and the role of the school in furthering personal development and adjustments.

2. Other model-builders conduct research as well. Paul Torrance has for 15 years conducted research studies on the improvement of creativity.[3] The essence of his models is in the character of his research. His frame of reference emphasizes the importance of helping students learn to originate solutions to problems. He envisions a world of cooperative, socially committed, but independently creative citizens.

3. Some of the researchers engage in studies in schools and other field situations. B. F. Skinner is an example of a psychologist who, after many years of laboratory work, developed models of teaching and began to engage in field studies.[4] He emphasizes the role of the environment in shaping the individual's behavior and he is concerned that the shaping be deliberate and humane rather than accidental, with unpredictable effects or side effects.

4. Still others engage in the development of models by thinking and speculating about the implications of the nature of the subject disciplines and how to teach them. We have identified a large number of models for teaching derived from persons who have developed or speculated on theories about child development, or theories about the learning process. For example, although the noted Swiss psychologist Jean Piaget has developed a massive line of research into the intellectual development of children, he has not interpreted his work extensively in terms of teaching or curriculum development. However, many others have given attention to this, and have attempted to develop models for teaching based on Piaget's theories about how intellectual development takes place. These educators stress the importance of developing the intellect and the role of the school in stimulating mental growth.[5]

In recent years many educators have sought to translate academic disciplines into teachable forms and wide varieties of curriculum projects have resulted, designed to teach the central ideas and research processes of the academic disciplines.

5. Many models have resulted from attempts to improve society, including

---

2 A. S. Neill, *Summerhill* (New York: Hart Publishing Company, 1960).

3 Paul Torrance, *Guiding Creative Talent* (Englewood Cliffs, N.J.: Prentice-Hall, 1962).

4 B. F. Skinner, *The Technology of Teaching* (New York: Appleton-Century-Crofts, 1968).

5 Edmund Sullivan, "Piaget and the School Curriculum: A Criteria Appraisal," *Bulletin No. 2 of the Ontario Institute for Studies in Education,* Toronto, 1967.

the desire to reform it radically. From Plato through Thoreau, Dewey,[6] and present-day social reformers, men have developed educational models designed to socialize children to an improved social order or to prepare citizens who will develop a more perfect society. Humanistic educators frequently stress the role of the school in improving social life and bettering the culture.

Over the years, then, a great many educational models have been developed by people engaged in distinctly different kinds of educational activity. Some are based on empirical work, others on theories, some on hunches, and some on speculation about the meanings of theories and research done by others. The purpose of this book is to draw together a number of these models for teaching and to analyze them in terms of their implications for curriculum (the planning of major programs of study), for the work of teachers when they are with children, and for the development of instructional materials. Educational models, in other words, can be used in three ways: for the making of curriculum plans, as guidelines for the teacher's interaction with students, and as specifications for instructional materials. All of these uses represent a form of teaching, although only the second represents interactive teaching (the engagement of a student with his teacher), which is what most people refer to when they speak of teaching.

## SELECTING THE MODELS OF TEACHING

So many people have developed positions on learning which can be used as models for teachers, curriculum-makers, and makers of materials, that the task of selecting the models to be treated was formidable. Educators, psychologists, sociologists, systems analysts, psychiatrists, and many others have produced theoretical positions about learning and teaching. Curriculum development projects, schools and school districts, and organizations representing particular curriculum areas or disciplines have also developed a large number of approaches to teaching and learning. The task of selection began with the development of a very long list of sources of models. Included on the list were the works of counselors and therapists, such as Carl Rogers, Erik Erikson, and Abraham Maslow.[7] Included also were sources by learning theorists such as Skinner, Ausubel, and Bruner.[8] The works of develop-

---

[6] See especially: Plato, *The Republic,* trans. Francis MacDonald Cornford (New York: Oxford University Press, 1945); Henry David Thoreau, *Walden* (New York: Heritage Press, 1939); John Dewey, *Democracy and Education* (New York: Macmillan, 1916).

[7] Carl Rogers, *Client-Centered Therapy* (Boston: Houghton Mifflin, 1951); Erik Erikson, *Childhood and Society* (New York: Norton, 1950); Abraham Maslow, *Toward a Psychology of Being* (Princeton, N.J.: Van Nostrand Reinhold, 1962).

[8] B. F. Skinner, *Verbal Behavior* (New York: Appleton-Century-Crofts, 1957); David Ausubel, *Psychology of Meaningful Verbal Learning* (New York: Grune & Stratton, 1963); Jerome Bruner, *Toward a Theory of Instruction* (New York: Norton, 1966).

mental psychologists such as Piaget, Kohlberg, Hunt,[9] and others were identified. Philosophers such as Dewey, James, and Broudy were represented.[10] Curriculum development projects in the academic subjects provided many examples. Specialists in group dynamics contributed models. The patterns of teaching from the great experimental schools, such as Summerhill, were on our list. Altogether, more than 80 theorists, schools, and projects were identified on the initial list.

As we examined the patterns of teaching in our first list, we discarded some because they seemed too vague to provide general models that could be communicated to many people. Others were eliminated because the advocates or developers of the models, while they were explicit enough about the specific things teachers or curriculums should do, paid inadequate attention to a rationalization for their model. In other words, it was not easy to tell *why* they advocated it, or why it could be reasonably expected to achieve its intended aims. The remaining models fit the criteria of being communicable and rationalized.

## GROUPING THE MODELS

Gradually, we began to group the models on the basis of the sources of reality which theorists drew on as they focused on the learner and his environment. Eventually we organized the models into four families which represent different orientations toward man and his universe. Although there is much overlap among families (and among models within families), the four are: (1) those oriented toward social relations and toward the relation between man and his culture and which draw upon social sources; (2) those which draw on information processing systems and descriptions of human capacity for processing information; (3) those which draw on personality development, the processes of personal construction of reality, and the capacity to function as an integrated personality as the major source; (4) those developed from an analysis of the processes by which human behavior is shaped and reinforced. At length we decided to organize this book around exemplars of these families. Let us define these sources more fully.

*families of models*

### 1. The Social Interaction Sources

The social interaction sources emphasize the relationships of the person to his society or his direct relationships with other people. They reflect a

9 Jean Piaget, *The Origins of Intelligence in Children* (New York: International Universities Press, 1952); Larry Kohlberg, "Moral Education in Our Schools," *School Review*, 1966, 74:1–30; David E. Hunt, "Matching Models and Moral Training," *Moral Education*, C. Beck, B. Crittenden and E. V. Sullivan, eds. (Toronto: University of Toronto Press, 1970).

10 See William James, *Talks to Teachers on Psychology and to Students on Some*

view of human nature which gives priority to social relations and the creation of a better society. They see the processes by which reality is socially negotiated as vitally important in the life of man. With respect to goals, consequently, models from this orientation were directed toward the improvement of the individual's ability to relate to others. Many of them developed from a desire to improve democratic processes and to educate students to relate to and improve the society.

It must be stressed that the social relations orientation does not assume that social relations is the only important dimension of life. Social relations may be emphasized more than other domains, but social theorists are usually concerned with the development of the mind, the development of the self, and the learning of academic subjects. Some of them, of course, have developed models *specifically* for the improvement of social relations or they use social relationships as the *primary* vehicle of education, but it is the rare teacher or theorist in education who is not concerned with more than one aspect of the learner's development, or who does not use more than one aspect of the environment to influence the learner's development. For instance, our first teacher emphasizes group investigation developed from encounters with conflict situations, but he leads his students to academic sources and he is concerned with their personal values and reactions.

## 2. *The Information-Processing Sources*

The second large family of models shares an orientation toward the information-processing capability of the student and systems which can be taught him so as to improve his information-processing capability. By information-processing we mean the ways in which people handle stimuli from the environment, organize data, sense problems, generate concepts and solutions to problems, and employ verbal and nonverbal symbols. Some of these models are concerned with the learner's ability to solve certain kinds of problems and use studies of problem-solving as a major source. Others concentrate on creativity or on general intellectual ability. Some emphasize the teaching of specific strategies for thinking, creative thinking, and thinking within academic disciplines.

Again, however, it must be stressed that nearly all models from this family are also concerned with social relationships, and the development of an integrated, functioning self. Yet their primary sources are the student's capacity to integrate information and to process it, and systems, especially academic systems, which can help individuals to process data. We refer to them as *information-processing oriented models*. Our second and third

---

*of Life's Ideals* (New York: Holt, Rinehart & Winston, 1889); Harry S. Broudy and J. R. Palmer, *Exemplars of Teaching Method* (Skokie, Ill.: Rand McNally, 1965).

teachers, the "Student of Cases" and the "Lecturer," emphasize the academic disciplines as information-processing systems which they teach. The second teacher is much concerned with group interaction, however, and both are concerned with the personal development of their students.

### 3. *The Personal Sources*

The third family of models shares an orientation toward the individual person as the source of educational ideas. Their frames of reference spotlight personal development and they emphasize the processes by which the individual constructs and organizes his reality. Frequently they emphasize the personal psychology and the emotional life of the individual. These models are directed toward the individual's internal organization as it affects relationships with his environment and himself. Some are concerned with his personality and with his capacity to reach out fearlessly into his milieu to make contact with others, and to venture where he has not been before. Others are more oriented toward the individual's feelings about himself, toward his self-concept, or his self-image. Yet others are concerned with helping him develop an authentic reality-oriented view of himself and his society.

Again, it is necessary to note that most of the models which are oriented around the development of the self are also concerned with the development of social relations and information-processing capacity. The distinctive feature of this category is its emphasis on personal development as a source of educational ideas. The focus of educational goals and means is on the self, at least as the avenue toward other aspects of development, rather than on the person as a processor or an interactor with others. Hence, while the focus is on helping the person to develop a productive relationship with his environment and to view himself as a capable person, and although most of the model-builders in this group believe that the relationship between individual learner and his teacher is central in the learning process, it is expected that one of the products will be richer interpersonal relations, and a more effective information-processing capacity. We refer to this family as the *person-oriented family*. None of our three teachers gave primacy to a person-oriented approach.

### 4. *Behavior Modification as a Source*

The fourth source of models has developed from attempts to create efficient systems for sequencing learning activities and shaping behavior by manipulating reinforcement. Students of reinforcement theory, such as B. F. Skinner, have developed these models and operant conditioning is their central procedure. They frequently are referred to as behavior-modification theories because of their reliance on changing the external behavior of the student and their description of him in terms of extremely visible behavior rather than underlying and unobservable behavior.

Operant conditioning has been applied to a wide variety of educational goals, ranging from military training to interpersonal behavior and even to goals of therapy. Its general applicability has led to its use in many domains of human behavior which characterize the other families of models. Although all of our three teachers shape the behavior of their students, none uses a conscious behavior-modification strategy.

## RELATIONSHIPS AMONG THE FOUR FAMILIES

Our families of models, therefore, are by no means antithetical to one another, and the actual prescriptions for developing learning environments that emerge from some of them are remarkably similar although we classified them into different families. Also, within the families certain of the models share many features, both with respect to goals and with respect to the kinds of means that they recommend.

A list of the models included in this book, classified by family, and annotated briefly, follows as Table 1-1.

**TABLE 1-1 The Models of Teaching Classified by Family and Mission**

| Model | Major Theorist | Family or Orientation | Missions or Goals for which Applicable |
|---|---|---|---|
| 1. Inductive Teaching Model | Hilda Taba | Information Processing | Primarily for development of inductive mental processes and academic reasoning or theory-building, but these capacities are useful for personal and social goals as well. |
| 2. Inquiry Training Model | Richard Suchman | Information Processing | |
| 3. Science Inquiry Model | Joseph J. Schwab (also much of the Curriculum Reform Movement; see Jerome Bruner *The Process of Education* for the rationale) | Information Processing | Designed to teach the research system of the discipline but also expected to have effects in other domains (i.e., sociological methods may be taught in order to increase social understanding and social problem-solving). |
| 4. Jurisprudential Teaching Model | Donald Oliver and James P. Shaver | Social Interaction | Designed primarily to teach the jurisprudential frame of reference as a way of processing information but also as a way of thinking about and resolving social issues. |

**TABLE 1-1** (con't)

| Model | Major Theorist | Family or Orientation | Missions or Goals for which Applicable |
|---|---|---|---|
| 5. Concept Attainment Model | Jerome Bruner | Information Processing | Designed primarily to develop inductive reasoning. |
| 6. Developmental Model | Jean Piaget, Irving Sigel, Edmund Sullivan | Information Processing | Designed to increase general intellectual development, especially logical reasoning, but can be applied to social and moral development as well. (See Kohlberg.) |
| 7. Advance Organizer Model | David Ausubel | Information Processing | Designed to increase the efficiency of information-processing capacities to meaningfully absorb and relate bodies of knowledge. |
| 8. Group Investigation Model | Herbert Thelen John Dewey | Social Interaction | Development of skills for participation in democratic social process through combined emphasis on interpersonal and social (group) skills and academic inquiry. Aspects of personal development are important outgrowths of this model. |
| 9. Social Inquiry Model | Byron Massialas Benjamin Cox | Social Interaction | Social problem-solving primarily through academic inquiry and logical reasoning. |
| 10. Laboratory Method Model | National Training Laboratory (NTL) Bethel, Maine | Social Interaction | Development of interpersonal and group skills and through this, personal awareness and flexibility. |
| 11. Non-Directive Teaching Model | Carl Rogers | Person | Emphasis on building capacity for self-instruction and through this, personal development in terms of self-understanding, self-discovery, and self-concept. |
| 12. Classroom Meeting Model | William Glasser | Person | Development of self-understanding and self-responsibility. This would have latent benefits to other kinds of functioning, i.e., social. |
| 13. Awareness Training Model | William Schutz Fritz Perls | Person | Increasing personal capacity for self-exploration and self-awareness. Much emphasis on development of interpersonal awareness and understanding. |

**TABLE** 1-1 (con't)

| Model | Major Theorist | Family or Orientation | Missions or Goals for which Applicable |
|---|---|---|---|
| 14. Synectics Model | William Gordon | Person | Personal development of creativity and creative problem-solving. |
| 15. Conceptual Systems Model | David E. Hunt | Person | Designed to increase personal complexity and flexibility. Matches environments to students. |
| 16. Operant Conditioning Model | B. F. Skinner | Behavior Modification | General applicability. A domain-free approach though probably most applicable to information-processing function. |

## CONCEPTS FOR ANALYZING AND DESCRIBING THE MODELS

The models coming as they do from many different sources, are written in many kinds of languages. Some were written in the symbol systems of the systems analysts. Others were written by psychologists, and appear in the language of learning theorists. Yet others are from curriculum materials, from descriptions of schools in operation, from therapists and from teachers, and use the languages common in those circles.

Our concern is to describe each model as explicitly as we can to make it useful to a diverse audience including teachers, curriculum-makers, and materials-makers. At the same time, we wish to avoid doing any more violence to the original theorists than we can help. To accomplish these purposes, we have developed several concepts for describing each model. The concepts stem from our conception of teaching as the creation of environments (systems of interrelated parts) which have both long- and short-term effects on the growth of children. Each of the following concepts describes the models in terms of its characteristic environment. Teaching has always created total environments but we have not always taken account of this. We have not always been aware of the multiple dimensions of the environment, their effect on each other, and their effects on the learner.

### The Orientation or Focus of the Model

This concept involves a description of the aspects of the student and the learning environment which are most emphasized. It includes the *thesis* of the model, that is, the kinds of goals the model-builder focuses on and the reasons he believes the particular means specified is likely to achieve those goals. It describes the aspects of the environment which are most important in the life of the student (from the view of the model).

## The Syntax or Phasing of the Model

The syntax of the model involves a description of the model in action. It tells us about the shape of the activities which typify the particular educational environment belonging to each model. For example, if a teacher were to use the model as the basis for his strategy, what kinds of activities would he use? Would these activities have a characteristic beginning and end? What should the teacher keep in mind as he responds to the activity of the learner? As we describe the structure of each model, we attempt to describe a practical example of the model in action, showing clearly the phases of activity that the teacher or curriculum would go through and their interrelationships to each other.

For example, one model begins with a presentation to the learner of a concept that is called an "advance organizer." This concept is given to the student verbally. That is, the teacher makes a statement of the concept or presents a written statement. In the second phase, the material to be learned is presented to the learner and he reads it, watches a film, or otherwise is exposed to the data. This phase is followed by another in which the learner is helped to relate the material to the organizing concept. These phases make up the structure or syntax of the model, the flow of events designed to influence the student or help him teach himself. In a different model, the first phase of a typical activity includes data collection by the students. The second phase involves organization of the data under concepts the student forms himself, and the third, a comparison of the concepts developed with those developed by other people. As shown in Table 1–2, these two models have a very different structure or set of phases, even though the same type of concept might emerge from both models, and they were in fact designed for somewhat different purposes. The first was designed for the mastery of material, and the second, to teach students inductive thinking processes.

**TABLE 1-2 Illustration of Phasing in Typical Activity of Two Models**

|  | *Phase One* | *Phase Two* | *Phase Three* |
|---|---|---|---|
| *Illustrative Model #1* | Presentation of Concept | Presentation of Data | Relating of Data to Concepts |
| *Illustrative Model #2* | Presentation of Data | Development of Categories by Students | Identification and Naming of Concepts |

By comparing the structural phasing of the activities of models we are able to identify the operational differences between them and to make clear the roles a teacher needs to fulfill in order to make a given model work. In Illustrative Model #2, for example, a teacher (or a mechanical agent) must trigger the concept-building activity of the second phase and shift the student's attention from the collection and identification of data to the development of concepts which group and otherwise make the data comprehensible.

### Principles of Reaction by Teachers or Other Agents

Some models provide the teacher with principles to guide his reaction to student activity. In Illustrative Model #2, the teacher during Phase Two might reward concept-building activity, and encourage students to compare their concepts. In some models the teacher overtly tries to shape behavior by rewarding some student activities and maintaining a neutral stance toward others. In others, the teacher tries not to manipulate rewards, but maintains carefully equal status with his students and helps them select their own means of judging and guiding their activities.

These principles help the teacher select the reactions he will make as his interaction with the students emerges. They provide him with rules of thumb by which he can gauge the student and select his responses to what the student does.

### The Social System Characteristic of the Model

To describe the social system we use three subconcepts: a description of the kinds of student-teacher *roles*, a description of the *hierarchical relationships* or authority relationships, and a description of the kinds of *norms* which are encouraged and the student behavior which is rewarded. The leadership roles of the teacher vary greatly. In some models, he is a reflector or facilitator of group activity. In others, he is a counselor of individuals. In some, he is a taskmaster. The second concept, hierarchical relationships, is explained in terms of the sharing of initiatory activity by teacher and learner, the location and the amount of control over activity that emerges from the process of interaction. Some models use the teacher as the center of activity and source of input; he is the organizer, pacer, and chief authority in the situation. Others provide for a relatively equal relationship between teacher and student, while some place the student at the center. Finally, different kinds of student behavior are rewarded in different models. In some models the student is rewarded for getting a job done and sticking to a prescribed line of inquiry. In others, he rewards himself by knowing that he has learned something.

One way to describe a model of teaching is according to the degree of structure in the learning environment. That is, as roles, relationships, norms, and activities become less prescribed or externally imposed, and more emergent and within the students' control, we can say that its social system is less structured. Roughly, we can classify models as highly structured, moderately structured, or relatively unstructured.

## THE CONCEPT OF SUPPORT SYSTEMS

We use this concept to describe not the model itself so much as the conditions necessary for its existence. What support, we ask, is needed in order to create the environment specified by the model? That is, what are the additional requirements beyond the *usual* human skills and capacities and technical facilities? For example, the Human Relations Model may require a trained leader; the Non-Directive Model may require a particular personality, i.e., an exceedingly patient, supportive one. Suppose that a model postulates that students should teach themselves, with the roles of teachers limited to consultation and facilitation. What support is necessary? Certainly a classroom filled only with textbooks would be limiting and prescriptive. Rather, support in the form of books, films, self-instructional systems, travel arrangements, and the like is necessary or the model will be empty.

The support requirements are derived from two sources—the role specifications for the teacher and the demands of the substantive nature or the experiences, i.e., experts and knowledge of the experts. Support requirements are real. Many able educational programs fail because of failure to consider or anticipate the support requirements. As a result, we feel that considering the support system is as much a part of making a model happen as learning the model itself.

## CLASSROOM IMPLEMENTATION

Under this concept we describe or illustrate the model as it operates to create actual classroom environments. In some cases we present transcripts or anecdotal descriptions of teaching episodes using a particular model. We also provide some analysis of these lessons in terms of the model and focus on critical aspects or special difficulties in moving from theory to practice.

## GENERAL APPLICABILITY OF THE MODEL

Under this concept we describe the primary purposes of the model, and any other applications which are claimed, or which seem reasonable. Some models are designed for very specific purposes, while others have very wide general application. For example, some are designed only to improve certain aspects of interpersonal relations, whereas others within the family of social-relations oriented models, are intended for a very wide range of academic purposes and for personal development as well. Some behavior-modification models are designed to affect *any* type of student behavior by changing responses to the environment.

The effects of an environment can be *direct* or designed to come from the content and skills which are the bases of the activities engaged in. Or, effects can be latent or implicit in the life of the environment. One fascinating question about models is the implicit learnings they engender. For instance, a model which emphasizes academic discipline can also (but need not) emphasize obedience to authority. Or one which encourages personal development can (but need not) beg questions about social responsibility. The examination of latent functions can be as exciting and important as the examination of direct functions.

Hence, the description of the effects of models can validly be categorized as the direct or *instructional* effects and the indirect or *nurturant* effects. The instructional effects are those directly achieved by leading the learner in certain directions. The nurturant effects come from "living" in the environment created by the model. High competition toward a goal may directly spur achievement, for example, but the effects of living in a competitive atmosphere may alienate one from his fellows. Alienation would be, in this case, *nurtured* by an *instructional* method. In choosing a model for teaching, curriculum-building, or as a basis for materials, the teacher must balance instructional efficiency, or directness, and questions about the nurturant effect, as shown in Figure 1-1.

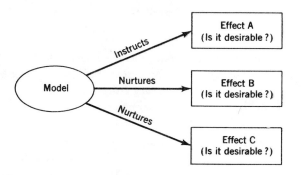

**Figure 1-1**

If we have two models whose instructional effects are both appropriate for our goal, we may choose between them because the nurturant effects of one further other goals or because the nurturant effects reinforce the direct instructional effects. Suppose we favor goal "A." Three models might be considered, as shown in Figure 1-2.

If we assume equal efficiency, we might choose Model I because its instructional and nurturant effects reinforce one another and there are no undesirable nurturant side effects.

It is possible to defend the selection of a model chiefly on the basis of its nurturant effects, even though it might not have high direct efficiency. The Progressive movement, for example, emphasized teaching academic subjects through democratic process less because it would be an efficient

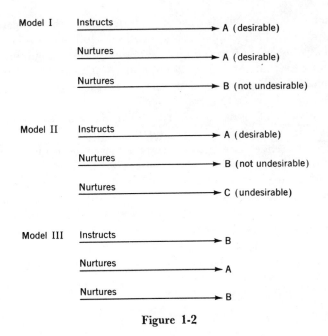

**Figure 1-2**

way to teach content (although many believed it would be) than because it would be likely to *nurture* later democratic behavior and citizen involvement and give an opportunity to *instruct* citizens in democratic skills.

We can diagram the situation as in Figure 1-3.

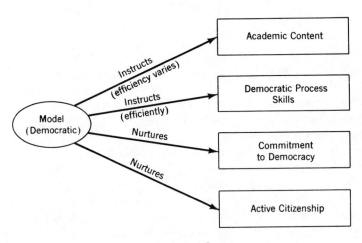

**Figure 1-3**

Our three civil rights teachers from the beginning of the chapter might consider the instructional and nurturant values of their approaches. The "Lecturer," for example, is concerned with his direct instructional effects. He might try to ascertain what his method nurtures at the same time. If he were to consider group investigation, he might question whether it was as efficient for achieving his instructional goals, but he might value its nurturant effects. He might feel that the "Student of Cases" had a good compromise, with strong instructional values over the content and desirable nurturant effects as well.

In the real world of education there are real decisions to be made among models which really differ from one another. By the models we choose, reality is created for our students. With so little empirical evidence to guide our choices, logic, awareness, and our own social values have to be most prominent in our selection.

## DIALOGUE IN THE CLASSROOM

What kind of dialogue can the model create within the walls of a busy classroom? The answer to this question depends on one's view of teaching.

One view is that teaching is a mysterious and exceedingly personal art. With that point of view, the task of each teacher is to find his own model. He may create it by adapting an existing model of teaching. He may create it rationally and consciously out of his beliefs about the kinds of conditions that will produce learning, or he may create it intuitively as he interacts with his students. Of course, he may not develop just one model at all; each time he teaches, a new kind of interaction may result out of the unique occurrence of his attempt to teach and his students' attempts to learn.

For the teacher who possesses such a viewpoint, knowing the models of teaching which have been developed by others provides a panorama of the beliefs of other people concerning effective teaching and learning. This panorama should help him test the adequacy of his own conceptions, and of the kinds of models that result from his work with his students. It should provide an intellectual stimulation to him as well. If he is interested in helping students develop more adequate self-concepts, then Rogers may offer something to him. If he is trying to teach a skill, he may be interested in what Skinner and Ausubel have to say about it. If he is trying to understand his learner, he may be interested in Hunt's, Piaget's, or Kohlberg's ways of looking at the learner, and the different kinds of things that are likely to affect him. The artistic view of the teacher would resist any notion that he should see any of the models as prescriptive of his own behavior. Rather they would be sources to stimulate his imagination and provide insight into his own work. The panorama of models creates a conceptual map through which the necessary artistic detachment and self-awareness can be filtered.

Another view of teaching is that most teachers need to develop a solid basic style or model that they can use as the "bread and butter" of their teaching. Many teacher-educators, for example, have attempted to present to teachers a good general-purpose model which they can master, modify, and eventually replace as they mature professionally. For example, the Group Investigation Model has been taught as a basic teaching strategy by teacher-educators, particularly those whose historical roots are in the Progressive movement. They reason that this model will give the teacher a good base for organizing the students to work with the teacher in a mutual way. If this model could be established, it would solve a good many potential discipline problems and if the beginning teacher can develop a mutual cooperative learning environment, then the children would work at teaching themselves, a state of affairs that would have applicability in almost every curriculum area. Emphasis on creative thinking could lead toward aspects of the Synectics Model or a similar way of looking at teaching and learning. An emphasis on inquiry would lead toward the Science or Social Inquiry models, and an emphasis on inductive thinking could lead toward the Taba or Suchman approaches to inductive reasoning. Models based on inductive thinking, or "inquiry," have also served as staples for teachers, and there are many who believe that these are the basic models which should be taught to the future teacher and used by him in most curriculum areas. Behavior modification models, such as Skinner's, are implicit in the methods of many other teacher education programs, and are suggested as basic models for the teacher.

The authors' position is that the models for teaching are best viewed by the teacher as potential strategies which are applicable to a wide variety of purposes. Since no single teaching strategy can accomplish every purpose, the wise teacher will master a limited repertoire of strategies which he can bring to bear on specific kinds of learning problems. For example, the Group Investigation Model *is* a good basic element for the teacher's repertoire. It gives him the means of organizing the students into a mutual group that can work well with him, and which will have the devices to improve its own processes. Unquestionably, it is broadly applicable, also. It can be used in the creative arts areas, in the teaching of skills, in the teaching of the sciences, and a number of other ways. However, models derived from other sources are also valuable. The models designed from the practice of the disciplines, such as those used by the Biological Sciences Curriculum Study, are clearly relevant to the teaching of the academic disciplines. The Rogerian Model is specifically applicable to helping people to become open, to free their inquisitiveness and their creativity and to help them to develop the drive and the sensitivity to try to educate themselves. Similarly, the Laboratory Method Model has great advantage for the im-

Use of various models

provement of human relations skills. To the extent that it is possible, therefore, we urge the teacher to master a very solid range of models which he can bring to bear on the variety of instructional problems that he is likely to face. This is particularly important if he is a self-contained classroom teacher, responsible for teaching many children in many curriculum areas. But it is also important for the subject-matter specialist, for his responsibilities, even if they are confined to the teaching of a single discipline to fairly mature students, imply teaching tasks for which no one single model can be completely adequate. For instance, the secondary teacher of English can draw on several models for teaching his discipline. He may also wish to make use of the models, such as Synectics, in the teaching of creative writing. He may wish to use Skinnerian techniques for the teaching of skills, and Rogerian methods to help open his students to a sense of their own potentialities and a willingness to capitalize on them.

Teams of teachers working together can discover the models which are most amenable to each member of the team and can orchestrate these to build a strong and balanced pattern of education for children. Some teachers will use the counseling models effectively, others will use the behavior modification strategies such as simulations to teach skills and particular problem-solving strategies. Yet others will be the democratic-process organizers. Together, a large team of teachers, able to draw on teacher-aides and support systems of various kinds, should be able to create a rather good panorama of opportunities for children.

To develop repertoire means to develop flexibility. Part of this flexibility is professional. The teacher faces a wide range of problems, and if he has a wide range of teaching models to draw from, he should be able to offer more creative and imaginative solutions to those problems. On the personal side, repertoire requires the ability to grow and expand one's potential, and the capacity to teach oneself more varied and interesting ways of coping with one's own need to develop. The environment for personal growth is greatly enhanced when people can define their present situations and see the alternative possibilities once this map is provided. The growing, developing teacher can reach out and embrace more forms of experience, explore more aspects of his students, and find more ways of helping them to grow.

The satisfaction of growth and exploration should be reason enough for the teacher to reach out and set as his goal, not one or two basic models which he uses for all purposes, but a variety which he explores for the potential they hold for his pupils and for himself.

## A DIALOGUE ON TEACHER EDUCATION

For the teacher-educator and teacher alike the models of teaching pose two problems. First, how does one choose which models to teach (learn) and second, how does one go about teaching (learning) them? While we have no formula-like answers to these questions, we do have some thoughts about them and some experience upon which to draw. For several years now, we have been carrying on instruction and research over the Models of Teaching with preservice students in elementary education.

Our initial instructional experiences with the models were very crude. The models themselves were not well-formulated or exemplified. Neither were the procedures for teaching them. Instructional materials for demonstrating or applying a model were virtually nonexistent. As far as classroom implementation goes, our own knowledge of the "ins and outs" of the model in the classroom has emerged simultaneously with the implementation by our students. In fact, in the beginning we differed very little from our students with respect to the Models of Teaching. Our conceptual understanding of a model was probably greater. Also, we had more emotional distance through which to view classroom implementation (that is, unless we ourselves were demonstrating a particular model for the first time). In addition, we had an intellectual and professional curiosity that is hard to ask in a beginning teacher. This combination gave the instructional staff the obligation to assume some leadership in uncovering or recognizing the subtleties of a model and figuring out how to learn it. Basically, however, students and staff alike were naive when it came to models and to the questions posed at the beginning of this section.

We feel the best way to share our thoughts about these questions is to recount some of our own experiences and share some of the decisions we have made and the patterns we now use. For example, our students in the Columbia University Teachers College elementary teacher education program, now begin by studying the four families of models and learning one example from each family. This introduces the four families of models, each of which creates different kinds of environments and learning experiences and reflects different values, and gives the students a chance to experience the different realities of the families. They thus have concrete experience on which to base their dialogue over how to teach. In terms of the goal of flexibility in teaching, it enables new teachers to develop a repertoire spanning the four families. Thus they are "stretched" from the type of routine teaching which could quite easily dominate them.

In addition to the "models" framework, the instructional staff and students have equipped themselves with a system for analyzing teacher and student verbal communication which analyzes several dimensions of the learning environment in terms especially designed to study models of teaching. We have all learned this multidimensional system for looking at pupil-teacher behavior and we use it to observe ourselves when we teach. We have learned something about the differences in interaction patterns which occur when particular models are used. For example, we can describe the initiation of the model "phases" in terms of teacher and student interaction patterns. We know that models whose social systems are less teacher-directed and more student-directed should differ in the amount and type of teacher behavior and student behavior. In our category system we would expect that models which focus on substantive information would have different coding patterns from those which focus on social interaction processes. Our knowledge of the models also grows the other way. That is, we may observe a model in the classroom and have certain intuitive thoughts about it which are then clarified by the coding pattern. Between our conceptual understanding of a model and the interaction analysis schema we are able to be more specific in our description of what a model looks like in practice and what prerequisite behaviors are necessary for teachers to carry out a model. This is our way of "getting into" a model and of refining our procedures for training teachers in the Models of Teaching.

## SELECTING MODELS TO LEARN (TEACH)

Aside from the decision to begin with one model from each family, we faced the decision of which family and model to begin with. The problems resulting from our decision illustrate the complexity of the problems of learning how to use the models to develop learning environments. Our initial decision was to select a highly-structured, teacher-directed model whose objective was quite operationally identifiable. We felt that such a model would be easier for beginning student-teachers than a loose, emergent model. Hence, during one year our students were introduced to the idea of models through the Information Processing family and, specifically, the Concept Attainment Model based on the work of Jerome Bruner. We felt that concept attainment was easier to learn than democratic process or group inquiry. The sequence of phases and role of the teacher are more identifiable and predictable in the Concept Attainment Model.

Much to our surprise the choice was seriously questioned by the students. Because it was all so delineated, the model seemed simplistic and mechanistic to the students and seemingly violated their "progressive" views of education. In truth, the relative clarity of steps somewhat blinded both students and staff from seeing the subtleties of the model and from decentering our attention from the model syntax to a richer, more general exploration of the whole concept-building process. We learned that we needed to explore the models (and specifically concept-attainment) as a way of looking at and explaining teacher-student interaction. One could not just learn "how to do" a model, he had to learn how to look at teaching and learning and how to "feel" the texture of a learning situation with the philosophical "lenses" of the models. As we explored this perspective with the students, the idea of a Model of Teaching took on greater richness and meaning. As we began the second model (Group Investigation), and the Social Interaction family, the staff carried with it a less recalcitrant but, nonetheless, highly skeptical student body, wary of being taught formulas but anxious for guidelines to teaching.

Our rationale for selecting the Group Investigation Model as the first representative of the Social Interaction family went something like this: First it seemed to combine more elements and more clearly represent the essence of this family than any other single model. It pays much attention to the social interaction process and at the same time bears a strong but flexible relationship to content and intellectual process. Thus, it finds many uses within the classroom and can easily be adapted to the field situations our students find themselves in. However, it is a complex model.

Generally, students *do* have many opportunities to use group investigation and it has been well-used. Its complexity *does* make it difficult to learn, however, and it stretches the repertoire almost too much. As a result, it also presents problems. At the end of Parts II, III, and IV of the book we will talk further about the selection of models and specific problems in learning and teaching some of them.

We will draw on our experience in teaching and learning the models and present general training procedures we have found helpful. In addition, we will continue to present ideas concerning the selection of models both for the teacher (to expand his repertoire) and for the student (to expand *his* possibilities for learning).

## SUMMARY

The remainder of this book is structured into two divisions. In the first division (Parts I, II, III, and IV), we present the four families of teaching models. Under each family several models or variations on models are described in terms of the concepts indicated above. Also, specific exemplars are given of the application of the models to practical curriculum and teaching situations. In the second division (Part V) there are five chapters. These describe the models way of thinking and the application of the models to curriculum development: to teaching, and to the design of instructional systems. The last chapter discusses the implications of the models for a dialogue on the nature of teaching and learning.

We believe that the four families of models provide a "present state of the art" repertoire for teachers and curriculum-makers, including a range of models broad enough to be useful for many types of educational purposes. The most creative teachers and curriculum-makers, however, will rarely take their repertoire from what exists. They will see these models as beginning points and they will go on and create their own. Models of teaching should not serve as recipes but as stimulators to activity.

Our basic stance can be represented in the following hypothesis: Teaching should be conceived as the creation of an environment composed of inter-dependent parts. Content, skills, instructional roles, social relationships, types of activities, physical facilities, and their use all add up to an environmental system whose parts interact with each other to constrain the behavior of all participants, teachers as well as students. Different combinations of these elements create different environments eliciting different educational outcomes.

Further, the effects of educational environments can be seen as:

1. Instructional effects consisting chiefly of the content and skills which are developed by the students through the activities which characterize the environment.
2. Nurturant effects consisting chiefly of changes in capacity (thinking, creativity, integrativeness) and values (including depth and flexibility as well as direction of values) which result from "living in" the environment.
3. Moreover, instructional and nurturant effects interact with and affect each other.

Models for teaching are models for creating environments—they provide rough specifications which can be used to design and actualize learning environments. Teachers and other educators can choose to employ models either:

1. for their instructional effects (because a model is likely to generate an environment efficient for teaching a skill), or
2. for their nurturant effects (to affect intelligence, flexibility, values, etc.), or
3. for both instructional and nurturant effects.

The personal, interactive, information-processing, and behavior modification "families" of models focus on characteristic types of goals and means. The personal models emphasize personal relationships and see growth resulting from them. The interactive models depend on the energy of the group and the process of group interaction. The informational models depend on activities which carry content and skills. Behavior modification focuses on rewards and on the control of activities.

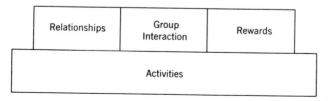

Figure 1-4

The activities produce the direct effects of the environment while the entire environment produces the slower nurturant effects. (Figure 1-4 shows the learning environment.)

By choosing to create some environments and not others, teachers and educational planners choose both kinds of effects—creating gently and subtly the world of the learner.

# I

## Social Interaction

### as a

## Source of Models

# INTRODUCTION

## Interaction-Oriented Models

Human interaction is the theme of Part I. In it we examine a number of models for teaching that place heavy emphasis on social relations either as a goal or as an educational means, or both. By social relations we mean both how individuals conceptualize and relate to each other as people and how they relate to their society as a social institution.

The interaction-oriented models actually represent a number of subfamilies from which we have drawn representatives. These subfamilies appear because theorists and practitioners with a social orientation use a variety of frames of reference which result in rather different approaches to education. Two subfamilies are given attention here out of a much larger possible number.

1. *Concepts of Society.* Models derived from a conception of society make up the first subfamily. This subfamily represents education whose chief point of departure is its view of society. Its creators usually envision what human beings would be like in a very good, even Utopian society. They set about the creation of educational methods which would develop citizens who could live in and enhance that society, fulfill themselves in and through it, and who would even be able to help create and revise it. The models for teaching which result are models for the education of ideal citizens. We have had such models from the time of the Greeks. Plato's *Republic* is a blueprint for an ideal society and the educational program

to support it.[1] Aristotle also dealt with the ideal education and society.[2] Since their time, many other utopians have produced educational models. Augustine (*City of God*), Sir Thomas More (*Utopia*), Comenius (*The Great Didactic*), and John Locke, among others, developed such approaches.[3]

Here we present only contemporary models[4] which are drawn from an interest in a more effective democratic process. This interest derives from an intellectual tradition which had its focus early in the century in John Dewey, who combined a view of society with a view of intellectual process to develop a conception of education in which democratic, problem-solving processes were central.[5] We have identified several models, all articulated during the 1960s, which appear to represent that tradition now. Our selections include a model drawn from the work of Herbert A. Thelen of the University of Chicago, a model for teaching young citizens to reflect on social issues developed by Donald Oliver and James Shaver at Harvard University, and a model for social studies teaching articulated by Byron Massialas of the University of Michigan and Benjamin Cox of the University of Illinois.[6] A host of others from this tradition are mentioned in the text.

It should be particularly noted that we have neglected conceptions of education stemming from even more revolutionary conceptions of society and education than these—conceptions produced by radical social reformers. This tradition is new in the United States; at least it is only newly "respectable" and widely known. Generally, it aims toward a "radicalized" or much changed social order and employs educational models designed to develop social reform-minded or even revolutionary young persons. Representing this area is the work of Herbert Marcuse and Paul Goodman,[7] but there are many theorists and practitioners who have developed radical conceptions of society and education. Although their work is stimulating and often

---

[1] See *The Republic,* trans. Francis MacDonald Cornford (New York: Oxford University Press, 1945).

[2] See *The Works of Aristotle,* J. A. Smith and W. D. Ross, eds. (Oxford: Clarendon Press, 1912).

[3] See especially: *The City of God,* trans. John Healy (London: J. M. Dent, 1931); *Utopia* (New York: Dutton, 1965); *The Great Didactic,* M. W. Keatinge, ed. (Glasgow: A & C Black, 1907); John Locke, *Some Thoughts Concerning Education,* R. H. Quick, ed. (Cambridge: Cambridge University Press, 1927).

[4] For a clear and brief overview of the classic historic models, see Harry Broudy, "Historic Exemplars of Teaching Methods," in N. L. Gage, ed., *Handbook of Research on Teaching* (Chicago: Rand McNally & Co., 1963), pp. 1–43.

[5] John Dewey, *Democracy and Education* (New York: Macmillan, 1916).

[6] H. A. Thelen, *Education and the Human Quest* (New York: Harper & Row, 1960); Donald Oliver and James Shaver, *Teaching Public Issues in the High School* (Boston: Houghton Mifflin, 1966); Byron Massialas and Benjamin Cox, *Inquiry in Social Studies* (New York: McGraw-Hill, 1966).

[7] Herbert Marcuse, *Eros and Civilization* (Boston: Beacon Press, 1955); Paul Goodman, *Compulsory Miseducation* (New York: Horizon Press, 1964).

forward-looking, it is difficult to describe operationally, partly because they oppose existing institutional forms of education and do not yet visualize many of the forms of the new social orders which they would create. Their work is frequently anti-institutional or anti-definitional in its form due to their pronounced emphasis on avoiding the apparent evils of existing social relations.

2. *Concepts of Interpersonal Relations.* The second subfamily to be considered among the interaction-oriented models is derived from stances toward the development of interpersonal relations. The model-makers in this group are concerned with improving interpersonal relations and their models have been developed to accomplish this. Among them are the theorists and clinical practitioners who have developed the various procedures for "sensitivity training" and "encounter groups" which have generated so much interest in recent years. Included also is the work of group dynamics specialists and analysts of interpersonal relations who have developed techniques for helping people reach one another more productively. We have included a model employed by the sensitivity training specialists of the National Training Laboratory.

We begin with models drawn from a conception of society—models which can be extremely useful for the classroom teacher because they provide him with ways of organizing classes into cohesive, productive groups.

## MODELS OF TEACHING
## DESIGNED TO IMPROVE DEMOCRATIC PROCESSES

It was natural that attempts would be made to use teaching methods to improve society. In the United States, extensive efforts have been made to develop classroom instruction as a model of democratic process. Variations on democratic process are probably more common than any other general teaching method as far as the educational literature is concerned. In terms of instructional models, democratic process has referred to organizing classroom groups to do any or all of the following tasks:

1. Develop a social system based on and created by democratic procedures.
2. Conduct scientific inquiry into the nature of social life and processes. In this case democratic procedures is synonomous with the scientific method and inquiry.
3. Engage in solving a social or interpersonal problem.
4. Provide an experienced-based learning situation.

The implementation of democratic methods of teaching has been exceedingly difficult. They require the teacher to have a high level of interpersonal *and* instructional skills. Also, democratic process is cumbersome and frequently slow; parents, teachers, and school officials often fear that it will not be efficient as a teaching method. In addition, a rich array of instructional resources is necessary, and these have not always been available. Probably the most important hindrance is that the school simply has not been organized to teach the social and intellectual processes of democracy. It has rather been directed toward and organized for basic instruction in academic subjects, and school officials and patrons have, for the most part, been unwilling to change that direction or organization.

*Difficulties w/ dem process*

## THE PHILOSOPHICAL UNDERPINNINGS

The dominating figure in the effort to develop models for democratic process has been John Dewey, and nearly all of the theoreticians who have devoted effort to reflective thinking since Dewey wrote *How We Think*[8] in 1910 have acknowledged their debt to him. However, those who have emphasized democratic process have by no means been homogeneous nor have they followed Dewey in the same ways or even directly. Charles Hubbard Judd in 1920s emphasized academic scholarship.[9] William Heard Kilpatrick, for many years a major spokesman of the Progressive movement, emphasized social problem-solving.[10] George Counts stressed not only problem-solving but also reconstruction of society.[11] Boyd Bode emphasized the general intellectual processes of problem-solving.[12]

A well-known statement of this group's concern with the democratic process and societal reconstruction was made in 1961 by Gordon H. Hullfish and Philip G. Smith in a book entitled *Reflective Thinking: The Method of Education*.[13] They stress the role of education in improving the capacity of the individual to reflect on the ways that he handles information, on his concepts, his beliefs, his values. A society of reflective thinkers would be capable of improving itself and preserving the uniqueness of individuals. Their philosophy contains many ideas or propositions common to democratic-process philosophies. It carefully delineates the inextricable relationship among the personal world of the individual, his intellect, social processes, and the functioning of a democratic society.

Hullfish and Smith see intellectual development and social process as inextricably related. For example, the development of skill in social process

[8] John Dewey, *How We Think* (Boston: Heath, 1910).

[9] C. H. Judd, *Education and Social Progress* (New York: Harcourt Brace Jovanovich, 1934).

[10] W. H. Kilpatrick, *The Project Method* (New York: Teachers College Press, 1919).

[11] George Counts, *Dare the School Build a New Social Order?* (New York: The John Day Company, 1932).

[12] Boyd Bode, *Modern Educational Theories* (New York: Macmillan, 1927).

[13] Gordon H. Hullfish and Phillip G. Smith, *Reflective Thinking: The Method of Education* (New York: Dodd, Mead, 1961).

requires skill in synthesizing and analyzing the viewpoints of those engaged in social interaction.

Next, they believe that knowledge is constructed and continuously reconstructed by individuals and groups. They stress that knowledge is not given to us merely through our sensory interactions with our environment, but that to have knowledge we must operate on experience to produce knowledge. As result, knowledge has a personal quality. It is necessarily unique for each individual. For example, a few hours before writing this, one of the authors stood on a rocky point looking into the Pacific Ocean against the brown of the California coast. He felt a quiet excitement and an appreciation of the sea and the rocks and the great peace of the scene about him. Yet the concept "sea," the concept "rock," and the concept "wave," and the excitement, peace, and appreciation he felt were not inherent in the experience themselves. These were constructed by the author in relation to that experience and to others he has had. He created some concepts and borrowed some from others. He generated some feelings and some beliefs and had been given some by imitating other people (the vast majority were borrowed in this way).

Thus, the individual's ways of reflecting upon reality are what make his world comprehensible to him and give him personal and social meaning. Therefore, the quality of an individual's ability to reflect on experience becomes a critical factor in determining the quality of the world he will construct about him. Someone who is insensitive to much of his experience and does not reflect on it will have a far less richly constructed world than someone who takes in a good deal of experience and reflects fully on it. It becomes critical for education to sensitize the individual to more and more aspects of his physical and social environment and to increase his capacity to reflect more fully on the environment.

The individual quality of knowledge is not without difficulties, especially when it comes to constructing a society. Nevertheless, Hullfish and Smith maintain that individual differences are the strength of a democracy and negotiating among them is a major democratic activity. The more an individual learns to take responsibility for reflecting on experience and developing a valid view of the world and a valid set of beliefs, the more it is likely that the resulting network of information, concepts, and values will be unique to the individual. In other words, the more fully reflective an individual is, the more he will develop his own personal processing system. A democratic society requires that we work together to reach each other's worlds and develop a shared perspective that will enable us to learn from each other and govern ourselves while preserving a pluralistic reality.

The perception of alternative frames of reference and alternative courses of action is essential to social negotiations. However, to do this requires very great personal development for one must have the ability and openness to examine not only one's own frame of reference but also the frames of reference of others. Only then can a mutual reality be constructed.[14]

The essence of a functioning democracy is the negotiation of problem definitions and problem solutions. The ability to negotiate alternative problem conceptions and to thrash out alternative problem solutions balances with helping each person negotiate his own world and helping him learn to negotiate a world with others.

Maintaining sense of meaning and life depends on the development of a valid and flexible way of dealing with reality. Failure to make life comprehensible and to negotiate reality with others will result in a feeling of chaos. The continual reconstruction of the value stances, and the ability to create value systems which are not unnecessarily dichotomous, are both essential to mature development.

Most models of teaching assume that one does something in particular in order to get a specific outcome from the learner. *On the contrary, those who emphasize democratic process hope that the outcome of any educational experience will not be completely predictable.* The democratic model-makers reason that if they are successful in persuading a student to inquire into the nature of his experience, and to develop his own way of viewing the world, it will be impossible to predict just how he will face any given situation. The alternative solutions that he generates to any problem should be unique to him and thus unpredictable on the basis of any educational experience which is given to him. Hence, if the student is taught an academic discipline, it is not so that he will know *exactly* the discipline which is known by others, but so that his exposure to a particular discipline will help him in creating his own frame of reference, and his own ways of ordering reality.

## SUMMARY

Those who have developed models of teaching based on a view of democracy-in-action have tended to be constructionists. They believe that each man constructs knowledge by reflecting on his own experience. The resulting world is pluralistic, and the essence of democratic process is the creation of interaction among the unique, personal worlds of individuals so that a shared reality is created. This shared reality should embrace the unique personal worlds and encourage their growth while providing for common investigation, growth, and governance.

[14] See Peter Berger and Thomas Luckman for a contemporary statement on the social construction of reality: Berger and Luckman, *Social Construction of Reality* (Garden City, N.Y.: Doubleday, 1966).

The Group Investigation, Jurisprudential, and Social Inquiry models focus on improvement of society through the practice of social processes and the intellectualization of social issues and concerns. The subfamily of interpersonal models share many of these same concerns but focus on conceptualizing the processes of social action, especially on understanding the emotional responses of members of a group to each other.

Theorists in this family reason that democratic processes call for well-functioning social groups. If human beings understand the dynamics of groups—especially the ways they reflect and affect individual responses—then interpersonal flexibility and the ability to respond to change can be increased and the possibilities for effective social membership enhanced.

# 2

# GROUP INVESTIGATION

## *Democratic Process as a Source*

The teaching models developed around democratic process have had prominent intellectual components, for most theorists of democratic process have combined their views of social process with views of the use of scientific or other intellectual strategies to help men create knowledge and a better social order. In *Democracy and Education*,[1] John Dewey recommended that the entire school be organized as a miniature democracy in which students would participate in the development of the social system and would, through this participation, gradually learn how to apply the scientific method to the perfection of human society. This, Dewey felt, would be the best preparation for citizenship in a democracy. John U. Michaelis has extracted from Dewey's work a formulation specifically for teaching the social studies at the elementary level.[2] Central to his method of teaching is the creation of a democratic group that defines and attacks problems of social significance.

In many respects Herbert Thelen's Group Investigation Model resembles the methods recommended by Dewey and Michaelis. Its goal is not to practice and learn the democratic process as such while indirectly instilling the scientific method. Rather, the Group Investigation Model attempts to combine in one teaching strategy, the form and dynamics of the democratic

[1] Dewey, *Democracy and Education* (New York: Macmillan, 1916).
[2] Michaelis, *Social Studies for Children in a Democracy* (Englewood Cliffs, N.J.: Prentice-Hall, 1963).

process and the process of academic inquiry. Like the Laboratory Method theoreticians, Thelen[3] is reaching for an experienced-based learning situation, conducive to the scientific method and highly transferable to later life situations.

## ORIENTATION OF THE MODEL

Thelen's conception of the democratic process and the basis of his teaching strategy come from a set of postulates regarding the social image of man. Education has to come from a conception of a social man, "a man who builds with other men the rules and agreements that constitute social reality. . . ."[4] Otherwise each man in his quest for self-maintenance and autonomy may well conflict with the similar efforts of other men. Any view of how man should develop has to make reference to the inescapable fact that life is *social*—and social man cannot act without reference to his fellows. In contributing to the establishment and modification of social agreements, each individual helps to determine both prohibitions and freedom for action. These rules of conduct, both implicit and explicit, in all fields—i.e., religious, political, economic, and scientific—constitute the culture of a society. For Thelen, this negotiation and renegotiation of the social order is the essence of the democratic process:

> Thus in groups and societies a cyclical process exists: individuals, interdependently seeking to meet their needs, must establish a social order (and in the process they develop groups and societies.) The social order determines in varying degrees what ideas, values and actions are possible, valid and 'appropriate'! Working within these 'rules' and stimulated by the need for rules the culture develops. The individual studies his reactions to the rules and re-interprets them to discover their meaning for the way of life he seeks. Through this quest, he changes his own way of life, and this in turn influences the way of life of others. But as the way of life changes, the rules must be revised, and new controls and agreements have to be hammered out and incorporated into the social order.[5]

The classroom is analogous to the larger society; it has a social order and a classroom culture and its students care about the way of life that develops there, that is, the standards and expectations that become established. Educational procedures should seek to harness the energy naturally generated by the concern for creating the social order. The Model for Teaching replicates the negotiation pattern of society. Through negotiation the students learn the academic domains of knowledge and ultimately to engage in social problem-solving. According to Thelen, knowledge in the

---

[3] Thelen is one of the founders of the National Training Laboratory.

[4] Herbert Thelen, *Education and the Human Quest* (New York: Harper & Row, 1960), p. 80.

[5] *Ibid.*, p. 80.

*process to knowledge is the important thing*

disciplines like the social order, is manufactured and revised by the process in other aspects of negotiation and renegotiation. One should not attempt to teach knowledge from any academic area without teaching the social process by which it was negotiated.

Thelen rejects the normal classroom order that develops around the basic values of comfort and politeness, or of keeping the teacher happy, substituting in their place the normative structure, teacher roles and student roles that support inquiry. He proposes that "...the teacher's task is to participate in the activities of developing the social order in the classroom for the purpose of orienting it to inquiry, and the 'house rules' to be developed are the methods and attitudes of the knowledge discipline to be taught. The teacher influences the emerging social order toward inquiring when he 'brings out' and capitalizes on differences in the way students act and interpret the role of investigator—which is also the role of member in the classroom."[6] To begin their process, the teaching strategy starts with a stimulus situation to which students "...can react and discover basic conflicts among their attitudes, ideas, and modes of perception. On the basis of this information, they identify the problem to be investigated, analyze the roles required to solve it, organize themselves to take these roles, act, report and evaluate these results. These steps are illuminated by reading, possibly by some short range personal investigation, and by consultation with experts. The group is concerned with its own effectiveness, and with its discussion of its own process as related to the goals of investigation."[7]

It would be reasonable to move from this point in our discussion to specific examples of Group Investigation. To do so, however, would short-circuit the fundamentals of the model and possibly commit the error of earlier interpreters and users of democratic process models. In their concentration on the overt activities of democratic process, many followers and interpreters of Dewey overlooked the underlying spirit which captures the essence of the democratic process and brings it to life. The overt activities of democratic process, if followed by rote, provide only lifeless empty applications quite unlike the democratic process and scientific method Dewey and Thelen have in mind. We may restate this point in the language of the *Models of Teaching*. That is, the syntax reflects the intent of the model, but merely carrying out the phases of the model—implementing the structure of interaction—does not ensure fulfillment of its spirit. Only in combination with the Principles for Reaction and the appropriate Social Organization aspects which incorporate the theory's underlying concepts, does the model take an organic quality. This is true, of course, for many of the models but is particularly so in this case. There is a rich educational literature on this

6 *Ibid.*, p. 81.
7 *Ibid.*, p. 82.

point. Many attempts to implement process did little to change educational outcomes because the implementation was superficial—the form but not the substance of democratic process was followed. To avoid a superficial interpretation let's return once again to Thelen's formulation, in an effort to identify and explore its theoretical underpinnings.

Three concepts are central to Thelen's strategy. These are his notions of inquiry, knowledge, and the dynamics of the learning group. The heart of Group Investigation lies in its formulation of inquiry. According to Thelen, the concern of inquiry is "to initiate and supervise the processes of giving attention to something; of interacting with and being stimulated by other people, whether in person or through their writings; and of reflection and reorganization of concepts and attitudes as shown in arriving at conclusions, identifying new investigations to be undertaken, taking action and turning out a better product."[8] The first element of inquiry is an event which the individual can react to and puzzle over—a problem to be solved. In the classroom the teacher can facilitate this by selecting content and casting it in terms of problem-situations. The provision of the problem itself will not generate the puzzlement, which is a major energy source for inquiry. The student must add an awareness of self and desire for personal meaning which will cause him to give attention to something and seek its reality. This requires the distinction between self and object. The student has to assume the dual roles of participant and observer characteristic of any experienced-based learner situation. That is, the student simultaneously inquires into something (participates in study) and observes himself as an inquirer. He tries simultaneously to learn and to improve himself as a learner. Inasmuch as inquiry is basically a social process, the student is aided in his self-observer role by the opportunity to interact with other puzzled people. In comparing his reactions to those of others, he is better able to see himself. This comparative interactive process occurs throughout the course of inquiry and serves different purposes at different points. At first, it illuminates one's own reaction and the conflicting viewpoints energize the student's interest in the problem. After the initial motivation, the differing viewpoints serve as parameters for the problem-situations providing a focus for their identification. This brings us to the second component of inquiry—the diagnostic process. That is, while the teacher can provide a problem-situation, it is up to the student as an inquirer to identify and formulate the problem and pursue its solution. Third, inquiry calls for first-hand activity in a real situation, and on-going experience that continually generates new data. This requires the student to possess a consciousness of method, so that he may collect data, associate and classify ideas recalling past experience, formulate and test hypotheses, study consequences, modify

[8] *Ibid.*, p. 85.

plans, etc. Finally, as a fourth element of inquiry, the student must develop the capacity for reflection, the ability to synthesize overt participative behavior with symbolic verbal behavior. Reflection requires the student to give conscious attention to his experience—explicitly formulate the conclusions and integrate these with his existing ideas. In this way ideas are shaken up and reorganized into new and more powerful patterns.

Let's examine a few examples that Thelen gives us to illustrate the flavor of inquiry and to point out the difference between inquiry and activity. The first example is drawn from a second grade social studies class dealing with the question "How do different people live?" The teacher proposed that the students select some group of people, find out how they live, and put this information in a play they would write themselves. Much to their surprise the students after some discussion selected prairie dogs as a focus for their study. Here is an account of their inquiry.

> They started their study by naming the characters for the play they would write, and of course the characters turned out to be baby, chicken, mother, father, farmer's boy, snake, etc. They made lists of questions to be answered: What do prairie dogs eat? Where do they live? What do they do with their time? How big are their families? Who are their enemies? etc. Individuals sought answers to questions from science pamphlets, books, the science teacher, officials of the local zoo, and I have no doubt at least a few of them talked to their parents to be taken to see the Disney opus. They reported their findings in compositions during the writing lessons. The plot of the play gradually took shape and was endlessly modified with each new bit of information. The play centered around family life, and there was much discussion and spontaneous demonstrations of how various members of the family would act. Most of these characterizations actually represented a cross-section of the home lives of seven-year-old children, as perceived by the children. But each action was gravely discussed and soberly considered, and justified in terms of what they knew about the ecology of prairie dogs.
>
> They built a stage with sliding curtains and four painted backdrops—more reference work here to get the field and farm right. The play itself was given six times, with six different casts, and each child played at least two different parts. There was never any written script; only an agreement on the line of action and the part of it to occur in each scene. And after each presentation the youngsters sat around and discussed what they had been trying to communicate, how it might be improved.[9]

Thelen contrasts this example with one drawn from a high school social studies class in which the students were to put on a series of television programs on the history of the community. As preparation, the students looked up information and visited historical sites taking pictures of important evidence.

[9] *Ibid.*, pp. 142–43.

Harry and Joe took pictures of an Indian mound, left there by original settlers. They took it from the south because the light was better that way; and they never discovered the northern slope where erosion had laid bare a burrow full of Indian relics. Mary and Sue spent two afternoons on a graph of corn production in the region; the graph was in a geography book the teacher gave them and the time was mostly spent in making a neat elaborately lettered document for the camera. The narrators were chosen for their handsome appearance, and much of the staging of the show (which used reports mostly) centered around deciding the most decorative way to seat the students. A lot of old firearms and household implements were borrowed from a local museum and displayed a sentence or two of comment for each.[10]

In this latter instance, Thelen acknowledges that the kids may have learned something about the region, but he points out that most of the energy, the measure of success, was the effectiveness of the television as a blend of entertainment and of information-giving. The roles in which the students inquired "were those of a *reporter* with a keen eye for human interest angles, rather than the sociologist's or historian's with a disciplined concern for the course of human events."[11]

These two examples illustrate the distinction between activity and inquiry. The actions of the second grade class investigating prairie dogs contained the elements of inquiry: puzzlement, self-awareness, methodology, and reflection. We may identify by looking at the examples given above and ask ourselves: Were there questions? Who formulated them? Who sought their answers? How was this information obtained? Was the information applied? Were conclusions drawn and who drew them? Activities are potential channels for inquiry but inquiry must emanate from the motivations and curiosity of the students. Activities cease to be inquiry when the teacher is the sole source of the problem identification and the formulation of plans or when the end product of inquiry takes precedence over the inquiry process.

If the development of knowledge is the goal of inquiry, knowledge must be defined. According to Thelen, it is not, as most schools presently hold, organized information, which he feels is only a knowledge byproduct. Thelen prefers to cast knowledge in behavioral terms, in the application of the universals and principles drawn from past experience to present experience. In the prairie dog example the process of discovering sciences was on center stage at all times; the principles of inquiry were what counted. The students were studying orientations for organizing experience-principles and rules which make experience coherent.

The continuous dialectic between ideas and experience is the means by which existing universals and principles are tested and new ones are generated. Thelen states:

[10] *Ibid.*, pp. 143–44.
[11] *Ibid.*, p. 144.

*Thelen:*
*knowledge*

Knowledge is unborn experience; it is the universals incorporated into the nervous system; it is a predisposition to approach the world with inquiry; it is meaningful past experience living within oneself; it is the seed of potential internal reorganization through which one keeps in touch with the changing world. Knowledge lies in the basic alternative orientations and the proposition through which new orientations can be built. . . .[12]

When students possess alternative orientations which they can scientifically apply to experience and which experience can alter, they possess the foundations of knowledge.

Why should investigation take the form of group investigation? The answer to this question is found in the relationship between Thelen's view of inquiry and learning and the dynamics of the group. Inquiry is more than the application of scientific method. There are emotional aspects of inquiry— emotions arising from student involvement and growing self-awareness, the seeking of personal meaning and the affect that accompanies conscious reflective behavior. Thus, we find Thelen's view of a learning situation as ". . . one which involves the emotions of the learner."[13] The group enhances the emotional context in two ways. The first is due to the interplay of interpretation in the group and the conflict between personal needs and the social purpose of the group. The group is both an arena for personal needs as individuals deal with their anxieties, doubts, and private desires and an instrument for solving social problems with the prerequisite of a common cause and culture. As these conflicting forces impinge on the individual, he finds himself inescapably involved in the social and academic dimensions of the inquiry. "He is driven by very profound and very pervasive psyche needs for the kind of classroom in which he can survive as a person and find a place for himself in the organization. Algebra may mean less than nothing to him, but self-esteem, freedom of sorts, feelings of growing adequacy and stimulation that provoke him into rewarding activity are important."[14] The social involvement of Group Investigation is a route, therefore, to disciplined academic inquiry. Initially, however, individuals become involved because the existence of the inquiry group forces upon them a conflict between their psyche needs and the group's socio or task requirements.

The second source of energy for emotional involvement is found in the incompatibility among the assumptions which underlie the varying reactions to the same phenomenon. As a group confronts a puzzling situation, the reactions of individuals vary widely, and the assumptive worlds which give rise to the different reactions are even more different than the reactions

[12] *Ibid.*, p. 51.
[13] Herbert Thelen, *Dynamics of Groups at Work* (Chicago: University of Chicago Press, 1954), p. 47.
[14] Thelen, *Education and the Human Quest,* p. 147.

themselves. The need to reconcile such difference generates a basic challenge. The newly perceived alternatives extend the student's experience by serving both as a source of self-awareness and a stimulant to his curiosity.

## STRUCTURE OF THE MODEL

Thelen feels that a "teachable group" is a prerequisite for any really deep group investigation. Ideally about 10 to 15 students should comprise the investigating group. This is large enough for a diversity of reactions and small enough for individual participation. There should be enough commonality of values that communication is easy and ways of working are similar but enough differences to generate alternative reactions. Finally, group members should possess a common level of sophistication and orientation toward the knowledge area to be investigated. If the range is too great, the levels of conceptualization will very likely be too far apart to enable the group to relate productively.[15]

In one of Thelen's examples the group is 11 adult women preparing to be elementary school teachers. This group manifests a common enough base to facilitate close relationship but contains enough diversity to generate the differing reactions that energize inquiry. They were investigating the skills, attitudes, and knowledge necessary to be an effective teacher. In effect, group inquiry was employed to build their teacher education program. The initial confrontation centered around seven elementary school classes that the teachers observed. They were given no instructions as to what to observe but simply told to report their findings to the group. Soon heated arguments developed over the interpretation of a kindergarten teacher's behavior. The discussion revealed a great many attitudes and ideas about teaching and learning as well as many submerged personal concerns about the course.

At that point the discussion dissolved into arguments and ceased being informative. Hence, the instructors broke in with the suggestion that the group accept the difference of opinion and more systematically examine the factors that influence classroom activities. Short filmstrip samples of classroom activities were then presented. The group listed all the factors they could think of to account for the differences among the samples. The purposes of the teacher seemed central. The next task, then, was to relate the observed behavior of children to the motivations of the teacher. Out of this task grew a checklist for studying the behavior and roles of the students. In other words, the original emotional conflict had led to the collection of new information, more disciplined analysis, and finally to an instrument for making judgments more objectively. The group continued to make and compare their observations. From these discussions individuals

15 *Ibid.*, p. 157.

were stimulated to pursue aspects of teaching that interested them and the instructors provided the appropriate source materials. The instructors then met on a private, personal basis with each person and developed further individual goals. But what were to be the next activities of the group as a whole? On the basis of their discussion with their students, the instructors were able to identify broad questions about child development that interested the group. Accordingly, they made a proposal to study the skills, attitudes, and orientations of children at different ages. The instructors proposed that conscious attention be given to how to conduct inquiry. The group began to study, calling in resource people, evaluating their progress gradually, and taking over responsibility for guiding their own action. The original inquiry into different reactions to the behavior of a teacher had been "recycled" into an inquiry into child development.

*Teacher's role*

The teacher's role in group investigation is one of counselor, consultant, and friendly critic. He must guide and reflect the group experience over three levels: the problem-solving or task level (What is the nature of the problem? What are the factors involved?) ; the group management level (What information do we need now? How can we organize ourselves to get this?) ; and the level of individual meaning (How do you feel about these conclusions? What would you do differently as a result of knowing about. . . .?).[16] This teaching role is a very difficult and sensitive one, for the essence of inquiry is student initiation and formulation. At the same time the instructor must (a) facilitate the natural processes of group development that are going to go on anyway so they won't use up all the energy of the group, (b) intervene in the group to harness its energy into potentially educative activities, and (c) supervise these educative activities so that educative learning that is personal meaning from the task-related experience actually occurs.[17] Intervention by the instructor should be minimal, however, unless the group bogs down seriously.

## CLASSROOM APPLICATION

Let us see how these roles might function in an example of group investigation with younger students. Imagine a sixth grade social studies class in a suburban school. The teacher has presented the students with a recent article in an urban newspaper vividly recounting the all-too-typical life of a twelve-year-old inner city child who died of an overdose of heroin. The children's reactions to the story and their speculation as to why it may have happened are very different. From this discussion the children decide to focus on an investigation of the drug problem. They begin by interviewing a physician and reading about drug use among children. Their investigation

---

16 Thelen, *Dynamics of Groups at Work,* pp. 52–53.
17 Thelen, *Education and the Human Quest,* p. 136.

is supplemented with a trip to a city neighborhood. As they try to formulate conclusions, they discover that the drug issue is a complex one with many contributing factors. On the basis of this finding the group "recycles" its investigation into the housing situation, the welfare system, and racial discrimination, as they relate to the plight of the drug-user. In fact, out of this initial group investigation confrontation evolves a semester of group investigation on urban life and problems.

## SYNTAX

The model begins with the confrontation of the students with a stimulating problem. The confrontation need not be a verbal one—it can be the provision of an experience. It can very well be a puzzlement which arises naturally—it might not be "provided" by a teacher. (Or it *might*!) If the students react, the teacher draws their attention to the differences in their reactions—the different stances they take, the variety of things they perceive, the different ways they organize things, and the various feelings they have. As the students become interested in their differences in reaction, the teacher draws them toward formulation of a problem, moving not to structure their problem for them, but to induce them to formulate it for themselves. After they formulate the problem, the students proceed to develop an attack on it, to analyze the required roles, and to organize themselves. Next, they act and report their result. Finally, the group evaluates its solution in terms of the original purposes of the group. Then the cycle begins to repeat itself, either with another confrontation or with a problem development growing out of the process of investigation itself.

## SOCIAL SYSTEM

The social system is democratic with governance by decisions developed from, or at least validated by, the experience of the group—within boundaries and in relation to phenomena identified by the teacher as objects to study.[18] The activities of the group are emergent with a minimal amount of external structure provided by the teacher. The students and teacher have equal status except for role differences.

## PRINCIPLES OF REACTION

The teacher is to function as an academic counselor, playing what one might think of as a vigorously recessive role in which the teacher is vigilant not to intrude structure, but equally vigilant to get the children to examine what they are doing in terms of the requirements of inquiry; that is, formulation and solution of a problem, consciousness of method, group management, and personal meaning and reflection.

[18] *Ibid.*, p. 148.

## SUPPORT SYSTEM

The support system for this kind of teaching needs to be extensive and responsive to the needs of the students. If this type of teaching is characteristic of a school, then that school needs to be equipped with a first-class library which provides information and opinion through a wide variety of media. The school also needs to provide access to resources outside of it. The children need to be able to go outside, both for their own investigation, and also to contact resource people as their experience is needed. One reason cooperative inquiry of this sort has been relatively rare is that the support systems were not adequate to maintain the level of inquiry.

## GENERAL APPLICABILITY OF THE MODEL

This model is highly versatile and comprehensive, blending the goals of academic inquiry, social interaction, and social process learning. It can be used in all subject areas, with all age levels where the teacher desires to emphasize the formulation and problem-solving aspects of knowledge rather than the intake of preorganized, predetermined information.

## INSTRUCTIONAL AND NURTURANT VALUES

Provided that one accepts Thelen's view of knowledge and its reconstruction, the Group Investigation Model (Figure 2-1) can be considered a very direct and probably efficient way of teaching academic knowledge as well as social process. It also appears likely to nurture interpersonal warmth and trust, respect for negotiated rules and policies, independence in learning, and a respect for the dignity of others.

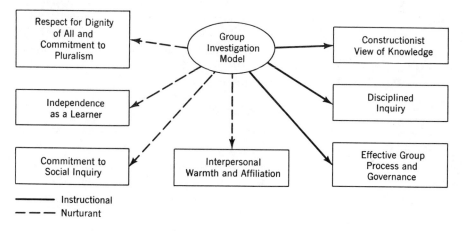

**Figure 2-1**

In deciding whether to use the model, the potential nurturant values may be as important as the likely direct instructional effects. Another model might be as appropriate for the teaching of academic inquiry, or even more likely, but the teacher might prefer group investigation for what it might nurture. Or, the teacher might prefer the nurturant effects of another model.

Certainly anyone who does not accept the constructionist view would probably select a model with a more highly structured view of how knowledge should be approached with children.

Later in the book, after we have considered more models, we will consider the question of comparative selection.

### TABLE 2-1 Summary Chart: Group Investigation Model

| *Syntax:* | *Phase One* | *Phase Two* | *Phase Three* |
|---|---|---|---|
| | Encounter with a puzzling situation (planned or unplanned). | Exploration of reactions to the situation. | Formulate study task. Organize for study (problem definition, role, assignments, etc.). |
| | *Phase Four* | *Phase Five* | *Phase Six* |
| | Independent and group study. | Analysis of progress and process. | Recycling of activity. |

| | |
|---|---|
| *Principles of Reaction:* | Teacher plays a facilitative role directed at group process (helps learners formulate plan, act, manage group) and requirements of inquiry (consciousness of method). Functions as an academic counselor. |
| *Social System:* | Democratic process, i.e., group decisions. *Low* external structure. Puzzlement must be genuine—it can't be imposed. Authentic exchanges are essential. Atmosphere of reason and negotiation. |
| *Support System:* | Environment must be able to respond to a variety of learner demands. Teacher and student must be able to assemble what they need when they need it. |

# 3

# THE JURISPRUDENTIAL MODEL

*A Social Model Propelled by the Artificial Creation of a Discipline*

Donald Oliver and James Shaver, in their Harvard Social Studies Project, created an intellectual structure which could serve as the basic strategy for teaching students to analyze and take positions on public issues in American society. Their achievement is unusual because there are several disciplines among the social sciences that provide structures which can be used to analyze values. Oliver and Shaver were well acquainted with these, and much of their rationale is built on a scholarly analysis which makes use of existing disciplines. However, in creating the structure which organized the Harvard Social Studies Project, they created a kind of quasi-discipline. The model that results has interest not only on its own terms (and it is exceedingly interesting on its own terms) but because it illustrates a potentially useful method for dealing with many curriculum-construction tasks. Teachers and developers might well consider the creation of intellectual structures when the ones that exist in the disciplines are not adequate for their purposes.

For our purposes, the work of Oliver and Shaver has several dimensions of interest. Their concern to develop a pluralistic society is in accord with that of Thelen and Dewey. With Thelen, their approach is a type of social inquiry characterized by vigorous intellectual activity and serious dialogue. Their model is distinguished, however, by having a specific scheme for guiding the discourse and leading students simultaneously toward greater sophistication and value commitment.

## ORIENTATION OF THE MODEL

### THE PHILOSOPHICAL POSITION

The conceptualization begins with the assertion "that the multiplicity of purposes in American society can be summarized in one very abstract phrase: to promote the dignity of each individual that lives in the society."[1] Oliver and Shaver hold commitment to human dignity as the fundamental value (goal) of our society. If human dignity is to exist, then individuals must be able to make choices between alternatives; choice is the essential defining characteristic of human dignity. Oliver and Shaver postulate that for this to be the case, there must be many groups, or subcultural groups, in the society that maintain different positions with respect to central questions. "A plurality of active groups—i.e., pluralism, is a necessary ingredient of a free society, because it is the only natural mechanism that can insure some freedom of choice. Pluralism, as we are using the term, implies the existence of not only different or political partisan groups within the society, but of various sub-cultures that claim the mutual respect of one another, at least to the extent that there is free communications among them."[2] In other words, Oliver and Shaver envision a free democracy as a society in which there are a multiplicity of positions with respect to the important issues in the society and there are groups which support the positions. Furthermore, these groups must be able to negotiate with one another rather than confront one another unilaterally.

They reason, therefore, that a free society requires open conflict among groups who represent different positions on important issues, but that the society must have a common standard as a means for dealing with the conflict and resolving it. Negotiation must characterize the conflict situations.

The framework for analyzing public issues emerges from their particular conception of the nature of social values and the ways of using social values. Oliver and Shaver note that social values operate at different levels of generality. "Some apply to specific groups; some apply to all men; some apply to specific situations; some apply to all situations. The more specific values often contradict the general values."[3] More difficult, however, is the fact that often those values we think of as the basic or general values—i.e., personal freedom, equality, consent or representation, due process, freedom of speech or conscience, cultural autonomy—are in conflict with each other, particularly at the operative level. Hence, we cannot resolve these practical, political, or social controversies on the basis of these general values alone. "If these values are final, permanent and universal, what do we do when

---

[1] Donald W. Oliver and James P. Shaver, *Teaching Public Issues in the High School* (Boston: Houghton Mifflin, 1966), p. 9.

[2] *Ibid.*, p. 10.

[3] *Ibid.*, p. 23.

one of them contradicts another? If both are final, both must be accepted as right; it is impossible to choose between them as criteria for action."[4] As a solution Oliver and Shaver posit a higher moral plane and put forth the more general value of "human dignity" as the final or root value. Human dignity, with choice as its defining characteristic, is most often expressed as a balance of values. If this conception of human dignity is to have any reality, however, new ways of using social values must be devised for our present means of approaching value conflicts does not lend itself to flexibility and choice. This requirement brings Oliver and Shaver to their second important distinction between the two ways of regarding social values.

They emphasize that values can be seen or used on what they call a dimensional basis, as contrasted to an "ideal" basis. If social values are construed as ideals, then they have to be dealt with on an either-or basis. In that case, either one lives up to a value or he does not. If, for example, one approves of equality of all races before the law in the ideal sense, he feels it either has been or has not been achieved. If, on the other hand, values are seen on a dimensional basis, then one can judge degrees of desirable conditions on a continuum. For example, one can accept a compromise that ensures some but not all possible equality. Politically one might opt for such a position in the hope of getting a little bit more next time around. Oliver and Shaver use the example of free speech, and suggest that if we see free speech as a total ideal, something to be preserved at all costs and all situations, then we are unable to cope with situations where it might be desirable to abrogate free speech temporarily in order to provide for public safety. (For instance, a speaker might be prevented from continuing a speech because a hostile crowd is about to do something violent to him. In such a case one might interfere and abrogate his free speech in order to provide for his safety and prevent the crowd from doing things that might be regretted later on.) Oliver and Shaver note that, "Both conceptions of value have particular strengths. Thinking of a value as an ethical ideal or ethical absolute tends to focus our attention on the essential defining characteristics of the value and prevents us from pretending that compromises with the value really don't matter. Thinking of the value as a dimensional construct, on the other hand, allows us to apply the value more flexibly in a broad range of situations and to deal more realistically with problems of value conflict. Rather than simply saying a value is or is not violated in a particular situation, we can describe degrees of violation and weigh the violation against other 'goods' protected in the same situation."[5] "When we consider social values on a dimensional basis our ethical

4 *Ibid.,* p. 25.
5 *Ibid.,* p. 25.

problem is to determine at what point on a value dimension an action should be categorized as intolerable or bad or at what point it should be given priority over another competing value."[6]

Oliver and Shaver identify a number of ways that value conflicts can be approached, and from this analysis they develop a conceptual framework within which the ethical commitment of a democratic society can be brought to bear on the analysis of public issues. It is this framework that provides the essence of their strategy.

They assume that our society needs to proceed by a process of rational consent—a process or a set of processes by which individuals consent to specific decisions or to procedures, such as legislative ones, for making decisions. The important kinds of decisions are those in which there is conflict among the alternatives, because these are the ones in which the alternatives are significantly different from one another. They represent different cultural solutions to important problems. Whenever conflict is involved three kinds of problems are likely to arise to some extent.

> One problem involves clarifying which values or legal principles are in conflict, and choosing among them. The second problem involves clarifying the facts around which the conflict has developed. A third involves clarifying the meanings or uses of words which describe the controversy.[7]

These can be regarded respectively as *definitional* problems, *value* problems, and *factual* problems. Definitional problems involve the clarification of words. Value problems involve the clarification of values, issues, or legal principles, and factual problems involve the establishment of the realities of the situation.

In order to cope with the value problems, definitional problems, and problems of fact, Oliver and Shaver have created the general strategy that they refer to as the "Jurisprudential Framework for Teaching the Analysis of Public Issues." The framework is complex because the analysis of public issues is complicated. For example, the three kinds of problems are often related. Value problems and definitional problems occur and are related in many controversial situations in which lack of clarity creates value conflict. This makes the problems of inquiring into value conflicts extremely complex and they turn away from simplified analysis.

## STRUCTURE OF THE MODEL

The jurisprudential framework consists of a set of intellectual operations which can "be made explicit in the analysis of political controversy," and a rough logical order in which these intellectual operations might take

6 *Ibid.*, p. 27.
7 *Ibid.*, p. 89.

place. Not all the intellectual operations need be followed in the analysis of any particular issue, nor need they be followed in the order they are listed; however, there is some logic to the order. It is assumed that several of the intellectual operations will be brought to play on any one issue.

1. *Abstracting general values from concrete situations.* The student should be aware of and understand ethical and legal concepts; and he should be able to translate concrete problem situations into ethical and legal terms. To use Oliver and Shaver's example, "If the problem is whether or not Congress should pass an anti-trust act...the student must be able to see that the decision can be construed in terms of such general values as property and contract rights, protection of equal rights for large and small businessmen alike, and protection of the interests of the community at large."[8] In other words, the student needs to take concrete problem situations, and attempt to put them into a general ethical-legal framework.

2. *Using general value concepts as dimensional constructs.* The student needs to characterize each value on a dimensional basis so that he is able to distinguish degrees of violation or dilution. In other words, students should learn not to use values as all-or-none categories, but to see the *possibility of the partial achievement of a value* in a concrete situation. For example, in the situation above it simply may not be possible to provide small businesses with equal power to that of large ones, using legal means. To do so might be to violate some of the rights of property of large businesses and others. The values of equality of opportunity and the right to hold property each have to be compromised, probably, in order to arrive at a situation that is not totally unfair to one interest or the other.

3. *Identifying conflicts between value constructs.* In dealing with a concrete situation, the student needs to determine whether more than one value can be abstracted from the situation, and if it can, whether the values abstracted conflict with one another. Returning to one of the examples presented above, the desire to provide equality of opportunity in certain respects can conflict with the desire to protect property rights equally, when it happens that the acquisition of property by one group gives it advantages over the other.

4. *Identifying classes of value-conflict situations.* In other words, the student learns to identify concrete problems in terms of their similarities and differences, and to develop a conception of the types of value-conflict situations that occur during controversial situations.

5. *Developing analogies to the problem which is under consideration.* Analogies enable us to see our consistencies and inconsistencies. If, for example, we identify five situations relating to the same value, we can tell whether our position on that value is consistent by making analogies which enable us to compare our value position in each situation.

8 *Ibid.*, p. 127.

6. *Working toward a general qualified position.* The student is pressed to work toward general policies by which he can make decisions when two values are in conflict, and to apply those policies to fresh situations. For example, the value of free speech in many situations comes into conflict with the need to protect the community. In time of war, should one permit the enemy to send over individuals who will advocate the overthrow of the government? After examining a number of situations in which the value of free speech in communication conflicts with the safety of the community, the student can gradually arrive at a policy statement which will say something like, "Under such and such circumstances, I will sacrifice such and such amounts of free speech, in terms of such and such kinds of community safety." And the other way around, "In the interests of free speech, I will sacrifice such and such amounts of public safety, and risk the security of the community in order to protect the free communication."

7. *Testing the factual assumptions behind a qualified value position.* When one makes a policy statement, or a qualified value position, he assumes that behaving in a certain way will have an effect of a certain kind. This assumption needs to be tested. For example, "Will permitting free speech of any kind during a war actually affect the public safety in any way?" If the fact is that it *will* endanger the public safety, then one might say that there is factual merit in the position that one will abrogate the right of free speech in order to protect the community. If, on the other hand, it does not decrease the public safety, that is another matter.

A good contemporary example of this is the controversy over capital punishment. Those who wish to see capital punishment abolished feel that it violates the right to life, and makes the state a legal murderer. Those who are in favor of capital punishment may agree with the preceding position, but feel that the punishment is worth it to protect the community from those who would commit murder. One of the factual controversies, involving both value positions, is whether capital punishment actually does or does not decrease the probability of a murderer committing a murder. If it turns out that capital punishment does not act as a deterrent, then one position obtains an advantage. If it does act as a deterrent, the other position gains an advantage.

8. *Testing the relevance of statements.* Once one develops policy positions, they must pass the test of relevance to any particular situation. For example, welfare payments to avoid destitution of children are sometimes attacked on the grounds that they contribute to the idleness of the parents. The question is, even if that were the case, whether the idleness of the parents has any relevance to the problem of protecting the children against hunger, lack of medical care, and so on.

These eight general operations are the intellectual framework which is to be applied to the analysis of public issues in order to teach students how to sort out the value problems, the definitional problems, and the factual problems, and to come to policy positions that reflect the balancing of values, and an appreciation of the dimensionality of values as they apply to particular situations.

The essence of the teaching strategy is to engage the students in a dialogue in such a way that these eight intellectual operations are continuously performed. Roughly, it can be said that there is a good possibility that they could be performed sequentially in relation to a given problem. As stated earlier, this is by no means always true, and it is not important to press for the sequence of operations. What is important is to see that they are performed in relation to ths particular issue, so that the student becomes increasingly skillful in performing each of them.

## CLASSROOM APPLICATION

The conduct of constructive controversy cannot take place in a vacuum. Students must have some familiarity with the broad historical, sociological, economic, and/or political background of the problem before they develop a position. On the other hand, students cannot be "told" how to conceptualize the problem; they must experience, become personally involved in the problematic situation as they formulate their positions. Oliver and Shaver have resolved this "chicken and egg" phenomena by building controversial case materials which provide non-analyzed, conceptual information as well as dramatic impact. These provide the focus for dialogue. Analysis of the controversy will center, as discussed earlier, on clarifying the conflicting values or legal principles, clarifying the facts of the controversy, and clarifying the meanings or uses of words which describe the controversy. Oliver and Shaver provide specific suggestions for dealing with each of these problems.[9] They also present a valuable framework for describing the teaching dialogue. This can serve as a map for guiding or lens for viewing one's discussion posture.

On a different level, we can see more clearly the general paradigm of their teaching strategy in the following two examples. In the first example, a short controversial case and analytical comments are presented. The second example is an annotated excerpt of student-teacher dialogue.

### Illustration One
### The Sidewalk Speech

On a raw, windy afternoon in March, a hot-headed, earnest young student named Barry Schwartz was making a speech to a crowd in a small shopping area. The street was in a Negro neighborhood in Poughkeepsie, New York. Schwartz stood on a large wooden box on the sidewalk and shouted at the crowd in a high-pitched voice through a loudspeaker system attached to an

---

[9] *Ibid.*, pp. 91–113.

automobile. He waved his arms, stamped his feet, and once in a while smacked a fist in his palm. He wanted to publicize a meeting of the Young Progressives of America that was to be held that evening. Among other things, Schwartz said,

"The mayor of this city is a champagne-sipping bum; he doesn't care who crushed the Negro people."

"The President of the United States is a bum."

"The Legion of American Veterans is a Nazi Gestapo."

"The Negroes don't have equal rights; they should rise up in arms and fight for their rights."

The crowd listening to Schwartz numbered 75 or 80 people, both Negro and white. It filled the sidewalk and spread out into the street. The people were restless. There was some pushing, shoving, and milling around. Some men picked up bricks and threatened to throw them at Schwartz. Lincoln Frost, who owned a nearby store, was afraid for his plate glass windows, so he phoned the police.

Lieutenant Collins and Sergeant Davis drove up in a squad car to investigate. For a while they just sat in the car and watched. Then one of the women onlookers who thought Schwartz should get a chance came over and said, "What's the matter? You scared? Can't you cops make people behave right?" A big, muscular man nearby turned around and said, "If you cops don't get that guy off his orange crate in two minutes, I'll shove it down his throat." Then he elbowed his way into the crowd until he was very close to Schwartz.

Lieutenant Collins pushed his way after him through the crowd and asked Schwartz to break up the crowd "to prevent it from resulting in a fight." He repeated the suggestion several times. Each time Schwartz ignored the policeman and went on talking. During all this time the crowd was pressing closer around Lieutenant Collins and Schwartz. The muscular man began urging the men near him to "Get Schwartz." Finally, Collins told Schwartz he'd have to arrest him for his own safety, and ordered him to get down from the box.

Schwartz got off the box, but as Collins took him through the crowd to the squad car, he shouted, "What's happening to free speech in this country? I've got a right to say what I think even if the big-wigs don't like it. I've got a right to talk even if some bigots standing around here want me to shut up."

Schwartz was tried and convicted of disorderly conduct and sentenced to thirty days in the county jail. Schwartz appealed the conviction because he said it took away his rights under the First and Fourteenth Amendments of the American Constitution.

In discussing the "Sidewalk Speech" we can ask a number of important questions to clarify the problem. Are any important values being violated? Barry Schwartz claims his freedom of speech is abridged. The Poughkeepsie police claim that the peace and order of the neighborhood is threatened. Clearly, there is a conflict over important values. Further questions: Is there any legal basis to support these values? Does the violation of a value in these circumstances also violate a law? And even more important: Does the government have the power under the Constitution to make the law which has allegedly been violated? In this particular case, is there any constitutional protection for freedom of speech? The answer is plain, as Barry Schwartz points out: in the First and Fourteenth Amendments. We might also ask: Does the community have the authority to make laws prohibiting disorderly conduct? Again the answer is surely "yes." We now have a conflict not only between values but also between laws which are designed to protect these values. Although we know that constitutional law is supreme, we also know that the First Amendment does not necessarily protect people from unreasonable use of free speech. Assuming that we want to protect peace and order, then, how is order to be preserved? By arresting the speaker or by restraining those who threaten the speaker with violence? Which course of action is taken depends to a large degree on how "reasonable" use of free speech is defined.

This is not only a definitional and a value problem. It is closely related to an important factual issue: What is a clear and accurate description of the problem situation? The relevant factual questions in "The Sidewalk Speech" center on how much violence actually occurred and to what extent there was an immediate threat of more violence. In this connection the following factual questions might be important:

How large was the crowd?
To what extent did the crowd obstruct traffic or pedestrians?
To what extent was there 'pushing, shoving and milling around'?
How many people actually threatened Schwartz?
How serious were their intentions?
How many policemen were available to keep order?

## Illustration Two
### Excerpt of a Discussion
### That Has Focused on the Question
### of Full Voting Rights for Negroes

| *Dialogue* | *Annotation* |
|---|---|
| Teacher: What do you think, Steve? | |
| Steve: I think that the police power of local government can go only so far, that the constitutional rights of voting—maybe the Negroes should have them. | |
| Teacher: Negroes should have the right to vote, even though there may be all kinds of violence and resistance. We should send troops into the South and protect every individual's right to vote? | The teacher suggests that providing voting rights may threaten a second important value: the safety of the community; and this in turn may threaten local control by the states, if federal intervention is required to keep order. |
| Steve: I'm not saying that. I don't | Questions factual assumption of |

| Dialogue | Annotation |
|---|---|
| think that we would have to send down troops. | teacher. The teacher can, at this point, choose to debate the factual assumption or treat the assumption hypothetically and clarify the value commitment of the student. |
| Teacher: But what if it did go that far? | The teacher chooses the latter course. |
| Steve: Probably; yes. | |
| Teacher: Suppose people called Negroes on the phone who intended to vote and said, "If you vote tomorrow, something might very well happen to your kids." Do you think we should send the FBI down there to investigate these intimidations? | The teacher modifies the hypothetical situation to determine the point at which the student's position will change in favor of local control and against federal intervention. He is shifting the meaning of "violence" to do this. |
| Steve: No. | |
| Teacher: Why not? | The student reverses his position with the shift in the situation. |
| Steve: If the threat is carried out; then I would send down troops or the FBI. | The student is aware of the reversal of his position and explains the essential criterion determining the reversal: overt use of force to prevent the Negro from voting. The student has qualified his position. |
| Teacher: After something has happened to the courageous Negro's family, then you would send someone down to stop it.   You don't go along with the notion that if there is an atmosphere of fear and intimidation we should do something to change the atmosphere so that people will be free to vote. We shouldn't do anything until there is actual violence? | Emphasizes the negative consequences of the student's position.   The teacher now raises the definitional question: Do we have to commit an act of physical violence against a person before we have violated his rights? Is threat of violence, to some degree, also "violence"? |
| Steve: In the case of Negroes, yes. | |
| Teacher: Why? | |
| Steve: Because I don't want to give them the complete power to vote. This is taking a little of it away. | |
| Teacher: You want to deny some Negroes the right to vote, a right you are willing to give to whites? | |
| Steve: Yes. | The student is operating with two categories of citizenship. The teacher is here asking him to justify classification on the basis of race. |
| Teacher: Why? | |
| Steve: Because I feel that Negroes are inferior to whites. | Children are classified as different from adults and denied full rights of citizenship. In a sense, it is because they are "inferior." This |

| *Dialogue* | *Annotation* |
|---|---|
| | response does have a rational component which the teacher feels obligated to explore. |
| Teacher: In what respect? | |
| Steve: In intelligence, in health, in crime rates. | The student states the criteria on which his classification is based. |
| Teacher: You are suggesting that if a person is tubercular or sick, you should deny him the right to vote. | The teacher is here challenging the relevance of a criterion on the basis of which the student is making his classification. |
| Steve: No. | |
| Teacher: But if a Negro is sick we don't let him vote? | |
| Steve: Let him vote, sure. It is just that I think they are inferior for these reasons. I'm not saying because of these reasons I'm not going to let him vote. | |
| Teacher: Then for what reasons aren't you going to let them vote? | |
| Steve: Because I think they are inferior because of these reasons. (Student then laughs self-consciously, aware of his inconsistency.)[10] | At this point the student has contradicted an earlier position. |

The essence of the Jurisprudential Teaching Strategy is embodied in the student-teacher dialogue. It is here that the student explores a controversial area, finds out where he stands and how he might best defend his position. In this interaction, the role of the teacher is a crucial one. Oliver and Shaver have characterized the teacher's position in the following way:

> The role of the teacher in such a dialogue is complex, requiring that he think on two levels at the same time. He must first know how to handle himself as he challenges the student's position and as his own position is challenged by the student. This is the Socratic role. Second, he must be sensitive to and aware of the general process of clarification or obscuration that takes place as the dialogue unfolds. He must, that is, be able to identify and analyze the complicated strategies being employed by various protagonists to persuade others that a stand is 'reasonable' or 'correct.' Nor is it sufficient for the teacher simply to teach a process of questioning evidence, questioning assumptions or pointing out 'loaded words.' In matters of public policy, factual issues are generally handmaids to ethical or legal stands which cannot be sloughed off as 'only matters of opinion.' Clarification of evaluative and legal issues, then, becomes a central concern.[11]

[10] Oliver and Shaver, *Teaching Public Issues in the High School,* pp. 89–91; 150–52. Copyright 1966 by Donald W. Oliver and James P. Shaver.
[11] *Ibid.,* p. 115.

## MODEL

### SYNTAX

The situation begins with the identification of a public issue. Oliver and Shaver provide a convenient analysis of a number of issues which would be likely to be fruitful. The issue may either be generated by the teacher and presented to the student, or it may arise from student study or from a conflict situation in the classroom or in the community. Then dialogue and study are engaged in over the particular issue, and the teacher works to see that the eight operations are performed as thoroughly as possible as they are relevant to the merits of the case, to the interest of the students, and to their ability to handle the material involved. The eight operations provide a kind of floating guide to the behavior of the teacher as he moderates the dialogue among the students and himself.

### SOCIAL SYSTEM

The jurisprudential framework was constructed with the assumption that there would be a rigorous dialogue, conducted more or less democratically with each individual's views and opinions equally respected, and also subject to the same scrutiny. Because of the nature of the operations, the social climate would be by no means mild, for a vigorous analysis of value is only possible in an open, abrasive climate. There is no reason for this climate to be unkind or intolerant, and, in fact, we can expect that the discussion would not remain open very long if the abrasive vigor were not tempered with a good deal of kindness and tolerance and respect for the dignity of each individual on his own terms. However, the teacher in the sense that he is continually pressing for the eight operations would play a leading role, and bears responsibility for seeing that the debate is solid and the issues are explored thoroughly.

### PRINCIPLES OF REACTION

The teacher insures an intellectual climate where all views are respected. He maintains the intellectual vigor of the debate by continually pressing for the eight operations.

### SUPPORT SYSTEM

Two kinds of support are needed. One serves to help students identify information about the problem situations which are focused on. The other provides access to those who have studied values and have identified ethical and legal positions that can be brought to bear in the discussion. Oliver and Shaver have developed sets of source documents which relate to value conflict in American society and these sets can serve as partial informational support as those issues are approached.

## GENERAL APPLICABILITY OF THE MODEL

Oliver and Shaver developed their model specifically to improve students' ability to analyze public issues and to develop and clarify value positions which they can use in the public domain. As such, they attempt to teach a framework which changes the ways that students process information about public issues, a framework designed to give them control over their own value positions and those of others. They do not pretend in any way that their teaching strategy would be applicable to a wider set of objectives.

It is interesting to note that they report an experiment in which they attempted to teach the framework, partly under what they call recitation analytic and partly under what they call Socratic analytic teaching methods. One group of children was taught by the Socratic method, and the other by the recitation method during the discussion of controversial cases. Recitation teaching is characterized by teacher control of knowledge. Students, in the extreme case, are called upon to fill in the sequence of information which the teacher wants to develop in class. Socratic teaching is "clearly adversarial. . . . Socratic teaching requires that the student do more than describe the controversy in the terms in which the teacher (or assigned material) has presented it. . . . Here the emphasis is not only on knowledge provided by the teacher as background for discussion but on the process by which the student arrives at a decision about the topic under consideration."[12] "The most striking result presented by these data, is that at the end of the experimental period, the groups taught by the two styles behaved similarly on every measure of learning administered."[13] Apparently, the jurisprudential method had about the same effect under both conditions. Nonetheless, it is our opinion that the jurisprudential method is designed to be worked under generally Socratic-type conditions with analytic discussion and not recitation being the mode of study.

As indicated earlier, one of the interesting aspects of Oliver and Shaver's strategy is the fact that it involved the deliberate creation of a discipline. As applied to curriculum construction problems there may be many other areas, particularly in the social domains, in which educators might well consider the development of a structure similar to that of a discipline if one does not exist pertinent to their pedagogical purposes.

### INSTRUCTIONAL AND NURTURANT VALUES

The Jurisprudential Teaching Model (Figure 3-1) was designed to teach, directly, the jurisprudential framework, a commitment to pluralism and respect for alternative views, and an ability to carry on a dialogue to develop social policy. Indirectly it seems likely that it will nurture a commitment

---

[12] Oliver and Shaver, *Teaching Public Issues,* p. 177.
[13] *Ibid.,* p. 301.

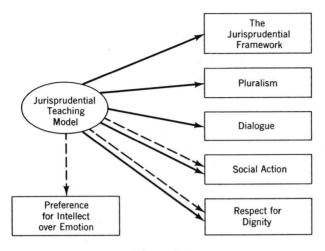

**Figure 3-1**

to social action and a respect for the point of view and dignity of one's fellow man. It seems probable that it will also nurture a preference for intellectual rather than emotional solutions to problems.

**TABLE 3-1 Summary Chart: Jurisprudential Teaching Model**

| *Syntax:* | *Phase One* | *Phase Two* |
|---|---|---|
| | Identification of public issue. | Dialogue in which the light operations described by Oliver and Shaver are guides for teacher-moderated discussion. |
| *Principles of Reaction:* | Teacher (1) insures an intellectual climate where all views are respected; (2) preserves the intellectual solidity of the debate by continually pressing for the right operations. | |
| *Social System:* | *Moderate* to *high* structure with teacher initiating and controlling discussion. However, an atmosphere of openness and intellectual equality prevail. | |
| *Support System:* | Source documents which can be focused on as problem situations and other informational supports that elaborate the ethical and legal value positions which relate to a particular issue. | |

# 4

# SOCIAL INQUIRY

*An Inquiry Model for the*
*Social Studies\**

For more than a decade, "inquiry" has been one of the rallying cries of educational reformers. However, the term has actually meant many kinds of things to its users. To some, inquiry has meant a general position toward child-centered learning, and has referred to building most facets of education around the natural inquiry of the child. To others, it has meant the use of the modes of inquiry of the academic disciplines as teaching models.

Many of the approaches to teaching described in this book share more or less academic definitions of inquiry: the Inductive Model developed by Hilda Taba (Chapter 7), the Scientific Inquiry Model built on the practice of biology by makers of the Biological Sciences Study Committee curriculum (Chapter 9), and the procedures for Inquiry Training developed by T. Richard Suchman (Chapter 8). Others are concerned with developing student capacity to inquire into and reflect on the nature of social life, particularly the course of their own lives and the direction of their society. This stance toward inquiry is generated from a philosophical belief that the promotion of a reflective and inquiring frame of reference will improve the quality of personal and social existence. Thelen and Oliver and Shaver share many of these concerns, although they have worked them out differently in the operational sense.

Byron Massialas and Benjamin Cox[1] are also representatives of the social

* Proponents: Byron Massialas and Benjamin Cox.
[1] Byron Massialas and Benjamin Cox, *Inquiry in Social Studies* (New York: McGraw-Hill, 1966).

inquiry approach as it applies to the social studies. Their concern is primarily with the improvement of society—the solution of societal problems. "It is our contention that in view of the prevailing conditions in our culture, the single, most important goal of education should be the reflective examination of values and issues of current import."[2]

Massialas and Cox take the position that the school has to be an active participant in what they call the "creative reconstruction" of the culture. The school has no business maintaining only one set of values which reflect a single segment of United States society. Neither does it have the right to avoid the value controversies that are necessary in a pluralistic democracy, nor can it reasonably avoid the difficulties in the culture and the problems which require systematic cooperation of all of its citizens. On the contrary, they believe that the school must deal actively with the serious and critical areas of public controversy; that the school must make a solid effort to teach citizens to reflect on their values and the values of others and to participate with others in the creative reconstruction of the society. The method of inquiry they recommend bears some resemblance to the general methodologies described by Hullfish and Smith and Thelen, but it also has a number of unique aspects that are worth noting, especially when we consider the popularity of "inquiry" today, and the number of people who are attempting to explore it as an educational method.

## ORIENTATION OF THE MODEL

### GENERAL CONDITIONS OF INQUIRY

There are three essential characteristics of the reflective classroom, as explored by Massialas and Cox. They stress first that the inquiry model cannot take place in any kind of classroom. The social aspects of the classroom are especially important as the setting in which inquiry can proceed as a general method. An open climate of discussion is a requirement. "All points of view and statements are solicited and accepted as propositions that merit examination."[3]

An emphasis on hypotheses as the focus of inquiry is the second characteristic of the reflective classroom. The discussion is oriented around hypothetical solutions of problem situations and the nature of hypotheses themselves. Knowledge is viewed as hypotheses which are continually tested and retested. The focus on the hypothetical nature of knowledge requires a continual negotiation as the members of a class and their teacher collect data relevant to the hypotheses, revise their notions, and try again. The atmosphere then becomes one of negotiation, and a willingness to modify one's ideas in the

[2] *Ibid.*, p. 12.
[3] *Ibid.*, p. 12.

face of evidence. Hypothesizing calls into play skills of logic, for the logical formulation and implication of the hypothesis is as much a part of inquiry as experimentation and observation.[4]

The third distinguishing aspect of the reflective classroom is the use of fact as evidence. "The classroom is recognized as a form where scientific inquiry is engaged."[5] In the classroom, the validity and reliability of facts are considered as well as the testing of a hypothesis. It is the validation of facts that is given the greatest consideration.

These characteristics then, the open climate of discussion, the focus on hypothesis, and the validation of facts are the social conditions within which the model can be enacted.

## THEORETICAL APPLICATION

Massialas and Cox describe phases for carrying out inquiry in the social studies classroom. They also provide a hypothetical illustration which we will follow through.

### Orientation

Orientation is simply the sensitization of the teachers and students to a particular kind of problem. The problem may have literally any origin, so long as it results in a problem in the social domain. It may arise from a real-life contemporary situation, from reflection on reading, from a conflict within the classroom itself, or from any number of other sources. The important thing is that the problem be one which is sensed by all concerned and which can be summarized as a genuine problem. That is, it is not simply an obstacle to "good behavior" for which a predetermined solution will be sought. There must be a genuine puzzlement (that word again!) about the problem, or a genuine conflict with respect to any quickly arrived-at solution. Without genuine puzzlement the subsequent inquiry would not be genuine. The teacher should work to help the problem sensitization become within the group, and also to help the group develop a general statement of the problem which defines its elements and can be accepted by all as a starting point for the inquiry. The starting point can be a question which calls for an explanatory relationship, solution, or policy.[6]

"In our hypothetical illustration of the process, the orientation is achieved through the use of a passage from a high school text. The springboard passage appears in Canfield and Wilder's text for high school United States history. It may be thought of as having constituted a part of a class's reading assignment, now to be focused on more directly.

[4] *Ibid.*, pp. 92–93.
[5] *Ibid.*, p. 115.
[6] The following excerpt is from *Inquiry in Social Studies* by Massialas and Cox. Copyright © 1966 by McGraw-Hill, Inc. Used with permission of McGraw-Hill Book Company.

During the next two centuries, however, trade was revived in an unusual way. From Western Europe whole armies, led by noblemen in armor, journeyed by land and sea to the Holy Land in Asia Minor. There they fought battle after battle with the Mohammedans in heroic attempts to rescue the Holy Land and bring it again under Christian control. These religious expeditions were known as the Crusades.

People who took part in the Crusades became acquainted with eastern luxuries that they had never dreamed existed. They brought home from the Orient spices, rare drugs, brilliant dyes, perfumes, jewels, ivory, glassware, fine silks, and gorgeous tapestries. More and more Europeans longed to possess such luxuries, so that the demand for them grew rapidly. The merchants of the Italian cities, especially those of Venice, were quick to see the importance of meeting that demand.

These merchants set out on buying trips to the ports of the eastern Mediterranean, returning to Europe with spices, perfume, and other items. For centuries some goods had been trickling from many parts of Asia along land and water routes to the cities of the eastern Mediterranean. Now the trade routes became crowded as the riches of Asia began to flow to the Mediterranean Sea, to be shipped by Italian merchants to all parts of Europe....

While Europeans were learning to enjoy new physical comforts, they were also waking up to new ideas. For centuries, under feudalism, people's interests had been limited to the simple affairs of the small estates on which they lived. They had almost completely lost the desire to educate themselves. Few men had written books or produced works of art.

Now the relations with the East were bringing about a new interest in learning. Europeans not only came in contact with the rich culture of the Mohammedans but also rediscovered the advanced learning of the Greeks and Romans. The booming trade relations which grew out of the Crusades also stirred up an exciting exchange of ideas between Europe and the East. The result was a great revival of learning and of the arts.

This revival took many forms. Universities were founded and grew. Scholars began to study and enjoy certain literature and art of Greece and Rome which had been neglected or forgotten. Architecture and painting flourished. Stories and travelers' tales were written in the simple languages which common people understood instead of in Latin. By the time of Columbus, this great intellectual movement was on the march. The movement is called the *Renaissance,* which means rebirth.[7]

"These passages constitute the springboard about which the teacher asks the following kinds of questions: How would you summarize the point of view the author is suggesting here? Or more specifically, How do you explain the fact that these Europeans in this episode were in the process of changing their values and cultural orientation?

"The forming of the summarizing statement is the result of discussing the above questions: European contact with the Orient as a consequence of the Crusades resulted in the buying trips of Italian merchants to eastern

---

[7] From Leon Canfield and Howard B. Wilder, *The Making of Modern America.* Copyright © 1966, 1950 by Houghton Mifflin Company. Reprinted by permission of the publisher, Houghton Mifflin Company.

Mediterranean ports for the acquisition of Eastern products with the effect of the infusion of new ideas and values. This summary statement then serves as the basis for the hypothesizing phase of the process."[8]

## Hypothesis

The second stage of the inquiry is the development of an hypothesis which expresses as clearly as possible the antecedents and consequents of the proposed relationship, an explanation, policy, or solution to the phenomenon. The hypothesis will serve as a guide to the inquiry which is to follow, to attempt to verify the elements of the problem, see whether those elements do indeed relate to the proposed solution, and whether the solution holds up or others need to be generated. There can be more than one hypothesis advanced at this stage in the model, and in fact many of the most interesting applications of the model occur when there appear to be more than one competing solution to the same problem.

From the summary statement in our example it is hypothesized that "Contact with different cultures results in changed values and desires." This hypothesis is now tested by the teacher and class in terms of (1) its validity as an explanation of the springboard episode, (2) its compatibility with previously devised generalizations and the experiences of the pupils and teacher, and (3) the existence of other historical facts and evidence which are relevant to its proof or disproof."[9]

Three kinds of testing take place, one being the general validity of the hypothesis, the second its compatibility with generalizations and experiences of teachers and students, and the third, its fit to the facts relevant to the problem situation. Before proceeding to validating a hypothesis, however, the members of the group should make sure it is clear to them that the terms have been defined adequately. Hence, the next phase.

## Definition

In this stage the terms of the hypothesis are clarified and defined, until all members of the group are able to communicate about the problem situation, and the language that each of them uses in relation to the problem situation is made clear and pinned down to verifiable experience.

"For example, with reference to our illustration it may have been hypothesized to begin with that contact with different cultures results in progress. Here an ambiguous term, *progress,* requires either clarification and definition or substitution by another term or terms, the meaning of which has more specific connotations to the teacher and class."[10]

[8] Massialas and Cox, *Inquiry in Social Studies,* pp. 116–17.
[9] *Ibid.,* p. 117.
[10] *Ibid.,* p. 118.

*Exploration*

During this phase the hypothesis is extended in terms of its implications, its assumptions, and the deductions which can be made from it. It is qualified and limited, and examined for logical validity and internal consistency. "In our example a logical implication could be stated as follows: If contact with different cultures results in changed values and desires, then people involved in trade outside their own territory are more likely to undergo cultural change. Or to state another possible implication, If a people live in isolation, then their culture will remain relatively static. The statement of implications leads directly to the searching for evidence to support the original hypothesis."[11]

*Evidencing*

In this stage, facts and evidence needed to support the hypothesis are gathered in terms of the conditions which have been hypothesized and defined.

"In pursuing the implications made in our illustrative case, questions like the following are asked: Do you know of people who trade(d) extensively and who in the process of exchanging goods also trade(d) ideas and cultural patterns? Or, with reference to the second implication, Do you know of any such isolated people; and is it true that their culture has (did) not change(d) over a long period of time?

"As evidence relevant to these deductions the early feudal experience of Europe presents a clear case of isolation whereas the Crusades and the Renaissance in Europe are examples and results of intercultural exchange. The transformation that took place in Japan following its opening to the Western trade in the mid-nineteenth century offers additional evidence applicable to both deductions. Other historical, anthropological, sociological and social science data relevant to these and other deductions are brought to bear on the hypothesis to prove or refute its validity in all times and places. In many cases, of course, insufficient data preclude any pursuit of the inquiry beyond this phase. In such an instance students and teachers should recognize that further examination without available evidence is not warranted."[12]

*Generalization*

The sixth and last phase of inquiry is an expression of the solution of the problem. More than likely if an honest problem has been approached, defined carefully, related carefully to evidence, and culled with sufficient complexity, no absolute general solution will be found. The generalization

[11] *Ibid.*
[12] *Ibid.*, p. 119.

is simply the best statement which can be arrived at. It may be that two or three hypotheses will seem about equally tenable at the conclusion of an investigation. If this is the case, they should be maintained together, with their alternative advantages and disadvantages identified as carefully as possible.

"If we assume that in the example sufficient evidence for its support, and no evidence leading to its refutation or major reconstruction is found, the warrantable conclusion to be drawn from the reflective procedure may be stated as follows: If a people of one culture contact a people of another culture, then a culture different from either of these but characterized by identifiable elements of each emerges."[13]

## CLASSROOM APPLICATION

One of the interesting aspects of this model is that it lends itself well to building upon the prescribed course of study and the mechanics of the "traditional" classroom. Ironically, the textbook is one of the most fertile sources of dilemmas for inquiry. These dilemmas can be created out of textbook generalizations, which often warrant further examination or statements of fact. Massialas and Cox provide us with the following examples.

"...the class may encounter the generalization in its government text: The orderly conduct of a society is dependent upon an accepted system of law. This statement expresses a relationship between constitutional government and an orderly society. A legitimate doubt could be raised, however, over the nature of this relationship. Do constitutions *cause* societies to behave in an orderly fashion? Do orderly societies insure tranquility *via* constitution—as suggested by one well-known statement of the relationship. Or is there a functional relationship between these two, both phenomena, perhaps, being the effects of the third factor?"[14] or:

"A social studies class might become oriented to a problem by way of a statement of fact like the following: The Spanish conquistadors and the colonists who followed, brought with them their religion, art, architecture, law and customs, and left the indelible mark of their culture in Mexico. A fact, as we have stated, is primarily used as evidence in the reflective classroom. So, in this case, the students must move inductively from the single episode to the statement of a hypothesis which explains the process of cultural infusion in a given region."[15]

It might be helpful at this point to examine some of the transcripts and anecdotal records of social inquiry discussion in order to see the flow of

[13] *Ibid.*
[14] *Ibid.*, p. 120.
[15] *Ibid.*

inquiry as it moves from phase to phase as well as to conceptualize better the phases themselves.

The first transcript captures the class in the orientation phase as it was just beginning to formulate the hypothesis that in order to adjust to a cultural region a state has to be like its neighbors.[16]

In another situation, students are directed to interpret a passage in a paperback book being used in class. The students in this case are becoming aware of the problem of Israel's accommodation to Arab-Islamic culture. The passage reads as follows:[17]

> The influx of immigrants from Yemen, Iraq, and other non-Western areas means that today 40 per cent of Israel's population is non-Western in origin. It is predicted that within a decade the population of the country will be 60 per cent non-Western. The more non-Western Israel becomes the sooner and more effectively it will fit into the Middle East, and we must remember that, whatever may be the intellectual and spiritual attachments of Israel's European-born population, the new state, for better or for worse, must live in the Middle East, and not in Europe or in the United States.[18]

Teacher: Who would like to interpret the passage?

Kathy: Well, it tells us about the immigration of non-Western Jews to Israel, and predicts that they will soon outnumber the European or Western Jews. I am not sure of this, but the author seems to be saying that as Israel's people become more Oriental so will Israel, and that this will help the country fit into the Middle East better.

Steve: I think this is a terrible passage.

Teacher: Why so?

Steve: Because it is wrong.

Teacher: Why?

Steve: Well, for one thing, how can Israel fit into the Middle East if the Arabs do not want it to happen? Maybe the author thinks they should become Arabs.

Randy: Also, as far as I know, the Arabs are having a great deal of trouble westernizing. Why should Israel become like them? That would be a step backward for Israel.

Helen: Well, maybe the author means that Israel should develop its own special brand of life that combines Western life with that of its Arab neighbors.

Steve: That might be, but she does not really say so. She says that as Israel becomes less Western, the better it will become a part of the Middle Eastern way of life.

16 *Ibid.*, p. 122.

17 The following is from *Inquiry in Social Studies* by Massialas and Cox. Copyright © 1966 by McGraw-Hill, Inc. Used with permission of McGraw-Hill Book Company.

18 From Vera Miles Dean, *The Nature of the Non-Western World* (New York: New American Library of World Literature, Inc., 1960), p. 65.

Bob: I have something to add. (pause) How can Israel fit in with its neighbors if they are at war with her? That is pretty hard to do, isn't it?

Mary: What is Israel supposed to fit in with? Since we have been studying something about the Middle East, I know that all those neighbors of Israel are not the same at all. Lebanon, I think, is more Christian than Moslem; whereas most Arabs are supposed to be Moslem. What exactly is Israel going to fit in with?

"The next steps after stating the hypothesis are to test its logical implications, usually by deductive statements which point the hypothesis toward the needed evidence and to test the social hypothesis by its evidential basis in fact—usually by comparing the factors in similar events. Let's see how this exploration and evidencing took place in a world history class exploring the topic of nationalism. This is a particularly interesting example because of the abstract nature of the phenomenon.

Chapter fourteen dealt with the development of nationalism in England and France in the thirteenth and fourteenth centuries and with the Protestant Reformation. In an earlier classroom discussion when we talked about William the Conqueror, the Capetian kings in France, certain political developments in Spain under Ferdinand and Isabella, and the fight of the Spanish people against the Moors, we made some causal generalizations concerning national consciousness. Students easily recalled the generalizations, and the supporting material. For example, they said that *if an aggregate of individuals speaks a common language, have the same religion, the same customs, the same enemies, identify themselves with the same heroes and symbols, and have one historic background, then national consciousness will emerge.* The authors, in the beginning of the chapter, provided a definition of a nation which was consistent with the definition that we had given to the term except for the addition of independent government as a characteristic factor. When Bob raised the question of how the Jews would be classified before they gained independence in 1948, much discussion followed. The general consensus was that the Jewish population justifiably could have been called a nation; but this would have required a reconstruction of the definition provided by the authors since the Jews did not have an independent government prior to 1948. Many students referred to the dictionary in an attempt to get a more adequate definition of a nation. However, several said that the dictionary provided circular definitions which did not really explain or illuminate the phenomenon. I brought in the notion of operational definitions and definitions by stipulation. From there, I asked how we knew when we had nationalism. Could we see it, feel it, measure it, etc.? This again, brought about much discussion. Lorraine said that the feeling of nationalism was the feeling of oneness, that of being related to other people. Jack said that all we could depend on was the declaration of a person purporting to be a national of a country, or claiming to have national feelings. This brought about the idea that national consciousness amounted to the conception that a person has of himself in relation to other persons. If the relationship is a positive one, then the people involved can identify themselves as a nation. I observed that my pupils were moving to another, higher level of analysis. Now they talked in terms of measuring the level of intensity of sentiments on the basis of overt behavior, they talked about identifying and isolating social phenomena, and they talked about variable analysis.[19]

Exploration and evidencing with a more concrete phenomenon can be found in the following example.

Peter had prepared what he called the pattern of revolution from *The Anatomy of Revolution*. He had identified six steps in the revolutionary pattern, the first of which was the breakdown of the financial system of the country. After discussing the meaning of this financial aspect of the hypothesis the class developed this deduction: *If it is true that there is a breakdown of the financial system of a state preceding a revolution, then we should find in the period preceding the American Revolution (1750–1775) events which show the government (England) unable to cope with tax, trade, money, and debt problems, in ways satisfactory to the colonies.*[20]

The definition phase can be a frustrating experience. However, in addition to its logical importance, defining terms reflects the process of inquiry. This can be seen in the following excerpt in which the word "environment" is used in relation to early colonial settlements in America.[21]

Teacher: I think you have got a problem on your hands here. Who sees a logical way out of it? Now, as I interpret it, Clara Sue was attempting to say that environment is a very broad concept. The people along with the climate, the land, the minerals, the buildings, and the production of the people become environment. And if you have a brother and sister, these people are part of this environment.

Clara: Isn't that true?

Teacher: Now, that is certainly one kind of definition. But over on this side, George says that environment as he has been thinking about it, is principally climate and land.

George: I did not say that it was principally climate and land. I said that I do not think that that would affect that type of environment where you would have just physical environment. What she was talking about would not affect physical environment.

Teacher: Well, that could be. I would not argue with that. What are you thinking of Clara? What happens within this family to change the environment?

Clara: I do not know. Anything could happen, I guess.

Teacher: What?

Clara: Anything could happen. But I thought environment was everything about you. But, I was not thinking of physical environment. I do not know.

Teacher: Let us determine some kind of meaning here. I do not think we are going to have any luck at all in this enterprise until we do.

---

[19] Massialas and Cox, *Inquiry in Social Studies*, pp. 126–127.
[20] *Ibid.*, p. 127.
[21] From *Inquiry in Social Studies* by Massialas and Cox. Copyright © 1966 by McGraw-Hill, Inc. Used with permission of McGraw-Hill Book Company.

Steve: Well, I want to go back to the colonists.

Teacher: All right.

Steve: I think it definitely meant a change in physical environment, meaning a change in the land and climate and possibly also the people in the colony and other things like this. I think it is the second thing.

Teacher: The second thing being what?

Steve: Things other than just the land, the climate, the people, ideas and all this.

Teacher: Here is a new dimension. The ideas which the society holds comprise a part of the environment.[22]

Finally, generalizations should be thought of as open-ended statements subject to change. Following are some examples developed by a world history class discussing the rise of civilization in India and China.

1. If a religion meets the needs and wants of the people better than the present religion, then the new religion will be adopted.

2. If the system of writing in a country is hard to understand and is difficult for the common people to use, then it will be changed or revised.

3. If the people have a relatively long period of peace and a government which does not change, then these people will advance the arts.

4. If a strong ruler dies or is overthrown and there is no strong ruler to succeed him, then the country will decline or fall.[23]

## MODEL

*Syntax:* The six phases of the model are:

*Phase One:* Orientation—sensitization to a dilemma or problem and development of a general statement of the problem as a starting point for inquiry.

*Phase Two:* Hypothesis—development of a hypothesis or hypotheses which can serve as guides to inquiry and can be tested.

*Phase Three:* Definition—clarification and definition of terms in the hypotheses.

*Phase Four:* Exploration—examination of the hypotheses in terms of their logical validity and internal consistence, on the basis of this examination.

*Phase Five:* Evidencing—the gathering and reconciliation of facts in terms of the hypotheses to be tested.

*Phase Six:* Generalizations—expressions of solutions or statements about the problems.

## Principles of Reaction

During all phases the teacher is a counselor to inquiry, helping the students clarify their positions, improve the process of study, and work out their plans. He should help them clarify language, improve logic, become

[22] *Ibid.*, pp. 130–31.
[23] *Ibid.*, p. 132.

aware of ways of being more objective, understand their assumptions, and communicate more effectively with one another. Consequently, his role is a reflective one, as he helps the students understand themselves and find their own way. He is sharpener, focusser, and counselor, rather than instructor.

## SOCIAL SYSTEM

The social system is *moderately structured*. The teacher initiates the inquiry and sees that it moves from phase to phase. Students, depending on their inquiry abilities, should take major responsibility for the inquiry itself, and even carry it through the phases they are able. The norms of inquiry call for free and open discussion among a body of equals.

## SUPPORT SYSTEM

The means which are needed to carry out the model are, primarily, a teacher who believes in the development of a leisurely, problem-solving approach to life, open-ended library resources, and access to expert opinion and other sources outside the school itself. A very rich environment of information is necessary to maintain an honest inquiry and this is particularly difficult to provide because one cannot tell in advance what problems will be identified, or just what kinds of evidence will be seen as relevant to them.

## GENERAL APPLICABILITY OF THE MODEL

The primary purpose of the model is to teach students how to be reflective about significant social problems. Through genuine inquiry, they should learn how to define these problems, how to work with others in exploring different ways of looking at them, and how to conclude on the basis of the data as much as possible. No claim is made that the model will be more efficient for learning facts than any other given method. However, the authors of the model clearly believe that learning facts in isolation is not a very productive enterprise. And they also believe that the social sciences should be learned in the course of the attempt to develop solutions to significant social problems, so that the structure and modes of inquiry of the disciplines will be seen as they apply to the arena of human concern.

## INSTRUCTIONAL AND NURTURANT VALUES

Massialas and Cox' model (Figure 4-1) is designed to teach students to explore social issues and develop a commitment to civic improvement. It stops short of social action although it clearly hopes to nurture such action. A respect for the dignity of all men and tolerance in dialogue with differing people also seem to be nurtured in the environment to be absorbed by the student.

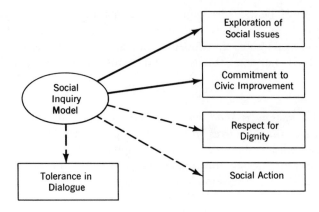

**Figure 4-1**

**TABLE 4-1 Summary Chart: Social Inquiry Model**

| *Syntax:* | *Phase One* | *Phase Two* | *Phase Three* |
|---|---|---|---|
| | Presentation and clarification of puzzling situation. | Development of hypotheses from which to explore or solve problem. | Define and clarify hypothesis. |
| | *Phase Four* | *Phase Five* | *Phase Six* |
| | Explore hypothesis in terms of its assumptions, implications, and logical validity. | Gather facts and evidence to support hypothesis. | Generalized expression or solution. |

| *Principles of Reaction:* | Teacher acts as sharperner, focuser, and counselor to inquiry. He helps students to clarify their position and improve the process of study. |
|---|---|
| *Social System:* | *Moderately Structured.* The teacher is generally initiator of inquiry and sees that it moves from phase to phase. Students, however, carry the responsibility for its development and the social norms call for open discussion among equals. |
| *Support System:* | A teacher with patience to carry out a problem-solving approach and the resourcefulness to locate the necessary information which the inquiry may call for. Open-ended library resources and access to expert opinion. |

*Group Inv - reactions*
*Social Inq - hypotheses*
*more specific*

# 5

# LABORATORY METHOD

## *The T-Group Model*

Beginning in 1947 in Bethel, Maine, Laboratory Training (also referred to as T-(training) Group and Process Analysis) grew out of a concern for increased understanding of the rapid personal and social changes taking place in modern society, and for new and improved methods of facilitating humane *responses to* and *control of* change. Basically, the methods that resulted are resocialization processes which have within their structure the elements for adaptation to change. The concern, however, was not only for an *adaptive* mechanism, but also for one which would serve both individual rehabilitation and social reconstruction.

The chronic change in contemporary society creates demands which are both personal and social in nature. Human beings are subjected to new and increasingly fragmented roles. For example, they must meet certain "intellectual" norms at work and other, often opposing "emotional" norms at home. (The working man must function as the man of leisure.) Despite a maelstrom of change, man must establish an identity and sense of personal wholeness. To complicate his task, complex bureaucratic organizations depersonalize human relations producing an "eclipse of community" and a sense of helpless isolation. To eliminate these self-defeating societal symptoms requires the integration of the cognitive and emotional aspects of one's life as well as the personal and social aspects. For in a complex, interdependent world, individual mental health is closely related to the larger social structure, to one's interpersonal relations. "Alone, people do not make and implement social decision adequately.... The ability to live with ambiguity and change, to work interdependently, to be socially inventive, to meet social requirements—all are requirements for effective social membership."[1] What is needed is a vehicle which serves both individual rehabilitation (toward greater integrity and self-understanding) and social reconstruction (greater behavioral effectiveness in managing personal and social change); a vehicle which furnishes a content that is individual and social and a method of inquiry that serves both. This is the purpose of process analysis. Briefly stated, "Laboratory training is an educational strategy which is based primarily on the experiences generated in the various social encounters by the *learners themselves,* and which aims to influence attitudes and develop competencies toward learning about human interaction."[2] It rests on the assumption that the skills of participation can be learned through the process of participation.

## ORIENTATION OF THE MODEL

### Description

A T-group is normally comprised of ten to twelve persons who spend anywhere from eight to forty hours together in an instructional, face-to-face group in which individuals participate as learners, at the same time helping others in their quest for understanding. The data for learning comes from the immediate experience of the group *as a group.* In other words, the conversation centers on the experienced behavior, feelings, perceptions, and reactions of the group members while they are together. Also present is a trainer, who, while taking an "actively passive" role, makes interventions that facilitate the development of valid communication and helps members make explicit the process of that development.[3] As a participant-observer, like the other group members, the trainer may serve as a model for participants to imitate. The participants are given the vague task of "constructing a group which will meet the requirements of all its members for growth."[4] We may say they are given the opportunity to share in the creation of a

---

[1] Leland P. Bradford, "Developing Potentialities Through Class Groups," *Human Forces in Teaching and Learning,* Leland P. Bradford, ed. (Washington, D.C.: National Training Laboratory, National Education Association, 1961), p. 39.

[2] Edgar H. Schein and Warren G. Bennis, *Personal and Organizational Change Through Group Methods* (New York: John Wiley, 1965), p. 4.

[3] Herbert A. Shepard, "The T-Group as Training in Observant Participation," *The Planning of Change: Readings in the Applied Behavioral Sciences,* Warren G. Bennis, Kenneth D. Benne, and Robert Chin, eds. (New York: Holt, Rinehart & Winston, 1964), p. 637.

[4] Leland P. Bradford, Jack R. Gibb, and Kenneth D. Benne, eds., *T-Group Theory and Laboratory Method* (New York: John Wiley, 1964), p. viii.

little society—to establish its goals, values, and procedures. In doing this, the participant is given the opportunity to clarify and reorient central life values that he has inherited and, perhaps, uncritically adopted. One source gives the following overview of a training group: "...structure is minimal. Members of the group are usually told they can learn much about their own behavior and that of others, and about group behavior, from continuous observation and analysis of experiences within the group. The trainer refuses to act as discussion leader, but proposes to help group members to find ways of utilizing their experiences for learning.

"Essentially a kind of social vacuum is produced. Leadership, agenda, expectations, usually preestablished by some authority, are blurred or missing. As tension produced by the vacuum mounts, members endeavor to supply the missing elements, and their behavioral output also mounts."[5] This format generates (1) behavioral output for analysis, (2) a climate of permissiveness, (3) collaborative relationships for learning, and (4) models for data collection and inquiry. Participants function as observer-participant, as diagnostician-actor, as planner-educator-evaluator, as theorist-practicioner, as expressor of feeling and critic of expression, and as helper-client."[6]

The goals of laboratory learning may be viewed along three dimensions—their focus or content, their level of learning, and the ultimate client. T-Group experiences may be designed to focus on one or more of four content areas: (1) intrapersonal, (2) interpersonal, (3) group dynamics, and (4) self-direction. The intrapersonal goal reaches for self-insight or increased self-knowledge, i.e., to know oneself more accurately and intimately. This may include identification of stress, management of hostility and tension, goal formation, and integration of emotionality and work. Interpersonal learning focuses on the dynamics of relationships among persons—relationship of influence, feedback, leadership, communication, conflict resolution, trust formation, leadership, giving and receiving help, intervention, power, and control. Understanding these aspects will increase one's ability to experience people and events more fully. Understanding the conditions which facilitate or inhibit group functioning is a third learning goal. That the group as a medium, apart from the collection of individuals which comprise it, possesses its own unique qualities is well established. Properties of the group include its norms and standards, its role, communication, power, and sociometric structure, its cohesiveness, its goals, and its interaction patterns. The fourth learning goal, self-direction,

---

5 Benne, Bradford, and Lippitt, "The Laboratory Method," *T-Group Theory and Laboratory Method,* Bradford, Gibb, and Benne, eds., p. 41.
6 Benne, "History of the T-Group in the Laboratory Setting," *T-Group Theory and Laboratory Method,* pp. 122–123.

shifts the emphasis from the cognitive (intellectual) to the behavioral. It develops the skills for diagnosing and for increasing competency in inter-personal and organizational behavior—"the ability not only to act but also to monitor the action and accuracy, assess its consequences for the actor in relation to others, and for the group in relation to its goals."[7]

Any one of these goals may be achieved at several levels or degrees. In their text on laboratory method, Schein and Bennis distinguish three: increased awareness, changed attitudes, and new behavior. Individuals may increase their *awareness* (and acceptance) of their own feelings and the feelings of others; of the complexity of the communication process; of the genuine differences in member needs, goals, and ways of approaching problems; of their own impact on others; of how groups function; of the consequences of certain kinds of group action; of learning how to learn (as observation analysis). Increased awareness may result in changed *attitudes* towards self, others, and groups. Finally, new *behavior* in the form of greater diagnostic and social skill competence may be built upon the previous levels.

To identify the last dimension, we ask the question, "Who is the ultimate client?" of training. Certainly the two possible answers, the individual and the organization or society, are mutually related. But distinguishing one above the other has practical consequences in terms of laboratory design and appropriate activities. (A training program whose purpose is to improve the functioning of a specific group, such as the staff of an embassy, is likely to include activities that are different from those of a group designed to help individual adolescents learn to reach out to others.) Usually, laboratory method, by stressing socially relevant aspects of behavior, is more concerned with society as a client than most other educational methods. But inasmuch as successful intrapersonal and interpersonal functioning is almost a prerequisite to the group dynamic goals, the individual is a significant beneficiary even when the group or society is the primary client.

Highly important to the purpose and climate of the T-group is its implicit values. Schein and Bennis identify these as the spirit of inquiry (an orientation toward truth and discovery), commitment to the democratic process, and choice. Each of these in turn has its own elements. For instance, a spirit of inquiry is partially hypothetical, involving a feeling for tentativeness and caution and at the same time a willingness to expose ideas to empirical testing. The ambiguity of the laboratory situation creates a need to define and organize the environment, naturally generating hypotheses about group process. Expanded consciousness is a second component of a spirit of inquiry. The laboratory situation brings into analysis social processes

[7] Shepard, "The T-Group as Training in Observant Participation," *The Planning of Change,* Bennis, Benne, and Chin, eds., p. 637.

usually taken for granted. Finally, a spirit of inquiry requires an authenticity in interpersonal relations and an openness of communication.

Acceptance of democratic values and adherence to its processes does not mean blind acceptance of "democratic shibboleths." Commitment to democratic values involves (1) mutual collaboration and interdependence as opposed to authoritarian interaction, and (2) conflict resolution through rational means and a problem-solving orientation rather than bargains, power plays, and compromise. Problem-solving in this case includes recognition and acknowledgement of conflict, full understanding of its causes and consequences, and exploration of all possible alternatives in an atmosphere of mutual trust. Finally, as the most fundamental value, there is choice—the application of the techniques and values only when appropriate and under the tight conditions. For example, as Schein and Bennis point out, there are circumstances when even authenticity is inappropriate and/or dysfunctional.[8] *Choice* involves autonomy of judgment as contrasted to slavish adherence to a formula.

Groups have been part of instructional methodology for many years but their value has been as an organizational setting rather than as a medium for learning. As such their structure, agenda, norms, and goals are usually prescribed either by habit or authority. The group can serve as a learning medium, according to laboratory method theorists, only when these forces are absent and ambiguity is present. If the behavior of the group is directed by an authority or by habit, laboratory method will not ensue. Besides this fundamental condition, Schein and Bennis have identified six necessary conditions that distinguish training groups from other learning groups.

The first is a "here and now" focus. That is, the content of laboratory training is the *experienced behavior* of the delegates, the data generated by individuals in interaction with each other. "In other words, here and now learning is based on experiences which are shared, public, immediate, direct, first-hand, unconceptualized and self-acknowledged."[9] In contrast, the traditional sharing of behavior is of past behavior, so the sharing is vicarious, detached, and filtered. The distinguishing feature of "here and now" learning is that concepts *follow* the emotions of experience. Learning thus has a point of reality in the concrete behavior to which words and concepts can be related.

If "here and now" learning establishes reality, the second condition, *feedback,* provides a mechanism to recognize it. Without an open and authentic communication, we cannot have adequate and trustworthy feedback mechanisms from which to obtain information about our behavior. Valid feedback "...should be based on publicly observed and experienced

8 Schein and Bennis, *Personal and Organizational Change Through Group Methods,* pp. 30–35.
9 *Ibid.,* p. 39.

behavior, sufficiently contiguous in time and space, and modified through all data sources available."[10] *Feedback* means that the members of the group interpret each other's reactions and feelings in an open, but descriptive, non-evaluative way.

A third learning condition involves a period of *unfreezing* or unlearning. The purpose of unfreezing is to create a desire to learn. This includes the idea of contrast (making the familiar strange) to generate curiosity, creating an ambiguous situation with unclear goals and lack of structure in order to make it difficult for individuals to use past habits to resolve the situation.

Unfreezing, however, can lead to anxiety instead of a desire to learn if the fourth condition, *psychological safety*, is not created. Psychological safety refers to the supportive nature of the environment, the group, and the support it gives to openness. This functions to help the participants feel comfortable and supported despite the ambiguity and frustration in the situation.

A fifth condition requires the *dual role of observant-participant* (observe, act, diagnose, and behave). Such a position blends the worlds of action and analysis. "To be detached without losing commitment is the aim of laboratory training."[11]

Finally, laboratory learning, if it is to be successful in supplying a mastery over previously perplexing phenomena, must provide *cognitive maps* or an intellectual framework for emotional experience, "rendering the dimly sensed feelings into words, into concepts, often helps to make the experience more understandable and hence, manageable."[12] Such a framework helps to make finer discriminations of the spectrum. It is also a link to the back home "there and then" world. Lastly, concepts help to build (or rebuild) a culture.

Behind these conditions are some basic assumptions on which laboratory training is built. One set of assumptions concerns the nature of the teaching-learning process. Learning is viewed as a transaction between the learner and the environment in which neither can be regarded as fixed. The target of education is "change and growth in the individual and his behavior."[13] As such it is a broader goal than intellectual learning: "...the desired direction of learning and change is toward a more integrative and adaptive interconnection of values, concepts, feelings, perceptions, strategies and skills."[14] Teaching is not just information dissemination and retrieval; it is a human relations problem in which the teacher and learner mutually

[10] *Ibid.*, p. 43.

[11] *Ibid.*, p. 45.

[12] *Ibid.*, p. 46.

[13] Leland P. Bradford, "The Teaching-Learning Transactions," *Human Forces in Teaching and Learning,* Leland P. Bradford, ed. (Washington, D.C.: National Training Laboratory, National Education Association, 1961), p. 5.

[14] Benne, Bradford, and Lippitt, "The Laboratory Method," *T-Group Theory and Laboratory Method,* p. 18.

explore and diagnose the needs for and resistances to learning and change. In addition, learners can acquire skills of participation in social process events.

Several assumptions have to do with visions of society. Rather than the current cultural norms, which deprecate feelings and emotions as immature and promote self-protective emotional masks and seeming protection of others' feelings, laboratory training places value on open and authentic communication. Through interpersonal training, laboratory method aims at social reform.

## Laboratory Theory

Only recently have the elements of laboratory theory been refined and combined to produce a coherent schema. An integrated frame of reference describing the structure (sequence of events) of the T-group experience can be found in the Dilemma-Invention-Feedback-Generalization (D-I-F-G) Model developed by Blake and Moulton.[15] For greater understanding, we may parallel this learning model with the typical classroom procedure. According to the model, the dilemma, created primarily by the participants, generates the anxiety or discomfort which is the main source of energy for the learning laboratory. The stage for the dilemma is set by bringing the group together without specifying goals or content. Tension develops as individuals attempt to structure the situation. They conflict, and each individual finds his perceptions of the situation are not confirmed by all of the others. The dilemma arises from the lack of structure compounded by the lack of confimation, and it provides most of the "here-and-now" content for the group. By analyzing the dilemma, the trainee can specify the appropriate subjects for the theory sessions and exercises which take place in addition to and outside of the basic T-group meeting.

In the beginning, solutions to the dilemma exhibit habitual patterns but when these fail, the need to invent becomes apparent, creating even more anxiety. In this emotional contest, analysis of the forces which are operative in the dilemma begins. The analysis leads to search thinking and creative behavior. At this point the participants supply emotional and conceptual evaluations of their own actions and reactions to others. On a group level, members may reflect on the direction and goal of the group. Finally, out of the feedback come generalizations. Delegates and trainer theorize together, formulate hypotheses, retest them, and recycle into the next learning phase.

The laboratory training process of inquiry-data collection, processing, feedback, and analysis of results is consistent with democratic methodology— gathering and furnishing information for valid decision, participating with others in interpretation of existing forms and the creation of new ones, experimenting with new forms, and facing value and power conflicts.

[15] Schein and Bennis, *Personal and Organizational Change*, pp. 47, 145.

Democratic methodology in this sense includes the validation of morals and values as well as knowledge.

The *content* of the T-group experience exhibits some predictable qualities despite the absence of a planned agenda. "The core of the theory of group development is that the principle obstacles to the development of valid communication are to be found in the orientation toward authority and intimacy that members bring to the group. Rebelliousness, submissiveness or withdrawal as the characteristic response to authority figures; destructive competitiveness, emotional exploitiveness, or withdrawal are the characteristic response to peers. . . ."[16] Problems of dependence (authority relations) and interdependence (personal relations) occur in a predictable sequence. Thus, the group will devote the initial D-I-F-G cycles to questions of broad role distinctions (concern with power) and after some resolution of these problems spend the remaining D-I-F-G cycles discussing personality, i.e., reaction to failure, warmth, anxiety, etc. (concern with affection).[17]

Finally, the multiple outcomes or levels of learning of laboratory training may be represented by the following cycle or sequence of learning.

Dilemma or Disconfirming Information
↓
Attitude Change (1)
↓
New Behavior (2)
↓
New Information
↓
Increased Awareness (2)
↓
Attitude Change (2)
↓
New Behavior (3)
↓
New Information
↓
Increased Awareness (3)
↓
Attitude Change (3)
↓
Until New Information or
Outside Event Terminates Process[18]

[16] Warren G. Bennis and Herbert A. Shepard, "A Theory of Group Development," *The Planning of Change: Readings in the Applied Behavioral Sciences,* Bennis, Benne, and Chin, eds., p. 323.

[17] For a detailed description of the dependence/interdependence stages in terms of emotional modality, content themes, dominant roles, group structure, group activity, group movement, and main defenses, see Bennis and Shepard, "A Theory of Group Development," *The Planning of Change,* pp. 331–39.

[18] Schein and Bennis, *Personal and Organizational Change,* p. 27.

## OPERATIONAL METHODOLOGY

Laboratory training may be designed in many ways, but it is usually comprised of four major training activities which may be integrated into the structure of the basic activity (the T-group) or handled outside the T-group. The four activities are:

(1) The T-group, the basic learning group described earlier, in which self-observation and diagnosis of the group's growth and development is the primary means of training.

(2) Theory sessions which provide a conceptual framework for group experiences. Such a framework might include the notion of group goals, norms, cohesiveness, power structure, sociometric structure, role functions including the various group task roles, group building and maintenance roles, and individual roles.[19]

(3) Focused exercises—activities with specifically enumerated learning goals. For example, role-playing may be utilized to enact group role problems, or listening skills may be improved with tape-listening using various rating scales. Other skill practices may include an observation task, again possible with various instruments, decision-making tasks, and feedback tasks. Consultation skills may be improved by having one group list its problems and discuss them with another group. Similarly, practice in giving-and-receiving help may include division into a four-man group in which one person presents a problem to two individuals who are already briefed by him. One raises questions (redefines) and probes for information while the other gives an action recommendation. The observer keeps notes on the reactions to the two styles. Learning about larger systems can be accomplished by designing tasks which include inter-group competition.

(4) Finally, there may be experimentation with a back-home problem, especially if the group shares a common work setting or profession.

Other activities designed to supplement the T-group structure may be seminars on a particular topic, two-man interviews, or trials in which a smaller group facilitates bringing more sensitive problems into the open, and informal cull-sessions.

## CLASSROOM APPLICATION

Elements from the model (basic learning group, theory sessions, or focused exercises) can be used by teachers to help classes become students of their own behavior and relations with others and to help groups of children work together more effectively. We have not included case illustrations of the basic T-group because a short segment of T-group interaction would not be meaningful and a complete transcript is beyond the scope of this book.

[19] See Mary Bany and Lois V. Johnson, *Classroom Group Behavior: Group Dynamics in Education* (New York: Macmillan, 1964); and Bennis and Shepard, "A Theory of Group Development," pp. 747–52.

However, excellent case episodes which provide some idea of the continuity and sequence of T-group behavior can be found in the book by Leland Bradford, Jack R. Gibb, and Kenneth Benne, *T-Group Theory and Laboratory Method.*[20]

In a recent project supported by the United States Office of Education, Springport High School developed a human relations handbook for high school students based on Laboratory Method.[21] The manual provides theoretical information on the basic concepts of laboratory training and a set of activities or focused exercises. We have included two of these tasks and their theoretical input. One task pertains to feedback and the other to decision-making.

## What Is Feedback?[22]

Feedback is communicating to a person or group about how their behavior has affected us or other people. The communication can be in the form of a spoken word, a gesture, or an action. If a person says or does something that makes me angry, I can give him feedback as to the effect his behavior had on me by 1) telling him about my angry feelings, 2) frowning or looking mad at him, or 3) punching him in the nose. As you can see, feedback can be either constructive or destructive, depending on whether it stems from the receiver's needs or the giver's needs.

One function of feedback is to make a person aware of the effects of his behavior on other people so that he may change or discard ineffective modes of behavior, or support certain kinds of behavior that are effective. Feedback lets a person know where he stands in the group and how he is seen by other members. It helps the person answer the question, "Who am I?" Finally, feedback helps the individual evaluate his progress toward his goals and how closely his behavior is related to his intentions.

To be useful to the person receiving the feedback, the giver should be able to 1) describe his *own reaction* to the behavior, 2) describe the specific behavior or incident that evoked the reaction, 3) give the feedback as soon as possible after the behavior occurred, and 4) take into consideration the needs of the person on the receiving end of the feedback. Feedback that is given out of anger or hostility is useless and only makes the receiver defensive and unable to benefit by it.

## CONSTRUCTIVE USE OF FEEDBACK

*All group members should read their program for five minutes.*

The next important goal for your group is to discover the use of constructive *feedback* in small group interaction. *Feedback* is reporting to an indi-

---

[20] Benne et al., *T-Group Theory and Laboratory Method,* pp. 136–67.
[21] *Human Relations Laboratory Training Student Notebook,* ED 018 834 (Washington, D.C.: U.S. Office of Education, 1961).
[22] From *Human Relations Laboratory Training.*

vidual the kind of impressions he is making on you or reporting your reactions to him. Constructive feedback is rarely effectively used in interpersonal communication. Our society puts a great deal of emphasis on the value of honesty. Children are taught in their homes and schools that it is bad to lie about their behavior. Stealing, lying, cheating, and other dishonest acts are denounced in every aspect of life. Yet all of us are guilty of a great deal of dishonesty in interpersonal relationships all of the time. (Since children are often very aware of this it makes the learning of the value of honesty very complex.) We rarely express our honest feelings toward others in home or in school. Often this involves simply avoiding the expression of reactions which we feel would be detrimental to others or ourselves. Often it involves what we call "little white lies" when we tell people something positive or reassuring rather than be direct, honest, or critical.

People often feel threatened by the introduction of feedback exercises. The notion that people will be hurt by criticism is very prevalent. Yet think of how many people you know who have good intentions but irritate, embarrass, or behave in ways which diminish their effectiveness. The range of operating efficiently and productively in many areas in life is seriously hampered if we never have a chance to become aware of our impact on others. Most of us are quite capable of improving our styles of interpersonal communication and becoming much more effective as people—parents, teachers, whatever—when we really become aware of our impact on others.

Before going on to an exercise designed to give and receive feedback to others in the group, it is useful to think about destructive versus constructive feedback. Feedback is destructive when it is given only to hurt or to express hostility without any goal of improving the communication between people. It may also be destructive when only derogatory or extremely critical statements are given without any balance of positive evaluation.

Feedback is useful to a person when:

1. It describes what he is doing rather than placing a value on it. Example: "When you yell at me it makes me feel like not talking to you any more." Rather than: "It's awful of you to yell at me."
2. It is specific rather than general.
3. It is directed toward behavior which the receiver can do something about.
4. It is well-timed.
5. It is asked for rather than imposed.
6. It is checked to insure clear communication.

## FEEDBACK TASK FOR GROUP

Your group should now divide into triads. Each triad should have paper and pencil and go to separate corners of the room. Each triad should then list all the members of the group on the paper. The task for the triad is to discuss each member of the entire group (exclude yourselves) in terms of what would be the most useful positive and negative feedback statements to give each member. You will probably find considerable disagreement in your triads about your reactions to the various members. You must develop the positive and negative feedback statements which include the reactions of everyone in your triad. The triad should think about how to state the feedback so it will be very clear, direct, and useful to the recipient. Each triad should complete two statements for each member.

Example:

The most negative behavior that Member A exhibits in this group is

_____

The most valuable behavior that Member A exhibits in this group is

_____

At the end of twenty minutes the group will reform and each triad will give each member of the group their joint feedback report *verbally.*

After the feedback report of each triad to the entire group is completed, the group should spend time comparing reports of different triads.

Were the triad's reports similar or quite different? Why? or Why not?

Were some triads more critical? Why?

Were some reports more useful? Why? Why not?

Learning to give constructive feedback to others is only one part of the process. Learning how to receive feedback from others is equally important. Two extreme reactions to receiving feedback is 1) to ignore the feedback and devalue it as being unimportant, hostile, or useless or 2) to pay too much attention to all feedback and to try to change in accordance with all feedback received. Neither reaction is constructive. It is important to learn to deliberately weigh feedback from others in terms of the motivation of the sender, the correctness of the sender's perceptions, and the appropriateness of the behavior when it occurred even if the consensus of the feedback received is negative. (An effective group leader or teacher must sometimes behave in a manner to which he will receive only negative feedback.) In some cases it is important to ignore negative feedback. However, consistently dismissing it is a different situation. While people generally have the most difficulty with critical feedback it is important to be aware that some people under-react or over-react to positive feedback also.

## RECEIVING FEEDBACK TASK

The group members should return to triads and discuss how the members of the triad felt about the feedback they received. (1) Discuss the feelings about the feedback. Were you hurt, did you feel attacked, pleased, or what? (2) Are there ways of changing your behavior that would be appropriate or possibly related to the feedback received? Members of the triads should help each other in turn to evaluate and suggest ways of effectively utilizing (or ignoring if appropriate) the feedback.

## DECISION BY CONSENSUS

*Instructions:* This is an exercise in group decision-making. Your group is to employ the method of *Group Consensus* in reaching its decision. This means that the prediction for each of the 15 survival items *must* be agreed upon by each group member before it becomes a part of the group decision. Consensus is difficult to reach. Therefore, not every ranking will meet with everyone's *complete* approval. Try, as a group, to make each ranking one with which all group members can at least partially agree. Here are some guides to use in reaching consensus:

1. Avoid arguing for your own individual judgments. Approach the task on the basis of logic.

2. Avoid changing your mind only in order to reach agreement and avoid conflict. Support only solutions with which you are able to agree somewhat, at least.

3. Avoid "conflict-reducing" techniques such as majority vote, averaging, or trading in reaching decisions.

4. View differences of opinion as helpful rather than as a hindrance in decision-making.

On the "Group Summary Sheet" place the individual rankings made earlier by each group member. Take as much time as you need in reaching your group decision.

## INSTRUCTIONS

Instructions: You are a member of a space crew originally scheduled to rendezvous with a mother ship on the lighted surface of the moon. Due to mechanical difficulties, however, your ship was forced to land at a spot some 200 miles from the rendezvous point. During re-entry and landing, much of the equipment aboard was damaged and, since survival depends on reaching the mother ship, the most critical items available must be chosen for the 200 mile trip. Below are listed the 15 items left intact and undamaged after landing. Your task is to rank order them in terms of their importance for your crew in allowing them to reach the rendezvous point. Place the number 1 by the most important item, the number 2 by the second most important, and so on through number 15, the least important.

Boxes of matches                                        _____

Food concentrate                                        _____

50 ft. of nylon rope                                    _____

Parachute silk                                          _____

Portable heating unit                                   _____

Two .45 calibre pistols                                 _____

One case dehydrated Pet Milk                            _____

Two 100 lb. tanks of oxygen                             _____

Stellar map (of moon's constellation)                   _____

Life raft                                               _____

Magnetic compass                                        _____

Signal flares                                           _____

First aid kit containing infection needles _____

Solar-powered FM receiver-trans. _____

5 gallons of water _____

## Scoring Instructions for Decision by Consensus

The prediction is that the group product will be more accurate than the average for the individuals. The lower the score, the more accurate. A score of "0" is a perfect score.

*Individual Score.* Each individual can score his own sheet. As you read aloud to the group the correct rank for each item, they simply take the difference between their rank and the correct rank on that item and write it down. Do this for each item and add up these differences—DISREGARD "+" and "−".

To get the average for all individuals, divide the sum of the individual scores by the number of individuals in the group. Compute the group score in the same way you computed each of the individual scores. If our hypothesis is correct, the group score will be lower than the average for all individuals.

## Possible Questions for the Group

1. Did the group really go by consensus? Or did we gloss over conflicts?
2. Did the group stay on the intellectual or task aspects or did we stop to examine our process to see how we could work more effectively?
3. How satisfied were we with the way the group worked? How efficient were we?

1 _____ 9

very poor                                    excellent

4. How satisfied are you (as members) with the group?
5. How much influence did you feel you had as an individual on the group decision?
6. Did the group listen to you? Ignore you?
7. Did you stay involved in the exercise or did you give up?
8. In what ways could you change or improve your interaction with others?

## Key

*Instructions:* You are a member of a space crew originally scheduled to rendezvous with a mother ship on the lighted surface of the moon. Due to mechanical difficulties, however, your ship was forced to land at a spot some 200 miles from the rendezvous point. During re-entry and landing, much of the equipment aboard was damaged and, since survival depends on reaching the mother ship, the most critical items available must be chosen for the 200 mile trip. Below are listed the 15 items left intact and undamaged after landing. Your task is to rank order them in terms of their importance for your crew in allowing them to reach the rendezvous point. Place the number 1 by the most important item, the number 2 by the second most important and so on through number 15, the least important.

GROUP SUMMARY SHEET
Individual Predictions

|  | 1 | 2 | 3 | 4 | 5 | 6 | 7 | 8 | 9 | 10 | 11 | Group Prediction |
|---|---|---|---|---|---|---|---|---|---|---|---|---|
| Box of matches |  |  |  |  |  |  |  |  |  |  |  |  |
| Food concentrate |  |  |  |  |  |  |  |  |  |  |  |  |
| 50 ft. of nylon rope |  |  |  |  |  |  |  |  |  |  |  |  |
| Parachute silk |  |  |  |  |  |  |  |  |  |  |  |  |
| Portable heating unit |  |  |  |  |  |  |  |  |  |  |  |  |
| Two 45 cal. pistols |  |  |  |  |  |  |  |  |  |  |  |  |
| One-case dehydrated milk |  |  |  |  |  |  |  |  |  |  |  |  |
| Two tanks oxygen |  |  |  |  |  |  |  |  |  |  |  |  |
| Stellar map |  |  |  |  |  |  |  |  |  |  |  |  |
| Life raft |  |  |  |  |  |  |  |  |  |  |  |  |
| Magnetic compass |  |  |  |  |  |  |  |  |  |  |  |  |
| Signal flares |  |  |  |  |  |  |  |  |  |  |  |  |
| First aid kit w/needles |  |  |  |  |  |  |  |  |  |  |  |  |
| Solar-powered radio |  |  |  |  |  |  |  |  |  |  |  |  |
| 5 gallons of water |  |  |  |  |  |  |  |  |  |  |  |  |

**Figure 5-1**

Little or no use on moon — *15* Box of matches

Supply daily food required — *4* Food concentrate

Useful in tying injured together, help in climbing — *6* 50 ft. nylon rope

Shelter against sun's rays — *8* Parachute silk

Useful only if party landed on dark side — *13* Portable heating unit

Self-propulsion devices could be made from them — *11* Two .45 calibre pistols

Food, mixed with water for drinking — *12* Dehydrated Pet Milk

Fills respiration requirement — *1* Two tanks of oxygen

A principal means of finding directions — *3* Stellar map

$CO_2$ bottles for self-propulsion across chasms, etc. — *9* Life raft

| | |
|---|---|
| Probably no magnetic poles; useless | *14* Magnetic compass |
| Distress call when line of sight possible | *10* Signal flares |
| Oral pills or injection medicine valuable | *7* First aid kit with injection needles |
| Distress signal transmitter, possible communication with mother ship | *5* Solar-powered FM receiver-trans. |
| Replenishes loss from sweating, etc. | *2* Five gallons of water |

## MODEL

Let us turn now to the definition of a model which can be applied in educational settings. There are four basic elements of the instructional strategy: First is the provision of an ambiguous situation in terms of goals, leadership, agenda, etc., which will produce and identify stress and ultimately self-direction. Second, is an orientation toward group growth and development, i.e., individual learning is the *common* goal and its realization involves collaboration. Third, the data for analysis are the experiences and feedback of the participants while they are together. In this way learning is active and concepts follow experience. Finally, members and trainer must take the roles of observant-participant which includes collection of data, analyses, experimentation, and generalization.

### SYNTAX

A precise sequencing of the structure of trainer-group, member-member, and/or trainer-member interaction should not be specified for two reasons. First, as mentioned earlier, the over-all design of laboratory training is adjusted to the development of the group. Focused exercises, theory sessions, and supplemental activities may occur within the context of the T-group and vary in their nature when they do occur. The syntax differs with each different training design. Second, while there is a theoretical structure of the laboratory experience, it is an approximate account of events. Each group is unique in its growth and development and, more importantly, is self-evolving. In other words, after the initial presentation of an ambiguous situation by the trainer, the nature and structure of interaction is emergent. Insofar as the basic T-group is concerned, no *planned* pattern of interaction moves the group through the predictable phases. The phases in their probable order of occurrence are the dilemma, invention, feedback, and generalization phases, but these are no rigid structure.

### PRINCIPLES OF REACTION

The trainer functions in several roles in the T-group (and throughout the training laboratory). As an observant-participant like the other group members, the trainer is memberlike in terms of his interventions and openness. In terms of his established skills, he provides a model of the observant-participant, and much of his "teaching" is mediated through modeling. As a T-group consultant and counselor, he interprets the group behavior, calling attention to the decision-making points (critical events) in the group, suggesting motivations and analyzing procedures for their effect on the group. As laboratory designer, the trainer provides additional concepts and skill-building exercises.

### SOCIAL SYSTEM

The trainer after establishing the initial ambiguous situation takes his place as a group member, albeit a highly skilled one. Structure is nonexistent and the group must take responsibility for directing its growth. Inherent however, in the nature of the T-group experience is a climate of supportiveness and collaborative relationships for learning along with a climate of permissiveness (nonevaluation). The group norms and a spirit of inquiry support open, authentic communication and individuality.

### SUPPORT SYSTEM

The optimal support system is, of course, an experienced trainer and, ideally, a haven in the woods where the group can meet away from established patterns. However, sensitivity-training procedures can and should take place within institutional settings, and can be incorporated in the ongoing life of any group, such as a class.

### GENERAL APPLICABILITY OF THE MODEL

Laboratory-training methods are specifically designed to improve interpersonal relations and, by doing so, to increase flexibility and the ability to respond to change. Every setting in which people live and work together potentially can be improved through interpersonal relations training and every organization that is involved with change is a potential site for laboratory training.

### INSTRUCTIONAL AND NURTURANT VALUES

The Laboratory Model (Figure 5-2) is so unstructured that it hardly seems proper to say that it operates at all directly, in the sense, say, that the Jurisprudential Model *teaches* the Jurisprudential Framework. However, the environment generated in training groups can be extremely powerful. Hence, we feel that its primary mechanisms are nurturant in character, but the effects are by no means side-effects. There are, rather, primary nurturant effects and secondary nurturant effects which roughly correspond to direct and indirect effects in the more structured models. These vary, depending on the nature of the group and the direction by the trainer.

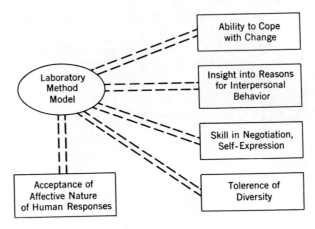

**Figure 5-2**

**TABLE 5-1 Summary Chart: Laboratory Method Model**

| | |
|---|---|
| *Syntax:* | Varies depending on the design of the laboratory training session(s). Usually the T-group structure is entirely emergent but in focused exercises this may be less true. |
| *Principles of Reaction:* | Training agent (1) assumes role of observer and assumes memberlike role in terms of his interventions and opinions; (2) provides a model and interprets group behavior, calling attention to critical events or motivations in the group. |
| *Social System:* | *Love to moderate external structure.* Norms are those of supportiveness and climate of permissiveness. |
| *Support System:* | Experienced trainer. |

# SUMMARY

## *Learning to Teach Interaction-Oriented Models*

In later chapters, we will examine various ways that models of teaching can be used in developing curriculums and preparing instructional materials. At this point we will consider the problems involved when we try to use the models as guides to our classroom teaching. Mastering the models in interactive teaching is, perhaps, more complex and taxing than to learn their use in curriculum construction and the development of materials. The reason for this is that the interactive teacher responds continuously to the unexpected—he interacts with learners simultaneously in many dimensions. He is responsible for leading children to comprehend subject matter and for modifying that subject matter so it is appropriate to the student. He has to help students grow in terms of emotional and interpersonal skills as well as intellectual skills. All these things happen simultaneously and in groups whose members are all different and whose motivations vary tremendously from situation to situation.

The classroom, even the special purpose classroom, is an extremely complex place in which to work. When a teacher employs a particular model of teaching, it makes the situation at once simpler and more complex. It renders the situation simpler in that the model provides the teacher with a framework for analyzing what is going on and for making decisions about what to do next. He furnishes guidelines for his behavior; and these, to some extent, reduce the enormous burden on him. At the same time, nearly all models of teaching that are worthwhile lead the teacher and his students into complex modes of interaction that are difficult to handle. Because models of teaching are directed to particular educational ends and provide the means for achieving those ends, the specifications for the teacher's behavior are more precise than when one simply interacts with students on an intuitive basis. Thus, in a sense, the models of teaching conceptualize rigorous standards of performance which make the teaching situation somewhat more demanding.

Probably no family of teaching models is more difficult to master than the interaction-oriented family because they deal with interpersonal relations and with intellectual operations simultaneously within frameworks that respond to differences among the students. In the interaction-oriented models, therefore, the teacher is simultaneously dealing with interactive matters, cognitive matters, and personal matters and he must keep these reconciled and balanced in order to operate with one of these models in an effective way.

We recommend that the novice teacher begin by mastering one of the models or variations of one of the models from each of the four families. These four models can give him a basic repertory and enable him to explore what the different frames of reference mean when they are worked out with youngsters. As the teacher develops control over these models, he will be mastering some of the techniques he will need in order to learn still other members of the families, and he will find that the mastery of the first model is the most difficult part and that they become successively easier as one proceeds to master others. One caution is in order. None of these models can be used as formulas for governing one's teaching behavior. They only provide guidelines for activity and they all have to be modified to to suit the teacher and the students he is working with. Some young teachers make the serious mistake of regarding the models as formulas which are to be followed rigidly. Their error can be seen dramatically in the interaction-oriented family; each of the models in this family depends on a course of events which has to be determined by the teacher and the student as they work together. The course of events cannot be laid out beforehand. Thus, although phases may be suggested to lead students through successive stages of activity toward particular goals, these phases have to be modified enormously depending on the events that occur as the teacher interacts with his students and the individual needs which emerge as the students respond to the teacher's behavior.

Thelen's distinction between group investigation and meaningless activities is a pertinent one. Group investigation will occur only when the students have a genuine puzzlement and when they authentically create the activities which will help them explore their puzzlement and the different responses they have to the puzzling situation. Simply to engage in an activity which is cooperatively planned but does not involve either the puzzlement or the engagement with the different responses to the puzzlement results in a hollow activity in which students go through the motions but do not generate the genuine inquiry and negotiation which is the purpose of the model.

## SELECTING A MODEL TO LEARN

In our teacher education work, the selection of the model to learn first has become an important consideration. Generally, we favor experimentation with Group Investigation as the initial experience with the interaction-oriented family. The model is quite complex and requires both a constructionist or personal view of knowledge and the ability to negotiate a shared reality with children; but these liabilities are really assets. While they render the model difficult to learn, they provide a basis for exploring all the other models. Our further reasoning for selecting this model may be of interest.

First, it combines intellectual and social process. In a sense, the Laboratory Model represents one end of a continuum within the family in that its rational objective is exclusively the group process. On the other end of the social interaction continuum are the Jurisprudential and Social Inquiry models. Both of these adopt an intellective approach to social reconstruction; the group process assumes a nurturant rather than direct instructional function.

Second, despite their free intellectual atmosphere both the Jurisprudential and Social Inquiry models retain a fair amount of structure and teacher initiation and control. Since our hope is to push the teacher toward greater variability in teaching style, we leaned toward the Group Investigation Model because it offered a substantially different role for the teacher and a significantly different reality for their students.

A third consideration is the grade-level applicability of these particular models. At first glance, the Jurisprudential and Social Inquiry models require verbal skills and mental processes, i.e., ability to generalize, that are probably beyond the scope of very young children. The same is true of the Laboratory Method. Since many of our students are working in the Early Childhood grades we did not want them to struggle with the impossible (or to sabotage our own framework). All of the models probably require some adaptation for each learning situation. We have certainly done our fair share of adapting or "stretching a model" as we call it.

Having made the decision to use Group Investigation, we are off and away into the social interaction mode.

## GENERAL PROCEDURES FOR TEACHING A MODEL

The basic paradigm we have used to teach a model is a simple one.

### *Theory*

First, the teacher candidates are introduced to the theory of the model. They read descriptions of the theory, a narrative account or annotated transcript of the model, and perhaps the original theoretical references. The narrative account or annotated transcript has proven to be a very helpful concrete referent for the theoretically-oriented sources, for it pins down the theory and makes it clear. Time is then provided to discuss students' reactions and questions. We have also found it useful to supplement this input with a brief lecture summarizing and clarifying the salient features of a model—its objectives, syntax, principles of reaction, social system, and conceptual points, and to have further discussion to clarify the model. Reading about the model, even several books, is not enough without help from a strong oral presentation and questioning.

*Demonstrational Practice*

Moving to the more applied level of demonstration and practice, the students view and analyze a video tape or live demonstration. We have found this presentation to be more meaningfully experienced *after* the session clarifying and reinforcing the students' conceptual understanding of the model. In the "early days" of our work with the models, we would next have the students teach the model in peer group situations soon after initial encounter with the theory. But as our knowledge of the process of learning the models becomes more sophisticated, (i.e., we have spotted points of difficulty) we have begun to develop exercises in which the students concentrate on implementing one aspect of the model or developing a particular behavioral skill before attempting the entire model. For instance, in the concept attainment model which is described in the next part of the book, the ability to recognize and identify the attributes of concepts, particularly the one being taught, is critical to the purposes of the model. At first, our students overlooked this and later wondered why they did not feel their lesson had increased the level of understanding of their students—why it had all seemed like a guessing game. Obviously, teachers cannot design substantive concept attainment experiences if they, themselves, are not clear on the attribute approach and make-up of concepts. We can foresee providing exercises in which the students are asked to specify attributes for given concepts. Such exercises will increase their awareness of the attribute make-up of concepts and precision in identifying them. This kind of task analysis breaks the complex behavior, in this case, the model of teaching, into its component behaviors and sequences them so that they become salient and prerequisite behaviors are acquired first.

The experiences with peer-teaching have proven quite productive for the students provided two procedures are followed. ("Peer-teaching is practice teaching with your peers [other teacher education students] acting as students.") First the learning task should not be at the peer level but should be one the student-teacher can use with his students. In this case, the peer-teaching group members (about five seems an optional number) become role-players. Second, it helps to specify for the students the peer-teaching assignment or topic. This eliminates the anxiety and frustration of pulling a topic or lesson "out of the air" and allows the student to concentrate his energy on simply understanding the model. Providing a list of suggested model topics or tasks across subject areas is a good procedure. It is vital that students experience the model from the learner's point of view. Peer teaching provides that opportunity. Often the students use these suggestions to build their first classroom experiences with a model. Focused exercises can be designed to provide practice with various aspects of the model.

*Application in the Classroom*

The third part of the procedure for learning a model is classroom application. Generally we have asked students to plan and carry out at least three teaching experiences with one model over different content areas. However, this requirement varies with the long-termness of the model. Behavior Modification can be practiced in many relatively brief sessions. Group Investigation takes a long time and can be applied over only one area at a time and the time needed varies considerably. Also, the democratic process does not conform to specified lesson plans or time blocks. Learning to cope with this kind of open-endedness is one of the important learnings to be gained from the model, but open blocks of time are needed and must be provided. As in the case of the peer-teaching experience, the student can be provided with specific lessons to help him get started with classroom practice. However, the more we are able to get the student teacher or intern to draw from the ongoing curriculum of the classroom, the better off we are. There is a tendency to see the models as content itself rather than as one possibility for dealing with the content and experience at hand.

A brief outline of these procedures follows:

## FRAMEWORK FOR TEACHING A MODEL

Part I: Theoretical Background
Read basic sources.
Read an annotated transcript or narrative account of a model.
Read related research or related theoretical references.
Listen to and discuss the summary lecture on the salient features of the model: objectives, syntax, social system, principles of reaction, and points of conceptual or practical difficulty.

Part II: Application of the Model
Watch and analyze a video-tape or live demonstration.
Practice exercises focusing on a component behavior or particular phase of the model.
Peer-practice teaching the model over specified lessons or topics.
Implement the model in the classroom over different content areas.

The following account provides some idea of our first experiences with the Group Investigation Model.

## TEACHING THE GROUP INVESTIGATION MODEL

We began by having our students read the general sources and a lengthy, (about 40 pages) narrative account of a Group Investigation experience developed by a teacher with her class. Although the teacher knew nothing about the Models of Teaching or Group Investigation, her account vividly portrays the democratic spirit and emergent character of the Group Investigation Model. Apparently this piece made the model come alive for our students; they seemed unusually responsive to the initial reading of material on a model. (We had not provided a similar experience with the earlier models that year). The instructional staff was able to draw upon this example to make many points—both theoretical and applied. Staff and students talked about the account in terms of phases of the model and of the social system and principles of reaction. Part of its instructional richness came from the fact that there were aspects of the model that it does and does not exemplify. In fact, throughout the exposure to Group Investigation, this narrative proved to be an invaluable common reference point for both students and staff.

The account, written by the teacher, documents her class's efforts to carry out a social action project and reveals her own reservations in playing the "facilitator" role. The project had grown spontaneously out of a conventional unit on India.[1] As part of their current events the students had read about the famine in India. Struck by the magnitude of starvation, one member of the class popped up with the suggestion: "Why don't we send them some food?" What ensued was three months of red tape that included contacts with shipping companies, customs officials, foreign embassies and organizations, wholesale food distributors, the school superintendent, and parents. The children made numerous telephone calls, wrote letters, collected food, and then had a food sale to collect money instead when they could not send the food directly. Throughout the experience their feelings and perceptions were the major part of the study experience.

Quite inadvertently the account paved the way for our students to experience a significant insight. The students' enthusiasm did not forestall the usual comments: "I think this is great, but how does this apply to me. I couldn't carry on something like that in my school. Her situation must certainly be an atypical one." They were responding to the length and complexity of the experience. At this point the preservice staff took the

---

1 For the account, see: Bruce R. Joyce, *New Strategies for Elementary Social Studies* (Chicago: Science Research Associates, 1971). The account is by Delores Greco.

opportunity to identify more limited confronting situations from which to build a Group Investigation, i.e., "Here is an eight-inch pie for our class of 40 students. Your task is to decide what to do with it." Without a word of explanation, the contrast sharply laid bare the purpose and range of possibilities of the Group Investigation. The differences in response to the simple pie-division task provided all the energy needed for a Thelenesque investigation.

In the summary lecture and discussion we tried to elaborate on several points. First, what we saw as the multiple dimensions of the model: learner initiative through curiosity, learner flexibility in inquiring into and reconciling different points of view; development of interpersonal and social skills and academic inquiry. Second, we tried to make operational terms like democratic process, inquiry, and group process. As much as possible, we related these to the Food for India piece or the illustrations in text of the model. As it later turned out, discussing these terms was a crucial aspect in helping our students carry out the model. In the course of practicing the model, our students often took voting simply as the symbol and substance of the democratic process. Yet, they did not seem totally satisfied with the process of democracy that had taken place. We often heard: "Next time the group will be more democratic." But when questioned, the students did not seem at all clear what "more democratic" would mean for their own behavior or that of their student group. They saw it in terms of legalistic procedures rather than as social negotiation.

Third, we explored the Phases of the Model as they related to the teacher's role in each phase. Lastly we discussed the general ways to bring about the needed—the social system. We pointed out that having students carry on independent investigation or group inquiry needs to be shaped very gradually and does not come about suddenly in children who are accustomed to passive roles in school. The teacher needs to vary the complexity of the tasks she gives to the students and to help the students break down a complex task into doable chunks. She can conceive of her own behavior as a model for the students, particularly interpersonal skills and flexibility. In addition, the teacher can orient the group to inquiry: "Can we make that testable?" and demonstrate the language of negotiation. "I'm not sure I understand what you mean. Could you explain that another way or is this what you mean...?" (clarification) or "Michael, how do you feel about Tom's suggestion?" (drawing out the researchable differences).

The first step toward application of the model began with a list of task situations drawn up by the instructional staff and given to the students. We had anticipated that one of their difficulties with this model might be selecting and formulating confronting incidents. The list included quite a range of suggestions covering different content areas, varying in length and complexity and in the degree of emotionality. Since we did not know in advance what makes a good Group Investigation task (what will "grab" any group of students), we looked at and rated each suggestion for emotionality, complexity, and academic background. Emotionality refers to the emotional value of the content for the students, i.e., a task related to the subject of stealing is probably more emotional than one related to math. Complexity refers to both the apparent number of dimensions of the task and to the lack of definition or structure in the task. For example, a task to "make a study of the traffic problems of New York" is replete with "where do we begin problems" whereas the pie problem mentioned earlier is narrow in scope and low in ambiguity. Our third dimension refers to the amount of academic background (content or methodology) that is necessary to carry out the task.

For peer-teaching, our students were divided into groups of five or ten. One person was asked to take the role of teacher. From the list of suggestions, she was to choose one, present the task to the group, and lead the first phase of group investigation. Part of the group acted as observers. They were given various instruments for looking at the group dynamics—measures for characterizing an individual's behavior in groups and the group's decision-making procedures. This experience tends to be intense, with a reluctance to break up the role-playing which identifies some of the serious problems they might encounter with youngsters.

As the student-teachers began their application of the model in the classroom, a number of issues to be clarified revealed themselves. The interactions among the youngsters were often unfocused and the exploration of individual suggestions often wandered. Our observations left us with the sensation that although a product often emerged from the engagements, i.e., a play, individual reports, or a decision to go to the zoo, the experience did not have the "feel" of group investigation in Thelen's terms; it tasted more of activity than inquiry. At first, we were not able to be more specific in what we meant. Finally, thanks to our observation instrument, we realized that students were not relating to each other. There were enough suggestions on how to solve the problem situation (Phase II) but they were directed toward the teacher for her cataloging and comment. The traditional student and teacher roles had not changed much. Although of a softer variety, the perceived authority relationships were the same and the teacher was still at the apex of conversation. Furthermore, each student idea seemed couched in its own berth; one student idea did not permeate or penetrate another. The pros and cons of each suggestion were not fully explored. The students, themselves, did not seem aware or concerned about the diversity of reactions. They did not feel a real need to resolve anything. The teacher unwittingly had become the recipient and mediator of ideas. As a result any social conflict to be resolved was held within the person of the teacher, rather than within the entity of the group. In neither the substance nor form of the interaction did a "group" exist.

In succeeding presentations of this model we include consideration of the development of group dynamics as well as demonstrations and discussion on ways to get youngsters relating to each other.

Another problem we found, which was touched upon earlier, is the conception of the democratic process. Some of the lessons we observed had the *appearance* of democracy—student participation, decision-making, voting, laissez faire instruction—but the inquiry and realities of social conflict and problem-solving were missing. Often, in fact, the "social" resolution was for each student to "do his own thing." No social order was negotiated. The students themselves when asked by the teacher: "We have four suggestions, how should we decide?" seemed to have a conditioned and almost passive response, "voting." They demonstrated no need for "a discussion of the issues," or a sense of personal investment. More than likely what we were probably observing is better characterized as a very cooperative, teacher-directed, activity-centered approach, which does not meet the learning objectives of the Group Investigation Model.

To summarize, we found that it is much easier to develop a cooperatively planned activity than to develop an inquiry into different responses to a genuine puzzlement. The essential energy of group investigation does not appear until the inquiry into alternative responses appears because the puzzlements are real and the concerns with different reactions become real also.

# II

# Information Processing

## as a

# Source of Models

# INTRODUCTION

*Models of Teaching*
*Designed to Affect Information Processing*

In this section we will explore models for teaching which emphasize the ways in which the student processes information. While all attempts to help students grow are, in a sense, directed at ways of processing information from their environment, either directly or indirectly, there have been a very large number of educational programs and theories which focus specifically on the information-processing process and which view education from that vantage.

These models operate from frames of reference which include a point of view about how people process information and a thesis about how to affect the ways they operate on information. It should not be assumed that all of these models are built on mechanistic theories about the human mind. On the contrary, some of them have rather free-flowing views of information-handling.

They vary in the breadth of their approach, as well. Some focus on narrow aspects of information processing; there are some specialized models designed to teach specific types of thinking. There are others which focus on the whole person—which conceptualize all dimensions of activity in terms of information processing and project ways of changing the general modes of behavior of the individual.

To many people, information is the primary business of the school, which gives particular interest to information-processing models and is probably the reason why there are so many of them.

Models focusing on information processing have come to us from several sources:

*1. One of these is from developmental studies of the intellectual capacity of the human being.* There have been quite a large number of investigators who have studied the development of the intellectual processes of the child and the adolescent. These provide what is still, for the most part, a fairly crude and tentative map of intellectual development. Even at this point of knowledge, however, it is possible to generate theories about how to increase intellectual development or to teach so that the demands of the environment are matched with the capacity of the student. It is in these theories that we find the models of teaching based on descriptions of intellectual development. To illustrate them, we have chosen models developed from the work of Jean Piaget who, probably more than anyone else, has mapped the intellectual development of children and whose work is frequently used as the basis for models of teaching.

*2. A second source is from conceptualizations of mental processes.* From the days of the earliest Greek philosophers there have been theories about how the mind works. Especially, various processes of induction and deduction have been described, sometimes in logical or mathematical language, and sometimes in more commonplace terms. During the present century studies of thinking have been carried on using laboratory experiments and observations of individuals in problem-solving situations. Computer simulations of mental processes have been developed and a whole science of information theory has grown up both to assist in the study of thinking and to assist us in problem-solving.

It is but a short leap of the imagination to move from a description of a mental process to the creation of a model of teaching designed to develop that mental operation or to use it to reach some other educational goal. For example, as a psychologist studies the ways individuals form concepts, the educator may want to use the psychologist's knowledge either to improve the processes by which people form concepts or to teach concepts within curriculum areas. We have many examples of models for teaching which are built around mental processes. These range from systems for teaching general problem-solving ability to procedures for teaching specific thinking processes. Teaching models of this sort are the Inductive Teaching Model of the late Hilda Taba and the Inquiry-Training Model of Richard Suchman.

*3. A third source comes from learning theorists who have developed systems for enhancing particular kinds of information processing.* Many are concerned with developing models for teaching concepts with the view that as a student learns concepts he uses them to process information. To teach a set of concepts would be, by this view, to change a portion of the thinking processes of the individual. Some of these theorists, such as David Ausubel, have confined themselves primarily to verbal learning whereas others have dealt with other kinds of learning. We have included the model contained in David Ausubel's theory of Meaningful Verbal Learning[1] and a creation of our own, generated from studies constructed by Jerome Bruner[2] and his associates into the strategies which people use to learn concepts.

4. *The scholarly disciplines, broadly construed, may be seen as systems for processing information.* A large quantity of educational models have been developed to teach either the major concepts or the systems of inquiry used by the disciplines with the assumption that as a student learns the processes and ideas of the discipline, he incorporates them into his own system and behaves differently as a result.

We have included a teaching model developed by Joseph Schwab and his associates of the Biological Sciences Study Committee.[3] The Committee developed the model as one of the chief methods for a biology course for secondary schools.

The range of information-processing models is considerable and they offer to the teacher several ways of thinking about the ways students think and a good variety of techniques for trying to improve thinking ability. Grasping the entire family of available models is a formidable task and we have tried to arrange our presentation of models so that the order will facilitate this task.

We begin with a model for teaching concepts because it explores the nature of concepts and focuses on a specific and detailed method for teaching concepts with some precision. We proceed to two models which are designed to teach students how to develop concepts and to theorize. Next we examine a model for teaching the research methods and "feel" of an academic discipline. This model is followed by one designed to teach the system of ideas of the academic disciplines (the "structure" of the discipline). We conclude the presentation of this family with the model developed from Piaget's work—one which tries to increase the rate of mental development.

After presenting this series of models, we will look at the problem of learning how to use some of them in the process of teaching. They are more highly structured than the interaction-oriented family and in some ways easier to master, at least for pre-service teachers.

[1] David Ausubel, *Psychology of Meaningful Verbal Learning* (New York: Grune & Stratton, 1963).

[2] Jerome Bruner, Jacqueline J. Goodnow, and George A. Austin, *A Study of Thinking* (New York: Science Editions, Inc., 1967).

[3] BSCS, Joseph J. Schwab, Supervisor, *Biology Teacher's Handbook* (New York: Wiley, 1965).

## A Theoretical Note

It is worth noting that some information-processing models focus on the *general* capacity of the student to process information while others focus on teaching him specific strategies for thinking. For example, the strategy developed from Piaget's work aims at increasing the abstractness with which a person thinks—it tries to accelerate his general intellectual development. The inductive strategies developed by Hilda Taba, on the other hand, teach inductive thinking techniques, albeit with the hope that a generally better thinker will emerge.

Generally speaking, the models which emphasize general changes in the character of the learner rely on *nurturant* processes while those which emphasize specific changes rely on activities to *instruct* the new *techniques*. Thus the activities receive the most attention in the latter group and the general environment is stressed in the former group.

# 6

# CONCEPT ATTAINMENT

## A Model Developed
## from a Study of Thinking

This chapter concentrates on the work by Jerome Bruner, Jacqueline Goodnow, and George Austin in 1956[1] and a model for teaching which we developed after studying this work.

### ORIENTATION OF THE MODEL

Bruner, Goodnow, and Austin study the process by which humans form concepts of categories which enable them to describe similarities and relationships among things in the environment. They begin with the assertion that the environment is so tremendously diverse and man is able to discriminate so many different objects that "were we to utilize fully our capacity for registering the differences in things and respond to each event encountered as unique, we would soon be overwhelmed by the complexity of our environment."[2] It is in order to cope with the environment that we engage in the process of categorizing, which means that we "render discriminately different things equivalent...respond to them in terms of their class membership rather than their uniqueness."[3] In other words, we invent categories.

These categories enable us to group together, mentally, objects which have real differences but which we classify together on the basis of what

[1] Jerome Bruner, Jacqueline J. Goodnow, and George A. Austin, *A Study of Thinking* (New York: Science Editions, Inc., 1967).
[2] *Ibid.*, p. 1.
[3] *Ibid.*, p. 1.

they have in common. We use them to manipulate our confusing world. This process of categorizing or forming concepts benefits us in three ways. First, it "reduces the complexity of the environment."[4] Second, it gives us the means by which we identify objects in the world. Third, it reduces the necessity of constant learning. For example, once we have learned what an automobile is, we do not have to discover, at each encounter with an automobile, that it is an automobile. We simply need to find out whether or not it has certain identifying properties. In the first case, categorizing gives us direction for activity. If we know that we've liked eggs before and that they are nutritious, it helps us select eggs rather than some other substance that we might eat for breakfast. In the last case, categorizing helps us to organize and relate classes of events, for example, the subject disciplines, or cognitive maps, or sets of interacting categories that we use for rendering the world comprehensible, ordering it, and making decisions about investigations and their meaning.[5]

Bruner, Goodnow, and Austin devote their major work to the description of a process by which we discriminate the attributes of things, people, and events and place them into categories.

In the discussion, they identify[6] three types of concepts. One is conjunctive, which means that the category is defined by the joint presence of several attributes, or characteristics. For example, "red-haired boys" is a conjunctive category. When we find a boy who is also red-haired, we have an example of the concept. The attributes "boy" and "red-haired" have joined. They also describe disjunctive categories, members of which share the presence and absence of attributes (red-haired boys who are not thin) and relational concepts (those in which there is a certain relationship between defining attributes). A relational category, for example, is that there are more accidents when people drive at higher speeds on narrow roads. (Accident frequency *relates* to automobile speed and narrowness of the road. Holding narrowness of road constant, drivers at higher speeds will have more accidents.) Mother, father, son, and daughter may also be thought of as relational concepts, for they *define* relationships.

Concept attainment, according to Bruner, Goodnow, and Austin, occurs by making decisions about what attributes belong in what categories. The process of attaining a concept which has been invented by someone else is the process of determining the criteria by which they have placed certain attributes into certain categories. For example, suppose that a college senior is trying to describe (to someone who is trying to get him a blind date) the kind of girl that he would like to be matched up with. In order to do this, he is trying to *communicate* his concept and his friend is trying to

4 *Ibid.*, p. 12.
5 *Ibid.*, pp. 12–13.
6 *Ibid.*, pp. 41ff.

*attain* the concept. Our senior communicates by identifying to his friend several girls both know who fit his concept of a desirable date and several who do not. In the middle of his description, his friend interrupts him and finally says, "Ah, I see. Aha!" he says. "You like short girls who laugh a lot and you tend to avoid girls who are very good students and are very intelligent."

"You've got it, but how did you know?"

"All the time you were talking, I kept thinking about why you put each girl on the preferred and not-preferred lists. Gradually, I began to get the idea that those were the reasons why you did it. For example, most of the preferred girls laugh a lot and are short and only one is a good student and she gets her grades by working hard and selecting her courses carefully."

The process used by the match-maker was one of concept attainment. His friend has the concept of the girls he likes to date, and they could be defined by several attributes. As soon as his friend began to see by what concepts the girls were being discriminated into the two classes, he had attained the concept and was able to act.

Concept attainment is essential to categorizing, for it is the process of learning what features (attributes) of the environment are relevant for grouping events into categories. An attribute (feature) of the environment is any descriptive, general property which may vary continuously or discretely, and which has a range of values. An attribute is a characteristic of an object or event, and may refer to size, shape, color, texture, weight, substance, and so on.

Two types of attributes are significant for concept attainment: defining attributes and critical attributes. A defining attribute is one set by law, by scientific convention, or by a statement of the degree of correlation between the defining attribute and an ultimate criterion. For example, the attribute "stealing" characterizes the category "thief." All who share the attribute "stealing" are defined as "thieves." A *critical* attribute is personal, derived from experience but having external referents. We define some people as affectionate, others as cold, from experiencing them. The criteria for the categories are formed by the individual and he decides what *attributes* are relevant to the categories.

In another example, safe driving for a given area of highway may be defined by law as 50 miles per hour. The concept is safe driving, the defining attribute is speed, and the range of values of the attribute is zero to 50 miles an hour. A driver using this area of highway may consider safe driving to be when his car feels under control to him, and he may then drive at more than 50 miles per hour. The concept is safe driving, the critical attribute for the driver is the feel of the car, and the range of values for the attribute is from "feels under control" to "feels out of control." In this case, the defining attribute and the critical attribute are not compatible. The categories developed personally differ from the public, lawful ones, and the attributes referred to are different also (speed in one case, and feel of the car in the other).

Generally, the identification of anything is not inferred from a single attribute but from a constellation of attributes in particular relation to one another. As stated earlier, concepts which are defined by the joint presence of the appropriate values of several attributes are called *conjunctive* concepts. Red-haired boy is a conjunctive concept. To be placed in this category a person must be a boy. The appropriate values for this are male, between one and approximately seventeen years of age, and red-haired (the appropriate values for red may be anywhere between dark reddish brown and carrot-red hair). Relational concepts are defined by a specific relationship between the defining attributes. Income tax bracket is a relational concept, for it is determined by the relation of income level and number of dependents. In either case, to form a concept one has to focus on certain attributes and their values until a category is perceived. For example, if one is studying the letters which Thomas Jefferson wrote to Alexander Hamilton and trying to determine where their views about financing the government were and were not congruent, one has to decide what aspects of the letters to focus on (what *attributes*) and how to assign values to the attributes (assess intensity of belief, for example). As attributes pile up, one may gradually attain the concepts which fit both men's views, and then, by matching them, arrive at a comparison.

We have developed a "concept attainment" teaching model to serve three purposes. One is to teach students about the nature of concepts—to help them understand how objects are distinguished by attributes and placed in categories. This understanding is exceedingly important, for it relates to the nature of knowledge, since concepts are the basis of personal and scientific knowledge. A second is to teach students to be more effective in attaining concepts (finding out categories which others use to organize the environment) and forming concepts (developing new categories). The third purpose is to teach specific concepts.

## APPLICATIONS

### FIRST CONCEPT ATTAINMENT EXERCISES

The model begins with a "concept-attainment" exercise. Students are first provided with samples of information, some of which represent a concept and some of which do not. They know only which samples reflect the concept and which do not and they are informed about the kinds of attributes which make up the concept. Gradually, they are presented with more samples until everyone in the group thinks he knows what the concept is. Each student keeps a record of his thinking during the procedure. After everyone believes he knows the concept, each one describes the process he went through, and the group discusses the relation between attributes, concept, and the thinking process. An example of this procedure will clarify it.

Each of the following passages is labeled "yes" or "no" depending on whether it represents a concept that I have in mind. As you read the passages, think of the concepts that the "yes" passages might represent: the principle by which they were designated "yes" and the others that were designated "no." The attributes which are relevant to the concept are actions by which people communicate emotions to one another.

*Sample One*

A group of children are playing on the playground. One child makes an error that lets the other side win a point. The other children crowd around him, shouting at him. Some take his side. Gradually, the hubbub subsides, and they all return to the game.

The previous passage *does* provide an example of the concept. What concept? Is it argument, or shouting, or punishment, or game-playing? What are the other possibilities? Let us turn to another passage in which the concept is *not* contained.

*Sample Two*

Four children are sitting on the floor of a room. There is a rug, and they are shooting marbles. At one point there is a dispute over a shot. However, the problem is soon settled, and the game resumes.

This passage contained a game, so we have to eliminate game-playing as an expression of mutuality. There was an argument, so we have to eliminate *that* possibility. What are some of the other concepts that are and are not exemplified in this passage and the previous one? Let us look now to another example in which our concept *is* represented.

*Sample Three*

It is bedtime. A harried mother is putting the children to bed. She discovers that one of the children has not scrubbed his teeth. The mother berates the child, sending him back to the bathroom and his toothbrush. When he returns, the mother smiles, the children crawl into bed, and the lights are put out.

What is our concept? Is it punishment? Is it, possibly, the resolution of conflict? Let us look at one more passage in which the concept is present.

*Sample Four*

It is a track meet. One boy crosses the finish line in the one-mile race far ahead of his competition. Yet, the next two runners cross the line, straining all the way as they vie for second place. As they slow down after the race, their parents and friends crowd around them, praising them for their effort.

Now, we must rule out punishment, for there is none in this sample. If we develop a more general concept, such as "things people do to influence one another's behavior" or a concept that includes "approval and disapproval," then we have identified the principle on which the selections were made. The concept is "expressions of approval and disapproval." The attributes were specific rewarding and punishing behavior. The "no" sample did not contain any attributes relevant to approval or disapproval, but all of the others, the "yes" samples, did.

This "game" could continue through several more passages. However, we have included enough to illustrate the purpose for this activity. It focuses attention on the basis on which we have made a categorization. Because that basis is not revealed clearly with the first "yes" or "no" samples, we have to keep several possibilities in mind. Gradually we receive more information that enables us to eliminate some possibilities and think of some new ones. Hence, we are involved in a search for the concept on which the division was made. This search can help throw light on the nature of the process of categorizing events.

### Analyzing Strategies for Attaining Concepts

A second purpose of the game is to help identify the mental processes we must go through if we are to make categories. In our last example, if you were to ask the participants how they decided on the concept, you would find several strategies being used. Some people seize on specific possibilities early in the game, e.g. punishment or shouting, while others begin with more general possibilities, e.g. human interaction. The ones who begin with a specific possibility carry their choice as far as they can, then discard it, going back and trying another. They may also carry several specific possibilities at one time discarding each along the way without going back to the beginning for a new one. The people who begin with a more general concept gradually narrow the field.

### SECOND CONCEPT ATTAINMENT EXERCISE

Let us now look at a more difficult example of the exercise. "Yes" or "no" is marked beside each nation in the following list. The task is to determine the principle on which the yeses and the noes were assigned. The attributes to consider are cultural characteristics of the countries. The principle emphasizes certain cultural characteristics and not others. It may refer to political characteristics, for example, or religious ones, or some other aspects.

Consider the following set:

| | |
|---|---|
| Ghana | yes |
| France | no |
| Kenya | yes |
| Germany | no |
| Chad | yes |
| Denmark | no |
| Egypt | no |

At this point, if "African" cultures was thought to be the basis for the division, it has to be discarded. What possibilities remain? How have the cultures been grouped?

| | |
|---|---|
| Peru | yes |
| Japan | no |
| England | no |
| Ecuador | yes |

Have you arrived at a concept? Are the nations being divided on a basis of the extent of their economic development? Is it their voting patterns in the United Nations (their international political stance)? What possibilities are there?

| | |
|---|---|
| Russia | no |
| Polynesia | yes |
| Indonesia | yes |
| Canada | no |

And on and on we might go, developing and discarding principles. This game, of course, presupposes considerable familiarity with world cultures and nations, for the student has to have enough knowledge to supply possible attributes for each nation.

## THIRD CONCEPT ATTAINMENT EXERCISE

Finally, let us look at the teaching of a simple concept to a young child. Let us present him with the following written words, saying each one as we present it.

| | |
|---|---|
| Fat | yes |
| Fate | no |
| mat | yes |
| mate | no |
| rat | yes |
| rate | no |

What concept can he attain from this exercise? What concept would he form if we were to reverse the positive and negative character of the exemplars? Can you make a concept-attainment task in which he could learn the two concepts and how they are related?

## ANALYZING CONCEPTS IN WRITTEN MATERIALS

The real payoff of the "concept attainment game" occurs when we begin to apply it to unarranged material to help us become aware of the categories that are being employed.

The analysis of concepts and attributes in written material is essential to any kind of meaningful and critical reading, for verbal assertions of concepts appear throughout written material—the attributes on which they are based being made explicit considerably less often. For example, consider the following passages in a secondary social studies textbook. The passage was constructed to teach students the attributes of one concept of United States military policy, the policy of containment.

"As the word itself, indicates, containment is a defensive policy: we react to Communist moves. . . .

"Our defensive military policy rests on the idea that the United States must be strong enough to endure any attack and still have the power to crush the aggressor. If the Communists are aware that we can destroy them even if they strike the first blow, they are unlikely to follow an aggressive course.

"In recent years the United States has taken the following steps to insure that we will be able to strike back after an atomic attack: the development of the Polaris submarine, which, because of its mobility, cannot be easily destroyed; the concealment of intercontinental missiles. . . . ; the development of a world-wide warning system against impending attack; and keeping nuclear bombers on around-the-clock alert.

"The defensive nature of the United States military policy creates certain difficulties. Not only can an enemy choose the time of attack, he can also choose the place and the manner. Therefore the United States not only must maintain troops in many parts of the world, but it must maintain highly mobile forces which can be dispatched to any trouble spot on short notice. The most serious problems, in some ways, grow out of the fact that the Communists are free to choose their manner of aggression. Because they prefer to attack from within, using subversion and guerrilla forces we, too, must adopt new tactics. To that end, the United States has undertaken the training of some of its forces in guerrilla warfare. Our government has sent such specially trained groups to allied countries that have needed help in fighting Communist rebels. In South Vietnam, for example, American special forces have taken an important part in the struggle against Communist guerrilla fighters."[7]

The concept of defensive military policy (containment) is explicated with several attributes. In addition, several other concepts are being taught. Communist military policy, or at least one concept of it, is being taught. What attributes are attached to it?

Can you identify other concepts and related attributes in these passages?

For another instance, let us look at two concepts of *criminality* as contained in the professional literature. Attributes are italicized.

It has been traditional to impute to the criminal certain distinctive and peculiar motivations and physical, mental, and social traits and characteristics.

7 Robert P. Ludlum *et al., American Government* (Boston: Houghton Mifflin, 1969), p. 333. Reprinted by permission of the publisher.

Historically, crime has been ascribed to *innate depravity, instigation of the devil, constitutional abnormalities, mental deficiency, psychopathology,* and many other conditions inherent in the individual. Criminals have been thus set off as a distinctive class, qualitatively different from the rest of the population.[8]

From this frame of reference, the dominant attributes of criminality are personal—the criminal is a different kind of person from the noncriminal. Compare this with the concept in the following passage about five delinquent brothers:

> The delinquent careers of the brothers had their origins in the *practices of the play groups and gangs* with which they became associated as children. The initial *acts of theft were part of the undifferentiated play life of the street.* From these sample beginnings, the brothers *progressed, by social means, to more complicated,* more serious, and more specialized forms of theft. The *situation in the home community not only failed to offer organized resistance to this development,* but *there were elements which encouraged it* and *made any other course of action difficult.*[9]

The concept attached to the word "criminal" now has social attributes rather than personal ones. The passages, in fact, succeed in helping us contrast two concepts of criminality.

## CONCEPT ATTAINMENT, CONCEPT FORMATION, AND INDUCTIVE TEACHING

Expository teaching, whether oral or written, is often criticized because it masks from students the nature (attributes) of the concepts which are being taught. Inductive teaching (we will consider two well-known inductive strategies in the next two chapters) presents data to students and either helps them organize it according to previously selected concepts (concept attainment) or helps them organize the data by making concepts of their own (concept formation). There is a vast difference between the induction of pre-selected concepts from arranged data and the induction of an original concept.

For example, when a student exposes various materials provided him to magnets and generalizes about the kinds of materials which are and are not sensitive to magnetism he gradually attains a concept preordained by the selection of materials. When he finds his own materials and tries to find out which ones will conduct electricity, he may form his own generali-

---

[8] Ernest W. Burgess and Donald J. Bogue, "The Delinquency Research of Clifford R. Show and Henry D. McKay and Associates," in Burgess and Bogue, eds., *Urban Sociology* (Chicago: University of Chicago Press, 1967), p. 308. Reprinted by permission of the publisher. Italics added.

[9] *Ibid.*, p. 308. Italics added.

zation although working with someone else's concepts. To collect data about various nations and develop one's own categories for classifying them requires invention of concepts, structuring of data collection, and other complex operations.

It is worthwhile for a teacher to include early in the year some lessons intended to establish an understanding between himself and his students of what a concept is and then to apply this as they analyze resources, whether books, objects, or visitors. The strategy can (and should) be used effectively not only with written or oral verbal material but also with a variety of media—films, drama, dance. It is possible to imagine a walking tour of the city or of a museum using the concept attainment strategy. Teachers can point out exemplars and non-exemplars of the concept.

Students also can develop their own categories, as we have illustrated— and concept-building activity should probably be one of the major activities in any social studies unit.

## MODEL

### SYNTAX OR STRUCTURE

*Phase One: Playing Concept-Attainment Games*

The first part of this phase involves presenting data to the learner. The data may be events or people or any other discriminable unit. The units of information are delineated to the learner as belonging or not belonging as examples of the concept, and he is told the kinds of attributes the concept was developed from. During the game the learner is encouraged to speculate about the concept or principle or discriminatory concept which is being used as the basis of selection of units of data. While doing so, students are encouraged to compare their hypotheses concerning the concepts and their reasons for their choices. In succeeding parts, further units of data may be presented as before, and the preceding procedure may be repeated until there is consensus about the concepts.

*Phase Two: Analyzing Strategies*

In this phase, students begin to analyze their strategies for attaining concepts. As we have indicated, some learners initially try very broad constructs and then gradually narrow the field or become more specific in their statement of the concept. Others move rather quickly to specific concepts and combinations of them. Concept-attainment strategies are particularly interesting when relational concepts are being considered. Suppose that units of data are presented which compare countries by agricultural productivity in relation to technological level (use of fertilizer, etc.), the climate, general level of development of the country, and so on, and the students are attempting to attain concepts of relationship among the several factors. In such a complex case the strategies students will use will be varied and interesting.[10]

*Phase Three: Analyzing Concepts in Reports,*
*Conversations, and Written Material*

During this phase students analyze the kinds of concepts and attributes used in a variety of materials appropriate to their age and experience. (A concept is identified and the material is presented to the students. They create the data units—exemplars—and specify the attributes of the concept.) Young children may analyze concepts like "flower pot," "neighborhood," "family," concepts for grouping things within their life experience. Older children may examine concepts like "social status" and others more complex than those appropriate for the young children. High school students can analyze even more sophisticated concepts, such as those used to categorize poets (romantics vs. realists), nations, and life-styles.

The purpose of this phase is to increase knowledge of the nature of concepts and how they are used.

*Phase Four: Practicing*

Students practice forming concepts, teaching them to others through concept-attainment games, and defending them. This phase is designed to help the student become aware of his concept-formation techniques and to sharpen the precision with which he develops and uses concepts.

### Social System or Structure

In the initial phase the teacher presents data and designates it as belonging or not belonging as an exemplar of the concept. (This designation is in sharp contrast to the typical move of the teacher who tells people what a concept is.) In the latter stages when students are beginning to analyze and compare their strategies for attaining the concept, the teacher shifts to an analytic role, but again draws the students into analysis, being exceedingly careful not to provide them with the criteria by which they can judge their strategies. If it is desired to improve students' efficiency in attaining concepts, successive concept-attainment lessons are necessary with subsequent analyses of the effectiveness of various strategies. The teacher is the controller, then, but the atmosphere is cooperative and his procedures stay closely in tune with the learners.

### Principles of Reaction

During the flow of the lesson, the teacher wants to be supportive of the students' hypotheses about concepts, but to emphasize that they are hypo-

---

[10] For examples of different strategies, see Bruner, Goodnow, and Austin, *A Study of Thinking.*

thetical in nature and to create a dialogue in which the major content is a balancing of one person's hypothesis against another's. In the latter phases of the model, the teacher wishes to turn the students' attention toward analysis of their concepts and strategies, again being very supportive. He should encourage analysis of the merits of various strategies rather than attempt to seek the one best strategy for all people in all situations.

## SUPPORT SYSTEM

Concept-attainment lessons require material which has been arranged so that concepts are embedded in the material. The material can be arranged either so that positive and negative exemplars are pointed out to the student *or* so that he may have to ferret out the concept-relevant material himself, as when he analyzes a political approach. It should be stressed that the student's job in a concept-attainment strategy is not to invent new concepts, but to attain the ones that have previously been attained by the teacher or teaching agent. Hence, the data sources need to be *known* beforehand.

## GENERAL APPLICABILITY OF THE MODEL

The Concept-Attainment Model is widely useful. In many senses, much of language learning can be viewed as concept attainment inasmuch as the society has already devised categories of things and labels for those categories, and the language learner attains those concepts and learns those labels. The same is true in terms of the grammar or the syntactic structure of every language in that the linguistic structure consists of relational concepts of various kinds that need to be attained, to learn the structure of the disciplines to attain the concepts of that discipline. In mathematics, for example, the basic properties of integers, the commutative, the associative and distributive properties, are existing concepts which become attained by the mathematics student. Whenever students seem not to be understanding something, the concept-attainment strategy can be brought into play in an effort to establish the fundamental ideas which are at the root of the difficulty. Because of its great flexibility, the Concept Attainment Model can be adapted to entire curriculums in the various disciplines and it can be the basis for extensive man-machine systems. It can function as a model for television teaching, both when the teacher is seen and when the medium is used to carry an instructional sequence without a visible teacher.

## INSTRUCTIONAL AND NURTURANT EFFECTS

As is the case with many members of the information-processing family, the Concept Attainment Model (Figure 6-1) is "cool" and intellectual. It contrasts almost starkly with the planned group dynamics of the interaction-oriented family which are advocated as much for their nurturant effects as their instructional effects. The Concept Attainment Model is designed to

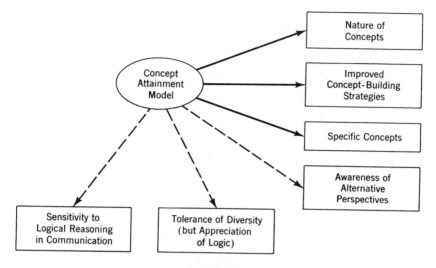

**Figure 6-1**

**TABLE 6-1 Summary Chart: Concept Attainment Model**

| *Syntax:* | *Phase One* | *Phase Two* |
|---|---|---|
| | Concept attainment games. Present data—indicative positive and negative exemplars. Students speculate about the concept, comparing and contrasting their hypotheses. Additional exemplars may be present until concept is identified. | Analyzing strategies. Students analyze their strategies for attaining concepts in Phase One. |
| | *Phase Three* | *Phase Four* |
| | Analyzing concepts from unorganized data. Students analyze given concepts for their attributes from unorganized data, material is presented, and identification of exemplars is done by the students (as in the analysis of historical documents). Analysis of the process. | Practicing concept formation. Formation of concepts, teaching and defense of concepts. Analysis of process. |

| *Principles of Reaction:* | Supportive. In Phase Two must turn discussion to concept-attainment strategies. Care must be taken to be sure students are clear about their task in Phase One. |
|---|---|
| *Social System:* | *Moderate Structure.* Teacher controls action, but it may develop into a free dialogue within phases. |
| *Support System:* | Data are needed in the form of discrete units that can be labeled as exemplars. Or—as students become sophisticated, *they* can share in making of data units (as when analyzing a document). |

have three direct instructional effects: to help students learn the nature of concepts and concept-building, to explore ways of improving their categorization processes, and to teach specific concepts. It has probable nurturant effects which may result from the student's living in the type of social system which is necessary to build the model. Awareness of alternative perspectives and how these affect concept-development should result. A critical view of knowledge and sensitivity to the logic of communication should also develop. Tolerance for diversity would very likely be tempered by critical habits and awareness of evidence and validity of concepts as a result of exposure to the process of balancing evidence and alternative concepts.

# 7

# AN INDUCTIVE MODEL

*A Model Drawn from Conceptions of*
*Mental Processes and Theory-Building*

Probably nothing has been more consistently pursued yet seemed more elusive than has the teaching of thinking. From the earliest days of educational writing, philosophers, social reformers, and educators have been trying to find some way of improving the ways human beings process information and solve problems. Thus, there are many models for teaching thinking. In this chapter, we will consider part of the sophisticated work of the late curriculum theorist, Hilda Taba, who developed a series of teaching strategies designed to develop inductive mental processes. Her models are designed to help students improve their ability to categorize and to use categories— they explore some of the same territory as the concept-attainment model.

## ORIENTATION OF THE MODEL

Hilda Taba was probably more responsible than anyone else for the popularization of the term "teaching strategy," and in her work with the Contra Costa School District she provided a first-rate example of the development of a teaching strategy designed to improved the student's ability to handle information. The strategy formed the backbone of a social studies curriculum.[1]

---

[1] Hilda Taba, *Teaching Strategies and Cognitive Functioning in Elementary School Children*, San Francisco State College, Coop Research Project No. 2404 (San Francisco, 1966).

Taba analyzed thinking from a psychological and logical point of view, and came to the following conclusion:

> While the processes of thought are psychological and hence subject to psychological analysis, the product and the content of thought must be assessed by logical criteria and evaluated by the rules of logic.[2]

She identified three postulates about thinking:

1. The first postulate was that thinking can be taught. We won't elaborate this. There is evidence pro and con. We'll live with the assumption.
2. The second was that thinking is an active transaction between the individual and data. This means that in the classroom setting, the materials of instruction become available to the individual (yield up their data) when he performs certain cognitive operations upon them—organizing facts into conceptual systems; relating points in data to each other and generalizing upon these relationships; making inferences and using known facts in generalization to hypothesize, predict, and explain unfamiliar phenomena. Mental operations cannot be taught directly in the sense of being "given by a teacher" or being acquired by absorbing someone else's thought products. The teacher can, however, *assist* the processes of internalization and conceptualization by stimulating the students to perform complex mental processes and offer progressively less and less direct support.[3]
3. Taba's third idea was that the processes of thought evolve by a sequence which is "lawful." She postulated that, in order to master certain thinking skills, you had to master certain other earlier ones and that this sequence could not be reversed. Therefore, "this concept of lawful sequences requires teaching strategies that observe these sequences."[4] In other words, Taba concluded that specific teaching strategies need to be designed for specific thinking skills and that, furthermore, these strategies need to be applied sequentially because thinking skills arise sequentially. One can argue with this assumption also, but we will live within it in order to explore the model.

## Structure of the Model: Three Teaching Strategies

Taba identified a set of cognitive tasks, or thinking tasks, and then developed sets of teaching moves, called teaching strategies, which would induce those tasks. The three cognitive tasks make up the process of inductive thinking as Taba described it. Each task represents a stage in the inductive process.

### Concept Formation

The first stage is that of concept formation. This cognitive task involves (1) identifying and enumerating the items of data which are relevant to

2 *Ibid.*, p. 36.
3 *Ibid.*, p. 34.
4 *Ibid.*, p. 35.

a problem, (2) grouping those items according to some basis of similarity, and (3) developing of categories and labels for the groups. In order to cause students to engage in each one of these activities within the task of concept formation, Taba identified teaching moves in the form of questions which she called "eliciting questions" that would be likely to cause the student to engage in the appropriate type of activity. For example, the question, "What did you see?" might induce the student to enumerate a list. The question, "What belongs together?" is likely to cause people to group those things which have been enumerated or listed. The question, "What would we call these groups?" would be likely to induce people to develop labels or categories.

An illustration of the concept-formation strategy can be drawn from a second grade unit of Taba's Contra Costa Social Studies Curriculum. The unit attempts to develop the following main idea. "The supermarket needs a place, equipment, goods and services."[5] As an opener for the unit the children are presented with the following hypothetical situation. "Mr. Smith wants to open a supermarket. What will he need?" The eliciting question might be posed that way or might be phrased, "What do you see when you go to the supermarket?" or even, "What do you see in this picture of the supermarket?" Depending on the wording of the eliciting question, children can be expected to identify individual food, items, stock boys, cashiers, equipment, a building (or place), deliveries of food. Their responses can be recorded and the listing continued until several categories are represented. After the enumerated list has been completed, the children are asked, perhaps on another day, to group the items, on the basis of similarity. "What belongs together?" Presumably, if the enumeration is rich enough, the children will identify "things the market sells" and "things done for the supermarket owner." These concepts can then be labeled "goods" and "services."

The purpose of the concept-formation strategy is to induce students to expand the conceptual system with which they process information. Thus in the first phases, they are required to do something with those data, something which requires them to alter or expand their capacity for handling information. In other words, they have to form concepts which they subsequently can use to handle new information as it comes their way.

Concept-formation activity elicited by the teaching strategy presumably reflects mental operations which are hidden from view, and which Taba refers to as "covert." The following chart (Table 7-1) illustrates the relationship between the overt activity in the concept-formation teaching strategy, the mental operations which the students presumably perform

[5] Hilda Taba, *Teacher's Handbook for Elementary Social Studies* (Reading, Mass.: Addison-Wesley, 1967), p. 52.

during the activity, and the appropriate eliciting questions which teachers use in order to lead the students through the concept-formation activities.[6]

### TABLE 7-1 Concept Formation

| Overt Activity | Covert Mental Operations | Eliciting Questions |
|---|---|---|
| 1. Enumeration and listing. | Differentiation. | What did you see? hear? note? |
| 2. Grouping. | Identifying common properties, abstracting. | What belongs together? On what criterion? |
| 3. Labeling, categorizing. | Determining the hierarchical order of items. Super- and sub-ordination. | How would you call these groups? What belongs to what? |

*Source:* Hilda Taba, *Teacher's Handbook for Elementary Social Studies,* 1967, Addison-Wesley, Reading, Mass.

*Interpretation of Data*

The second cognitive task around which Taba built a teaching strategy is the mental operation that she refers to as interpreting, inferring, and generalizing. These three mental operations are the base of the cognitive task that she refers to as Interpretation of Data. In the following chart (Table 7-2) we find specification of the overt activity involved in the interpretation of data and the questions a teacher can use to elicit the activity.[7]

### TABLE 7-2 Interpretation of Data

| Overt Activity | Covert Mental Operations | Eliciting Questions |
|---|---|---|
| 1. Identifying points. | Differentiating, | What did you notice? see? find? |
| 2. Explaining items of identified information. | Relating points to each other. Determining cause and effect relationships. | Why did so-and-so happen? |
| 3. Making inferences. | Going beyond what is given. Finding implications, extrapolating. | What does this mean? What picture does it create in your mind? What would you conclude? |

*Source:* Hilda Taba, *Teacher's Handbook for Elementary Social Studies,* 1967, Addison-Wesley, Reading, Mass.

6 *Ibid.,* p. 92.
7 *Ibid.,* p. 101.

It can be seen that the three main activities which the teacher is to elicit are those of identifying points (which requires the student to differentiate among the characteristics of particular data), explaining items which have been identified (which requires students to relate points to each other and determine the cause and effect relationships which relate data), and making inferences (which is the identification of implications which lie beyond the cause and effect relationships which have been identified). As in the case of the concept-formation strategy, the interpretation of data strategy is propelled by eliciting questions on the part of the teacher. It is assumed that the teaching strategy takes place during a group discussion activity, and in the first phase, the teacher's eliciting questions attempt to teach students to identify certain aspects of selected data. For example, students may be asked to identify features of the economic systems of the Union of South Africa, Great Britain, and Germany. After they have completed reading about these nations the teacher might ask, "What did you find about the economic systems of those three countries?" Secondly, the students are to explain the items of identified information, relating the points to each other. The teacher leads them to this by asking questions which would dig into causes and effects. For example, he might simply ask, "Do you think that the economic systems of the three countries are very similar? Why?" "Could you describe a product and show the ways in which they might handle that product, similarly and differently?" He might even say, "Are the economic systems of the three countries based on the value of the same metal? If so, how does this make them similar and different from each other?" The third phase involves the activity of making inferences. The teacher elicits this phase with sets of questions, saying things which would require the students to go beyond the data given. For example, the teacher may say, "What effect does the economic system have on the relative position of a country?" or "If the currency of all three countries is based on the value of gold, what does this mean for the relative position of the countries?" No one could be certain of a "correct" answer to this question but it could give rise to conjectures and inferences which would require the students to go beyond the data which is given about the countries, and to try to come to conclusions based on inferences about them.

## The Application of Principles

The third cognitive task upon which Taba built a teaching strategy is that of applying principles to explain new phenomena, or predicting consequences from conditions which have been established. As she saw it, a unit or series of student activities would lead the students from concept-formation activities through to activities requiring the interpretation of data, and then into activities requiring the application of principles. At each one of these stages, the student would be required to expand his capacity to handle information, first developing new concepts, and then developing new ways of applying principles that have been established so that he can use them in new situations.

The following chart (Table 7-3) is reproduced from Taba's handbook and describes the overt activities, the covert mental operations, and the eliciting questions appropriate to the application of principles teaching strategy.[8]

### TABLE 7-3 Application of Principles

| *Overt Activities* | *Covert Mental Operations* | *Eliciting Questions* |
| --- | --- | --- |
| 1. Predicting consequences. Explaining unfamiliar phenomena. Hypothesizing. | Analyzing the nature of the problem or situation. Retrieving relevant knowledge. | What would happen if . . . ? |
| 2. Explaining, and/or supporting the predictions and hypotheses. | Determining the causal links leading to prediction or hypothesis. | Why do you think this would happen? |
| 3. Verifying the prediction. | Using logical principles or factual knowledge to determine necessary and sufficient conditions. | What would it take for so-and-so to be generally true or probably true? |

*Source:* Hilda Taba, *Teacher's Handbook for Elementary Social Studies,* 1967, Addison-Wesley, Reading, Mass.

The first phase of the strategy requires the students to predict consequences, explain unfamiliar data, or hypothesize. In the second phase, they attempt to explain or support the predictions or hypotheses which were made, and in the third case, they proceed to try to verify the predictions, or to identify the conditions which would verify the predictions. Suppose that we are dealing with the economics of South Africa, Germany, and Great Britain, and we are again dealing with the question of the currencies of the three nations. We might continue our previous study by asking the students "How would it change the picture if the value of currency was based on iron ore?" Or the teacher might change the emphasis by asking the students for various hypotheses about things which might stabilize the international monetary situation as exemplified by the currencies of the three countries. In the second phase, they might be asked to support or explain their hypotheses. For example, if someone feels that a fixed currency rate for all countries should be established, and held in the same way for a long time, he would attempt to explain why he thought this system would work, and how he thought it would cope with such factors as the relative

[8] *Ibid.,* p. 109.

prosperities or production ratios within the countries. In the third phase, the students would be led to attempt to establish the conditions under which the hypotheses would hold, and to defend these against scrutiny by others who would attempt to find out whether the hypotheses meet the tests of both fitting the facts and dealing with the complexity of questions which are involved.

## CLASSROOM APPLICATION

Taba's Inductive Teaching Model has been developed to *create* inductive thinking in children and her Contra Costa Social Studies curriculum is organized to *facilitate* this process. Carefully sequenced content and suggested learning experiences build the necessary basis of information that students must draw on if they are to proceed inductively. As the learning tasks suggested in the unit call for students to form concepts, interpret data, generalize or apply principles, the teacher calls upon the appropriate teaching strategy. Taba's *Teacher's Handbook for Elementary Social Studies* provides several illustrations of these strategies "in action" as well as some useful interpretative comments and cautions.

The first example is one of enumeration and grouping that took place in a second grade class

### Example 1

### Discussion Excerpt: Enumeration and Grouping (Grade 2)

*Sequence*
*and Speaker*

| | |
|---|---|
| 1. Teacher | Let's start listing on the board things that you would buy if you went to the store. |
| 2. David | Apples. |
| 3. Paul | I'd buy a steak. |
| 4. Randy | Shrimp. |
| 5. Denny | I'd buy a puppy. |
| 6. Teacher | A puppy is different, isn't it? |
| 7. Mike | Watermelon. |
| 8. Carla | Candy bar. |
| 9. Ann | Scooter. |
| 10. Teacher | Scooter, that's something different again, isn't it? |
| 11. Teacher | We've almost filled up our board with things that we would buy. What can we do with these things? Do some of them belong together? Which ones could you find in the same place? |
| 12. Denny | You can buy a doll and scooter in the same place. |
| 13. Teacher | You would buy one of them in a toy shop, wouldn't you? Let's pick out the ones that you might buy in a toy shop. |

You might buy the scooter and the doll. What else would you buy in the toy shop?

14. Ricky          Squirt gun.
15. Teacher        All right, we would buy a squirt gun in the toy shop. What else would we buy in the toy shop?[9]

Taba notes several points with respect to enumeration. Students tend to persist in the mode established by the first speaker, for example, the listing of food. If the concepts to be developed are goods and services, such a unidimensional list would not be very productive for grouping. It's not clear from this excerpt that this was the purpose of the discussion. The teacher could have been distinguishing the concept of grocery store from other stores. However, if her ultimate objective was to induce the concept of goods and services (as seen earlier in the chapter) a broader opening question such as the one presented earlier in the chapter "What does Mr. Smith need if he is to open a grocery store" or "What do you see when you go to the grocery store" would be more apt to elicit a multidimensional list. By requesting the students to list "things that you would buy if you went to the store" the teacher is in effect providing the grouping or category for the children to which they merely add the appropriate items. It's very easy in the opening question for the teacher to suggest inadvertently the groups instead of letting them emerge from the students on the basis of their lists. Taba also points out another problem inherent in categorizing— the provision of such a broad category that it encompasses items in the other groups. For instance, the teacher called for a category label and was given "facilities and conditions" along with "education" and "transportation." In this case, "pavement," an item listed earlier, could have been put under both transportation and "facilities and conditions."[10] The following courses of action are suggested for directing discussion when problems of grouping and categorizing arise:

1. Generally, when a category is given, proceed to identify any other items which belong to it. In the case of "facilities and conditions" it would be possible to do some double subsuming—group "pavement" under "facilities and conditions" and also under "transportation."

2. When one category is of a different order from the others, it sometimes can be eliminated once the other categories are established. Items of the eliminated category can be subsumed under those remaining.

3. When the meaning of the category is not clear, clarification should be sought from the contributor. He should either explain what he means or name items which he thinks belong to the category.

4. In many cases, it is not necessary to press for a final decision, since the

9 *Ibid.*, p. 95.
10 *Ibid.*, p. 96.

emphasis is on the process rather than the content. An open procedure will encourage students to offer items which are too difficult to deal with for the time being. In other instances, the category or item in question may even be irrelevant to the content of the unit.[11]

The second strategy in the process of inductive thinking is intrepretation of data. The important aspect of this strategy is that to be meaningful the inferences have to be within the confines of the data. Often students will either make inferences totally apart from supporting information or will bring prior knowledge (ethnocentricism in the case of cultural comparisons) to bear upon the data being interpreted that often distort (also can enrich) the inferences. The teacher can increase the soundness of the inferences by following up student responses with questions that cull unprocessed information.

In this excerpt most of the discussion is at the generalization level. The teacher's focusing questions were primarily responsible for sustaining the discussion at this level.

## Example 6

### Discussion Excerpt: Interpreting Data (Grade 6)

*Sequence and Speaker*

| | |
|---|---|
| 1. Teacher | Now let's get back to intermarriage. You said that inter-marriage was so important. What about that? |
| 2./3. Seth | They marry freely, whoever they want to. They just pick. If they want to marry a Negro, an Indian, or a white person, they just do. It doesn't seem to bother them. |
| 4. Teacher | What do you have to say about that? |
| 5. Cathy | In Argentina they marry very young, and they are restricted and can't go out on dates. I mean free dates. |
| 6. Teacher | Let's get back to this intermarriage. What does that show about the country of Brazil? |
| 7. Tom | People aren't prejudiced and for segregation. |
| 8. Teacher | Why do you suppose they are not prejudiced? |
| 9. Bob | I think because they did it before. |
| 10. Amy | And there are more percentage of Indian and Negro than there are in different countries. |
| 11. Teacher | All right, do you want to carry that a little further? You thought that was a good idea, didn't you, when we talked about it? |
| 12. Karl | When the Portuguese came over to colonize, they |

[11] *Ibid.*, p. 96.

married. They found out that the Indians were there many hundreds of years before and they married them freely, and then there was an intermingling of bloods.

| | |
|---|---|
| 13. Teacher | A melting pot, isn't it? All these different peoples and they seem to get along together, which is wonderful. |
| 14. Amy | In Argentina there are not many Indians because of the war of 1888. |
| 15. Teacher | What happened to the Indians then? |
| 16. Amy | They were almost wiped out because of the war. They were against the people and they were almost wiped out. |
| 17. Karl | The intermarriage came in places that are lightly settled. |
| 18. Teacher | Why is that? |
| 19. Seth | Because there is not very many to pick from. |
| 20. Karl | They used what is around. |
| 21. Tom | Another thing about intermarriage is that they have married freely, but they didn't lose the language. |
| 22./23. Teacher | That's a good thing. What language? Where did this happen? |
| 24. Gwen | Well, intermarriage shows that everybody is created equal.[12] |

In the third teaching strategy, the application of principles, the students must apply known principles and facts either to explain unfamiliar phenomena or to predict consequences. The alternating movement between prediction and explanation to which individual students contribute as the entire class builds to a more complete explanation (or prediction) is demonstrated in the following excerpt.

EXAMPLE 7

DISCUSSION EXCERPT: APPLICATION OF PRINCIPLES (GRADE 5)

Focus of Content and Operation: "Suppose that America suddenly discovered a large, beautiful island out in the Pacific Ocean close to California. Also suppose that this island was inhabited by non-literate people who were farmers. What would happen?"

| *Operations* | *Content* | *Speaker* | |
|---|---|---|---|
| Prediction | Tools | Carla | They would have to import tools. |
| Reason | | Ned | They don't know how to make tools. |

12 *Ibid.*, pp. 106–7.

| | | | |
|---|---|---|---|
| Informational<br>support | | Teacher | All right. How are most of our tools made? |
| | | Ned | By machines. |
| Prediction | Machines | Teacher | Do you think that they would have machinery as we have it? |
| | | Ned | No. |
| | | Teacher | Why do you think that they wouldn't? |
| Support by logical<br>reasoning | | Ned | Because they wouldn't have schools. |
| | | John | Electricity would run the machines. |
| Prediction | Electricity | | They probably wouldn't have electricity over there. |
| | | Teacher | Why do you think they wouldn't have electricity? |
| Support by logical<br>reasoning | | John | Well, they wouldn't know about electricity. |
| | | Rita | But they could still have machines if they knew how to use water power. |
| Prediction | Water<br>Power | Teacher | Do you think that perhaps they would know how to use water power? |
| Support by logical<br>reasoning | | Rita | Maybe.[13] |

The third step of the strategy involves verifying the prediction or hypothesis by checking its probability or universatility. For instance, in one class students were asked what would happen if the desert had water. If the students had reached the conclusion that the presence of water makes the soil productive and that water would transform the desert way of life, the teacher could move the discussion to questioning whether the presence of water is the only condition to making the soil productive and transforming the way of life (i.e., what about need for a transportation system? How will the products be distributed?).[14]

[13] *Ibid.*, p. 110.
[14] *Ibid.*, p. 111.

## MODEL

### Syntax

All three of these teaching strategies bear strong resemblances to each other. Each of them is built around an idea of a mental operation. In one case the mental operation involves concept formation. In the second case, it involves the application of principles or ideas. In each case, the teaching strategy involves types of activity which assume that students must go through certain operations which are not visible in order to perform the activity. The sequence of activities forms the syntax of the teaching strategies and is presumably accompanied by "covert," that is, underlying mental processes. In each case, the teacher's activity is that of moving the strategy along by means of eliciting questions which pull the student from one phase of activity into the next when it is appropriate. In the case of concept-formation strategy, for example, the grouping of data would be premature if the data had not been identified and enumerated, and there would be no basis for group discussion of the data, if the data were not known to all and had not been enumerated and identified in a public way. Consequently, although the strategies have definite phases, the teacher is to apply those phases by the use of eliciting questions when it is the right time, and not before. Again, however, to delay too long would be to lose opportunities to help the students increase their capacity to handle the information in more complex ways.

### Social System

In the case of all three strategies, the atmosphere of the classroom is cooperative, with a good deal of pupil activity, but the teacher is generally to be the initiator of phases, and thus is the major controller of information. The sequence of the activities is determined in advance, so the teacher is in a controlling, if cooperative position.

### Principles of Reaction

Taba provides the teacher with rather clear guidelines for reacting and responding within each phase, for if he matches his eliciting questions or moves to the specific cognitive tasks within each strategy, he must be sure that the cognitive tasks occur in optimum order, and also occur at the right time. That is, the teacher should not direct a grouping question to a person who has not yet enumerated or listed, and if the teacher is working with a large group, he must be sure that the enumeration and listing activity is completed and understood by all before he can proceed effectively to the grouping questions. The prominent moves by the teachers are questions, and there are also the eliciting questions which are modeled after the cognitive functions. The teacher's primary mental task in the course of the strategies is to monitor the ways in which the students are processing information, and then to use the eliciting questions as appropriate to move things along. If the enumeration is fairly adequate, he then moves on to elicit grouping. If he finds that the students are still unclear about the data and are not grouping it effectively, then he may return to the earlier phase. In other words, Taba provided a rather complete map which the teacher can use in order to monitor his behavior as he attempts the strategies. The teacher's task is to sense the student's readiness for new experience, and his readiness for new cognitive activity with which to assimilate and use those experiences.

### SUPPORT SYSTEM

Taba built these strategies for a curricular system in the social studies, but they could be applied in other curricular areas as well. In any case, large quantities of raw data which can be organized by the students are necessary. For example, if the students were studying economic aspects of various nations of the world, they would need large quantities of data about the economics of those countries, statistics about world affairs, and the like, so that they could collect their data. Then the teacher's job would be to help them process the data in more complex ways, and to increase the general capacity of their systems for processing data at the same time.

### GENERAL APPLICABILITY OF THE MODEL

Taba's teaching strategies were designed specifically to increase thinking capacity. Each one was built upon a particular mental task, or cognitive task, which was to improve thinking capacity in a specific way. Thus, the primary application is to the development of thinking capacity. However, in the course of developing the thinking capacity, obviously the strategies require the students to ingest and process large quantities of information. Furthermore, although the strategies were developed specifically during the construction of a social studies curriculum, obviously they could be applied to a very large number of other curriculums. In fact, there are a great many examples of inductive strategies in science curriculums, English curriculums, and many other curriculums which are not based on specific subject areas. In addition, the third strategy, by inducing students to go beyond the data given, is a deliberate attempt to increase productive or creative thinking. Inductive processes thus include the creative processing of information, as well as the convergent processing of information in order to solve problems.

In the accompanying summary chart (Table 7-4) there is an outline of the elements of the concept-formation strategy, which is typical of the three which Taba used as the backbone of the Contra Costa Social Studies Curriculum Plan. All the strategies have relatively distinct syntaxes, with the reactions of the teachers coordinated with the syntaxes, a cooperative but teacher-centered social system, and the support systems requiring ample sources of raw ungrouped data. Their applicability is extremely wide.

## TABLE 7-4 Summary Chart: Inductive Teaching Model

*Strategy One: Concept Formation*

| Syntax: | Phase One | Phase Two | Phase Three |
|---|---|---|---|
| | Enumeration and listing. | Grouping. | Labeling categories. |

*Strategy Two: Interpretation of Data*

| | Phase Four | Phase Five | Phase Six |
|---|---|---|---|
| | Identifying dimensions and relationships. | Explaining dimensions and relationships. | Making inferences. |

*Strategy Three: Application of Principles*

| | Phase Seven | Phase Eight | Phase Nine |
|---|---|---|---|
| | Hypothesizing predicting consequences. | Explaining and/or supporting the predictions and hypothesis. | Verifying the prediction. |

From the point of view of the classroom teacher, probably a repertoire of basic inductive strategies like these should be considered an essential, and any person who is to have a reasonable opportunity of being effective as a teacher at any level should find inductive procedures, flexibly applied, to be one of his more important tools.

### NURTURANT AND INSTRUCTIONAL VALUES

The Inductive Model (Figure 7-1) is designed to instruct students in concept-formation and, simultaneously, it serves to teach concepts. It very likely nurtures attention to logic, to language and the meaning of words, and to the nature of knowledge.

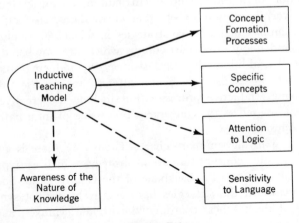

**Figure 7-1**

# 8

# INQUIRY TRAINING MODEL

## *Theory-Building as a Source*

Whereas Hilda Taba (Chapter 7) developed a model of teaching from a specific kind of thinking which underlies scientific inquiry, J. Richard Suchman developed a generalized model of inquiry from a general analysis of the methods employed by creative research personnel. He developed a training program in scientific inquiry and later, after studying the effectiveness of the training program, created a series of materials for schools built around the inquiry training concepts. He, too, is concerned with concept development, but his emphasis is on the complex concept-building that is part of creative theory-building.

## ORIENTATION OF THE MODEL

The goals of the Inquiry Training Model are, in Suchman's words, "to develop the cognitive skills of searching and data processing, and the concepts of logic and causality that would enable the individual child to inquire autonomously and productively; to give the children a new approach to learning by which they could build concepts through the analysis of concrete episodes and the discovery of relationships between variables; and to capitalize on two intrinsic sources of motivation, the rewarding experience of discovery and the excitement inherent in autonomous searching and data processing."[1]

---

[1] J. Richard Suchman, *The Elementary School Training Program in Scientific Inquiry,* Report of the U.S. Office of Education, Project Title VIII, Project 216 (Urbana: The University of Illinois, 1962), p. 28.

This model begins with the assumption that inquiry is "the pursuit of meaning."[2] Suchman feels that individuals are motivated to increase the complexity of their intellectual structure and they seek continually to make their encounters more meaningful, that is, "to obtain a new level of relatedness between and among separate aspects of one's consciousness."[3] Thus, the inquiry, meaning, and expansion of the intellect are intimately related and interdependent. Furthermore, conscious awareness of the process and strategies of inquiry is an essential aspect of autonomous inquiry. While all of us often inquire intuitively, we cannot analyze and improve our thinking unless we are consciously aware of it.

The general procedures developed in the Inquiry Training Model reflect the processes which a student goes through in order to inquire into his environment, and to develop an increasingly complex schema of the world. "Left to his own devices, man feeds his expanding intellect through the process of inquiry. These processes are carried on through three interacting and complementary functions: (1) encountering the environment, (2) processing the data obtained, (3) reorganizing one's own knowledge."[4] Similar to Piaget, who believed in mechanisms of assimilation and accommodation, Suchman believes that the individual, as he encounters a puzzling environment, needs to explore the data surrounding the puzzlement, and as he obtains this data, to put it together in new ways so that he reorganizes his knowledge. He hopes to capitalize on this natural process by developing a training program to teach students about their processes of inquiry, to teach them more effective ways of encountering the environment, obtaining and processing data and encounters, and reorganizing one's knowledge in order to increase one's ability. If this could be done, he reasons, the individual would be in the position to consciously control his intellectual development, that is, he would be able to use his knowledge of how to inquire to increase the effectiveness with which he inquires and to accelerate his intellectual development.

## THEORETICAL APPLICATION

The instructional conditions for inquiry and the inquiry process as they appear in the classroom have been described by Suchman.

> The process of inquiry can be made observable in the classroom setting by allowing children to formulate theories and gather data to test them in a group setting. Having seen discrepant physical events, they are challenged

2 J. Richard Suchman, "A Model for the Analysis of Inquiry," *Analysis of Concept Learning,* Herbert J. Klausmeier and Chester W. Harris, eds. (New York: Academic Press, 1966), p. 178.
3 *Ibid.*
4 J. Richard Suchman, *Inquiry Box: Teacher's Handbook* (Chicago: Science Research Associates, 1967), p. 1.

to formulate and test their own theories to account for the events. They have access to data through question-asking and can at any time verbalize their explanatory or theoretical formulations. Since no attempt is made by the teacher to either explain the events to the children or to render judgments about their theories, the children quickly learn that they have to judge the power of their own or each other's theories and that this can be done through verbally mediated empirical tests or experiments.

Because of these specific conditions, the transactions between teacher and pupil represent true and open inquiry where the responsibility for initiative and control in the learning situation rests squarely and consistently on the shoulders of the inquirers, the children.[5]

From this conceptualization Suchman developed a strategy which had the following format. First, materials for encounters were developed and presented to the student; second, the student was led to inquire into the puzzling situation; and third, he was prompted to examine his process of inquiry. The teacher helped him identify how he inquired and formulated more effective ways of inquiring.

One may ask why he feels it is necessary to develop special training materials, why one cannot simply have the children inquire into the world about them more or less as they are motivated to do so, and then teach them how to inquire as they go along. Suchman responds to this question in the following way. "When a person embarks on a search for new understandings in a particular discipline, often he becomes too absorbed in the substance itself to observe his own thought or action. Therefore he has little opportunity to learn about the dynamics of his own strategy of pursuit. The Inquiry Development Program brings this process into focus in the context of a given content area. But there are times when a close look at the process, undistracted by the structure of any particular discipline, is desirable. Inquiry in a vacuum is clearly impossible. What is needed is inquiry in a highly circumscribed domain in which the variables are few, the theory simple, and the ways of collecting data restricted."[6]

We can see better the conditions and strategy for inquiry operationalized and described in a classroom experience. "The children were confronted by an episode to explain, or in other words, a series of discrepant events to be assimilated. We used short physics demonstrations as the problem episodes. They were recorded on motion picture film and accompanied by a title which simply asked why a particular outcome of the demonstration has resulted."[7] Suchman uses the examples of a bimetallic strip which is bent when it is held over a Bunsen burner flame. "The strip is made of a lamination of unlike strips of metal (usually steel and brass) that have

[5] Suchman, "A Model for the Analysis of Inquiry," *Analysis of Concept Learning,* pp. 177–78.

[6] Suchman, *Inquiry Box: Teacher's Handbook,* p. 1.

[7] Suchman, *The Elementary School Training Program,* p. 29.

been welded together to form a single blade. With a handle at one end it has the appearance of a narrow knife or spatula. When this apparatus is heated, the metal in it expands, but the rate of expansion is not the same in the two metals. Consequently, half of the thickness of this laminated strip becomes slightly longer than the other half and since the two halves are attached to each other the internal stresses force the blade to assume a curve of which the outer circumference is occupied by the metal which has expanded the most.

"The child who encounters this problem must contend with the following variables: the temperature of the blade, the structure and composition of the blade, the length of the blade. These are all highly relevant to the problem at hand and the inquirer must sample them at various times during the demonstration to determine changes. In addition there are innumerable other variables which, although irrelevant to the bending, must be considered by the child before he can determine this fact. The position in which the blade is held during the heating, the composition of the handle, the source of heat, the upward pressure of the gas flame are just a few of the variables which concern the typical inquirer, but which do not affect the bending appreciably. If the child immediately tries to hypothesize complex relationships among all the variables that seem relevant to him, he could go on testing indefinitely without any noticeable progress, but by isolating variables and testing them singly he can eliminate the irrelevant ones and discover the relationships that exist between each relevant independent variable (such as the temperature of the blade) and the dependent variable (which in this case is the bending of the blade)."[8] The bending of the strip when it is held over the flame is the kind of episode that is used to confront the learner and to begin the inquiry cycle. Suchman and his collaborators deliberately selected episodes that would have sufficiently surprising outcomes to make it difficult for a child to remain indifferent after the encounter.

How does the child proceed? He proceeds by asking questions of the teacher, and the teacher attempts to respond to the child's questions by facilitating his discovery. However, he structures the situation. "First, the questions must be so structured as to be answerable by 'yes' or 'no.' This eliminates all open-ended questions and forces the children to focus and structure their probes. In a sense each question becomes a limited hypothesis. For example, the child *may not* ask: 'How did the heat affect the metal?' but he *may* ask, 'Did the heating change the metal into a liquid?' In the first instance the child does not state specifically what information he wants, and is asking the teacher to conceptualize relationships for him, to teach him something."[9] The child is permitted to continue to ask ques-

---

8 *Ibid.*, pp. 15–16.
9 *Ibid.*, p. 30.

tions, and whenever he phrases one which cannot be answered in a "yes" or a "no," the teacher or training agent reminds him of the "rules of the game" and waits until he finds a way of stating the question in the proper form. As the children attempt to inquire in the proper fashion, the teacher tries to lead them to a strategy whereby they confine their early questions to an analysis of the situation they have observed—trying to find out what things have been made of, what actually happened, and that type of thing. Then they can turn their questions to relationships among variables. At this point the children, in addition to questions, may conduct verbal or actual experiments—selecting new data, or putting it together in new ways to see what would happen if things were done differently.

In the last phase the teacher works with the children to help them analyze their inquiry and to try to formulate principles about the "logical structure of causality and strategies of inquiry. Each time, the children check their performance against these rules. Against this background of very concrete experiences, revived and made immediate through the recordings, the children can begin to conceptualize the structure of inquiry and see the shape of the strategies they are being urged to use, and the consequences of using them or not. With each session the children see more clearly the success they achieve by following this pattern which reinforces the use of these systematic and productive operations."[10] In addition, the teacher attempts to help the students learn a set of concepts, or a structure, as Suchman calls it, for the analysis of causality.

The crux of inquiry is in the data gathering operations. "The inquirer uses data as a means of suggesting theories and as a means of checking the validity of his theories. Thus, we can arbitrarily divide data gathering into two categories: verification and experimentation."[11] The structure for the analysis of causality provides a set of concepts for looking at both of these inquiry processes. Thus, the inquirer can verify and experiment with (1) the nature of *objects;* (2) the occurrence of *events;* (3) the *conditions* or states of objects; and (4) the *properties* of objects. These concepts are described and illustrated as follows:[12]

"He may verify the nature of the various objects or substances in the event: 'Was that a knife?' 'Was that liquid in the tank water?' 'Was the knife blade made of two different metals?' These are typical examples of verification of *objects.* Verification of a complex arrangement of objects could also be placed under this category: 'Was that a vacuum pump?' 'Was that an ordinary automobile?'

[10] *Ibid.,* p. 35.

[11] J. Richard Suchman, *Inquiry Development Program: Developing Inquiry* (Chicago: Science Research Associates, 1966), p. 28.

[12] From *Inquiry Development Program: Developing Inquiry* by J. Richard Suchman. © 1966, Science Research Associates, Inc. Reprinted by permission of the publisher.

"Events can also be verified: 'Did the blade bend upward the second time?' 'Was water evaporating from the blade when it was in the flame?' 'Did the man press on the blade as he wiped it?'

"Another category is the verification of *conditions,* the states of objects or systems. For example: 'Was the blade hotter than room temperature when he held it up and showed that it was bent?' 'Was the blade about six inches long?' 'Was he holding the blade perfectly horizontal in the flame?' 'Did the blade bend so that the tip was about two inches from its original position?' In verifying conditions one must always specify a given point in time, since the conditions vary with time. The teacher cannot answer a question such as 'Was the blade hot?' until the student specifies the time at which he wants to verify the condition. In fact, the change of conditions with respect to time often gives important information. If the student finds that the blade was always hotter than room temperature when it was curved, and always at about room temperature when it was straight, he has information that will be very helpful in the formulation or testing of a theory about the cause of the bending.

"Finally, verification can be used to ascertain the *properties* of objects or systems: 'Does a strip of copper always bend when it is heated?' 'Does an ordinary kitchen knife bend if it is held in a flame?' 'Does a Bunsen burner flame always give about the same amount of heat?' 'Does a vacuum pump take longer to pump the air out of something than it does to put the air back in?' These are typical probes from inquirers who are trying to ascertain the properties of various objects as a way of finding new data that will help in building a theory. In one sense these are theory questions, but they are close enough to being pure data questions that the teacher should usually answer them with a yes or no, or a properly modified answer. He may have to ask the inquirer to be more specific: 'What do you mean by an *ordinary* kitchen knife?' He may have to qualify his answer: 'A Bunsen burner can be adjusted to give different amounts of heat, and the different parts of the flame have different temperatures. But the temperature of each part of the flame in the film remained about the same during the film.' "[13]

In addition to providing a set of concepts for looking at the inquiry process, Suchman also describes a general schema for inquiry. Before he does this, however, he qualifies the purpose of his description. "There is no formula for discovery. Inquiry strategies vary over a wide range. Most of Inquiry Training has been a matter of letting the children experiment freely with their own question structuring and sequencing. In the critique sessions we tried to call their attention to the consequences of their strategies without imposing a system on them that would limit their creative thinking.

[13] *Ibid.,* pp. 28–29.

"Nevertheless, inquiry can be divided into broad phases which on the whole should be undertaken in a logical order simply because they build upon one another. Failure to adhere to this order leads either to erroneous assumptions or to low efficiency and duplication of effort. We have tried to help the children recognize these phases and see the value of planning their questioning in accordance with the schema."[14]

Let's summarize these phases. In Phase One the students (1) learn as much as possible about the properties of the objects either by verifying questions or by verbal experimentation; (2) ascertain the conditions of each object before and after the occurrence of events; and (3) assemble the data from (1) and (2), perhaps in chart form, so they are better able to discover the relationship between conditions and events. In Phase Two the students isolate and identify the *relevant* variables and necessary conditions, perhaps by experimentally manipulating one variable at a time, necessary to produce the original outcome in the encounter. Finally, in Phase Three, students, knowing the necessary conditions for a given event, attempt to *explain* the changes that occur, to hypothesize causal relationships. "Here is where the individual brings to bear his existing conceptual system in hypothesizing causal relationships and testing them. Here too is where conceptual systems are expanded through the dual process of assimilation and accommodation."[15]

## CLASSROOM APPLICATION

Suchman has provided a number of interesting teaching devices. One of these is a set of films and film strips to provide the confrontations with the environment and an "Inquiry Box" which poses problems and provides a fairly compact means for the examination of the puzzling encounters with the box. All of these add up to an Inquiry Development Program[16] which is quite extensive. It also includes a series of text books, resource books, and idea books in the physical science area. These are organized according to units which begin with puzzling situations designed to stimulate inquiry. The same teaching strategy is applied over these materials as the one which we have described here. The following examines a few of these presentations.

Suchman's description of the uses of the inquiry box is typical. "The Inquiry Box is a device that poses problems for inquiry. Inside the box, various pieces of apparatus can be assembled in a mechanical linkage which is almost completely concealed. Part of the linkage extends outside the box. The student manipulates this part and observes the consequences

[14] Suchman, *The Elementary School Training Program,* p. 38.
[15] *Ibid.,* p. 42.
[16] Suchman, *Inquiry Development Program.*

of what he does. In other words, he observes the output of the box in response to his input.[17]

"The box poses the problem: what pieces are inside, where are they located, and how are they hooked together? The inquirer can gather information about this problem in two ways: by manipulating the external portion of the linkage and observing the results, and by probing into the box with a stick to test theories about the location of objects.

"The Theory Sheet is a map of the inside of the box showing the permanent features (holes, slots, and eyes) and the components that can be used in the linkage. The inquirer uses this sheet to record his theories as he manipulates, probes, and observes.

### "Use of the Inquiry Box"

"The Inquiry Box can be used in three ways. Its first function is to illustrate the inquiry process to students. Because the box is a concrete thing used in concrete ways, it lends itself well to a demonstration of the elements of inquiry.

"The inquirer is faced with the problem of developing a *theory* about the linkages inside the box. He *gathers data* about the linkages by probing and manipulating and observing the results. Sooner or later he builds a theory about the linkage, based upon the data he has gathered. From this theory he deduces *hypotheses* about the expected results of particular probes or manipulations. He then *experiments* by trying these operations and observing the results. If the results do not support his hypotheses, he may be forced to revise his theory or to build a new theory.

"Thus the Inquiry Box enables the teacher to clarify for students the role of theories, the way in which hypotheses are deduced from theories, the function of exploratory investigations in gathering data and formulating theories. In other words, the fundamental elements of all inquiry have their counterparts in the use of the Inquiry Box.

"The box is an ideal introduction to inquiry processes for children, because the use of it requires no academic learning or formal system of knowledge, no special vocabulary or background information. Each encounter with the Inquiry Box focuses the child's attention on the processes of inquiry, void of traditional subject-matter content.

"Many different problems can be set up, so that students can work with the box again and again. As they become more sophisticated in their strategies of inquiry, more difficult problems can be set up for them to solve.

"The second function of the Inquiry Box is to give students experience in developing their own strategies for inquiry. They can gain this experience

[17] The following is from *Inquiry Box: Teacher's Handbook* by J. Richard Suchman. © 1967, Science Research Associates, Inc. Reprinted by permission of the publisher.

without becoming immersed in the facts and theories of any particular subject. The box enables them to study inquiry processes with a minimum of distraction.

"The third function of the box is to provide a means of analyzing and evaluating the inquiry of individuals or groups. Because the information available to the inquirer and his means of gathering information are restricted, it is possible to record and analyze his strategies under fairly controlled conditions. A standard problem can be set up and used with many students at different times, permitting comparison and study of the individual styles and strategies. Each operation that the student performs can be systematically recorded and analyzed later at leisure. Using the Inquiry Box for such study enables the teacher to observe general strengths and weaknesses in problem attack unrelated to specific disciplines or areas of knowledge."[18] Figure 8-1 depicts the Inquiry Box as it is set up with two linkage problems.[19]

## ILLUSTRATION ONE

A teacher-student interaction with the inquiry box might occur as follows "...the inquirer says, 'I think there's a spring in there,' and he draws a spring on the Theory Sheet or blackboard diagram where he believes it is located. At this point the teacher can ask: 'What makes you think there's a spring there?' The child might respond that as he pulls the dowel he feels a certain amount of tension, and then as he lets go of the dowel it withdraws into the box again. This suggests to him that there is a spring stretching out as he pulls the dowel, and then pulling the dowel back in again when he lets go. As a matter of fact, this student is saying that there must be a structure called a spring inside the box to account for the springlike function he has observed in his manipulation. At this point the teacher might say: 'From the data you have gathered so far, you now have formed a theory that there is a spring inside. Instead of stopping here, can you think of some way you could gather more data to test your theory further?' The teacher might even suggest that the student try probing in the spot where he believes the spring is, to see if he can gather additional evidence to support or question his theory—for instance, hearing the characteristic sound of the probe striking coiled metal."[20]

## ILLUSTRATION TWO

The following excerpt from the *Teacher's Guide* of the Inquiry Development Program gives a description of an encounter situation, which appears on film, information on the background conditions, and an analysis of probable inquiries. It is interesting to assume the teacher's role and imagine

[18] *Ibid.*, pp. 1–2.
[19] *Ibid.*, p. 25.
[20] *Ibid.*, p. 4.

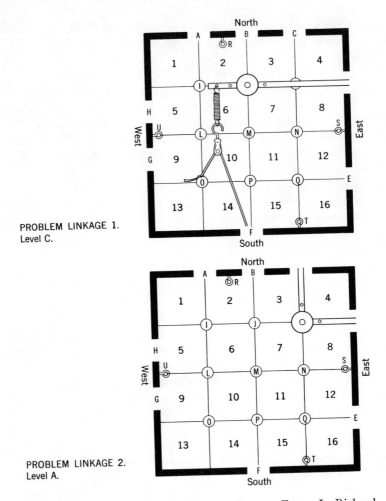

PROBLEM LINKAGE 1.
Level C.

PROBLEM LINKAGE 2.
Level A.

**Figure 8-1** Some Problem Linkages. *Source:* From J. Richard Suchman, *Inquiry Box: Teacher's Handbook.* © 1967, Science Research Associates, Inc. Reprinted by permission of the publisher.

the inquiry session that would take place and the moves you as a teacher might make.

PROBLEM 16[21]

FILM 6: THE ICE CUBES

Synopsis. At the beginning of the film a glass of clear liquid is sitting on a table and a man is just filling a second glass with clear liquid from a

21 From *Inquiry Development Program in Physical Science: Teacher's Guide* by J. Richard Suchman. © 1966, Science Research Associates, Inc. Reprinted by permission of the publisher.

pitcher. He places the glasses side by side on the table and drops an ice cube into each. The ice cube in the glass on the left, which he has just filled, floats, while the ice cube in the glass on the right sinks to the bottom. After a few moments the cube on the right slowly begins to rise. With a plastic spoon, the man pushes both cubes to the bottom of the glass. The one on the left again rises to the top when released, but the cube on the right rises only about halfway and floats there. It continues to rise very slowly. Again he pushes both cubes to the bottom with the spoon and releases them. The cube on the left again rises to the surface, and this time the one on the right also rises almost to the surface.

*Questions.* Why does one cube float and the other sink?

Why does the right-hand ice cube rise slowly?

Why does the right-hand cube remain near the middle of the glass after being pushed by the spoon the first time?

Why does the right-hand cube rise to the surface after being pushed by the spoon the second time?

Why is the left-hand cube white and right-hand cube clear?

Why are there streams of some liquid draining down from the right-hand cube?

*Conditions.* Both cubes are ordinary ice cubes. The cube on the left contains some air bubbles which cause it to appear white and opaque. However, both cubes would float in ordinary water. The right-hand glass was filled with a warm alcohol-water mixture before the beginning of the film. The temperature of the liquid in the left-hand glass is about room temperature (80°F) at the beginning of the film, and decreases to about 40°F by the end of the film. The temperature of the liquid in the right-hand glass is about 100°F at the beginning of the film and also decreases during the film. The right-hand glass contains about 60 percent alcohol and 40 percent water at the beginning of the film. As the ice cube melts, the percentage of water becomes greater.

*Principles.* Archimedes' principle. Newton's first law of motion. Change of state.

*Analysis.* This film begins with a problem in observation. Many students will be certain that they saw the man fill both glasses from the same pitcher. This, of course, is not true. The right-hand glass was already filled with the warm alcohol-water mixture at the beginning of the film, and the man was seen filling only the left-hand glass from the pitcher of water.

The density of the warm alcohol-water mixture is somewhat less than the density of ice, so the ice cube in the right-hand glass in unable to displace enough liquid to balance its own weight and it sinks. Because of the unusual crystal structure of ice, water expands slightly upon freezing, so the density of ice is slightly less than that of water and the ice floats in the left-hand glass.

As the ice cube in the right-hand glass melts, two effects occur which increase the density of the liquid in the glass. To melt the ice, heat is required, and this heat is taken from the liquid. As the liquid becomes colder, it contracts slightly and becomes denser. Also, as the ice melts, more water is added to the mixture, increasing its density. Because the water is denser than the alcohol, it tends to collect in a layer in the bottom of the glass instead of mixing evenly with the alcohol. Therefore, by the time the man puts in the spoon the first time there is a layer of nearly pure water in the bottom of the right-hand glass on which the ice cube can float, and a layer of the alcohol-water mixture on top. The cube floats at the boundary between these layers. As more water is added and the mixture becomes colder, the cube floats closer to the surface. When the spoon is put in the second time, the mixture is stirred fairly thoroughly, and the density of the whole mixture becomes great enough that the cube floats at the surface.

While the cube is floating on the boundary near the middle of the glass, you can see streams of pure water flowing off the ice and sinking in the alcohol-water mixture.

The difference in appearance of the two cubes, caused by air bubbles in the left-hand cube, is irrelevant, the same things would have happened.

If the liquid in the right-hand glass had not been warmed, the cube would still have sunk, but it would not have melted as fast or risen again as quickly. If the liquid in both glasses had been warm, the results of the experiment would have been the same.[22]

## MODEL

### SYNTAX

Generally speaking, inquiry training has three phases. The first phase is the confrontation with a problem (in such a way that would be puzzling to the student). The second phase is a period of inquiry. Sometimes this is a series of questions that the teacher has found can be answered with yes or no answers. In other cases, the children may operate on the environment, that is, they may conduct experiments or try to analyze problems by selecting new data and putting it together in new ways. In any event, during this phase, students inquire by collecting data and trying to generate ideas or hypotheses which will explain them and therefore resolve the puzzling situation in a meaningful way. In the third phase the teacher and the students working together analyze the student's strategies, emphasizing the consequences of particular strategies. This attempts to help the students become more causal in their questioning and to follow a general scheme of establishing the facts first, determining what is relevant second, and

---

[22] J. Richard Suchman, *Teacher's Guide: Inquiry Development Program in Physical Science* (Chicago: Science Research Associates, 1966), pp. 47–48.

building concepts of explanation or relationship third. In addition, they may be taught during the third phase and subequent activities, a systematic scheme for approaching puzzling situations. The sequence of phases then is:

1. Phase One       Encounter with the problem.
2. Phase Two       Inquiry through questioning, the collection and analysis of data, and the generation of hypotheses.
3. Phase Three     Analysis of the inquiry strategy with an emphasis on the development of more effective strategies.

## SOCIAL SYSTEM

Suchman's intention is that the social system be cooperative and rigorous. The teacher's moves are critical: He needs to move the inquiry sessions from phase to phase, and to insist that students turn their inquiry into their own strategies for examining their own environments. Although the structure of the inquiry training model is quite high and the social system is largely controlled by the teacher, the intellectual environment is open to all relevant ideas and teachers and students participate as equals when ideas are concerned. Moreover, the teacher should encourage students to initiate inquiry as much as possible.

## PRINCIPLES OF REACTION

The most important reactions of the teacher are during the second and third phases. During the second phase the teacher's task is to help the students to inquire, but not to do the inquiry for them. If the teacher is asked questions, he must turn the questions back to the students in such a way that they phrase their questions so as to further their own attempt to collect data and relate it to the problem situation. The teacher can, if necessary, keep the inquiry moving by making new information available to the group and by focusing particular problem events or raising questions. During the third phase the teacher's task is to keep inquiry turned back onto the process of investigation itself. Thus, he should not respond to behavior which confuse or defend the inquiry from examination, but instead, should respond in such a way as to turn the students' attention to their own processes of thinking and to the process or schema which might be used in place of or in addition to that which they employ during phase two.

## SUPPORT SYSTEM

If one accepts Suchman's notion that inquiry should focus on particular types of problems or subject matter in order that the process of inquiry can be examined, then one needs prepared sets of materials that cause fairly valid and puzzling confrontations. We have provided several interesting examples of this in the Classroom Application section of this chapter. Secondly, one needs a training agent who understands alternative strategies of inquiry and enjoys helping the student analyze his own patterns and work toward greater effectiveness.

## GENERAL APPLICABILITY OF THE MODEL

The model was designed for and is most useful for attempts to teach children scientific methods of inquiry. Particularly, it helps them to analyze their own inquiry and to compare the effectiveness of various strategies. At the same time, however, the model seems applicable to teaching an open-ended attitude toward inquiry, a receptivity to the examination of one's own behavior by others, and a willingness to examine it oneself. Consequently, side effects of the inquiry training model should be improvement in interpersonal relations and in the openness of the self toward new possibilities, especially new possibilities for organizing data and relating to other people over it.

## Instructional and Nurturant Values

Suchman's model (Figure 8-2) is designed specifically to teach children to improve their strategies of inquiry and to nurture a spirit of creativity

### TABLE 8-1 Summary Chart: Inquiry Training Model

| *Syntax:* | *Phase One* | *Phase Two* | *Phase Three* |
|---|---|---|---|
| | Encounter with the problem. | Inquiry through questioning, verbal or actual experimentation and generation of hypotheses. | Analysis of inquiry. |
| *Principles of Reaction:* | The teacher: | | |
| | 1. insures that questions are phrased so that they can be answered in yes or no and that their substance doesn't require the teacher to do the inquiry. | | |
| | 2. acts to provide a free intellectual environment. | | |
| | 3. responds to learners' requests for information and provides maximal stimulus for inquiry by focusing, refocusing, or summarizing the inquiry. | | |
| *Social System:* | *Highly structured.* Teacher is the controller of the interaction and prescribes the inquiry procedures. However, the norms of inquiry are those of cooperation, intellectual freedom, and equality. | | |
| *Support System:* | The optimal support is a prepared set of confronting materials and a training agent who understands process and strategies of inquiry. | | |

and independence in learning. There are other possible values but these seem so predominant and clear that any other probable effects, including the learning of specific concepts, seem subordinate.

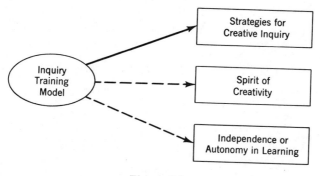

Figure 8-2

# 9

# BIOLOGICAL SCIENCE INQUIRY MODEL

*The Modes of Inquiry Approach*

From the early 1950s to the late 1960s, innovation in American education was the product of the Academic Reform movement more than any other given thrust. The Academic Reform movement was an effort to reform curriculum and instruction within curriculum areas by centering instruction around conceptions of the major ideas and research methodologies of the academic disciplines. In the area of mathematics for example, the reform movement attempted to affect the way students would think about mathematics, both the major ideas that they would use and the methods they would use to inquire into mathematical reality. Similarly, in the sciences attempts were made to update curriculum so that it would effect the major ideas of the sciences and the research methods and attitudes of the scientific community. One way of describing this effort is to say that it attempts to teach students information processing systems drawn from the academic disciplines.

Whereas many of the sets of curriculum materials and instructional procedures developed by the Academic Reform movement used rather straightforward, unimaginative teaching strategies such as simply presenting in didactic fashion the ideas and research methods of the disciplines to the student, some of the curriculums which were produced utilized very sophisticated curricular and instructional strategies designed to induce students to practice the methods of the disciplines. A very articulate exemplar of this is the approach taken by the Biological Science Curriculum Study

(BSCS) which produced curricular and instructional patterns for use in high school biology.[1]

## ORIENTATION OF THE MODEL

The essence of the BSCS approach was to teach students to process information in the ways similar to the research biologist as they engage in their inquiry, that is, conceptualizing problems and applying a particular methodology toward their solution.

The emphasis in the BSCS is two-fold. First is the stress on ecological and behavioral aspects of biology. The biologists maintain that "The problems created by growing human populations, by depletion of resources, by pollution, by regional development, and the like, all require intelligent government or community action. These are, in part at least, biological-ecological problems, and every citizen should have some awareness of their background."[2] Second is the great emphasis, in some of the three versions of the course, on scientific investigation. With respect to the blue version, they say, "Although one of the major aims of this version is to describe the major contributions modern molecular biology has made to the general understanding of scientific problems, a second aim will also be apparent. Measured by almost any standard, science has been and continues to be a powerful force in our society. A difficulty has arisen, however. This difficulty, expressed by C. P. Snow in his book, *Two Cultures,* arises from the fact that although many people may understand the *products* of science, at the same time they may be very ignorant of the nature of science and its methods of inquiry. It is probably a safe generalization to say that the understanding of the *products* of science cannot be attained unless the process is also understood. It is apparent that in a free society such as ours, much will depend on the average citizen's evaluation of science."[3]

As a consequence of this concern for an understanding of the nature of science, the strategies developed by the BSCS Committees introduce students to the methodologies of science at the same time that they introduce them to ideas and facts from the sciences. The BSCS Committee put it rather pungently, "If we examine a conventional high school text, we find that it consists of mainly or wholly of a series of unqualified, positive statements. 'There are so many kinds of mammals.' 'Organ A is composed of three tissues.' 'Respiration takes place in the following steps.' 'The genes are the units of heredity.' 'The function of A is X.'

"This kind of exposition (called rhetoric of conclusions) has long been

[1] Biological Sciences Curriculum Study, Joseph J. Schwab, Supervisor, *Biology Teachers' Handbook* (New York: Wiley, 1965).

[2] *Ibid.*, p. 19.

[3] *Ibid.*, pp. 26–27.

the standard rhetoric of textbooks even at the college level. It has many advantages, not the least of which are simplicity and economy of space. Nevertheless, there are serious objections to it. Both by omission and commission, it gives a false and misleading picture of the nature of science.

"By commission, a rhetoric of conclusions has two unfortunate effects on the student. First, it gives the impression that science consists of unalterable, fixed truths. Yet, this is not the case. The accelerated pace of knowledge in recent years, has made it abundantly clear that scientific knowledge is revisionary. It is a temporary codex, continuously restructured as new data are related to old.

"A rhetoric of conclusions also tends to convey the impressions that science is complete. Hence, the fact that scientific investigation still goes on, and at an ever-accelerated pace, is left unaccounted for to the student.

"The sin of omission by a rhetoric of conclusions can be stated thus: It fails to show that scientific knowledge is more than a simple report of things observed, that it is a body of knowledge forged slowly and tentatively from raw materials. It does not show that these raw materials, data, spring from planned observations and experiments. It does not show that the plans for experiment and observation arise from problems posed, and that these problems, in turn, arise from concepts which summarize our earlier knowledge. Finally, of great importance, is the fact that a rhetoric of conclusions fails to show that scientists, like other men, are capable of error, and that much of inquiry has been concerned with the correction of error.

"Above all, a rhetoric of conclusions fails to show that our summarizing concepts are tested by the fruitfulness of the questions that they suggest, and through this testing are continually revised and replaced.

"The essence, then, of a teaching of science as inquiry, would be to show some of the conclusions of science in the framework of the way they arise and are tested. This would mean to tell the student about the ideas posed, and the experiments performed, to indicate the data thus found, and to follow the interpretation by which these data were converted into scientific knowledge."[4]

The BSCS uses several techniques in teaching science as inquiry. First, they use many statements which express the uncertainty and the tentative nature of science. Current theories are expressed simply as current theories which may be replaced by others as time goes by. BSCS materials are filled with expressions of tentativeness such as, "We do not know." "We have been unable to discover how this happens." "The evidence about this is contradictory."[5] Second, in place of a "rhetoric of conclusions" they

[4] BSCS, *Biology Teachers' Handbook* (New York: Wiley, 1965), pp. 39–40. By permission of the Biological Sciences Curriculum Study.
[5] *Ibid.*, p. 40.

use what is called a "narrative of inquiry" in which the history of concepts of major ideas of biology are described and the course of inquiry in that area is followed. Third, the laboratory work is arranged to induce students to investigate problems, rather than to just illustrate the text. As they put it, "They treat problems for which the text does not provide answers. They create situations in which the students can participate in the inquiry."[6] Fourth, the laboratory programs have been designed in blocks which involve the student in an investigation of a real biological problem. At first students may be presented with materials already familiar to scientists and problems whose solutions are already disclosed, but, "As the series of problems progresses, they come nearer and nearer to the frontier of knowledge."[7] Thus, the student gets to simulate the activity of the research scientist. Finally, there is the use of what are called "Invitations to Enquiry." Like the functioning of the laboratory, the Invitations to Enquiry involve the student in activity which enable him to follow and participate in the reasoning related to a frontline item of investigation or to a methodological problem in biology.

It is the model of the Invitations to Enquiry that we will focus on in this chapter as the model of teaching drawn from the BSCS materials.

### Structure of the Model

Probably developed more by Joseph A. Schwab of the University of Chicago than anyone else, the strategy was designed to teach science as inquiry. This means "...to show students how knowledge arises from the interpretation of data. It means, second, to show students that the interpretation of data—indeed, even the search for data—proceeds on the basis of concepts and assumptions that change as our knowledge grows. It means, third, to show students that as these principles and concepts change, knowledge changes too. It means, fourth, to show students, that though knowledge changes, it changes for a good reason—because we know better and more than we knew before. The converse of this point also needs stress: The possibility that present knowledge may be revised in the future does *not* mean that present knowledge is false. Present knowledge is science based on the best-tested facts and concepts we presently possess. It is the most reliable, rational knowledge of which man is capable."[8]

The Invitation to Enquiry (or lesson) specifies both a subject and a topic. While the subject may be "The Cell Nucleus" or "Muscle and Bone" the topic and the focus of inquiry is "Interpretation of Data" in the first instance and "Function in a System" in the second. The subjects, then, are primarily illustrative of the topics which are either the major concepts

6 *Ibid.*
7 *Ibid.*, p. 41.
8 *Ibid.*, p. 46.

or the methodology of the discipline. Even when the topics are concepts, however, BSCS develops them through inquiry. An invitation is designed to teach inquiry in two ways. First, "it poses example after example of the process itself. Second, *it engages the participation of the student in the process.*"[9]

Invitations to Enquiry bring before the student a sample of the operations of inquiry, but within each sample there are omissions, blanks, or curiosities left uninvestigated, which he is invited to help to fill. "This omission may be the plan of an experiment, or a way to control one factor in an experiment. It may be the conclusion to be drawn from given data. It may be an hypothesis to account for data given."[10] In other words, the format of the invitation insures that the student sees biological inquiry in action and is involved in it.

In addition to "planned omission," the sets of invitations are sequentially patterned in order to build up the students' conceptions of certain aspects of inquiry. The students begin with fairly simple experiments of inquiry operations, for example, and build up to more complex ones. Thus, the invitations are graded in terms of difficulty and are built up sequentially in terms of developing a conception of how inquiry works.

We can see this sequencing in the first group of Invitations to Enquiry which focus on topics related to methodology—with the role and nature of general knowledge, data, experiment, control, hypothesis, and problems in scientific investigation. The subjects and topics of the invitations in Group I appear in Table 9-1.

**TABLE 9-1 Invitations to Enquiry, Group 1**
**Simple Enquiry: The Role and Nature of General Knowledge, Data**
**Experiment, Control, Hypothesis, and Problem in Scientific Investigation**

| *Invitation* | *Subject* | *Topic* |
|---|---|---|
| 1 | The cell nucleus | Interpretation of simple data |
| 2 | The cell nucleus | Interpretation of variable data |
| 3 | Seed germination | Misinterpretation of data |
| 4 | Plant physiology | Interpretation of complex data |
| Interim Summary 1, Knowledge and Data | | |
| 5 | Measurement in general | Systematic and random error |
| 6 | Plant nutrition | Planning of experiment |
| 7 | Plant nutrition | Control of experiment |
| 8 | Predator-prey; natural populations | "Second-best" data |
| 9 | Population growth | The problem of sampling |
| 10 | Environment and disease | The idea of hypothesis |

[9] *Ibid.,* p. 47.
[10] *Ibid.,* p. 46.

| 11 | Light and plant growth | Construction of hypotheses |
| 12 | Vitamin deficiency | "If . . . , then . . ." analysis |
| 13 | Natural selection | Practice in hypothesis |

Interim Summary 2, The Role of Hypothesis

| 14 | Auxins and plant movement | Hypothesis; interpretation of abnormality |
| 15 | Neurohormones of the heart | Origin of scientific problems |
| 16 | Discovery of penicillin | Accident in inquiry |
| 16A | Discovery of anaphylaxis | Accident in inquiry |

*Source:* from BSCS, *Biology Teachers' Handbook* (New York: John Wiley and Sons, Inc., 1965), p. 52. By permission of the Biological Sciences Curriculum Study.

Probably the best way to appreciate the model is to look at some of the exemplars of it. For example, Invitation 3 in Group I is to lead students to deal with the problem of misinterpretation of data.

INVITATION 3[11]

(SUBJECT: SEED GERMINATION)

(TOPIC: MISINTERPRETATION OF DATA)

(It is one thing to take a calculated risk in interpreting data. It is another thing to propose an interpretation for which there is no evidence—whether based on misreading of the available data or indifference to evidence. The material in this Invitation is intended to illustrate one of the most obvious misinterpretations. It also introduces the role of a clearly formulated *problem* in controlling interpretation of the data from experiments to which the problem leads.)

To the student: (a) An investigator was interested in the conditions under which seeds would best germinate. He placed several grains of corn on moist blotting paper in each of two glass dishes. He then placed one of these dishes in a room from which light was excluded. The other was placed in a well-lighted room. Both rooms were kept at the same temperature. After four days the investigator examined the grains. He found that all the seeds in both dishes had germinated.

What interpretation would you make of the data from this experiment? Do not include facts that you may have obtained elsewhere, but restrict your interpretation to those from *this experiment alone.*

(Of course, the experiment is designed to test the light factor. The Invitation is intended, however, to give the inadequately logical students a chance to say that the experiment suggests that moisture is necessary for the sprouting of grains. Others may say it shows that a warm temperature is necessary. If such suggestions do not arise, introduce one as a possibility. Do so with an attitude that will encourage the expression of unwarranted interpretation, if such exists among the students.

[11] From BSCS, *Biology Teachers' Handbook* (New York: Wiley, 1965), pp. 57–58. By permission of the Biological Sciences Curriculum Study.

(If such an interpretation is forthcoming, you can suggest its weakness by asking the students if the data suggest that corn grains require a glass dish in order to germinate. Probably none of your students will accept this. You should have little difficulty in showing them that the data some of them thought were evidence for the necessity of moisture or warmth are no different from the data available about glass dishes. In neither case are the data evidence for such a conclusion.)

To the student: (b) What factor was clearly *different* in the surroundings of the two dishes? In view of your answer, remembering that this was a deliberately planned experiment, state as precisely as you can the specific problem that led to this particular plan of experiment.

(If it has not come out long before this, it should be apparent now that the experiment was designed to test the necessity of light as a factor in germination. As to the statement of the problem, the Invitation began with a very general question: 'Under what conditions do seeds germinate best?' This is not the most useful way to state a problem for scientific inquiry, because it does not indicate where and how to look for an answer. Only when the 'question' is made specific enough to suggest what data are needed to answer it does it become an immediately useful scientific problem. For example, 'Will seeds germinate better with or without light?' is a question pointing clearly to what data are required. A comparison of germination in the light with germination in the dark is needed. So we can say that a general 'wonderment' is converted into an immediately useful problem when the question is made sufficiently specific to suggest an experiment to be performed or specific data to be sought. We do not mean to suggest that general 'wonderments' are bad. On the contrary, they are indispensable. The point is only that they must lead to something else—a solvable problem.)

To the student: (c) In view of the problem you have stated, look at the data again. What interpretation are we led to?

(It should now be clear that the evidence indicates that light is *not* necessary for the germination of *some* seeds. You may wish to point out that light is necessary for some other seeds (for example, Grand Rapids Lettuce) and may inhibit the germination of others (for example, some varieties of onion).

(N.B.: This Invitation continues to deal with the ideas of data, evidence, and interpretation. It also touches on the new point dealt with under paragraph (b), the idea of a *problem*. It exemplifies the fact that general curiosity must be converted into a specific problem.

(It also indicates that the problem posed in an inquiry has more than one function. First, it leads to the design of the experiment. It converts a wonder into a plan of attack. It also guides us in interpreting data. This is indicated in (c), where it is so much easier to make a sound interpretation than it is in (a), where we are proceeding without a clear idea of what problem led to the particular body of data being dealt with.

(If your students have found this Invitation easy or especially stimulating, you may wish to carry the discussion further and anticipate to some extent the topic of Invitation 6 (planning an experiment.) The following additions are designed for such use.)

The format of this investigation is fairly typical. The students are introduced to a problem of the biologist and given some information about the investigations that he has carried on. The student is then led to attempt to interpret the data and to deal with the problems of warranted and unwarranted interpretations. Next, he is led to try to design experiments which would get at the factor with no likelihood of data misinterpretation. This syntax—to pose a problem, introduce students to authentic experiments, lead them to a problem about that kind of investigation, and then induce them to attempt to generate ways of going about the inquiry that will eliminate the particular difficulty in the area is a very typical one.

The essence of the model is to involve the student in a genuine problem of inquiry by confronting him with an area of investigation, helping him identify a problem within that area of investigation, and inviting him to participate in ways of overcoming that particular kind of problem. Thus, he sees knowledge in the making and is initiated in the community of seekers. At the same time, he gets a healthy respect for knowledge, as such, and particularly is expected to learn both the limitations of current knowledge and its dependability.

## CLASSROOM APPLICATION

Let's look at another Invitation to Enquiry—this time to a more concept-oriented topic. The following illustration is from the Invitation to Enquiry group dealing with the Concept of Function.

The objective is to introduce the student to the concept of function. Instead of a didactic presentation, the topic has been structured, in keeping with the instructional premise of inquiry, so that it is approached as a methodological problem, i.e., how can we infer the function of a given part from its observable characteristics (what is the evidence of function)? In this model the question is not posed directly. Rather the student is guided through an area of investigation, which in this invitation has been framed in such a way as to embed the methodological concern and spirit of inquiry. Questions are then posed so that the student himself identifies the difficulty and later speculates or infers on the basis of experienced evidence the ways to resolve it.

INVITATION 32[12]
(SUBJECT: MUSCLE STRUCTURE AND FUNCTION)
(TOPIC: SIX EVIDENCES OF FUNCTION)

(We concluded Interim Summary 3 by pointing out that the concept of causal lines has no place for the organism as a whole. Instead, the concept treats the organism simply as a collection of such causal lines,

---

[12] From BSCS, Biology Teacher's Handbook (New York: Wiley 1965), pp. 173–76. By permission of the Biological Sciences Curriculum Study.

not as an organization of them. Each causal line, taken separately, is the object of investigation. The web formed by these lines is not investigated. The conception of function is one of the principles of inquiry which brings the web, the whole organism, back into the picture.

(This Invitation introduces the student to the idea of *function*. This concept involves much more than the idea of causal factor. It involves the assumption that a given part (organ, tissue, and so on) encountered in an adult organism is likely to be so well suited to the role it plays in the life of the whole organism that this role can be inferred with some confidence from observable characteristics of the part (its structure, action, and so on). As we shall indicate later, this assumption, like others in scientific research, is a *working* assumption only. We do not assume that organs are invariably perfectly adapted to their functions. We do assume that most or many of the organs in a living organism are so well adapted (because of the process of evolution) that we proceed farther in studying an organ by assuming that it is adapted to its function than by assuming that it is not.)

*To the student:* (a) Which of the various muscle masses of the human body would you say is the strongest?

(Students are most likely to suggest the thigh muscles, or the biceps, on the grounds that they are the largest single muscle in the body. If not, suggest the thigh muscle yourself, and defend your suggestion on grounds of size.)

*To the student:* (b) We decided that the thigh muscle was probably the strongest of our body muscles, using *size* as our reason for choosing it. Hence size seems to be the datum on which we base this decision. But why size, rather than color or shape? Behind our choice of size as the proper criterion, are there not data of another sort, from common experience, that suggest to us that larger muscles are likely to be stronger muscles?

(In considering this question students should be shown that their recognition and acceptance of this criterion of muscle strength is derived from associations from common experience: A drop-kick sends a football farther than a forward pass, a weight lifter has bulkier musculature than a pianist, and so on.)

*To the student:* (c) Now a new point using no information beyond common experience. What can you say happens to a *muscle* when it contracts?

(The question here is *not* what a muscle does to other parts of the body, but what the muscle itself does—its change of shape in a certain way— becoming shortened, thicker, firmer by contraction. Have the students feel their arm muscles as they lift or grasp.)

*To the student:* (d) To the fact that the motion of a muscle is as you have found it to be, add two further facts: Many muscles are attached to some other parts of the body, and many such muscles are spindle-shaped, long, narrow, and tapering. From these data alone, what do you think muscles do?

(The motion, attachment, and shape taken together suggest that muscles in general move one or all of the other parts of the body to which they may be attached. Such inferences about function are only probable.

But so are practically all inferences in science. In (e) and later queries, we shall make a point of the doubtful character of functional inference.)

The example continues in this vein.

## MODEL

### SYNTAX

The syntax floats and can take a number of forms. Essentially it contains the following elements or phases, although they may occur in a number of sequences.

Number 1. An area of investigation is posed to the student, including the methodologies which are being used in the investigation.

Number 2. The problem is structured so that the students identify a difficulty in the investigation. The difficulty may be one of data interpretation, data generation, the control of experiments, making inferences, and so on.

Number 3. The student is then asked to speculate about the problem, so that he can identify the difficulty involved in the inquiry.

Number 4. The student is then asked to speculate on ways of clearing up the difficulty, either by redesigning the experiment, organizing data in different ways, generating data, developing constructs, etc.

### PRINCIPLES OF REACTION

The teacher's task is to nurture the inquiry, emphasizing the process of inquiry and inducing the students to reflect upon it. He has to be careful that the identification of facts does not become the central issue, but at the same time is to encourage a good level of rigor in the inquiry. His task is to turn the students toward the generation of hypotheses, interpretation of data, and the development of constructs, which are seen as emergent ways of interpreting reality.

### SOCIAL SYSTEM

A cooperative, rigorous climate is desired. The student is to be welcomed into a community of seekers who use the best techniques of science. The climate, therefore, includes a certain degree of boldness as well as humility. The students need to rigorously hypothesize, challenge evidence, criticize research designs, and so on. In addition to the necessity for rigor, students must also recognize the tentative and emergent nature of their own knowledge as well as that of the discipline, and in doing so develop a certain humility with respect to their approach to the well-developed scientific disciplines.

## SUPPORT SYSTEM

A flexible instructor who is skilled in the process of inquiry, a plentiful supply of "real" areas of investigation and their ensuing problems, and the necessary data sources from which to conduct inquiry into these areas provide the necessary support system for this model.

## GENERAL APPLICABILITY OF THE MODEL

The purpose of this model is to teach the modes of inquiry of biology and to effect the ways that students process information by enabling them to develop the major concepts and modes of the discipline. No claims are made as to what this does for an individual's self-concept or for the demo-cratic process in general. On the other hand, it could easily be argued that the derivative side effects would be feelings of confidence and adequacy in the face of problems and an awareness of how to work with others, at least in the domains of developing knowledge, but perhaps in others as well. Nonetheless, the purpose of the strategy is primarily to effect informa-tion processing by teaching the strategies of inquiry which characterize the biological sciences.

## NURTURANT AND INSTRUCTIONAL VALUES

The Biological Science Inquiry Model (Figure 9-1) is designed to teach the processes of research biology and to nurture a commitment to scientific inquiry. It is also probable that it nurtures open-mindedness, and an ability to suspend judgment and balance alternatives. Through its emphasis on the community of scholars it also nurtures a spirit of cooperation and an ability to work with others in scientific inquiry.

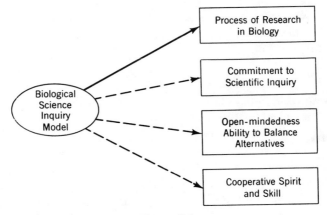

**Figure 9-1**

**TABLE 9-2 Summary Chart: Biological Science Inquiry Model**

| Syntax: (Floats) | Phase One | Phase Two |
|---|---|---|
| | Area of investigation is posed to the student. | Students identify problem in the investigation which has been prestructured. |
| | *Phase Three* | |
| | Student speculates on way to clear up difficulty. | |
| Principles of Reaction: | Teacher nourishes inquiry, turning students toward inquiry process rather than identification efforts. | |
| Social System: | *Moderate structure.* Cooperative, rigorous intellectual climate. | |
| Support System: | Flexible instructor skilled in process of inquiry and supply of problem areas of investigation. | |

## OTHER ACADEMIC INQUIRY MODELS

There are quite a number of models for teaching the disciplines as processes of community inquiry, but few as well-rationalized as that of the BSCS. One of them is worth some description here because of its promise in getting at areas of high emotional response while teaching processes of academic inquiry. It is especially interesting because it is directed at elementary school children.

It is the Michigan Social Science Curriculum Project, directed by Ronald Lippitt and Robert Fox, who have developed an approach which is potentially very powerful but is startling in its simplicity. Their strategy is to teach the research techniques of social psychology directly to children over human relations content, including their own behavior. The result presents social psychology as a living discipline whose concepts and method emerge through continuous application to inquiry into human behavior. Another result is a direct demonstration of the relevance of social science to human affairs.

Both the conception of social psychology held by these curriculum-makers and their teaching strategy, which is essentially to lead the children to practice social psychology, are probably best illustrated by looking at their materials and the activities they recommend.

They have prepared seven "laboratory units" which are developed around a resource book or text and a series of project books.

The seven units begin with an exploration of the nature of social science, "Learning to Use Social Science," and proceed to a series of units in which the students apply social science procedures and concepts to human behavior: "Discovering Differences," "Friendly and Unfriendly Behavior," "Being and Becoming," "Influencing Each Other."

The first unit is structured to introduce students to social science methods such as :

"What is a behavior specimen?" (How do we obtain samples of behavior?)

"Three ways to use observation" (Introduces the children to *description, inference,* and *value judgment* and the differences among them.)

"Cause and Effect" (Introduces the inference of cause, first in relation to physical phenomena, then in relation to human behavior.)

"Multiple Causation" (Teaches how to deal with several factors simultaneously. For example, the children read and analyze a story in which a central character has several motivations for the same action.) [13]

The children compare their analyses of this and other samples so that they check observations and inferences against one another and come to understand problems of obtaining agreement about observations as well as learning to analyze interaction using the technique of circular analysis.

Finally, a series of activities introduce the children to experiments by social psychologists which have generated interesting theories about friendly and unfriendly behavior and cooperation and competition.

This type of approach focuses the children's study on human interaction, provides an academic frame of reference and techniques for delineating and carrying out inquiry, and involves the student in the study of his own behavior and that of those around him. The overall intention is that he will take on some of the characteristics of the social scientist as he makes his way through the interpersonal world.

Thus, the instructional values are in the interpersonal domain as well as the academic domain.

---

[13] Ronald Lippitt, Robert Fox, and Lucille Schaible, "Cause and Effect," *Social Science Resource Book* (Chicago: Science Research Associates, 1969), pp. 24–25.

# ADVANCE ORGANIZER MODEL

*An Approach to Expository Teaching*

From a philosophical point of view, the Theory of Meaningful Verbal Learning developed by the psychologist David Ausubel represents an almost purely information-processing approach to education. Ausubel turns to information-processing sources both for his subject matter and for his description of mental processes, uniting them for the Theory of Meaningful Verbal Learning.[1] Perhaps no other educational theorist has confined himself to information-processing sources to the extent that Ausubel has; in contrast, there may be no other theorist who is quite as ready to admit that his educational theories, based as they are on information processing, may have limited application within other domains of human functioning.

## ORIENTATION OF THE MODEL

### THE DISCIPLINES AS SOURCES

Ausubel firmly espouses the view that each of the academic disciplines has a structure of concepts which form the information-processing system of the discipline. He takes the position that each of the disciplines consists of sets of concepts which are hierarchically organized. That is to say, at the "top" of the discipline are a number of very broad concepts which include

[1] David P. Ausubel, *The Psychology of Meaningful Verbal Learning* (New York: Grune & Stratton, 1963).

or subsume less inclusive concepts at lower stages of organization. He conceptualizes the discipline as levels of these hierarchically organized concepts that begin with perceptual data at the bottom and proceed through increasing levels of abstraction until the most abstract concepts appear at the top. Thus, we may imagine a discipline as being composed of a pyrimidal or conical set of concepts all linked together, and all firmly linked to data at the bottom and concepts of high abstraction at the top.

Ausubel believes that each discipline has its own unique set of such concepts and that the greatest power in the discipline is when it is considered on its own terms rather than being integrated with others. Thus, he has written strongly in favor of teaching the disciplines separately rather than integrating them together in broad curriculum areas where a number of disciplines are combined. His position then is that chemistry, physics, and biology should be taught separately, rather than being united together in an integrated framework or structure. His rationalization for this is that a discipline grows through research and other types of scholarship and that to the extent that a group of scholars work together to extend the discipline, then that discipline of concepts will have a unique structural character that cannot be simply folded into an integrated structure without a complete overhaul of its conceptual system.

Like Bruner, Ausubel believes that the structural concepts of each discipline can be identified and taught to the students and they then become an information processing system for him: an intellectual map which can be used to analyze particular domains and to solve problems within those domains of activities. For example, Bruner and Ausubel assume that political science contains sets of concepts which can be used to analyze political events. This set of concepts can be taught to the learner in such a way that when he tries to analyze political and social behavior and solve political problems, he can use the information-processing system from political science. Nearly all of the "national" curriculum projects of the late 1950s and 1960s which are described as the new math, the new science, the new social studies, and so on, have made the same assumptions and have attempted to organize their materials accordingly, although in many cases the projects have integrated the disciplines, an occurrence which Ausubel has criticized strongly.

The task of the school according to Ausubel is to identify clear, stable, and organized bodies of knowledge within the disciplines. The most important kind of learning which the school can foster is the acquisition of these bodies.

The major task of the educator is to transmit these stable bodies of knowledge in such a way that the learner will incorporate them meaningfully into his own system and they become his own and function for him.

## The Nervous System as Source

Ausubel describes the human nervous system as an information processing and storing system which may be analogized to the conceptual structure of an academic discipline. The information-processing system of the human being is a set of ideas which provide anchors for new information or ideas as these are received and which provide a storehouse when new meanings are acquired. As this information-processing system acquires new information and new ideas, it reorganizes itself to accommodate to those ideas, and thus it is in a perpetual state of change. However, "new ideas and information can be usefully learned and retained only to the extent that they are relatable to already available concepts or propositions which provide ideational anchors."[2] In other words, although a new set of ideas can be incorporated into the existing cognitive structure and in fact must be so incorporated for learning to persist, if new material conflicts too strongly with the existing cognitive structure or is so unrelated and no linkage is provided, the information or ideas may not be absorbed.

As the learner acquires clear, stable, and organized bodies of knowledge, these "constitute in their own right the most significant *independent variable* influencing the meaningful learning and retention of new subject matter."[3] In other words, as education transmits new hierarchical structures of ideas to the students, these provide him with power to continue his own learning. The new structure becomes part of his information-processing system and is used by him to scan the environment for new information, and provides anchors for new ideas and information as he encounters it. Thus, as the disciplines are taught to the students, they help to evolve his information-processing system into a new form. Because the disciplines have such power as information processing systems, the learner acquiring them achieves greater power as a learner and as a problem-solver.

## The Pedagogical Processing of Information

Ausubel conceptualizes the information-processing system of the discipline and the information-processing system of the mind as analogous, both with hierarchical organization of ideas "... in which the most inclusive concepts occupy a position at the apex of the structure and subsume progressively more highly differentiated sub-concepts from factual data."[4] When the major job of education consists of helping the learner to acquire

2 David P. Ausubel, *Learning Theory and Classroom Practice,* The Ontario Institute for Studies in Education, Bulletin No. 1 (Toronto, 1967), pp. 10–11.
3 *Ibid.,* p. 12.
4 *Ibid.,* p. 11.

the disciplines and to absorb those into his structure, two conditions must be satisfied in order to achieve this.

One is to ensure that the concepts presented to the student are *stable* with respect to those in his existing cognitive structure. The learner's own information processing system tends to absorb ideas which he learns and by gradual incorporation reduces and obliterates them in his system. In other words, one tries to help the learner incorporate new ideas into his cognitive structure in such a way that the structural ideas of the discipline become stabilized in his cognitive structure and do not simply become absorbed in the existing ideas and thus obliterated in their own right. Ausubel's insistence on stabilization of new ideas rather than integrating and absorbing them comes from his position that the hierarchical organization of ideas within each discipline is extremely powerful and that the learner can make maximal use of these ideas by having them stabilized within his structure, rather than by integrating them with his old ideas and making new kinds of structures.

The second condition is to ensure that the material is *meaningful* to the learner. Information and ideas acquire psychological meaning for the student when those ideas or that information is relatable to the relevant ideas within his own cognitive structure. To facilitate *both* stability and meaning, one needs to create ideational linkages between the student's own cognitive structure and that of the discipline to be taught. In this way the information and ideas which are to follow will have greater meaning for him.

To restate Ausubel's point, educators must provide the student with a structure of ideas representing the disciplines in such a way that these ideas and information are *meaningfully related* to the student's cognitive structure and implanted in the learner's information-processing system in a *stable* way. In order to accomplish this, Ausubel suggests two principles which should govern the programming of content in the subject fields, progressive differentiation and integrative reconciliation.

The first is the idea of *progressive differentiation*. "The most general and inclusive ideas of the discipline are presented first and then are progressively differentiated in terms of detail and specificity. . . . The assumption you are making here, in other words, is that an individual's organization of the content of a particular subject matter discipline in his own mind, consists of a hierarchical structure in which the most inclusive concepts occupy a position at the apex of the structure and subsume progressively less inclusive and more highly differentiated concepts and factual data."[5] Instead of beginning with the presentation of facts and helping the learner to build up the ideas of the discipline and move to progressively higher levels of

[5] Ausubel, *The Psychology of Meaningful Verbal Learning*, p. 79.

abstraction, Ausubel suggests that we begin with the most abstract ideas first so that they can include any material which is to follow. Then one would move slightly down the scale to somewhat less abstract ideas which are included at the higher level and so on until the "bottom" of the discipline had been reached.

The second principle which Ausubel operates on is that of *integrative reconciliation*. This simply means that new ideas should be consciously reconciled with and integrated with previously learned content. In other words, the sequence of the curriculum is organized so that successive learning is carefully related to what has gone before. Hence, if one begins with a certain idea in a discipline and establishes that idea and relevant examples of it so that it becomes established in the learner's cognitive structure, a following lesson in that discipline or domain should relate the new material to the idea previously established so that it builds on it and becomes integrated with it. Furthermore, the nature of the relationship should be explicitly identified and discussed. By following both the principles of progressive differentiation and integrative reconciliation, the discipline is gradually built in the mind of the learner. However, it must be kept in mind that it is built from the top down, rather than from the bottom up.

Before considering how this might be done, we should consider an important distinction that Ausubel makes between inductive, or inquiry-centered, learning and reception learning. By inductive learning, Ausubel means essentially the application of inductive learning models such as those of Taba, Suchman, and Schwab, among the information processing sources, and Massialas and Cox among the social interaction sources. Ausubel feels that the continuous use of inquiry-oriented strategies would be very inefficient because it would consume so much time and involve so many false steps. In addition, he feels that if learners are allowed to air their own ideas, many of those ideas will not be efficient. Therefore, they will not get the power that is to be derived from the hierarchical structure of the discipline. As a consequence, he feels that much learning needs to be organized as "reception learning," that is, in situations where the learner is the receiver of information and ideas. He presents the argument that reception learning can be very meaningful and should not be confused with rote learning. "Although rote reception learning of subject matter is common at all academic levels, it need not be so if expository teaching is properly conducted. We are gradually beginning to realize that not only can good expository teaching lead to meaningful reception learning, but also that discovery learning or problem solving is not necessarily meaningful learning. Problem solving in the classroom can be just as rote a process as the procedure whereby Thorndike's cats learned to escape from their problem boxes. This is so, for example, when students memorize the sequence of steps involved in solving each of the type problems in a mathematics course, without having the faintest idea of what they are doing and why, and then apply these steps mechanically to the solution of a given practice or examination problem after using various rotely memorized cues to identify it as an exemplar of the problem type in question. They get the right answers and undoubtedly engage in discovery learning. But is this learning any more meaningful than the memorization of a geometrical theorem as an arbitrary series of connected words?"[6] *In other words, Ausubel feels that discovery learning can be rote learning, while reception learning can be meaningful learning, although the converses are also the case.* What he is trying to do is avoid equating discovery learning with meaningful learning and reception learning with non-meaningful learning or rote learning.

Although meaningful reception (verbal) learning—the understanding and integration of new meaning into cognitive structure—is the focal point of Ausubel's theory, he does point out its drawback, the danger that the learner will delude himself and others to create an appearance of knowledge by learning verbal responses by rote, without reorganizing his cognitive structure. In order to counteract the "appearance of knowledge" possibility, Ausubel proposes supplementing meaningful reception (verbal) learning with a critical-thinking approach to subject matter. This may include tasks which induce students to recognize the challenge assumptions underlying new propositions or to distinguish between facts and hypotheses. (See the Jurisprudential Model [Chapter 3] and the Group Investigation Model [Chapter 2] for the kinds of approaches that induce students to analyze material in ways that could hardly be managed by rote principles.) Ausubel adds the observation that "Much good can be made of Socratic questioning in reconciling contradictions and in encouraging a critical attitude toward knowledge."[7]

Ausubel calls a middle ground between discovery and expository learning "guided discovery," and recommends it to ensure that students "work" new material and to prevent them from receiving it passively. This is a variant of expository teaching similar to Socratic questioning. It elicits the learner's active participation by requiring him to reformulate his own generalizations and integrate his knowledge in response to carefully programmed leading questions. But it is obviously much more structured than most discovery methods.[8]

Whether one uses reception or discovery learning, Ausubel emphasizes that a meaningful process is essential. Material has to be related to estab-

---

6 David P. Ausubel, "Cognitive Structure and the Facilitation of Meaningful Verbal Learning," *Readings in the Psychology of Cognition,* Richard C. Anderson and David P. Ausubel, eds. (New York: Holt, Rinehart & Winston, 1965).

7 Ausubel, *The Psychology of Meaningful Verbal Learning,* p. 21.

8 *Ibid.,* p. 31.

lished ideas in the cognitive structure of the learner in terms of ideas which enable the material to be learned in a logically coherent way. In order to accomplish this, the learner needs access during the learning process to sets of ideas that can subsume the new material to be learned, and which, by being incorporated into the cognitive structure of the learner, provide him with anchors for the new material.

## THEORETICAL APPLICATION

Given Ausubel's theoretical formulation, the job of facilitating meaningful verbal learning and retention has two aspects. First is the development of appropriate strategies to increase the clarity and stability of the learning material or, preferably, of the ideas in the cognitive structure. Second is to supplement or integrate with this teaching model others that facilitate a critical approach to subject matter.

The strategy with respect to the first task and the heart of Ausubel's approach entails the use of advance organizers. "Advance organizers consist of introductory material at a higher level of abstraction, generality and inclusiveness than the learning task itself. The function of the organizer is to provide ideational scaffolding for the stable incorporation and retention of the more detailed and differentiated material that follows the learning passage, as well as increase discriminability between the latter and related inferring concepts in the cognitive structure."[9] The advance organizer strategy operates both substantively and programmatically on the learning material. Substantively, it utilizes the basic organizing concepts and principles with the widest explanatory power, inclusiveness, generality and relatability of a given discipline.[10] In this way the availability of relevant subsumers in the cognitive structure is ensured. For example, a general model of class relationship is first provided as a general subsumer for a new class, subclasses, and species before more limited subsumers (classes and subclasses) are provided for the particular subclasses or species. Thus, varying kinds of forests are first distinguished from each each other before component subforests and trees are differentiated.[11] Organizers of this type are called expository organizers; they provide ideational anchorage for completely unfamiliar material. The relevant *substantive* organizational problem for this strategy is the identification of the basic organizing concepts to a given discipline.

*Programmatically,* the one advance organizer strategy advocates those methods of presenting and ordering the subject matter sequence that best enhance the clarity, stability, and integratedness of the cognitive structure.

[9] *Ibid.,* p. 29.
[10] Ausubel, "Cognitive Structure and the Facilitation of Meaningful Verbal Learning," *Readings in the Psychology of Cognition,* p. 108.
[11] Ausubel, *The Psychology of Meaningful Verbal Learning,* p. 214.

These methods follow the principles of progressive differentiation and integrative reconciliation and consolidation. "When subject matter is programmed in accordance with the principle of progressive differentiation, the most general and inclusive ideas of a discipline are presented first and are progressively differentiated in terms of detail and specificity."[12] A given discipline has many units of detailed differentiated material. Progressive differentiation is followed both in intra- and inter-unit planning. That is, each component unit has an organizer and, in relation to each other, the units are progressively differentiated in descending order of inclusiveness so that each unit serves as an organizer for the ones which follow. This programming corresponds to the postulated hierarchical way in which knowledge is organized and stored in the mind.

Integrative reconciliation refers to the practice of interrelating or cross-referencing these units or ideas so that significant similarities and differences are recognized and real or apparent inconsistencies are reconciled. Very often with relatively familiar learning material or material organized along parallel lines this involves the use of *comparative organizers*. These are designed to integrate new concepts with basically similar concepts existing in the cognitive structure and yet increase their disciminability in order to avoid confusion caused by their similarity. Progressive differentiation and integrative reconciliation increase the *stability* and *clarity* of existing ideational anchorage and ensure *discriminability* of the learning task. Consolidation, or the mastery of essential prior concepts before the introduction of new materials, ensures readiness. Deferring new material until the prior learning sequence is consolidated reinforces the *stability* of the existing cognitive structure.

In other words, each unit or lesson should be preceded by the presentation to the learner of an advance organizer—an idea that can provide the learner with the conceptual framework on which he can hang the new material. Progressively, from lesson to lesson, new organizers relate the new material to ideas that have been presented previously. As these organizers accumulate, they duplicate in the learner's mind the information-processing structure from the discipline. Thus, by the end of a series of units or activities, the learner possesses a new set of ideas. These will serve in his mind to keep the new material distinct and clear by providing an ideational scaffolding to which the new ideas are attached and which may help him to remember the new material. In addition, they provide ideas to which he can relate his present cognitive structure so that the new material can be integrated with, at least related to, the ideas that he was

12 David P. Ausubel, "Some Psychological Aspects of the Structure of Knowledge," *Education and the Structure of Knowledge,* S. Elam, ed., Fifth Annual Phi Delta Kappa Symposium on Educational Research (Skokie, Ill.: Rand McNally, 1965), p. 24.

previously using for processing information. Hence, the salient feature of Ausubel's "Organizer Technique of Didactic Exposition," as he puts it, is to program sequences of content for learners so that each segment of learning material is preceded by a conceptual "organizer," which we can think of as an advance organizer.

An organizer, if it is to function in the manner Ausubel describes, must possess certain properties in relation to the material which it organizes. The organizer has a higher level of "abstraction, generality and inclusiveness of" the material and is selected on the basis of its "suitability for explaining, integrating, and interrelating the material."[13] An organizer is not to be confused with an overview or summary, which is ordinarily at the same level of abstraction as the material which is to be learned. An organizer is an idea, a general idea, which is fairly abstract relative to the material and which precedes the material. It functions cognitively to organize the material as it is presented; that is, it provides a kind of conceptual framework into which the learner will integrate the material.

Ausubel describes two types of organizers and identifies their optimal application. He recommends using a general "expository" organizer with unfamiliar material. This will provide a wholistic conceptual structure to which the learner can relate the new material. The organizer in this case provides "ideational anchorage in terms that are already familiar to the learner."[14] When relatively familiar material is being presented to the learner, Ausubel recommends a "comparative" organizer which will help the learner integrate new concepts with "basically similar concepts in cognitive structure, as well as to increase discriminability between new and existing ideas which are essentially different but confusable."[15] Let us look at an example of this. Suppose that the material to be presented to learners is a matrix of multiplication facts. This matrix might be preceded by the commutative property with respect to multiplication (that is, that $A \times B = B \times A$). In this way, the exposition of the material in the multiplication matrix can be at least partly organized by the learner in terms of commutation. He will be prepared for ideas like $3 \times 2 = 2 \times 3$, and his memory task will be considerably reduced. The organizer, the commutative property, is more abstract than the multiplication facts themselves, but they are explainable in terms of it. In fact, they could be presented in commutative pairs. Later on, when the learner is being introduced to long division, a comparative organizer might be introduced that would stress the similarity and yet differentness of the division facts from the multiplication facts. For example, whereas in a multiplication fact the multiplier and multiplicand can be reversed without changing the product, that is $3 \times 4$ can be

---

[13] Ausubel, *The Psychology of Meaningful Verbal Learning,* p. 81.
[14] *Ibid.,* p. 83.
[15] *Ibid.*

changed to $4 \times 3$, the divisor and dividend cannot be reversed in division without affecting the quotient, that is, 6 divided by 2 is not the same as 2 divided by 6. This comparative organizer can help the learner see the relationship between multiplication and division and therefore anchor the new learning about division in the old ones about multiplication. At the same time, the comparative organizer can help him discriminate the new learnings so that he does not carry over the concept of commutability to a place where it does not belong.

## CLASSROOM APPLICATION

The advance organizer strategy is far more versatile than appears at first glance. While it is especially suited for written, verbal material and for conveying the disciplines of knowledge, it can be used quite effectively for many purposes and with much versatility in the interactive teaching situation. This is especially true if we conceive of an advance organizer as "...any idea, image, recollection, abstraction—any available pattern that can add to the meaningfulness of an encounter."[16] This conception permits a rather broad interpretation of both the form and function of an organizer. Before we discuss the feasible variations, however, it might be helpful to provide a few more illustrations of an organizer.

Before students read descriptive studies of communities from different cultures, the lesson or unit task (covering several lessons) might be preceded by an organizer from anthropology, like: "Culture may be viewed as sets of solutions to problems. Different cultures solve problems in different ways." In another example, a lesson or text describing the caste system in India or elsewhere might call forth an organizer to the effect that the caste system is a form of social stratification. Both of these examples draw on the hierarchical power of the major concepts of the disciplines to organize the pertinent material.

A generalization can also serve as an organizer. For instance, the generalization that technological changes can produce major changes in the society and culture could serve an organizing function for the study of many historical periods and places. Contrast this with what we might recognize as a topic sentence: "Three technological changes during this period contributed to changes in society." In the latter, the concept organizing the material is the concept of three, a concept whose organizing power is considerably less than the earlier organizer. Three as an organizer is not generic to the particular material in any way and is not at a significantly higher level of abstraction than the material it is organizing. To state the

16 Richard J. Suchman, "A Model for the Analysis of Inquiry," *Analysis of Concept Learning,* Herbert J. Klausmeier and Chester W. Harris, eds. (New York: Academic Press, 1966).

point in another way, imagine all the occasions text or verbal materials are presented to students organized in this fashion. In what way would this concept of three help them meaningfully learn or distinguish those diverse areas from one another? To what construct in their mental storage and retrieval system are they able to meaningfully attach the information?

The kinds of organizer we have illustrated here seem to emerge from or are in some way closely related to the material they organize. We can also envision a more creative function for an organizer, that is, to provide a new perspective. For instance, the concept of balance or form, though generic to the arts, may be applied to literature, to mathematics, to the functioning of the branches of government, or even to our own activities. Conversely, specific material (such as a study of churches) can be viewed under the rubric of many different organizers. Some can generate the economic implications, others cultural implications, still others sociological perspectives, and yet others can cause the material to be viewed from an architectural perspective. In other words, the meaning and significance of the material can vary with the organizers or perspectives that are applied to it.

In addition to having multiplicity of functions, the organizer and the material to which it relates can take on a variety of forms. The organizer can be a statement, a descriptive paragraph, a question, a demonstration, or even a film. It might be one sentence or it might be an entire lesson which precedes the other lessons in a unit of work. The form of the organizer is less important than the fact that its substance must be clearly understood and continuously related to the material it is organizing. The material itself can have great variety in its form. Although Ausubel stresses written, verbal material, and expository or didactic presentation, this need not be a hard and fast rule. Particularly in an interactive situation, who would want to keep lively second graders silent in their seats? It has been our experience that advance organizer models are never purely expository in the interactive situation. Children often break in to an interesting topic with their own questions. Provided the teacher continuously relates the organizer to the material, we cannot see where these divergences interfere with the essence of the model. The material bing organized, then, can take the form of a dialogue. It can also be contained in a film, a demonstration, or stories. Students in our teacher education program have created banks of tapes on different topics using advance organizers. Some student-teachers have used organizers with worksheets designed to teach skills. For instance,[17] for her second grade reading group, a student-teacher had made up a unit of worksheets on simple research skills, i.e., exercises requiring students to

[17] We are grateful to Miss Jane Shapiro who was in the Pre-Service Program for Elementary Teachers at Teachers College, Columbia University 1969–1970 for providing us with this illustration.

identify and use an index, looking up words and circling the page numbers, etc. The young students filled out these sheets over a period of weeks. Advance organizers relating or related to the concept of research might have made their activities more meaningful. There are many potential applications of organizers to "methodology of the disciplines" and related skills.

## MODEL

### SYNTAX

The first phase of the activity is the presentation of the organizer, which must be at a more general level than the material that is to follow. The second phase is the presentation of the material itself. In a sequence of learning activities, the first organizer and its materials should be hierarchically more abstract than succeeding ones which get more specific and elaborate the original ones. For example, in English, if the content were to deal with metaphors, the first organizer would deal with the general idea of metaphor and the content would illustrate that general idea. The next lessons would go into more and more specific kinds of metaphors and the ways they are used, so that the first unit of work with its organizer would intellectually anchor the material that was to come in the successive unit activities.

### SOCIAL SYSTEM

Many people at first find startling Ausubel's proposition that an abstract idea should be presented and should precede the material rather than later being discovered by learners who have analyzed the materials. One reason is that structured teaching has become associated in many people's minds with authoritarian social structures. To the extent that the use of organizers heightens the structure of the model, the social system is a structured one and the teacher is, in fact, the initiator and controller of norms. However, beyond the presentation of the organizer, the learning situation can assume a less structured posture and teacher and students can be very interactive. The teacher retains control of the intellectual structure, however, as it is necessary to continuously relate the learning material to the organizers and to help students discriminate new material and differentiate it from previous material.

### PRINCIPLES OF REACTION

In the flow of the lesson, the training agent can function to point out the conceptual anchorages for the material and to help learners see the relationship between the material that is being presented and the organizer. The teacher or the instructional material is the controller in the situation. The content has been selected for the learner, and the teacher should function to hem the discussion around the material at hand.

## SUPPORT SYSTEM

Well organized material is critical. The advance organizer depends on an integral relationship between the conceptual organizer and the rest of the content. It may be that it works best as a paradigm around which to build instructional materials so that the time can be taken to ensure complete relevance of content and organizer. However, the model was designed for use in face-to-face teaching and can be, if the time is given to prepare lectures or other types of material carefully.

## GENERAL APPLICABILITY OF THE MODEL

The Advance Organizer Model is another extremely versatile model in the sense that it can be applied to any material which can be organized intellectually. It can be used in nearly every subject area, although it was designed for use with verbal material rather than with skills and the mastery of problem-solving paradigms. However, Ausubel assumes that it will be useful in the transfer of materials to new problem settings, and he presents some evidence to that effect.

As a model it provides very good discipline for lectures, especially because the content of the lecture would have to be very carefully related to the organizer and the lecturer would not be permitted to ramble or digress without cause. Also, it can serve very well in the analysis of expository materials in textbooks and other instructional materials where abstractions and information alternate in various patterns. It is worthwhile to examine lessons and units in several of the disciplines and to look for the ways in which organizers are handled either consciously or unconsciously; for it should be obvious by now that a teacher who is not careful can unwittingly present a poor organizer that will confuse the learner.

In one sense this model is rather delicate. The essence of the strategy rests on the advance organizer functioning as a conceptual linkage from the material to the learner, and Ausubel has given us several principles of construction to ensure that this will happen. However, what happens if the organizer is not heard or perceived? This is especially possible in a face-to-face teaching situation, particularly coming as it does at the beginning of the lesson when the class may not yet be "settled-down." Obviously, if the student never receives or perceives the organizer, the strategy is lost. Perhaps, in interactive teaching situations and even over written materials, teachers will have to devise ways of ensuring that the organizer is received and continuously linked to the material. Restating the organizer or pausing momentarily to set it off from the rest of the material may be helpful, perhaps even stating its organizing function or later questioning the student on the relationship. The same precautions can hold for written material, i.e., underlining the organizer, setting it off spatially from the body of the material.

Ausubel's model also raises some interesting questions of applicability, especially as related to some of the other models which were presented. For example, the model which is described in the next chapter stresses the differences in intellectual capability between younger and older children partly in terms of the ability to handle abstract ideas. Ausubel does not discuss at any length the types of maturity that must be present before the learner can be expected to handle ideas that are at the hierarchical apex of the discipline. If there is anything to Piaget's theory of development or the descriptions which he uses to describe development, then children would not be able to handle the Ausubel strategy until ages ten or eleven at a minimum because it is not until those ages that the child begins to reach the stages of abstract thinking which he presumably would have to reach in order to handle such complex ideas. Similarly, Ausubel makes no attempt to handle the tasks which are necessary in order to utilize advance organizers in inductive as well as reception learning. It seems logical that some modification would have to be made of the usual discovery procedures to accommodate the use of organizers, and it would be interesting to hear him on this subject.

## INSTRUCTIONAL AND NURTURANT VALUES

It is difficult to determine whether the Advance Organizer Model (Figure 10-1) would be likely to produce nurturant effects or what they might be. The probable instructional values seem quite clear, however, and Ausubel does not make any claims beyond them.

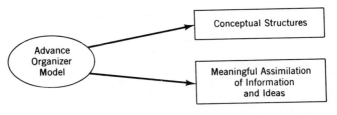

**Figure 10-1**

**TABLE 10-1 Summary Chart: Advance Organizer Model**

| *Syntax:* | *Phase One* | *Phase Two* |
|---|---|---|
| | Presentation of organizer. | Presentation of verbal material to be learned. |
| *Principles of Reaction:* | Teacher is seen as presenter. No consistent principles characterize the model. | |
| *Social System:* | *High Structure.* Teacher defines roles and controls norms. Learner roles carefully defined. | |
| *Support System:* | Development of organizer and system for presenting it is crucial. Material, however, must be organized so it *pertains* to the organizer. | |

# DEVELOPMENTAL MODEL

*An Approach Derived from a Study of Intellectual Development*

A major contemporary thrust in psychology strives to understand how the intellectual capacity of human beings develops. What are the types of thinking that characterize us as infants? That characterize us later on in life? How does the progression of intellectual development proceed, and what are the conditions that result in the progression? There are essentially two ways to design conceptions of teaching from views of the development of cognition in human beings. The first uses the developmental picture to gear the things that are done educationally for the youngster to his stage of development at any given moment. The second way uses the developmental pattern to generate teaching strategies that are likely to increase mental development or to accelerate it so that it will occur more rapidly than would be the case if the intervention did not take place. In this chapter we will consider both types of strategy-building activity. That is, we will examine ways of generating activities which are matched to the cognitive level of the child so that he can operate smoothly in the environment which is provided for him, and activities which are generated in order to accelerate his development into a new level of activity.

The developmental psychologist who has focused on intellectual development to the extent that he is at present preeminent in the field is the Swiss psychologist Jean Piaget. Piaget's students have been published from the mid-nineteen twenties until the present.[1] The mass of his work, while con-

---

[1] Jean Piaget, *The Origins of Intelligence in Children* (New York: International University Press, 1952).

troversial in many respects, has had wide influence on the activity of other developmental psychologists specializing in cognition and is the work most often interpreted by educators. In this chapter we will develop a model of teaching from Piaget's work simply because of his eminence in the field and the fact there are more curriculums developed from his work than from any other developmental psychologist who focuses on cognitive development.

## ORIENTATION OF THE MODEL

### THEORETICAL BACKGROUND

Summaries of Piaget's developmental theory can be found in many sources including Flavell, Hunt, and Furth.[2] However, to discuss models drawn from the theory, it is necessary for us to have at least a sketchy definition of the way he views development, and the stages which characterize his description of the pattern of human growth. Sullivan summarizes Piaget in the following way:

> Piaget's description of intellectual development is concerned with the formulation and description of coherent and meaningful stages which reflect the direction and course of mental development. Intelligence, in the Piaget model, is a process of adaptation and organization. Adaptation is seen as an equilibrium in the interaction of the organism and the environment. Organization involves a structual concept called the *schema*. Piaget (1960) defines schemas as essentially repeatable psychological units of intelligent action. Schemas may best be interpreted as types of "programs" or "strategies" that the individual has at his disposal when interacting with the environment.
>
> Adaptation involves the two invariant processes of assimilation and accommodation. Assimilation is the incorporation of the environment into present patterns of behavior. Accommodation is the change in the intellectual structures (schemas) which is necessary in order for the person to adjust to demands which the external environment makes on the individual.[3]

The schemas or structures that the child develops mediate between him and the environment and link the processes of assimilation and accommodation. Furth provides an illustration of this relationship. He gives the example of a baby who has acquired the ability to grasp things in his environment. In this case, Piaget would say that grasping is the baby's scheme or structure governing the sensory-motor operation of grasping. "The grasping scheme

[2] See J. H. Flavell, *The Developmental Psychology of Jean Piaget* (Princeton, N.J.: Van Nostrand Reinhold, 1963); J. McV. Hunt, *Intelligence and Experience* (New York: Ronald Press, 1961); Hans G. Furth, *Piaget and Knowledge* (Englewood Cliffs, N.J.: Prentice-Hall, 1969).

[3] Edmund Sullivan, "Piaget and the School Curriculum: A Critical Appraisal," Bulletin No. 2 of the Ontario Institute for Studies in Education (Toronto, 1967), pp. 2–3.

functions by assimilating a great variety of external things to itself; in other words the baby is observed to grasp and handle many different objects. These things have in common that they are all amenable to grasping even though their specific figural outlines may differ one from the other."[4] If the individual does not have the structure or schema to assimilate aspects of the environment, it does not exist for that particular individual. "Thus, the ordered arrangement of the sticks, even though present objectively— that is, to a critical adult intelligence—does not exist for the four-year-old who fails to perceive an ordered arrangement from an unordered arrangement. The four-year-old's intelligence cannot assimilate serrated order."[5]

We also know that a child's intellectual capacities grow, that is, in Piaget's terms of reference, he develops more and more complex schemas or structures through which to assimilate the environment. Accommodation is the process by which this is accomplished. "Accommodation applies a general structure to a particular situation; as such, it always contains some element of newness. In a restricted sense, accommodation to a new situation leads to the differentiation of a previous structure and thus the emergence of new structures."[6] It appears also that accommodation can consist of the selection and application of more than one structure to a given problem, i.e., the application of the existing schemas of both time and space to a problem of distance. "How long does it take to walk a certain distance?" Essentially, accommodation works to adjust the general schemes to the particular here and now situation which the individual has taken in or assimmilated. In this way as different but meaningfully similar (i.e., there is an existing structure or schema to permit assimilation) events are encountered and taken in by process of assimilation, the existing schemes are further differentiated, forming new ones and intellectual growth takes place.

However, the process of intellectual growth, described above, is carefully regulated, according to Piaget, by physiological maturation. Piaget conceptualizes an internal principle of organization which governs the changes in human beings, including the development of intelligence. Intellectual growth is a product of internal changes in interaction with external forces. Environmental factors are the medium for the physiological factors. Both can serve as constraints on the other but both are crucial for intellectual growth. "It follows that for Piaget physiological factors of maturation, physical objects in the world and the social environment are absolutely necessary for normal growth. The entire accommodative activity of the knowing person is directed to the environmentally given, the objective situation."[7] Piaget gives the name equilibration to the self-regulating coordina-

---

[4] Hans G. Furth, *Piaget and Knowledge,* p. 14.
[5] *Ibid.*
[6] *Ibid.,* p. 259.
[7] *Ibid.,* p. 207.

tion of the forces from physiological maturation with the forces from the physical and social environment. We may speak of Piaget as setting forth an equilibration model of cognitive development. In other words, intellectual growth takes place when there is a cognitive reorganization as a result of the imbalance in the forces of equilibration, that is, when the data from the environment is assimilable but conflicts with the existing cognitive structure and necessitates a cognitive reorganization.

The implication of Piaget's formulation of intellectual development is that the development of the schemas or structures occurs in a predetermined sequence and at a predetermined rate. The state of development of the schemas at any particular time in the life of the individual are the basis of attempts to classify his stage of development. Thus, Piaget classifies cognitive development in terms of certain stages that characterize the functioning of the schemas. Generally speaking, nearly everyone goes through the stages in about the same order, and when he is in a particular stage, he is able to perform certain kinds of thinking, and not other kinds of thinking. The earlier stages, however, lay the basis for the development through assimilation and accommodation of the thinking that is to characterize the later stages. The stages are as follows, again in Sullivan's words:

1. Sensorimotor stage (0 to 2 years)
2. Preoperational stage (2 to 7 years)
   a) preconceptual thought (2 to 4 years)
   b) intuitive thought (4 to 7 years)
3. Operational stage (7 to 16 years)
   a) concrete operational thought (7 to 11 years)
   b) formal operational thought (11 to 16 years)

Sensorimotor thought (birth to about 2 years) refers to those behaviors which are preverbal and are not mediated by signs or symbols. At birth the child mediates with the world with inborn reflex schemas and has no conception of object permanence. During this period the child is concerned with objects as objects. Thus, when a toy is hidden from his view, he shows no searching movements, since he has no internal representation of the objective world (i.e., object schemas) when not perceiving it. Gradually object permanence develops through repeated experiences with the world. As the child constructs object permanence through experience, primitive concepts of space, time, causality, and intentionality, which were not present at birth, develop and are incorporated into present patterns of behavior.

The second of Piaget's stages is preoperational thought (about age 2 to 7 years). This stage is further divided into two sub-stages: preconceptual thought (transductive), which extends from age 2 to about 4, and intuitive thought, which extends from about age 4 to 7.

a) The substage of preconceptual thought marks the beginning of what Piaget (1960) calls conceptual intelligence. In contrast to sensorimotor intelligence, adaptations are not beginning to be mediated by signs and symbols, particularly words and images. During this period, the child develops what Piaget calls the "symbolic function," or imagery. The main concern during this period will be with such activities as imitation, play, and the preconcepts shown in language behavior.

b) The substage of intuitive thought appears at approximately age 4 and marks the halfway house between preconceptual thought and the more advanced stage of concrete operations. The thought exemplified in this stage is illustrated in the following problem. The child is presented with two small glasses, A1 and A2, which are identically the same in height and width dimensions. The child places one bead in each glass alternately until both are filled. Glass A2 is emptied into a taller but thinner glass B. The child in the preconceptual stage thinks that the amount of beads has changed in the process, even though he says no beads were removed or added. The child says that there are more beads in B, since it is taller than A, or that there are more beads in A1, since it is wider than B. The child is centered on one aspect of the situation, 'height' or 'width.' Because the child can not hold the centerings simultaneously, he is unable to solve the conservation problem. The child in the intuitive stage still remains prelogical, but decenterings occur where previous centerings led to absurd conclusions. Thus the child who estimated that there are more beads in the taller glass because the level has been raised centers his attention on height and ignores width. If the experimenter continues to empty the beads into the thinner and taller glass, there will be a time when the child replies that there are fewer beads in the taller glass, since it is too narrow.

The stage of operational thought marks the advent of rational activity in the child. Up to this time the child demonstrates a logic (transductive) which is quite different from that of the adult members of his species (i.e., inductive and deductive).

a) Concrete operational thought. The first substage of operational thought is labelled 'concrete operations.' Piaget (1960) defines an operation as an internalized action which can return to its starting point, and which can be integrated with other actions also possessing this feature of reversibility. Operations are 'mental acts' which were formerly actions with reversible properties. Piaget calls the operational structures between the ages of 7 and 11 years 'concrete' because their starting point is always some real system of objects and relations that the child perceives; that is, the operations are carried out on concrete objects. The emergence of concrete operations is often a sudden phenomenon in development. Piaget (1960) attributes their emergence to a sudden thawing of intuitive structures which were up to now more rigid, despite their progressive articulation.

b) Formal operational thought. The substage of formal operations (11 to 16 years) marks the emergence of *vertical decalages*, that is, the ability to make vertical separations by solving problems at a level which transcends concrete experience (the area of *horizontal decalages*). Formal thinking marks the completion of the child's emancipation from reliance on direct perception and action. In contrast to the concrete action-oriented thought of the child, the adolescent thinker goes beyond the present and forms theories about everything. This thought is considered 'reflective' since the adolescent reasons on the basis of purely formal assumptions. He can consider hypotheses as either true or false and work out inferences which would follow if the hypotheses were true.[8]

_____

[8] Edmund Sullivan, "Piaget and the School Curriculum: A Critical Appraisal," Bulletin No. 2 of the Ontario Institute for Studies in Education (Toronto, 1967), pp. 4–9. Reprinted by permission.

The descriptions which have been provided so far are too meager to give any adequate view of the richness of Piaget's theory. However, they may provide enough substance so that we can discuss meaningfully the development of teaching strategies which are built from reflection on Piaget's view of the growth of human intelligence. We may restate the major points that we have covered here. First, intelligence is defined as operations for transforming data from the environment (i.e., grasping). The operations which define intelligence and which change with age are described as logical structures or schemes for processing information. Second, development is associated with passage from one stage of operation to another. Third, development is a function of experience and maturation.

### Theoretical Application

In order to build a model of teaching around a model of intellectual development, one is required to extrapolate. That is, we cannot move directly from the description of cognitive development directly to the production of a model. We have to make some guesses about the kinds of things that will make a difference. Piaget's theory provides the basis on which certain kinds of guesses can be made.

The psychologist Irving Sigel has extrapolated the propositions that he feels are most relevant to an educational strategy developed from Piaget's theory. "These are as follows: 1) intellectual development is dependent on confrontations with the social as well as physical environment; 2) intellectual development proceeds by orderly invariant sequences (stages) with transitions from stage to stage; 3) acquisition of new knowledge comes about through appropriate assimilations and accommodations resulting in equilibrated cognitive structure; 4) language is a facilitator varying in significance as a function of the developmental level of the child."[9]

The first proposition focuses essentially on the setting for learning. Piaget has described the type of interactions with the physical and social environment that result in cognitive growth. For example, as the child has repeated experience with certain objects, he comes to believe in their permanence. This changes his conception of the world, and the kinds of thoughts that he is able to have with respect to it. The second factor is social experience, which arises through interaction with other people and through the development of language. For example, with respect to moral development, Piaget describes the child as moving in a general direction away from egocentric and individualized ways of thinking to more socially-centered, publicly-validated ways of thinking. In the egocentric stages, the child tends to judge actions solely by their consequences. As for example,

[9] Irving E. Sigel, "The Piagetian System and the World of Education," *Studies in Cognitive Development,* David Elkind and John Flavell, eds. (New York: Oxford University Press, 1969), p. 472.

if someone bumps into him, he tends to judge the act by whether or not he is hurt. As a person moves towards a more socio-centric organization, he judges acts also by their intentions, and he becomes concerned not only with whether he was hurt, but also with whether perhaps anyone intended to hurt him. His participation with others is on a basis of equality and mutual respect; he moves from the egocentric and towards the socio-centric stages. Thus, the opportunity to exchange viewpoints and share personal experiences produces the cognitive conflict that is fundamental to intellectual development. This concern for the setting of learning (and to some this is the learning situation itself) can be translated into the following classroom practices. The first stipulates the availability of a rich objective world which the child can freely explore and manipulate and which is matched to his stage of development. The second practice places importance on free peer interaction in the classroom activities.

The next consideration for a teaching strategy involves more familiar aspects and roles of the learning environment such as the roles of the teacher and subject matter. Against the Piagetian frame-of-reference the logic of the subject matter becomes important, as does the nature of the learner (the logical structures of schemes of the child) and the requirements of the equilibration model of cognitive growth. Reflecting on these, Sigel feels that the teaching strategy designed to further cognitive development in Piagetian terms should have two parts. The first part confronts the student with a situation in which he must come to grips with the illogic of his thinking. "A major thrust of a teaching strategy is to confront the child with the illogical nature of his point of view. The reason for confrontation is that it is a necessary and sufficient requirement for cognitive growth. The shift from egocentric to socio-centric thought comes about through confrontation with the animate and inanimate environment. These forces impinge upon the child, inducing disequilibrium. The child strives to reconcile the discrepancies and evolves new processes by which to adapt to new situations. Strategies employing confrontations must be consistent with the child's stage of development."[10] In other words, what one tries to do is to confront the student with a situation which is puzzling, but one which is nonetheless relatively well-matched to his stage of development. The puzzlement leads to inquiry as he tries to resolve difficulties which are raised by the confrontation. In this struggle, he rearranges his thought processes and moves another imperceptable step toward a more mature cognition.

The form of the confrontation as well as its nature depends upon the developmental level of the child. "Confrontation can take a number of

10 Sigel, "The Piagetian System and the World of Education," *Studies in Cognitive Development*, p. 473.

forms depending on the developmental level of the child. Verbal and/or nonverbal techniques ranging from questions, demonstrations and/or environmental manipulations can be employed in the service of confrontation."[11]

## CLASSROOM APPLICATION

In setting forth the two-phase teaching strategy, Sigel cautions prospective users against assuming the child's level of development from his contextual use of language. Often children will use terms such as "brother," but these words do not accurately reflect the child's ability to understand the logical basis of the term. For instance, for the concrete-stage child, brother is "the boy who lives in my house" while to the adolescent, brother is defined in terms of kinship—it is a relational term.[12] Hence, Sigel speaks of a kind of prephase in which the teacher might make a clinical assessment, i.e., questioning which determines the child's ability. She is then in a better position to select the logical operation which needs strengthening.

Sigel provides us with a transcript which illustrates the teaching strategy of confrontation and guidance: ". . . the child was encouraged to label the various object attributes as a preliminary step to constructing, decomposing and reconstructing of classes, i.e., decentration. The child was free to use any one or more criteria for defining the classes. The teacher in this case did not superimpose class names."[13]

### TABLE 11-1 Portion of Verbatim Transcript of a Training Session Dealing with Multiple Attributes of Objects

| | |
|---|---|
| Teacher: | Can you tell me what this is, Mary? |
| Mary: | A banana. |
| Teacher: | What else can you tell me about it? |
| Mary: | It's straight. |
| Teacher: | It's straight. What else? |
| Mary: | It has a peel. |
| Teacher: | It has a peel. . .Tom, what can you tell me about it? |
| Tom: | Ummm. . .It has some green on it. |
| Teacher: | Uh-huh. |
| Tom: | It has some dark lines on it. |
| Teacher: | What can you do with it? |
| Tom: | You can eat it! |
| Teacher: | That's right!. . .Now let's see. . . |
| Children: | . . .I love bananas! |
| Teacher: | What is this? |
| Children: | An orange. |

11 *Ibid.*
12 *Ibid.*, p. 475.
13 *Ibid.*, p. 477.

| | |
|---|---|
| Teacher: | Is it really an orange? |
| Children: | Uh-huh...Yes |
| Teacher: | Look at it closely. |
| Child: | It's an artificial one. |
| Teacher: | Oh, that's right, it's an artificial one...But what else can you tell me about it?[14] |
| Children: | You can eat it...It's round. |
| Teacher: | Uh-huh. |
| Children: | ...Orange. |
| Teacher: | That's right! |
| Child: | It has a stem. |
| Teacher: | Now look at this one...What's this? |
| Children: | An orange...Orange. |
| Teacher: | And what can you do with it? |
| Children: | You can eat it...and it's round. |
| Teacher: | It's round... |
| Child: | It has a peel... |
| Teacher: | It has a peel...Now, look at these two things. Are they the same? |
| Children: | No. |
| Teacher: | What's different? |
| Children: | This one...This one here is pressed in on the side a little...this one is lighter. |
| Teacher: | Do you know what this really is? This is a tangerine...and this is an orange. Now, tell me in what ways they are alike. |
| Children: | This is smaller and that's bigger. |
| Teacher: | I said, 'In what way are they alike?' |
| Children: | They are both round...they both have a stem...both orange. |
| Teacher: | They both have a stem, both round, both orange. Anything else alike about them? |
| Child: | They're both fat. |
| Teacher: | Uh-huh. What can you do with them? |
| Children: | We can eat them... |
| Teacher: | We can eat them...Now, tell me, what's the same about all these things? |
| Child: | These are round, but this isn't. |
| Teacher: | I said, what is the same about them, not what's different about them. |
| Children: | They're both round...they're round...they're round...and they are both artificial. |
| Teacher: | They're all artificial, and...are they all round? |
| Child: | No. |
| Teacher: | What about the banana? |
| Child: | It's straight. |
| Teacher: | But...tell me something else that's the same about all of these things. |
| Child: | ...They have...all have a peel. |
| Teacher: | That's right too, but what can you do with all of them? |
| Children: | You can eat them! |

14 *Ibid.,* pp. 479–81. Reprinted by permission.

| | |
|---|---|
| Teacher: | That's right! That's the same about every one of them. Do you have a name for all of them? |
| Children: | Yes! |
| Teacher: | What? |
| Child: | A banana. |
| Teacher: | A banana? No...is there something that you can call all of them? |
| Children: | Fruit...fruit! |
| Teacher: | And what's the same about all fruit? |
| Children: | They are all round except bananas. |
| Teacher: | No...why do you call all of these things fruit? |
| Children: | Because you can eat them. |
| Teacher: | You can eat them. |
| Children: | And they are food. |
| Teacher: | And they are food. If I had a piece of bread here, would that be fruit too? |
| Children: | No. |
| Teacher: | Why not? |
| Children: | Because it is not sweet...not round... |
| Teacher: | Because it is not sweet. I think that's a good reason...and you eat bread too? |
| Children: | Yes. |
| Teacher: | But it is still is not fruit...right? |
| Children: | Yes. |
| Teacher: | Now, can you tell me again what this is? We talked about it yesterday. |
| Child: | A pencil. |
| Teacher: | What else can you tell me about it? |
| Children: | It's round...you said you were going to put it in... |
| Teacher: | That's right...ah...Tom, what is this? |
| Tom: | Chalk. |
| Teacher: | What else can you tell me about it? |
| Tom: | It's white. |
| Teacher: | Gail, tell me what's the same about these two things? |
| Gail: | They are both round. |
| Teacher: | What else? |
| Gail: | ...Ummm... |
| Teacher: | John, tell me what's the same about these two things? |
| John: | ...both write. |
| Teacher: | That's right! There are two things that are the same about it. Tell me what they are. |
| John: | Well...I don't know. |
| Teacher: | What are they Mary? |
| Mary: | They're round and they write. |
| Teacher: | Very good! |

A number of educators working at Ypsilanti, Michigan have developed an approach to preschool education based on Piagetian concepts. "In this preschool, an attempt is made first of all to consolidate the practical knowledge of objects, space, time and causality which was acquired during the sensory-motor period, so that there will be a solid foundation upon which to build later structures."[15] Following Piaget's description of development as it relates to the preschool child, the Ypsilanti educators have designed their program to teach the operations related to two types of knowledge, the child's physical knowledge and his logical knowledge. "Physical knowledge for the preschool child means learning about objects by finding out how they react when acted upon in different ways."[16] Logical knowledge refers to mathematical relationships such as classification (uniting, disuniting, and reuniting), seriation (comparing and ordering) and numbers; spatial relationships and temporal relationships. In other words, the program concentrates on activities which develop* these relationships.

Generally speaking, the Ypsilanti educators follow the type of teaching strategy that Sigel recommends, although they do not describe their teaching strategy in the same terms that Sigel uses. However, the essence of their model is to confront the student with encounters with reality that will cause him to have to modify and sophisticate his conceptions of things. The main difference between the two examples lies in the social structure. In the Ypsilanti program the student often guides himself through the instructional phases which are induced by the materials and activities in the environment. In order to increase the physical knowledge of the student, they provide him with a number of objects. Suppose that what is desired is to help the student discover that some objects return to their original state while others do not. In this case, the student is presented with an assortment of objects, some of which will and some of which won't return to shape after they are moved from their original state. The students are encouraged to play with the objects, squashing them, dropping them, pulling them, folding them, stretching them, and gradually discovering that some objects return, and others do not. In addition, by working with others, the students discover that the results are the same, no matter who does the experimenting on the objects.

The development of logical schema such as classification is taught by confronting the students with real life problems in which they need to classify. "The children can put together those things which are the same, and separate those that are different. Games can be developed for them to find identical objects from an array of grossly different things (e.g., two cups, three sponges, and three crayons.) Sorting games in which children find identical objects by touch alone also strengthens awareness of similarities and differences."[17] By being asked to group objects in these ways,

[15] Hanne Sonquist, Constance Kamii, and Louise Derman, "A Piaget Derived Pre-school Curriculum," *Educational Implications of Piaget's Theory: A Book of Readings,* J. J. Athey and D. O. Rubadeau, eds. (Waltham, Mass.: Blaisdell Publishing Co., 1971), p. 2.

[16] *Ibid.*

[17] *Ibid.,* p. 4.

students begin to develop presumably logical ways of dealing with the classification problem. For example, after the children have grouped like objects together, they would be asked to form groups in which objects which are partly alike and partly different are placed together. In this way, they learn a somewhat more complex way of grouping. Also, the students are confronted with problems where the objects that they are accustomed to grouping need to be grouped by criteria that they have not been accustomed to using. "For example, given a kit of four red and blue combs, and four red and blue cups, a child can make two groupings according to use (the cups and combs) and then shift into grouping by color. Having four or five children working with the same kit helps them realize that there are different ways of classifying objects."[18] In other words, these simple exercises are designed to help students develop structures relative to multiple classification of objects. This provides a logical foundation which they can use to cope with other situations as these occur.

The strategies used to induce schema relative to seriation are interesting. Placing things in series can be developed through commonplace situations in the classroom. Dolls can be grouped according to size for example, with the smallest at one end of the row and the biggest at the next end. To begin this, they suggest that students be confronted first with problems requiring them to classify objects of very different sizes by comparison. For example, putting the very big dolls in one pile and the very little dolls in another pile. They suggest that these activities be embedded throughout the day so that the student has a great many experiences with seriation problems. As they put it, "In the doll corner, the children use and arrange big and little pots, plates, spoons, dolls, etc. The block and truck area has shelves with two sizes of blocks, cars, trucks and animal figures. In art, big and little brushes and paper are used. At juice time, cups and cookies can be of two different sizes. On the playground children can take big or little steps, make long and short shadows, swing on swings of two sizes and heights, and play with big and little balls and hoops."[19] In this way, the student is continuously confronted with a comparison problem, so that he is given the opportunity to develop the schema necessary for making serials based on sizes. After the students are able to classify two sizes of objects, it is suggested that the environment be enriched so that students can order objects of three or more sizes. Students can be led gradually to seriation by "objects such as nesting cups or blocks [which] are particularly good for beginning the ordering of sizes because of their self-corrective nature. Making different sizes of objects out of playdough or clay is also good."[20]

[18] *Ibid.,* p. 5.
[19] *Ibid.,* p. 6.
[20] *Ibid.*

The Ypsilanti team also provides us with examples of the model as it is used to assist in the development of spatial concepts. The first phase confronts the student with a problem, and the second gives him the opportunity to explore the problem and learn from feedback from his own senses. "Two strategies may help the child to structure his representational space more geometrically. One is a variety of mystery box games using perception by touch alone. When the child cannot see a shape, he is forced to structure his mental image of the shape. The other strategy is a variety of rhythmics activity, involving the imitation of the teacher's body movements. When the child has to imitate the movement of one arm forward and the other arm to the side for example, he has to mentally structure the ninety degree angle and the parallel of both arms in relation to the floor, thereby strengthening his geometric notions on the representational plane. Watching the movements of his body in a wide, full-length mirror has been found helpful to the child who has difficulty in these activities."[21] The Ypsilanti team emphasizes that all of the activities should require the child's activity. For example, they contrast having him learn to order representational space by imitating their teacher, with attempts to teach children spacial relations by having them assemble a puzzle. It is their belief that the former activity is much more effective than the latter because the child cannot engage in the activity at all without coming to a concept of representational space, whereas there are quite a number of ways of solving a puzzle that do not require a revision of his logical structure.

Much of the developmental conception of the child's intellectual growth focused on physical concepts available to young children such as space, shape, weight, and number and children's ability to classify, to compare, and order, and to specify spatial and temporal relationships with respect to these concepts. The content and instructional strategy of the Ypsilanti Program is built around our knowledge of these areas. However, researchers have also been exploring less physical concepts. For instance a study by Karl Schuessler and Anselm Strauss explored stages of children's conceptual development with respect to the concept of money.[22] They were able to distinguish three aspects of the concept-coin recognition (naming coins), comparative value (which money is worth more), and equivalence (making change). For each of these aspects, they were able to scale tasks of increasing difficulty (much like Sigel's teacher did when she kept adding different items to the original classification problem of the banana and the orange). For instance, recognition includes distinguishing buttons from coins, recognizing all U.S. coins, knowing three nickels are nickels but not being able to state why. Their findings attest to the argument that "a concept is not grasped fully at the onset of the child's ability to verbalize the concept.

[21] *Ibid.*, p. 9.
[22] Karl Schuessler and Anslem Strauss, "A Study of Concept Learning by Scale Analysis," *American Sociological Review*, 15, 1950, 752–62.

Full comprehension is developed gradually. Put another way, a concept can be understood at different levels of complexity."

These findings have important implications for broadened use of the developmental model. Teachers of social studies, language arts, and science can become more cognizant of levels of complexity available on the concepts they use and the child's conceptual development in respect to them. They can then design learning activities to pull children toward more complex use of the same concept.

## MORAL DEVELOPMENT:
## ANOTHER STRATEGY BASED ON PIAGET'S WORK

Kohlberg has followed Piaget's work with an extensive analysis of moral development which provides us with a framework for analyzing stages of moral growth and generating teaching strategies which can move the child toward moral maturity. The basic framework consists of six stages of moral growth and 25 aspects of growth through the six stages. Let us begin by looking at the six stages and one of the aspects, for these can give us a fix on Kohlberg's definitions of moral growth.

### LEVEL I—PREMORAL

*Stage 1*—obedience and punishment orientation. Egocentric deference to superior power or prestige, or a trouble-avoiding set. Objective responsibility. *Stage 2*—Naively egoistic orientation. Right action is that instrumentally satisfying the self's needs and occasionally other's. Awareness of relativism of value to each actor's needs and perspective. Naive egalitarianism and orientation to exchange and reciprocity.

### LEVEL II—CONVENTIONAL ROLE CONFORMITY

*Stage 3*—Good-boy orientation. Orientation to approval and to pleasing and helping others. Conformity to stereotypical images of majority or natural role behavior and judgment of intentions.
*Stage 4*—Authority and social-order-maintaining orientation. Orientation to "doing duty" and to showing respect for authority and maintaining the given social order for its own sake. Regard for earned expectations of others.

### LEVEL III—SELF-ACCEPTED MORAL PRINCIPLES

*Stage 5*—Contractual legalistic orientation. Recognition of an arbitrary element or starting point in rules or expectations for the sake of agreement. Duty defined in terms of contract, general avoidance of violation of the will or rights of others, and majority will and welfare.
*Stage 6*—Conscience or principle orientation. Orientation not only to actually ordained social rules but to principles of choice involving appeal to logical universality and consistency. Orientation to conscience as a directing agent and to mutual respect and trust.[23]

[23] Larry Kohlberg, "Moral Education in the School," *School Review*, 74, 1966, 7.

By this conception the child moves from egocentricity, in which he makes decisions in terms of personal want, on one hand, and avoidance of punishment or catering to authority. He proceeds toward a stage of seeking approval and being a "good boy," conforming to rules and authority for their own sake. Finally, *if* he matures, he develops self-accepted principles, considers the negotiable character of rules and agreements, and is concerned with the establishment of mutual respect and trust.

Each of the aspects of moral growth proceeds through the six stages. Kohlberg illustrates with an aspect which is referred to as "The Basis of Moral Worth of Human Life." In terms of each stage the "basis of moral worth" proceeds in the following way:

*Stage 1*—The value of a human life is confused with the value of physical objects and is based on the social status or physical attributes of its possessor. Tommy, age ten: (Why should the druggist give the drug to the dying woman when her husband couldn't pay for it?) "If someone important is in a plane and is allergic to heights and the stewardess won't give him medicine because she's only got enough for one and she's got a sick one, a friend, in back, they'd probably put the stewardess in a lady's jail because she didn't help the important one."

(Is it better to save the life of one important person or a lot of unimportant people?) "All the people that aren't important because one man just has one house, maybe a lot of furniture, but a whole bunch of people have an awful lot of furniture and some of these poor people might have a lot of money and it doesn't look it."

*Stage 2*—The value of a human life is seen as instrumental to the satisfaction of the needs of its possessor or of other persons. Tommy, age thirteen: (Should the doctor "mercy kill" a fatally ill woman requesting death because of her pain?) "Maybe it would be good to put her out of her pain, she'd be better off that way. But the husband wouldn't want it, it's not like an animal. If a pet dies you can get along without it—it isn't something you really need. Well, you can get a new wife, but it's not really the same."

*Stage 3*—The value of a human life is based on the empathy and affection of family members and others toward its possessor. Andy, age sixteen: (Should the doctor "mercy kill" a fatally ill woman requesting death because of her pain?) "No, he shouldn't. The husband loves her and wants to see her. He wouldn't want her to die sooner, he loved her too much."

*Stage 4*—Life is conceived as sacred in terms of its place in a categorical moral or religious order of rights and duties. John, age sixteen: (Should the doctor "mercy kill" the woman?) "The doctor wouldn't have the right to take a life, no human has the right. He can't create life, he shouldn't destroy it."

*Stage 5*—Life is valued both in terms of its relation to community welfare and in terms of life being a universal human right.

*Stage 6*—Belief in the sacredness of human life as representing a universal human value of respect for the individual. Steve, age sixteen: (Should the husband steal the expensive drug to save his wife?) "By the law of society he was wrong but by the law of nature or of God the druggist was wrong and the husband was justified. Human life is above financial gain. Regardless of who was dying, if it was a total stranger, man has a duty to save him from dying."[24]

It can be seen that the basis of worth develops from an egocentric position toward an appreciation of the various positions from which any situation can be judged and, finally, toward universal ideals which embrace alternative positions and give a basis for action.

Kohlberg's description of moral development has several implications for the treatment of valuing in school. First, as indicated earlier, his position implies that values cannot be dealt with, educationally speaking, unless we deal with moral development also.

> In our view, there is a third alternative to a state moral-indoctrination system and to the current American system of moralizing by individual teachers and principals when children deviate from minor administrative regulations or engage in behavior personally annoying to the teacher. This alternative is to take the stimulation of the development of the individual child's moral judgment and character as a goal of moral education, rather than taking as its goal either administrative convenience or state-defined values. The attractiveness of defining the goal of moral education as the stimulation of development rather than as teaching fixed virtues is that it means aiding the child to take the next step in a direction toward which he is already tending, rather than imposing an alien pattern upon him.[25]

The second implication of Kohlberg's work is that we can use his matrix to diagnose moral development. For example, some children in Unit B may try to make judgments that always accord with the teacher and/or cliches about right and wrong. For example, if they believe that Miss O'Donnell approves of Councilman Wooten, they will tend to support her judgment. If children act like this, our educational task is to move them toward greater analysis and independence.

The third implication of Kohlberg's formulation is in terms of methods of moral education. He believes that the most promising method consists of exposing the student to conflict situations and introducing him to new levels of reaction to them. For example, if he is involved in an argument and cannot make judgments with reference to general moral grounds, the teacher would try to confront him with the need to cope with a more general moral level. Specifically in Unit B, if the student reacted to city council action only in terms of "I like that" or "I don't like that" the task would be to help him try to find whether general principles underlie his judgment and move toward more general bases of judgment.

Kohlberg stresses this is no minor point, that teaching should be matched to moral levels. To provide a "stage one" child with "stage five" tasks would

[24] *Ibid.*, pp. 8–9.
[25] *Ibid.*, p. 19.

be unproductive. Teaching optimally should aim one level or thereabouts above the student's level of functioning.

How can we interpret this goal in terms of specific educational practice? The first task, of course, is to learn about the children's levels of moral judgment. Probably the most direct way is to observe their behavior in conflict situations. For example, if students studying the patterns of bills passed by a legislature find that pressure groups have been getting their own way by lobbying, we can expect that the student's responses will vary substantially in terms of moral judgment. Some may be reluctant to believe that councilmen are anything but wise and just. (Probably an indication of stage four—"authority and social-order-maintaining orientation.") Others may be quick to condemn, especially if the majority leans that way. ("Orientation to pleasing.") In these cases the teacher can introduce them to a more complex analysis by getting them to look at the general implications of their position. ("Should we say a pressure group should *never* have access to lawmakers—what are the pros and cons?") ("What are the positions of other groups in the community who have not been able to lobby successfully?")

What the teachers should *not* do is preach a set of principles for the behavior of lawmakers. This both denies the student the new elements he needs for development *and* it is ineffective as a method.

## MODEL

### SYNTAX

The models consist of two phases. In the first phase the student is presented with a situation in which he is confronted with the illogic of his thinking or which is puzzling. The confronting situation must be relatively well matched to the learner's developmental stage both in its substance and form. There must be enough familiarity in the confronting situation to permit assimilation yet enough newness to require accommodation. The choice of form for the confrontation, i.e., verbal, nonverbal, or environmental manipulations, also depends on the learner's developmental stage. In Phase Two the learner is guided in his inquiry to resolve the discrepancy.

### PRINCIPLES OF REACTION

The teacher must create a facilitating physical and social atmosphere. Students should have the opportunity to manipulate objects and to freely exchange ideas in interactive situations. As a prelude to the strategy of confrontation and guidance, the teacher needs to assess the child's level of thought. Only then is she able to select the learning experiences that will be optimally mismatched in terms of the child's developmental stage in order to induce cognitive growth.

### SOCIAL SYSTEM

The social system can range from highly structured to minimally structured. On one hand the teacher's role can be one of environmental provider with student-guided inquiry induced largely through the activities and materials provided in the environment. For the most part, however, we have been describing a fairly high structured teaching model set amidst a free and open intellectual and social atmosphere in which the teacher initiates and guides the inquiry. The high structured approach may be more suitable for certain age-stage levels and to particular problem areas. For instance, the film-centered discussion about the differences between consequences and intentions might require more structuring than the goal of increasing the student's physical knowledge of the world about him.

### SUPPORT SYSTEM

The optimal support system is a rich object and resource environment and a teacher well-grounded in developmental theory who can create and tolerate a free social environment that permits the student to work out the cognitive problems developed in the confrontations.

### GENERAL APPLICABILITY OF THE MODEL

The Developmental Model drawn from Piagetian theory appears to be widely applicable both in terms of cognitive and social development and across all subject areas in which illogic or problems in thinking arise. It can be used for diagnosis and evaluation as well as for instructional purposes. Finally, the model, inherently interwoven with developmental considerations, can be employed to ensure that a child can operate smoothly in his environment or to specify activities that will accelerate his cognitive growth.

### INSTRUCTIONAL AND NURTURANT VALUES

To bring about cognitive development in the Piagetian sense means to affect all aspects of functioning. Thus, concentration on one aspect of cognition (such as moral development) means to nurture development in

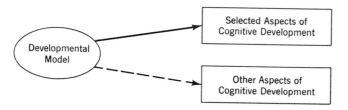

**Figure 11-1**

all other areas. Hence the Developmental Model may be illustrated as in Figure 11-1.

### TABLE 11-2 Summary Chart: Developmental Model

| *Syntax:* | *Phase One* | *Phase Two* |
|---|---|---|
| | Presentation of confronting situation as related to the learner's developmental stage and needs. | Guidance in the student's inquiry of the problem. |
| *Principles of Reaction:* | Teacher (1) creates a rich physical and free social atmosphere; (2) selects learning activities according to student's developmental level with objective to create optimal mismatch. | |
| *Social System:* | Can vary from *low* to *high* structure but is generally highly structured with the teacher initiating and guiding inquiry. | |
| *Support System:* | Instructor who is well-acquainted with the developmental sequence and tolerant of an active classroom, and a rich material environment. | |

# SUMMARY

## Learning to Teach
## the Information-Processing Models

In contrast with the interaction-oriented models, learning to use the information-processing models has its own set of problems. In some ways the models are easier to master, at least in the early stages, because many of them are fairly highly structured; and, in several cases, they provide clear guidelines to the activities of the teacher. However, they are quite demanding in that all require that we diagnose the student's activity rather precisely and then match our behavior to his. For example, in the inductive model, one cannot productively move from the data collection phase to the data analysis phase until all of the students in the group have fairly well mastered the data which are to be analyzed. Thus, one has to keep his mind on the children and to engage them in discourse over the material in such a way as to determine the extent of their mastery and to induce them to greater mastery of the material in order to prepare them for the next phase of activity. Then, as one does lead them into the next phase of activity, not all the students will receive the teacher's communications signaling the beginning of data analysis in the same way. Some of the students will move quite rapidly into the data analysis phase, while others will tail along. Also some will begin to build categories, while others will begin to analyze the data in different ways; and the teacher has to find these things out and behave in such a way as to unify the group activity without squelching the individual variation of the children.

In other words, the models are fluid structures which have to be applied flexibly to the interactive teaching situation; and while the structure reduces somewhat the complexity of the teacher's behavior by providing guidelines so one can follow, they, at the same time, require him to process a good bit of information about the activity of the students and to respond to the students in such a way as to induce the cognitive operations which lie at the essence of each of the models. Too rigid an application of the models to teaching results in empty activities which are not matched by the appropriate information processing operation.

It is also important to recognize that the information-processing models, for the most part, require complex social activity and careful attention to individual differences. The biological inquiry model, for example, actually tries to create a community of young scholars who practice biological science with their teacher and he and they are seen as scholars interacting over scholarly material in really highly complex ways.

### Selecting a Model

The selection of models from the Information-Processing family depends largely on the particular aspect of information processing the teacher wishes to foster. There is, however, some overlap among the models, although some emphasize the generation of new ideas and others emphasize existing structures. Taba's Inductive Teaching Model consists of three teaching strategies, designed to develop one inductive mental process in the hierarchy of inductive processes that Taba has identified. These processes are represented by three cognitive tasks—forming concepts, interpreting data, and applying principles to explain new phenomena or predict consequences. The Concept Attainment Model and Inquiry Training both bear some relationship to the Taba model though neither is as comprehensive. Like Taba, Concept Attainment focuses on concepts and the Inquiry Training Model involves the student in interpreting data and making inferences. However, in the Suchman Model the students formulate their own questions, whereas in the Taba models, they are guided in this effort by the teacher's questions. In addition, the Suchman Model and Concept Attainment call for the students to analyze the pattern of their questions to see if they can formulate general principles of inquiry.

In contrast to the focus on systems for generating information, Ausubel's Advance Organizer Strategy is concerned with the learner's efficient incorporation of new information. He believes that if knowledge is first "stably organized" in the mental structure then the learner is better able to use his existing knowledge to interpret and generate new data. Ausubel's teaching strategy attempts to provide, then, for stable and meaningful incorporation of information.

The Developmental Model, built upon the findings of developmental psychology, attempts to nurture and accelerate general intellectual development. Environments and instruction are constructed to take students through general stages of intellectual development characterized by specific mental activities, i.e., classification, serial ordering.

Finally, the Modes of Inquiry Approach focuses on knowledge through the methodology used by the disciplines. The learning objective is both the major concepts of the discipline and a system of inquiry by which those concepts were originally developed.

## DIFFICULTIES IN LEARNING THESE MODELS

As we have worked with pre- and in-service teachers with this family we have identified several problems which teachers could give special attention to in order to learn the models effectively.

For example, in working with the Concept Attainment model one source of difficulty has been the teacher's failure to identify for herself the attributes of the concept she is trying to get the students to attain. (This reflects a basic misconception of the intent of the model which is not to get students to identify the concepts, as such, but to become aware of the attributes). As a result of this omission, the teacher cannot construct the exemplars to systematically manipulate the attributes of the concept. In fact, the tendency has been for teachers to think in dichotomous terms and to set up a series of dichotomous exemplars (i.e., pictures showing winter and summer if the concept is winter). If there is no range in the exemplar attributes, the student can not fully explore the concept. He is more likely to "guess" at the concept rather than induce its attributes.

Failure to clarify the attributes of the concept also allows for selection of concepts that are inappropriate to the intellectual level of the children. For instance, children can verbalize such concepts as city, electricity, family, long before they are able to comprehend their attributes. The concept of electricity turns out to be beyond the grasp, attribute-wise, of many elementary school children unless one deals with it in a highly superficial manner, i.e., cord, plugs, which does not increase the understanding of the concept. City is a multi-layered concept. At one level there are all the observable phenomena we associate with a city, i.e., tall buildings, traffic, etc., but the heart of the concept probably lies in the particular character of the economic and social configurations that make up a city. Unless the possible levels of a complexity are recognized and attended to, selection of concepts can be inappropriate and, worse, treatment of concepts can be erroneous. The beauty of the Concept Attainment Model is that it quickly makes one aware of our tenuous or superficial grasp of most of the concepts we use and attempts to overcome this deficit. Understanding the attributes of the concept, then, is the prerequisite for carrying out the intent of the model.

We have also spotted recurring problems of a more mechanical sort. For instance in Phase I, when presenting the exemplars or giving them to the students for their analysis, teachers often spatially group all the Yes's and all the No's thereby biasing the comparison and contrasting and, again, circumventing the full exploration of the concept.

Another interesting point has emerged as we worked with this model. Students, especially younger children, often do not fully grasp the comparing and contrasting procedure and how the Yes's and No's function to tell them about the concept. If students are to perform Phase I of the model they need to understand the procedure. Teachers with young children often need to pause and teach comparing and contrasting and how to use the labels. ("Do you know what comparing means? Let's just take these two pictures. What is in this picture that isn't in this one? How are they alike and how are they different?" "Okay, in this picture there is a red circle [Yes]. Here is another picture with a blue circle [Yes]. What ideas do you get from the first picture? How does the second picture change them?")

The Concept Attainment Model can be an exceedingly rich experience from the standpoint of the mental operations involved and the substantive exploration of the concept. What is crucial, however, is that the teacher fully understand the attributes of the concept herself and also be prepared to guide or demonstrate the learning steps. If the students make random guesses at the concept without sufficient attention to the attributes they are using or to the function of the negative and positive labels much of the value is lost.

The chief conceptual difficulty with the Advance Organizer Model has been the question "What is an organizer?" Ausubel is not very specific on this point. We have attempted in the chapter to clarify this question and in doing so, we have been rather liberal in our interpretation. We would hope that teachers can now see the full range of possibilities in both form and function of the Advance Organizer Model and that the interpretation eliminates some of the difficulties in recognizing an organizer. In fact, if we are correct, the emphasis of the problem for the teacher may have changed from *identifying an* organizer to *selecting the* organizer from among many possible focuses and subsumers. For instance in studying different communities, does the teacher want to focus the learning on social norms in the community or on the economic activity? In studying a novel or play, the idea of theme or character development *or* the particular theme could precede the learning experience and enhance its meaning.

Two other aspects are crucial to the successful implementation of the model. In Phase I, Presentation of the Organizer, whether in interactive teaching or with written materials, the teacher must make sure the organizer has been heard and somehow mentally distinguished from the material it is organizing. Probably, this means restating the organizer, and perhaps questioning the student on the substance of the organizer. We do not feel that the presentation of a written organizer without discussion is a sure enough way to establish the organizer especially because an erroneously-perceived organizer could result in learning quite different from that anticipated. In Phase II, Presentation of Verbal Material to be Learned, the teacher must take care to continuously relate the organizing thought to the material particularly when the organizer has been presented in an earlier lesson. The teacher must work to establish the connection between the material and the organizer, especially for the younger children.

Taba's Inductive Thinking Model has its own special problems. In our experience we have found that teachers and students often do two things that inhibit the development of the students' ideas. First, teachers often are over-anxious and suggest a category system to the student: "What things were in the village? What things were outside the village?" "What other ways can you group these pieces? Can you group them by color?" rather than letting them induce the categories or concepts. Second, students often omit some of the items that do not fall into their categories. When this happens, the student is probably not expanding or stretching his conceptual system but simply matching examples to concepts readily available in his conceptual system. In order to account for the remaining items, he has to reach for different categories. The teacher should encourage students to reconcile all the items in one grouping or another.

The Developmental Model has the special difficulty that one must perceive the student's cognitive level fairly precisely or the activities to increase development will be useless either because they do not induce new development or they are too far above the student's level and are too difficult for him.

Schwab's approach, like most models focusing on the modes of inquiry of the disciplines, is difficult chiefly because one has to learn those modes and how to practice them. The teacher has to become a kind of practicing scholar in order to practice authentic inquiry with his students.

## INSTRUCTIONAL VS. NURTURANT EFFECTS IN INFORMATION-PROCESSING MODELS

Whereas many of the interaction-oriented models emphasize the rather gradual nurturing of behavior through the effect of the entire social system, the information-processing models are built around structured activities designed to produce specific instructional effects. Ausubel's Advance Organizer Model is a prime example, for it is designed to shape activities to facilitate the transmission of ideas and information.

However, the environment resulting from the use of the information-processing models consists of much more than learning activities. In the "Advance-Organizer" environment, the teacher lives as a structurer and giver of information and the student as a receiver of data and ideas. Over time, these roles may have an effect equal in importance to the instructional effects.

One caution we would raise is that we believe every effort should be made to weight the various probable effects of each model and to consider the gradual, nurturant effects as well as the more direct, instructional effects. It would be an error to permit a series of short-term decisions resulting in learning environments with desirable short-term instructional effects but less desirable nurturant effects. This statement should *not* be taken to imply that the information-processing models in general, or advance-organizers in particular, have adverse nurturant effects. What is important is to increase awareness of the complexity of such decision-making. It would be a pity to select strategies to increase intellectual development in one way (as through the Piaget-based models) and have social and intellectual side-effects which would nullify the positive instructional effects or be otherwise undesirable.

Becoming sensitive to these issues is as important a part of learning the models as is mastery of the behavior necessary to create the learning environments themselves.

# III

## The Personal Sources

# INTRODUCTION

## *The Individual to the Fore*

From time immemorial, people have dreamed of the day when education would respond to the needs of the individual and help him develop on his own terms. Fortunately, we live in an age when many people who share this concern with the individual have gone to work and developed theoretical or practical positions from which models for teaching can be described.

The "personal" and "social" familes of models share a concern which creates a certain paradox in the act of teaching. It is that placing the concerns of the individual students (or group of individuals) in the most prominent place and attempting to help them develop on their own terms causes one to wonder about the extent to which one can impose his own desires on them. To develop an individual fully or to help a group develop its unique possibilities, how much advance planning can we do? Must we not simply provide avenues and support for the desires of the student and let him choose his own direction?

Can one, in short, teach at all if one's purpose is to put the student in the center of the teaching-learning process?

The developers of educational approaches which give the individual person the greatest prominence have solved this paradox in various ways. First, they have emphasized the nurturant potential of educational environments. Their models tend to produce environments which gently nudge the learner rather than coming on strong through sets of definite activities.

In a different vein, David Hunt, a psychologist who focuses on personality, has developed an interesting teaching model which is designed for two purposes.[1] One of these is to adapt teaching to the characteristics of the individual in order to increase his personal flexibility and his ability to relate to others productively. The second purpose is to provide an environment which is matched to the ways that the student's personality relates to the environment so that the individual student will be comfortable and able to carry on his tasks. Hunt's model is interesting also because it can be applied "over" the other models. That is, Hunt's model provides a way for adapting other teaching models to individual differences by modifying them according to his theories about the relationships between personality dynamics and training environments. (We will deal with it in a later section after the other models have been examined and we can better see how Hunt applies to them.)

Other educators and psychologists have emphasized personal creativity as a desirable goal. A major function of education, seen from their reference point, is to help individuals to create new solutions to their own problems and the problems of their society. Among those sharing this viewpoint are E. Paul Torrance, who has devoted an enormous amount of energy to the development of teaching models,[2] and William J. Gordon, who has developed a group procedure for increasing the creativity of individuals and for creating functioning groups within organizations that can serve as "creativity cells," taking on problems and generating interesting solutions to them.[3]

Second, they tend to give the student control of the selection of activities, so that, in a sense, he selects his own instructional effects. Thus, many of the personal models are "non-directive" or "facilitating" with respect to activities.

Third, they tend to shape environments which are likely to increase the student's capacity to develop himself. Glasser, for example, has developed a method which helps groups of students to increase their capacity to reflect on themselves and plan better environments to live in.

Some of the personal theorists have been therapists. For example, Carl Rogers and Abraham Maslow have developed positions derived from their work as clinicians,[4] and each of them, together with many other personal counselors, has created models for teaching which place personal develop-

---

[1] David Hunt, "A Conceptual Level Matching Model for Coordinating Learner Characteristics with Educational Approaches," *Interchange,* OISE Research Journal, 1, June 1970.

[2] E. Paul Torrance, *Guiding Creative Talent* (Englewood Cliffs, N.Y.: Prentice-Hall, 1962).

[3] William J. Gordon, *Synectics* (New York: Harper & Row, 1961).

[4] See especially: Carl Rogers, *Client-Centered Therapy* (Boston: Houghton Mifflin, 1951); Abraham Maslow, *Toward a Psychology of Being* (Princeton, N.J.: Van Nostrand Reinhold, 1962).

ment at the center of the process. They are concerned with changes in the self which enable individuals to function in more integrative and effective ways. Members of the group who founded the Esalen Institute at Big Sur, California, have developed a wide variety of teaching models devoted to personal realization based on Gestalt Therapy. One of the best known of these has been articulated by William Schutz: it emphasizes training to increase the individual's capacity to feel and to receive experience from his environment, and to develop warmer and more effective ways of relating to other human beings.[5]

This section of the book includes two models developed from the therapeutic stances by Rogers and Glasser,[6] an aspect of Awareness-Readiness Training as Schutz expresses it, and Gordon's Synectics Model, which exemplifies a large number of models emphasizing creative information processing as their goal.

Philosophically, it is the emphasis on the maximization of unique personal development which characterizes the models in this section. Each one gives a central place to the individual's construction of his own reality—to his task of finding personal identity and living a life in which his own dignified search for meaning is recognized on its own terms. His life validates itself—his unique existence and "feeling life" is what counts. The long-term dispositional changes in the student are thus more important to this group of model makers than the short-term instructional effects, for they hope to nurture development of the whole personality.

[5] William Schutz, *Joy: Expanding Human Awareness* (New York: Grove Press, 1967).

[6] William Glasser, *Reality Therapy* (New York: Harper & Row, 1965).

# 12

# NON-DIRECTIVE TEACHING

## Rogerian Counseling as a Source

The psychologist Carl R. Rogers describes in *Client-Centered Therapy* a comprehensive approach to therapy, and in later chapters of the book he extends the position on therapy to teaching and other endeavors (Chapter IX, "Student-Centered Teaching").[1] Rogers reasons that if this basic hypothesis regarding human relationships facilitates the learning which is called therapy, it might also be the basis for learning which is called education.[2] Recently, he has applied his position on teaching in a book devoted entirely to education.[3]

### ORIENTATION OF THE MODEL

#### THEORETICAL

At the heart of Roger's theory lies the assumption that the individual is able to handle his own life situations in constructive ways. The counselor has to respect the client's capacity and use this relationship to help the counselee to identify his own problems and formulate solutions to them: "...the individual has sufficient capacity to deal constructively with all those aspects of his life which can potentially come into conscious awareness. This means the creation of an interpersonal situation in which material may come into the client's awareness, and a meaningful demonstration of

---

1 Carl R. Rogers, *Client Centered Therapy* (Boston: Houghton Mifflin, 1951).
2 *Ibid.*, p. 384.
3 Carl R. Rogers, *Freedom to Learn* (Columbus, Ohio: Charles E. Merrill, 1969).

the counselor's acceptance of the client as a person who is competent to direct himself."[4] Such an interpersonal relationship will facilitate the individual's reorganization of himself so that he will (1) be more integrated, more effective, (2) have a more realistic view of himself, and (3) be less defensive and more adaptive to new situations and information.

In this context learning refers to growth which involves changes in the self. Learning is the process or disorganization and reorganization in which a "new or revised configuration of self is being constructed. It contains perceptions which were previously denied. It involves more accurate symbolization of a much wider range of sensory and visceral experience. It involves a reorganization of values with the organism's own experience clearly recognized as providing evidence for the valuations.[5] Teaching is the implementation of the interpersonal situations which facilitate learning. We may now restate Roger's basic premise in terms of the classroom. "You can trust the student. You can trust him to desire to learn in every way which will maintain or enhance the self; you can trust him to make use of resources which will serve this end; you can trust him to evaluate himself in ways which will make for self progress; you can trust him to grow, provided the atmosphere for growth is available to him."[6]

Toward the creation of the atmosphere for growth the counselor attempts to (1) adopt the client's frame of reference, and (2) clarify the client's attitudes: "...it is the counselor's function to assume, in so far as he is able, the internal frame of reference of the client, to perceive the world as he sees it, to perceive the client as he sees himself, to lay aside all perceptions from the external frame of reference while doing so and to communicate something of this empathetic understanding to the client."[7] The counselor, by adopting this posture temporarily divests himself of his own selfhood, his own needs, views, etc., and in doing so, communicates to the client an understanding and acceptance of the client's attitudes and an expression of confidence in his problem-solving abilities. In the classroom this implies that the teacher keeps the students' feelings and problems at the center of the teaching process, and mutes his own. In addition, the client, seeing his own attitudes, confusions, ambivalences, feelings, and perceptions accurately expressed by another, but stripped of the complication of emotion with which he himself invests them, paves the way for acceptance into self all of those elements which are now clearly perceived. Reorganization of the self and more integrated functioning of the self are thus furthered.[8] To clarify the student's attitudes, the counselor (teacher) adopts

---

[4] Rogers, *Client Centered Therapy*, p. 24.
[5] *Ibid.*, p. 193.
[6] *Ibid.*, p. 427.
[7] *Ibid.*, p. 29.
[8] *Ibid.*, pp. 40–41.

a non-directive approach consistent with the basic hypothesis of respect for the individual and with the need to adopt the client's internal frame of reference. The non-directive stance permits most control to reside in the student and also, by drawing him out, permits the counselor (teacher) to learn about the client's frames of reference. The therapist's set of attitudes and techniques are best understood by examining the following example:

> Client: "I don't feel very normal, but I want to feel that way...I thought I'd have something to talk about—then it all goes round in circles. I was trying to think what I was going to say. Then coming here it doesn't work out.... I tell you that it seemed that it would be much easier before I came. I tell you that I just can't make a decision; I don't know what I want. I've tried to reason this thing out logically—tried to figure out which things are important to me. I thought that there are maybe two things a man might do; he might get married and raise a family. But if he was just a bachelor, just making a living—that isn't very good. I find myself and my thoughts getting back to the days when I was a kid and I cry very easily. The dam would break through. I've been in the army for four and a half years. I had no problems then, no hopes, no wishes. My only thought was to get out when peace would come. My problems, now that I'm out, are as ever. I tell you, they go back a long time before I was in the army.... I love children. When I was in the Philippines—I tell you, when I was young I swore I'd never forget my unhappy childhood—so when I saw these children in the Philippines, I treated them very nicely. I used to give them ice cream cones and movies. It was just a period—I'd reverted back—and that awakened some emotions in me I thought I had long buried." (A pause, he seems very near tears)

If the counselor had the following thoughts while this material was being expressed, he would be operating on an external frame of reference.

> "I wonder if I should help him get started talking. Is this inability to get under way a type of dependence? Why this indecisiveness: What could be its cause? What is meant by this focus on marriage and family? He seems to be a bachelor. I hadn't known that. The crying, the dam sound as though there must be a great deal of repression.
> He's a veteran. Could he have been a psychiatric case?
> I feel sorry for anyone who spent four and a half years in the service.
> Some time he will probably need to dig into those early unhappy experiences.
> What is this interest in children? Identification?
> Vague homosexuality?"[9]

If the counselor had an internal frame of reference his thoughts might be:

[9] *Ibid.,* p. 33.

"You're wanting to struggle toward normality, aren't you?
Is it really hard for you to get started?
Decision making just seems impossible to you.
You want marriage, but it doesn't seem to you to be much of a possibility.
You feel yourself brimming over with childish feelings.
To you the army represented stagnation.
Being very nice to children has somehow had meaning for you.
But it was—and is—a disturbing experience for you."[10]

The first set of responses, those indicating an external frame of reference, try to interpret the client in terms of concepts that exist outside of him. They categorize the student, albeit hypothetically (as a veteran, a bachelor, one vaguely interested in children). The latter responses take the views entirely from the client himself—"You want marriage" and "you saw the army as stagnation." In the latter case, the counselor is beginning to see how the client sees the world and is reflecting this back to him so he can apprehend it.

## STUDENT-CENTERED TEACHING

Rogers proceeds from his stance on therapy and theory of the self to develop the following principles or hypotheses about teaching.

We cannot teach another person directly; we can only facilitate his learning.
—Thus, instead of asking teacher focused questions such as, What shall I teach? What topics? How much shall I cover? How do I prove I taught it? an instructor should ask, What are the student's purposes? What does he want to learn?

A person learns significantly only those things which he perceives as being involved in the maintenance of, or enhancement of, the structure of self.
—To learn then, a student must see what is to be learned as having relevance for his own purposes.

Experience which, if assimilated, would involve a change in the organization of self tends to be resisted through denial or distortion of symbolization.
—It is painful and threatening to discover internal contradictions. Much learning material is threatening. For instance, to learn facts about prejudice or even arithmetic threatens old methods and attacks previous levels of understanding.

The structure and organization of self appears to become more rigid under threat; to relax its boundaries when completely free from threat. Experience which is perceived as inconsistent with the self can only be assimilated if the current organization of self is relaxed and expanded to include it.
—A supportive, non-evaluative environment, one in which the student is responsible for his own learning and evaluation, reduces external threat.[11]

[10] *Ibid.* Copyright 1951 by Carl R. Rogers. Reprinted by permission of the publisher, Houghton Mifflin Company.
[11] *Ibid.*, pp. 389–91.

Following from the above, "The educational situation which most effectively promotes significant learning is one in which (1) threat to the self of the learner is at a minimum, and (2) differentiated perception of the field of experience is facilitated." (This conditions allows the student to begin to see alternative ways of interpreting and assimilating experience.)

What do these principles look like in action—what are the general characteristics of a student-centered classroom or therapeutic encounter? Although specific methods may vary, a student-centered classroom begins around the purposes of the student. For example, Roger opens each class with a variant of the question, "What do we wish to do today?" The class then takes its start from some individual question. As might be expected, the personalized problem-solving in student-centered classes is characterized by loose discussion, jumping from topic to topic, and is exploratory in nature. The instructor does not attempt artificial closure of issues but expects that individuals will carry on vital thinking outside of class and that the unresolved nature of issues will be a stimulus to learning. After conducting a psychology course in both directive and nondirective fashions Rogers concluded that in the latter, the students came to grasp with the deeper issues in the field earlier in the course. At first the students were puzzled; feelings ranged from perplexity to confusion and frustration at being on one's own. Gradually, most students worked harder and at a deeper level. During the beginning of a course, the role of the leader should be largely one of acceptance of the students and understanding of their output. He should be non-judgemental in his desire not to intrude upon the value system of the students. He engages in what we call mood-setting action. It removes threat and subsequent defensiveness. The leader functions as an emotional and ideational sounding-board. His attitude is one of respect for and reliance upon the group members to plan activities and derive satisfaction and growth according to the needs and intent of each individual member. As the group develops and the atmosphere is a known consistent quantity to the students, the actions of the leader should subtly change to match the altered relationship. He is then in a position to participate more freely on a "this is how I feel about it" basis without preventing continuing analysis and exploration by members of the group.[12]

A first-hand description of the teaching strategy in operation is presented in Roger's most recent book *Freedom To Learn*. A sixth-grade teacher, exhausted by the failure of her more traditional attempts to cope with the discipline problems and the lack of interest in her class, decided to experiment with student-centered teaching. She has provided an account of that experience from which excerpts are presented here.

[12] *Ibid.*, pp. 399–400.

March 5, We Begin:

A week ago I decided to initiate a new program in my sixth grade classroom, based on student-centered teaching—an unstructured or non-directive approach.

I began by telling the class that we were going to try an "experiment." I explained that for one day I would let them do anything they wanted to do—they did not have to do anything if they did not want to.

Many started with art projects; some drew or painted most of the day. Others read or did work in math and other subjects. There was an air of excitement all day; many were so interested in what they were doing that they did not want to go out at recess or noon!

At the end of the day I asked the class to evaluate the experiment. The comments were most interesting. Some were "confused," distressed without the teacher telling them what to do, without specific assignments to complete.

The majority of the class thought the day was "great," but some expressed concern over the noise level and the fact that a few "goofed off" all day. Most felt that they had accomplished as much work as we usually do, and they enjoyed being able to work at a task until it was completed without the pressure of a time limit. They liked doing things without being "forced" to do them and liked deciding what to do.

They begged to continue the "experiment" so it was decided to do so, for two more days. We would then re-evaluate the plan.

The next morning I implemented the idea of a "work contract." I gave them ditto sheets listing all our subjects with suggestions under each. There was a space provided for their "plans" in each area and for checking upon completion.

Each child was to write his or her contract for the day—choosing the areas in which he would work and planning specifically what he would do. Upon completion of any exercise, drill, review, etc., he was to check and correct his own work, using the teacher's manual. The work was to be kept in a folder with the contract.

I met with each child to discuss his plans. Some completed theirs in a very short time; we discussed as a group what this might mean, and what to do about it. It was suggested that the plan might not be challenging enough, that an adjustment should be made—perhaps going on or adding another area to the day's plan.

Resource materials were provided, suggestions made, and drill materials made available to use when needed.

I found I had much more time, so I worked, talked, and spent the time with individuals and groups. At the end of the third day I evaluated the work folder with each child. To solve the problem of grades, I had each child tell me what he thought he had earned.

. . .

March 12, Progress Report:

Our "experiment" has, in fact, become our program—with some adjustments.

Some children continued to be frustrated and felt insecure without teacher direction. Discipline also continued to be a problem with some, and I began to realize that although the children involved may need the program more than the others, I was expecting too much from them, too soon—they were not ready to assume self-direction yet. Perhaps a gradual weaning from the spoon-fed procedures was necessary.

I regrouped the class—creating two groups. The largest group is the non-directed. The smallest is teacher directed, made up of children who wanted to return to the former teacher-directed method, and those who, for varied reasons, were unable to function in the self-directed situation.

I would have waited longer to see what would have happened, but the situation for some disintegrated a little more each day—penalizing the whole class. The disrupting factor kept everyone upset and limited those who wanted to study and work. So it seemed to me best for the group as a whole as well as the program to modify the plan.

Those who continued the "experiment" have forged ahead. I showed them how to program their work, using their texts as a basic guide. They have learned that they can teach themselves (and each other) and that I am available when a step is not clear or advice is needed.

At the end of the week they evaluate themselves in each area—in terms of work accomplished, accuracy, etc. We have learned that the number of errors is not a criterion of failure or success. Errors can and should be part of the learning process; we learn through our mistakes. We also discussed the fact that consistently perfect scores may mean that the work is not challenging enough and perhaps we should move on.

After self-evaluation, each child brings the evaluation sheet and work folder to discuss them with me.

Some of the members of the group working with me are most anxious to become "independent" students. We will evaluate together each week their progress toward that goal.

I have only experienced one parental objection so far. A parent felt her child was not able to function without direction.

Some students (there were two or three) who originally wanted to return to the teacher-directed program are now anticipating going back into the self-directed program. (I sense that it has been difficult for them to readjust to the old program as it would be for me to do so.)[13]

Rogers points out later in the book that the use of student contracts is a device which gives the student both security and responsibility within an atmosphere of freedom. It provides a transitional experience between complete freedom and learning within institutional demands. Not incidental, the contract also helps assuage the uncertainties of the teacher.[14]

Focusing for a moment on the teacher's activities rather than the students', how does a teacher spend his time and effort when he does not prescribe the curriculum, assign readings, set lessons, lecture frequently or administer grades?

Instead of spending great blocks of time organizing lesson plans and lectures, he concentrates on providing all kinds of resources which will give his students experiential learning relevant to their needs. He also concentrates on

[13] Carl R. Rogers, *Freedom to Learn,* pp. 12–16. Reprinted by permission of Charles E. Merrill.

[14] *Ibid.,* p. 133.

making such resources clearly available, by thinking through and simplifying the practical and psychological steps which the student must go through in order to utilize the resources. For example, it is one thing to say that a given book is available in the library. This means that if the student looks it up in the catalogue, waits around to find that it is already on loan, returns the next week to ask for it, he may obtain the book. Not every student will have the patience or interest to go through these steps. But I have found that if I can make a shelf of books and reprints available for loan in the classroom, the amount of reading done, and the resulting stimulation to use the library in pursuing individual needs, grows by leaps and bounds.[15]

As a resource, the teacher can make himself available for individual consultation, set up channels so that learning experiences can be easily arranged; lecture on his particular interests or act as a class recorder by providing feedback sheets on the class progress and problems.

### RATIONALE AND GOALS OF STUDENT-CENTERED EDUCATION

Rogers reaches to the conditions of contemporary society as the rationale for and the subsequent goals of student-centered education. "As our culture has grown less homogeneous, it gives much less support to the individual. He cannot simply rest comfortable upon the ways and traditions of his society, but finds many of the basic issues and conflicts of life center in himself. Each man must resolve within himself issues for which his society previously took full responsibility."[16] Accordingly, in such a society, "This would seem to mean that the goal of democratic education is to assist students to become individuals:

who are able to take self-initiated action to be responsible for those actions;
who are capable of intelligent choice and self-direction;
who are critical learners, able to evaluate the contributions made by others;
who have acquired knowledge relevant to the solution of problems;
who, even more importantly, are able to adapt flexibly and intelligently to new problem situations;
who have internalized an adaptive mode of approach to problems utilizing all pertinent experience freely and creatively;
who are able to cooperate effectively with others in these various activities;
who work, not for the approval of others, but in terms of their own socialized purposes."[17]

Undergirding Rogers' statement of the outcomes of a democratic education is his conceptualization of a fully functioning person.

I find such a person to be a human being in flow, in process, rather than having achieved some state. Fluid change is central in the picture.

15 *Ibid.*, p. 131.
16 Rogers, *Client Centered Therapy*, p. 4.
17 *Ibid.*, pp. 387–88.

...I find such a person to be sensitively open to all of his experience—sensitive to what is going on in his environment, sensitive to other individuals with whom he is in relationship, and sensitive perhaps most of all to the feelings, reactions and emergent meanings which he discovers in himself. The fear of some aspects of his own experience continues to diminish, so that more and more of his life is available to him.

Such a person experiences in the present with immediacy. He is able to live in his feelings and reactions of the moment. He is not bound by the structure of his past learnings but these are a present resource for him insofar as they relate to the experience of the moment. He lives freely, subjectively, in an existential confrontation with this moment of life.

Such a person is trustingly able to permit his total organism to function freely in all its complexity in selecting from the multitude of possibilities that behavior which in this moment of time will be most generally and genuinely satisfying. He is thus making use of all the data which his nervous system can supply, using this data in awareness but recognizing that his total organism may be, and often is, wiser than his awareness.

Such a person is a creative person. With his sensitiveness and openness to his world, and his trust of his own ability to form new relationships with his environment, he is the type of person from whom creative products and creative living emerge.

Finally, such a person lives a life with a wider range, a greater richness than the constricted living in which most of us find ourselves. It seems to me that the clients who have moved most significantly in therapy live more intimately with their feelings of pain, but also more vividly with their feelings of ecstasy; that anger is more clearly felt, but so also is life, that fear is an experience they know more deeply but so is courage; and the reason they can thus live more fully in a wider range is that they have this underlying confidence in themselves as trustworthy instruments for encountering life... the adjectives which seem more generally fitting are adjectives such as enriching, exciting, rewarding, challenging, meaningful. This process of healthy living, is not, I am convinced a life for the fainthearted.[18]

## MODEL

Let us analyze the specific aspects of the non-directive strategy according to the concepts which we have been using to present models in operational terms.

### SYNTAX

The development of student-centered instruction occurs in two interrelated but distinct phases: (1) the creation of an acceptant climate by the instructor, and (2) the development of individual and/or group purposes. Prerequisite to the development of an acceptant climate is the genuine trust in the student—his desire to implement his purposes as the motivational

---

18 Carl R. Rogers, "Toward Becoming a Fully Functioning Person," *Perceiving, Behaving, Becoming,* Association for Supervision and Curriculum Development Yearbook, 1962 (Washington, D.C.: National Education Association, 1962), pp. 31–32. Reprinted by permission.

force behind learning—and the implementation of this permissive atmosphere from the beginning. General guidelines for creating an acceptant climate are:

*(handwritten margin note: acceptant climate)*

Encourage self-revelation rather than self-defense. Give each person a feeling of belonging. Create the impression that difference is good and desirable. Encourage children to trust their own organisms. Emphasize the existential, ongoing character of learning. Finally, acceptance requires the establishment of an atmosphere which is generally hopeful. Such an atmosphere gives the child the feeling that he can be more than he is—the feeling that he has something to bring to this business of education rather than the feeling that all of education means acquiring something from somewhere else for some unpredictable time in the future.[19]

An acceptant climate can be accomplished initially by having students define the purposes and problems they are facing regarding the course. "I suspect each of us had some sort of purpose in enrolling, even if that purpose was only to gain another credit. If we would begin by telling what our purposes were, perhaps we can, together build the course is such a way to meet them." The teacher accepts all purposes—both intellectual content and accompanying emotions. He endeavors to elicit and clarify these purposes and helps the students identify their common and unique objectives. An acceptant climate is also evidenced in the physical aspects of the setting—as in a seating arrangement in which the instructor takes equal place.

In the second phase the individuals and group identify purposes on which they wish to act. The learning experience is shaped from these purposes. The instructor stresses that in a teaching situation the purposes may change from session to session and that purposes which were set several weeks before should not be followed automatically later on, but that each meeting of the group should begin with a reassessment and restatement of purpose. In this phase the instructor endeavors to organize and make easily available the resources the students may wish to use. For example, he may point out untapped resources as well as ways students might implement their purposes, i.e., lecture, observation, reading, discussion. The instructor, himself, must be a flexible resource capable of being utilized by the group in ways most meaningful to them. If it seems the instructor is playing a more active role during the second phase, this is because having established a truly acceptant climate, he can now participate on an equal basis without fear of unduly influencing the group. Corresponding roughly to the phases, the instructor first takes the leader role in order to establish an acceptant climate. His leadership is characterized,

[19] Carl R. Rogers, "Acceptance and the Accurate View of Self," *Perceiving, Behaving, Becoming,* Association for Supervision and Curriculum Development Yearbook, 1962 (Washington, D.C.: National Education Association, 1962), pp. 125–26.

however, by non-directive principles; he is the leader in the traditional sense only insofar as he does not attempt to become a participant. Gradually, in the second phase, he can participate—expressing his views as those of one individual only. The two roles are not as dichotomous as they appear and require continuous shifting back and forth.

### PRINCIPLES OF REACTION

The training agent's behavior is governed by two principles: (1) the assumption by the instructor, except when speaking for himself as a participant, of the student's frame of reference, understanding but not judging the individual's reactions and omitting his own concerns; and (2) clarifying the student's attitudes by reflecting them back to the learner so that the student himself can be assisted in deciding what to do next.

### SOCIAL SYSTEM

The teacher is to be non-directive. The student must take responsibility for initiating and maintaining the learning activities that emerge from the interactive process. Since learning according to Rogers is idiosyncratic and takes place only when it is meaningful to the student, he, alone, can decide what has meaning for him.

### SUPPORT SYSTEM

The optimal support system, is, of course, the non-directive teacher and an open-ended intellectual resource, such as a contemporary library in which the students can have random access to resources as they move along and identify their purposes. They also need access to resources—both people and things—throughout their community if these are needed for fulfillment of their purposes.

## GENERAL APPLICABILITY OF THE MODEL

Non-directive teaching is primarily aimed at improving the general functioning of the individual and especially his ability to develop himself on his own terms. An integrated self, reaching out to others and the physical world, able to develop and modify goals and means, emphathetic with others yet independent, is the goal. However, this stance leads one quickly to apply non-directive environments to attain less broad goals. If social and academic development depends on the growth of the self, then that environment which most enhances the self becomes also the most appropriate for social and academic ends. Consequently, non-directive teaching is the recommended avenue for teaching academic subjects, increasing interpersonal effectiveness, and developing fully functioning persons.

## Nurturant and Instructional Values

Since the activities are not prescribed but are determined by the learner as he interacts with the teacher and other students, the non-directive environment depends largely on its nurturant values, with the instructional values dependent on its success in nurturing nore effective self-development (Figure 12-1).

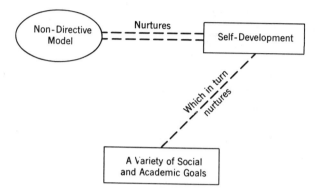

**Figure 12-1**

The model, thus, can be thought of as entirely nurturant in character, dependent for effects on "living in" the non-directive environment rather than carrying content and skills through specifically designed activity.

**TABLE 12-1 Summary Chart: Non-Directive Teaching Model**

| *Syntax:* | *Phase One* | *Phase Two* |
|---|---|---|
| | Teacher establishes an acceptant climate | Individual and/or group identifies and pursues their learning goals. Activities are emergent. |
| *Principles of Reaction:* | Training agent: 1. assumes student's frame of reference or, when he speaks for himself, does so as an equal participant. 2. attempts to clarify student's attitudes by reflecting them back to the learner. | |
| *Social System:* | Very *low external structure*. Assumes that purposes and structure flow from students. | |
| *Support System:* | Non-directive teacher and open-ended intellectual resource. | |

# 13

# CLASSROOM MEETING MODEL

## *A Model Drawn from a Stance*
## *Toward Mental Health*

In his therapeutic innovation, Reality Therapy, William Glasser challenges the fundamentals of personality theory as well as the basic conception of the traditional therapeutic and teaching relationships. In doing so, Glasser lifts most individual problems out of the realms of mental illness and assistance only by highly trained specialists, into the domain of positive mental health and skilled laymen, particularly parents and teachers. More fundamentally, he contends that individual failures occur not at the individual level of human functioning but at the interpersonal, the *social* level. Therefore, development of individual success must be channeled through the social medium. Following his belief that Reality Therapy is for everyone ("its percepts and principles are the foundation of successful satisfying social life everywhere"),[1] Glasser has applied his principles to the classroom through the mechanism of the Classroom Meeting, a 30- to 45-minute time at least once a week when students and teacher set aside their on-going curricular activities and instructional norms to engage in open-minded, non-judgmental discussions of problems (personal, behavioral, or academic) of concern to them in an effort to find collective solutions.

1 William Glasser, *Reality Therapy* (New York: Harper & Row, 1965), p. xv.

## ORIENTATION OF THE MODEL

### THEORY AND METHOD

According to Glasser, traditional psychology postulates that psychological disorders occur because of "cultural" interference with the basic human biological needs for sex and aggression. In addition, human beings get into emotional binds because their standards are too high. Accordingly, traditional therapy attempts through fostering an understanding of one's past and of one's unconscious to lower these standards to a more "realistic" level. It *interprets* rather than *evaluates* behavior and seeks change through *insight*. Reality Therapy departs from this conception in both theory and practice. Glasser's thesis is that individuals have problems because of their failure to satisfy their basic human needs for relatedness (love), and respect (self-worth). "First is the need to love and be loved. In all its forms, ranging from friendship through mother love, family love and conjugal love, this need drives us to continuous activity in search of satisfaction. From birth to old age we need to love and be loved. Throughout our lives, our health and happiness will depend upon our ability to do so. To either love or to allow ourselves to be loved is not enough; we must do both. When we cannot satisfy our total need for love, we will without fail suffer and react with many familiar psychological symptoms, from mild discomfort through anxiety and depression to complete withdrawal from the world around us.

Equal in importance to the need for love is the need to feel that we are worthwhile both to ourselves and to others. Although the two needs are separate, a person who loves and is loved will usually feel that he is a worthwhile person, and one who is worthwhile is usually someone who is loved and who can give love in return. While this is usually the case, it is not always so. For example, although an overindulged child may receive an abundance of love, the parents do not make the critical distinction between loving him and accepting his behavior, good or bad. . . .

But, whether we are loved or not, *to be worthwhile* we must maintain *a satisfactory standard of behavior*. To do so we must learn to correct ourselves when we do wrong and to credit ourselves when we do right. If we do not evaluate our own behavior, or having evaluated it, we do not act to improve our conduct where it is below our standards, we will not fulfill our need to be worthwhile and we will suffer as acutely as when we fail to love or be loved. Morals, standards, values, or right and wrong behavior are all intimately related to the fulfillment of our need for self-worth. . . ."[2] Together, love and self-worth form the pathways to a successful identity,

[2] Glasser, *Reality Therapy*, pp. 9–11.

man's single basic need. Love in the context of the classroom takes the form of social responsibility, a responsibility to help and care for each other.

Reality Therapy not only reverses the theory of neuroses in contending that human problems are incapacities or failures of interpersonal, social functioning, but also reverses the intent of therapy. It holds that problems arise not because standards are too high but because performance is too low. Reality Therapy, therefore, seeks not to lower aims but to raise performance according to the theory. Performance is raised and basic needs are satisfied by doing what is: (1) real (reality), (2) responsible (responsibility), and (3) right, and these three concepts are central to Reality Therapy's methodology. An action can be called realistic or unrealistic only when its remote as well as immediate consequences are taken into consideration and compared, weighed. Reality requires this kind of temporal integration. In the classroom, reality also involves relevance. "Responsibility, a concept basic to Reality Therapy, is defined as the ability to fulfill one's needs, and to do so in *a way that does not deprive others of the ability to fulfill their needs....* A responsible person also does that which gives him a feeling of self-worth and a feeling that he is worthwhile to others. He is motivated to strive and perhaps endure privation to attain self-worth. When a responsible man says that he will perform a job for us, he will try to accomplish what was asked, both for us and so that he may gain a measure of self-worth for himself. An irresponsible person may or may not do what he says, depending upon how he feels, the effort he has to make, and what is in it for him. He gains neither our respect nor his own, and in time he will suffer or cause others to suffer."[3] Finally, Reality Therapy calls for individuals to maintain a standard of behavior, one which they set and evaluate. Traditional psychotherapy avoids morality, but according to Glasser, standards of behavior are part of reality and self-worth. "When a man acts in such a way that he gives and receives and feels worthwhile to himself and to others his behavior is right or moral."[4] In raising the performance Reality Therapy relies not upon insight or understanding but upon the individual's commitment to action. It rarely asks *why* something *was* done, but *what is* done now. Although a portion of the problem may depend upon the past, the crucial element is facing up to the present and preparing action for the future. Reality Therapy searches not for insights but teaches patients better *ways* to fulfill needs.

We now come to the key of Reality Therapy—the process through which performance is raised and basic needs are fulfilled—the process of involvement. The love of a parent or personal involvement of a teacher provide substitute satisfaction, compensation for the primitive pleasure principle

3 *Ibid.,* p. 13.
4 *Ibid.,* p. 57.

one is being asked to give up. "The guiding principles of Reality Therapy are directed toward achieving proper involvement, a completely honest, human relationship in which the patient, for perhaps the first time in his life, realizes that someone cares enough about him not only to accept him but to help him fulfill his needs in the real world."[5] At present, however, teachers, like conventional psychiatrists, are trained not to become involved with students but to remain objective and detached. Glasser's formulation attempts to transform the class from a pedagogical to a personal experience. Emotional involvement requires more than caring and being cared for; involvement, according to Glasser, is a combination of love and discipline. "In essence, we gain self-respect through discipline and closeness to others through love. Discipline must always have within it the element of love."[6] Thus, the overindulgent parent whose love does not include discipline stifles the child from acquiring responsibility and the ultimate ability to fulfill his needs.

We are now in a position to set forth the three general requirements of Reality Therapy: (1) an intense personal involvement; (2) facing reality and rejecting irresponsible behavior, and (3) learning better ways to behave.

### CLASSROOM PRINCIPLES

Let us apply Glasser's theory of neurosis and these therapeutic requirements to the classroom. The problem of failure in school is a failure not in terms of academic performance but a failure to make the warm constructive relationships essential for success, a failure caused by loneliness. "To begin to be successful, children must receive at school what they lack: a good relationship with other people, both children and adults."[7] "*Thus, those who fail in our society are lonely.* In their loneliness they grope for identity but to the lonely the pathways to success are closed; only anger, frustration, suffering and withdrawal—a failure in identity—are open."[8] In isolation, children cannot develop the capacities to fulfill their needs for a successful identity. A teaching strategy based on reality therapy would aim at reducing this loneliness and would include the following six elements. The first and most fundamental would be the development of a warm, positive *involvement* within the classroom group, including the teacher. Second, the group must concern itself with *present behavior* rather than emotions, for the latter is the result of behavior. "*Emotion is the result of behavior,* but it is the behavior and the behavior alone that can be im-

5 *Ibid.,* p. xx.
6 *Ibid.,* p. 17.
7 William Glasser, *Schools Without Failure* (New York: Harper & Row, 1969), p. 16.
8 Glasser, *Reality Therapy,* p. 17.

proved. When behavior is improved, it leads to good feelings that in turn will snowball toward better behavior."[9] Third, the child must make a *value judgment* on his own behavior, what he is doing now that contributes to his failure. For example, if the child misbehaves the teacher must ask "What are you doing?" and get the child to reply honestly. The teacher may then ask whether his behavior is helping him, her, the class, etc. In other words, the child's world should not be manipulated by the teacher so that he doesn't suffer the reasonable consequences of his behavior. Fourth, the child must *select a better course of action.* The teacher may suggest alternatives and assist the child in planning a better course of action. Glasser gives the example of the talkative, disruptive child. Together he and the teacher work out a better seating arrangement. Fifth, the child after identifying and selecting a better way must make a *commitment* to enact it. Finally, once the value judgment, the selection, and the commitment to behavioral change is made, the teacher who cares exercises *discipline,* accepting no excuse for non-performance. The educational problem as Glasser sees it and the outlines of a solution are summarized in the following statement:

> Today increasing numbers of students fail to gain a successful identity and react illogically and emotionally to their failure. Because they are lonely, they need involvement with educators who are warm and personal and who will work with their behavior in the present. They need teachers who will encourage them to make a value judgement of their behavior rather than preach or dictate; teachers who will help them plan behavior and who will expect a commitment from the students that they will do what they have planned. They need teachers who will not excuse them when they fail in their commitments, but who will work with them again and again as they commit and recommit until they finally learn to fulfill a commitment. When they *learn* to do so, they are no longer lonely; they gain maturity, respect, love and a successful identity.[10]

These six elements alone will not recast the character of American education. Taking a closer look at the school, Glasser cites the additional needs for relevance and thinking as part of the teaching of social responsibility and fostering a successful identity: ". . . little of a success identity can be attained by using one's brain as a memory bank. Merely retaining knowledge, without using it to solve problems relevant to oneself and one's society, precludes extensive involvement with other people and with the world. The certainty principle (i.e., right or wrong) emphasizes isolation rather than cooperation and involvement."[11]  ". . . little or no effort is

[9] Glasser, *Schools Without Failure,* pp. 20–21.
[10] *Ibid.,* pp. 23–24.
[11] *Ibid.,* p. 41.

directly devoted to teaching children social responsibility. Learning to help one another solve common problems of living, learning that when we have educational difficulty we are not alone in the world, are ideas few people associate with school. . . . When students are not asked to think about the problems of their own world and how they relate to the whole world, when they are rewarded for remembering what others deem necessary and important, they begin to believe that right answers will solve all problems, or, as they discover more difficult problems, that problems are generally insoluble through formal education. . . ."[12]

## CLASSROOM APPLICATION

Education for social responsibility involves thinking, problem-solving, and decision-making as individuals and groups about subjects of concern to the students. This can be accomplished through the mechanism of the daily (preferably), open-ended, non-judgmental Classroom Meeting in which students and/or teacher can introduce for discussion behavioral problems, personal problems, or academic or curriculum issues. Glasser distinguishes three types of classroom meetings, each with a slightly different focus. The Social-Problem-Solving Meeting usually concerns itself with behavioral and social problems. However, other possible subjects include friendship, loneliness, vocational choice, etc. Students attempt to share the responsibility for learning and behaving by resolving their problems within the classroom. The orientation of the meeting is always positive, that is, toward a solution rather than fault-finding. Obviously many problems don't have a single answer. For example, in the case of coping with a bully, the solution is often in the discussion itself, which serves to decrease the intimidation of other students and increase their strength. If this is the case, further discussion of the "bully" should be avoided unless he does something constructive.[13] In Glasser's opinion, the whole disciplinary structure of the school should revolve around the Classroom Meeting.[14]

The second type of meeting is the Open-ended Meeting. "In the open-ended meeting children are asked to discuss any thought-provoking question related to their lives, questions that may also be related to the curriculum of the classroom. The difference between an open-ended meeting and class discussion is that in the former the teacher is specifically not looking for factual answers. He is trying to stimulate the children to think and relate what they know to the subject being discussed."[15] The teacher might start out the meeting with the question "What is interesting to you?" Glasser

[12] *Ibid.*, p. 31.
[13] *Ibid.*, p. 129.
[14] *Ibid.*, p. 133.
[15] *Ibid.*, pp. 134–35.

gives the example of the elementary class which responded to this question with an interest in ears and eyes. This starting point led to a discussion of the functions of eyes and ears and also of blindness. Having stimulated the students' involvement, the teacher then introduced a problem for solution, "Could a blind man read?" After some experimentation, hypothesizing, and guidance from the teacher the students expressed the idea that a blind man could read if he could feel the letters on the page. But how might this be done? Once again the children thought, experimented, and formulated a Braille-type system.

The third type of Classroom Meeting is the Educational-Diagnostic Meeting. This meeting is directly related to what the class is studying. Its purpose is to get an idea whether the class has understood the lesson. The Educational-Diagnostic Meeting is not to evaluate or grade students but to find out what they know and don't know: "...the leader should not incorporate value judgments into the discussion. The students should feel free to voice their opinions and conclusions any way they see fit."[16] Glasser used this approach with a class which had been studying the Constitution for a semester and a half. After a few penetrating questions, it was obvious that the class had no real understanding of the Constitution, its principles, how these might apply to them, or even if the Constitution actually existed in a physical form!

Although Glasser identifies three distinct foci or types of meetings, the basic mechanism, the Classroom Meeting, is the same. In the case of the Open-end and Educational-Diagnostic meetings, two types more closely related to the academic domain, the ingredients of thought-provoking questions as opposed to factual ones, relevant topics, student-initiated discussions, and non-evaluative responses, should be a part of any sound teaching strategy. In reality, classroom teaching is so culture-bound that apparently only the creation of a special mechanism, i.e., the Classroom Meeting, set apart in time and space (chairs in a circle rather than rows) can suspend the norms.

However, a distinction between the academic and the interpersonal functions of the classroom is a spurious one and both can be incorporated into the strategy of the Classroom Meeting. In fact, Glasser would have the strategy become so pervasive as to encompass all class time activities, losing its "special meeting" status. The special meetings, however, ensure some institutionalization of the method and are probably necessary initially.

Explicit or implicit in all teaching strategies is a conception of learning and teaching. Reality Therapy is no exception. For Glasser the most important aspect of learning is the ability to fulfill a commitment to behav-

16 *Ibid.,* p. 141.

ioral change. The outcomes of learning are emotional ones—self-worth, love, and identity. Teaching is the establishment of involvement and development of responsibility.

## MODEL

How does Reality Therapy look when we describe it as a model of teaching?

### SYNTAX

The structure of interaction for the Classroom Meeting Model includes six phases: (1) Establishing a Climate of Involvement; (2) Exposing the Problem for Discussion; (3) Making a Personal Value Judgment; (4) Identifying Alternative Courses of Action; (5) Making a Commitment, and (6) Behavioral Follow-up. The first phase, although essential for the strategy optimally or additionally occurs outside the parameters of the Classroom Meeting at an earlier period of time, when the teacher works to involve students and to help them bring their emotions freely into discussion. Phase One is a constant prerequisite undergirding all successful Classroom Meetings, but Phases Two through Six are repeated for each problem but may take place over the course of several meetings. To make these stages concrete, we may parallel their description with a case study presented by Glasser in which he (as an outsider) held one Social-Problem-Solving Meeting with an eighth-grade class over the problem of truancy.[17]

Phase One consists of the establishment by the teacher of a warm personal relationship with her students. In addition, a creditable non-evaluative, non-judgmental atmosphere should exist. Ideally this climate is established prior to the introduction of the classroom meeting in order to avoid aborted meeting attempts which fail for lack of a conducive climate discouraging both teachers and students. But here one runs into the circular problem discussed earlier. Very often, the uniqueness of the meeting mechanism itself is crucial to establishing a new kind of classroom climate. In Glasser's case study, immediate involvement with a total stranger is difficult to establish especially for social-problem-solving. Presumably, his skills in conducting such meetings compensated for the lack of familiarity. Glasser's goals were modest—simply to get the class to think about their own motives for cutting school and to suggest possible ideas to foster better attendance.

The second phase, Exposing the Problem for Discussion, may be initiated by either students or teachers. It may take the form of a confronting situation or simply a question. In either case what follows should be an open,

17 *Ibid.,* pp. 124–27.

honest discussion clarifying and reacting to the problem. Glasser began the meeting by asking if everyone were present that day. "There was considerable discussion, timid at first but shortly more frank, revealing that about eight students were absent and that those present knew that most of the absentees were not ill that beautiful spring day. When I asked whether some of the students present also frequently skipped class, many admitted they did."[18] The discussion continued, centering on the gains from cutting school, the problems it caused, the methods of handling truancy, etc. The students claimed that this was the last year they could cut school since next year they entered high school and would have to "toe the mark." Glasser challenged their rationalization.

In Phase Three the teacher attempts to get the students to make a personal value judgment about their behavior. In the case study, Glasser wanted the students to make a value judgment that going to school is worthwhile. Given the irrelevancy of much of the curriculum to their present and future lives, this point proved difficult to establish.

In Phase Four alternative courses of action are identified by the teacher and students. Inasmuch as going to school is a binary state, i.e., one either goes or doesn't go, Glasser's example doesn't lend itself to identifying alternative solutions. Nevertheless he did push the students for a commitment, which is Phase Five. He asked them to sign a statement promising to come to school the next day. Many students refused to make such a commitment. Countering, Glasser proposed they put their lack of commitment in writing, "If you won't sign a paper stating you will come to school tomorrow, will you sign a paper saying you won't sign a paper?" A third list circulated for those who refused to commit themselves in any way on the truancy issue. Commitment need not always be so dramatic or as overt, but it must be clear and recognizable both to the individual(s) involved and to the remainder of the group. This is necessary if Phase Six, Behavioral Follow-up, is to take place. Working with students until they fulfill their commitment is primarily the responsibility of the teacher but may also be a responsibility of the group. The recognition of fulfillment (as well as non-fulfillment) of commitment is also part of the behavioral follow-up. The group may choose to discontinue discussion of a particular problem, if the group's further attention to the problem reinforces rather than reduces the behavioral problem. Knowing when to continue or discontinue discussion is a follow-up skill.

## PRINCIPLES FOR REACTION

The teacher's behavior is governed by three principles. First is the principle of involvement; she must develop a warm, personal, interested,

[18] *Ibid.,* pp. 124–25.

and sensitive relationship with her students (as opposed to objective and detached). Second, the teacher though non-judgmental herself, must get the students to accept responsibility for diagnosing their own behavior, rejecting irresponsible behavior in themselves and their classmates. "It is important, therefore, in class meetings for the teacher, but not the class to be non-judgmental. The class makes judgments and from these judgments works toward positive solutions. The teacher may reflect class attitudes but she should give opinions sparingly and be sure the class understands that her opinions are not law."[19] Third, together teacher and students identify, select, and follow through with alternative courses of behavior.

## SOCIAL SYSTEM

The Classroom Meeting is moderately structured. Leadership, that is responsibility for guiding the interaction through the phases, ultimately resides with the teacher. However, the students may and hopefully will initiate topics for discussion and the whole behavioral change process may after many experiences establish itself on its own. While leadership remains with the teacher, moral authority rests with the students. The students express value judgments and make decisions; the teacher is non-judgmental.

## SUPPORT SYSTEM

The optimal support for this strategy depends upon the qualities of the classroom teacher. Ideally, she has a warm personality and is skilled in interpersonal relations as well as group discussion techniques. She must be able to create a climate of openness and non-defensiveness, yet at the same time guide the group toward behavioral evaluation, commitment, and follow-up.

## GENERAL APPLICABILITY OF THE MODEL

The model is specifically designed to help individuals understand themselves and take responsibility for their own development. This would obviously have latent benefits for all kinds of social and academic functioning, were it to take place. However, the primary application is to further personal functioning and it is toward this end that the structure of the model is developed.

## INSTRUCTIONAL AND NURTURANT VALUES

Glasser is primarily concerned with the general development of the student—toward a more responsible, integrated, responsive person who can direct and monitor his own growth. While he plans some activities, he depends on the development of a climate which nurtures responsibility,

[19] *Ibid.,* p. 13.

openness, and self-directedness. The Classroom Meeting Model (Figure 13-1) is thus primarily a nurturant model.

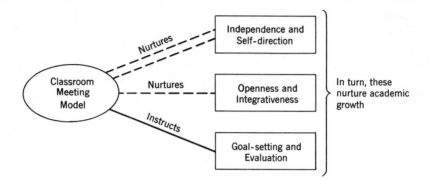

**Figure 13-1**

**TABLE 13-1 Summary Chart: Classroom Meeting Model**

| *Syntax:* | *Phase One* | *Phase Two* | *Phase Three* |
|---|---|---|---|
| | Teacher establishes climate of involvement. | Teacher or student exposes problem for discussion. | Teacher gets student to make a personal value judgment. |
| | *Phase Four* | *Phase Five* | *Phase Six* |
| | Teacher and students identify alternative courses of action. | Student makes a behavioral commitment. | Teacher or group provide behavioral follow-up. |

*Principles of Reaction:* Teacher's behavior is governed by three principles:
1. principles of involvement.
2. teacher, but not the class, is non-judgmental.
3. together with the class, the teacher identifies, selects, and follows through with alternative courses of behavior.

*Social System:* *Moderate Structure.* Teacher controls much of the action but in certain phases she shares the initiation or closure of activity with the students.

*Support System:* Chief qualities of the classroom teacher:
1. warm personality.
2. skillful in interpersonal and discussion techniques.

# 14

# SYNECTICS

## *A Model to Develop Creativity*

Synectics is an interesting new approach to the development of creativity designed by William J. J. Gordon and his associates. Gordon's initial work with Synectics procedures was confined to the development of creativity groups within industrial organizations, that is, groups of men who are trained to work together to increase their creativity and who function as problem-solvers or product-developers within the organization. In recent years, Gorden has adapted Synectics for use with school children, and materials containing many of the Synectics activities are now being published.

The Synectics procedure depends on a number of assumptions about the processes of creativity themselves and also on a stance toward group dynamics and its relationship to the development of creativity.

## ORIENTATION OF THE MODEL

### BASIC ASSUMPTIONS

Gordon begins with the important assumption that the creative process is not mysterious—it can be described and it is possible to train persons to increase creativity. "This assumption places Synectics theory in direct conflict with the theory that any attempt to analyze and train imagination, and those aspects of the human psyche associated with the creative process, threatens the process with destruction."[1] The assumption is directly opposed to those stances toward creativity which allege that by bringing a creative process into consciousness we would destroy it. By holding that creativity is enhanced by conscious behavior, it makes creativity amenable to description and thus to training procedures which can be learned and applied in a wide variety of settings.

A second assumption is that creativity or invention in the arts or in science and engineering are similar and characterized by the same fundamental intellectual processes. In other words, the theatre and the sciences are seen to be similar, describable, and trainable. Again, this goes counter to many people's beliefs that creativity in the arts is a special and mystical process which cannot be described or trained and which is quite different from the process of creativity in the sciences and engineering.

A third assumption is that the process by which an individual invents is directly analogous to the processes of group invention. This is an important assumption because it makes it possible to assume that there is no conflict between the way an individual will work alone and the way he will work in a group as far as the fundamental processes are concerned. This does not mean that some people do not work better alone than in a group. No doubt that is the case, but if the fundamental intellectual processes of group and individual creativity are the same, then we can study and train creativity under group conditions without feeling that we are violating the way individuals invent. More positively, the multiplicity of ideas and reactions generated as a result of the emotional and experiential diversity in the group will facilitate the initial development or strengthening of creativity in the individual so that he is able at a later time to function more creatively alone. A group following Synectics procedures can, according to Gordon, "compress into a few hours the kind of semi-conscious mental activity which might take months of incubation for a single person."[2]

The actual Synectics procedures are developed from a further set of assumptions or hypotheses. The first of these is that by bringing the creative process to consciousness and by developing conscious aids to creativity, we can increase the creative capacity of individuals and of groups—"creative efficiency in people can be markedly increased if they understand the psychological processes by which they operate."[3] If we teach people to understand what they do as they create, then we give them symbolic control over the process of creativity and thus the ability to increase their creative capacities.

The second hypothesis is that "...in creative process, the emotional component is more important than the intellectual, the irrational more

1 William J. J. Gordon, *Synectics* (New York: Harper & Row, 1961), p. 5.
2 *Ibid.,* p. 10.
3 *Ibid.,* p. 6.

important than the rational."[4] Nonrational interplay leaves room for open-ended thoughts, and it is part of the process which spirals up toward increasing coherence. "Ultimate solutions to problems are rational; the process of finding them is not."[5] Gordon does not by any means undersell the intellect. In fact, if one wishes to train persons to inventions in engineering, he assumes that technical competence of various kinds would be very useful, and that intelligent, well-educated people who can grasp the field are more likely to develop solutions than persons who do not have those characteristics. However, he does operate on this hypothesis, that creativity is essentially an emotional process, and that it actually requires elements of irrationality and emotion which capitalize on or enhance intellectual processes.

The third hypothesis on which Synectic processes are created is that "it is these emotional, irrational elements which must be understood in order to increase the probability of success in a problem-solving situation."[6] In other words, although the irrational is the key to creativity, it is assumed that the irrational and the emotional can be subject to analysis, and that this analysis can actually give the individual and the group control over their irrationality and their emotionality in order to increase their creativity.

## THE ESSENCE OF SYNECTICS TRAINING

After many years of working with creativity groups, Gordon was able to identify four interrelated "psychological states" that are present when an individual reaches breakthroughs en route to his final solution. These four states which he feels are basic to the creative process are: (1) detachment and involvement, (2) deferment, (3) speculation, and (4) autonomy of the object.[7] Unfortunately, Gordon also found that these states cannot be directly induced. We can't persuade a person to be intuitive, detached, or involved by merely naming or even describing these complex activities. The goal of Synectics theorists, then, was to design procedures which would draw individuals into the "psychological states" necessary to bring about creative activity.

The basic mechanism for generating creativity is metaphoric activity. Metaphor introduces conceptual distance between the student and the subject matter which is conducive to innovation and imagination, to breaking set! It provides the freedom and the structure for moving into creativity. Analyzing the adequacy of the metaphor forces the individual into seeing familiar situations in new contexts and from new viewpoints. But the creative state is also helpful for getting unfamiliar topics or problems under control and internalized. That is, a familiar analogy puts unfamiliar subject-matter

4 *Ibid.*
5 *Ibid.*, p. 11.
6 *Ibid.*, p. 6.
7 *Ibid.*, p. 18.

into a recognizable language so that it can be clarified and organized. The activities in this process are referred to by Gordon as "Making the Familiar Strange" and "Making the Strange Familiar."

Synectics procedures are actually built upon three metaphorical forms. The first is personal analogy and entails getting the individual subjectively involved with the problem so that he actually identifies with and feels that he has become part of the physical elements of the problem. It involves identification with a person, plant, or animal, or non-living thing. The emphasis is on empathetic involvement. Gordon gives the example of a problem situation in which the chemist personally identifies with the molecules in action. He might ask, "How would I feel if I were a molecule?" and then feel himself being part of the "stream" of "dancing molecules." Gordon notes that the application of the personal analogy demands extensive loss of self. Some individuals habitually are so wed to rigid inner control and rational behavior that any alternative behavior is anxiety inducing.

The second metaphorical form is direct analogy. This involves making analogies which are inclusive, though not necessarily identical in all respects, of the conditions of the real problem situations but which transpose them to another situation. For example, Gordon cites the experience of an engineer watching a shipworm tunneling into a timber. As the worm ate its way into the timber by constructing a tube for itself and moved forward, the engineer, Sir March Isumbard Brunel, got the notion of using caissons in order to construct underwater tunnels.[8] Another example of direct analogy occurred when a group was attempting to devise a new kind of can that could be opened so that the top could be used to cover the can once it had been opened. In this instance, the analogy of the pea-pod gradually emerged. Further analysis of the analogy produced the idea of the seam which could be placed a distance below the top of the can, thus permitting a removable lid. To use direct analogy, the Synectics trainees practice analogizing the conditions of their problems into new settings. This involves (1) selecting the new setting so that it will be productive (as Alexander Graham Bell analogized the problem of creating an earpiece for a telephone to that of creating sound within the human ear), and (2) working out the analogies in an attempt to generate problem solutions, as the canning group did once they came upon the pea-pod idea.

The third metaphorical form, compressed conflict, is a two-word description of an object where the words seem to be opposites or contradict each other. "Life-saving destroyer" and "nourishing flame" are two of the examples Gordon gives. He also cites Pasteur's expression, "safe attack." Compressed conflict, according to Gordon, provides the broadest insight into a new subject and maximizes the surprise factor. It is developed by an ana-

[8] *Ibid.,* pp. 40–41.

lytical process and requires the subject to observe the object from two frames of reference. A compressed conflict is developed from the traits used to define the characteristics of the object in the personal or direct analogy. Compressed conflicts reflect the student's ability to incorporate two frames of reference with respect to a single object. The greater the distance between the frames of reference (opposition), the greater the mental flexibility to creative development.

## CLASSROOM APPLICATION

In recent years, Gordon and his associates have turned their attention to the application of Synectics procedures in the classroom. Synectics techniques as applied to teaching embrace the following purposes: "(1) to increase the depth of students' understanding, (2) to use metaphors to link areas of substantive knowledge, and (3) to teach a method of hypothesis formation."[9] In other words, metaphoric activity can be used by classroom teachers to learn substantive information as well as to solve problems. In general, acquiring substantive information relates to the function of exploring unfamiliar content, and problem-solving relates to creating something new, i.e., a new perspective on a familiar phenomenon. "The metaphorical tool is not intended to replace substantive knowledge. Rather it is designed to enhance and enliven the substantive world by showing children how to interact personally with the world—how to bring into their own selves the facts and theories that would otherwise be external to them."[10] Metaphoric activity is designed to provide a supportive structure in which students can free themselves and develop imaginative insight into everyday activities.

The classroom procedures and materials employ the three metaphorical forms of direct analogy, the personal analogy, and the compressed conflict. However, in transferring the Synectics industrial techniques to the classroom, Gordon provides teachers with additional conceptual, instructional, and evaluative tools by distinguishing different qualitative gradations of metaphoric activity (or levels of involvement) for each metaphoric form. The gradations of strangeness provide the means by which we can further refine Synectics procedures and modulate our instruction according to the student's level of creative development. They also provide an evaluative tool for assessing the student's progress. We will review the forms only briefly here. A more thorough explanation and a plentiful supply of examples are provided in Gordon's work.[11]

[9] William J. J. Gordon, *The Metaphorical Way of Learning and Knowing* (Cambridge, Mass.: Synectics Education Press, 1970), p. 5.
[10] *Ibid.*, p. 4.
[11] *Ibid.*

The direct analogy, as discussed earlier in the chapter, is a simple comparison of two objects or concepts. Gordon points out that the comparison can be very close or very distant and that the usefulness of the analogy is directly proportional to the distance. The greater the distance, the more likely the student has come up with something new. Gordon has identified five levels of strangeness which can separate the inorganic-inorganic comparison from an organic-organic. For instance, an automobile wheel can be compared to the following objects that rotate as they move:

1. the cutter on a can opener
2. the rotor of a helicopter
3. the orbit of Mars
4. a spinning seed pod
5. a hoop snake[12]

Gordon provides us with an analysis of each of these comparisons in terms of the level of strangeness and comparative degree of imagination.[13]

Personal analogy emphasizes empathetic involvement. Gordon discriminates between the role-playing type of personal analogy and empathetic identification with inorganic elements. As in the case of direct analogy, he describes different levels of involvement in personal analogy:

1. First Person Description of Facts: the person recites a list of well-known facts but he presents no new way of viewing the object or animal and shows no empathetic understanding.
2. First Person Identification with Emotion.
3. Empathetic Identification with a Living Thing: the student identifies both emotionally and kinesthetically with the subject of the analogy.
4. Empathetic Identification with a Non-Living Object.[14]

Gordon and his associates have trained teachers to use Synectics procedures in all grades, with all kinds of students and in most subject areas. In addition they have developed a math and science curriculum, a language arts curriculum, and a social studies curriculum using Synectics principles. We are fortunate that the available Synectics material includes many excellent illustrations of the use of Synectics procedures in the classroom. As we examined the protocols which Gordon has provided, they fell into three categories. The first, Stretching Exercises, simply attempts to get the students to loosen up, to get familiar with and comfortable in metaphorical activities. These exercises are a series of short, rather loose comparisons to which the student is asked to make a verbal or written response. They may be direct analogies, personal analogies, or compressed conflicts. Here

12 *Ibid.,* p. 3.
13 *Ibid.*
14 *Ibid.,* p. 8.

are some examples that Gordon has used with students getting them to make a written response.

How is a beaver Chewing On a Log like a typewriter?[15]
Which is softer—a Whisper or a Kitten's Fur?[16]
Imagine that you are a spider who is trying to spin a web on a rainy, stormy day, BE THE THING! As the spider, what does the storm do to you and how do you feel about it?[17]
Delicate Armor describes _____   [18]
An example of REPULSIVE ATTRACTION is _____   [19]

The second category of Synectics materials illustrates a teaching strategy (as we use the term) which we call Exploring the Unfamiliar. Its objective is to increase the student's understanding and internalization of substantially new or difficult material.

The format consists of presenting (can be an oral or written experience) the student with the substantive material, then providing him with a relevant (familiar) metaphor. At first he is asked simply to describe the analogy and then to "Be the Thing." Next, he is asked to make connections with the substantive material and then to explain the connections. Secondly, he is asked to explain where the analogy doesn't hold. Finally, as a measure of his understanding, the student is asked to present his own analogy for the new material. The instructional mediator in this strategy can be the teacher or the materials themselves.

## EXPLORING THE UNFAMILIAR

The following illustration complete with sample student responses demonstrates the process of Exploring the Unfamiliar. The strategy, as we have described it earlier, includes a personal analogy. We feel that asking the student to "Be the Thing" before asking him to make intellectual connections will increase the richness of his thinking. The sample presented here does not include that phase.[20]

"In this example the student first is presented with a short, substantive paragraph:

Democracy is a form of government that is based on the highest possible respect for the individual. All individuals have equal rights, protected by law. Since each person has a vote, when the people so desire they can change

15 *Ibid.*, p. 13.
16 *Ibid.*, p. 17.
17 *Ibid.*
18 *Ibid.*, p. 19.
19 *Ibid.*
20 *Ibid.*, pp. 2–7.

the law to further protect themselves. The role of education in a democracy is critically important because the right to vote carries with it the responsibility to understand issues. An uneducated voting public could be led by a power-hungry political group into voting away their right to freedom. Thus democracy puts all its faith in the individual, in all the people...democracy's respect for the individual is expressed in the right of individuals to own property such as industries whose purpose is to make profit in competition with others.

"Next the student is told:

List the connections you see between the description of democracy and the human body. Certain elements of the human body are written in the left-hand column. In the right-hand column jot down the elements in the paragraph on democracy that you think are parallel.

| BODY | DEMOCRACY |
|------|-----------|
| each cell | each individual |
| muscles | education |
| brain | law |
| body as whole | democratic country |
| disease | loss of freedom |

.    .    .

"After the student has filled in his connection list he is asked to: 'Write a short paragraph showing your analogical connections. Be sure to point out where you think the body analogue fits and where it doesn't.'

"A sample response:

Each body cell is an individual. It may not look like it to the naked eye, but that's how it looks under a microscope. The muscles are education because they must be taught (except for automatic things such as blinking and digestion and there may be teaching here that we don't know about) to do certain acts; walking, games, knitting, etc. The brain is the law. If I do something wrong my mind tells me and my brain is in my mind. The body as a whole is democratic because it depends on the health of all the cells. When there is disease the body loses freedom and a power-hungry disease takes over. The body dies when the disease takes over all the cells.

Non-fit. In democracy the people control the government by voting, and they can always repair bad laws. You can't always repair a body that is growing older...it will finally die.

.    .    .

"So far in this sample exercise the student has been held by the hand. An analogue was presented to him, and all he had to do was make the connections as he saw them. The final skill taught in this exercise is *application*. The student's program tells him:

Now think up your own analogue for democracy. Draw on the non-living world to make sure that your analogue is not like the body analogue. Write your choice of analogue on the line below. If your analogue doesn't fit, pick a new one. REMEMBER that analogues never fit exactly, they are just a way of thinking.

Use this list form to get you going. Fill in the elements of your analogue and add more elements about democracy if you want.

Your Analogue
automobile                          democracy
each part                           each individual
education                           design of parts
car itself                          democracy
no gas                              loss of freedom

"In the final phase of the programmed exercise he is told:

Now write your connections in the best prose you can. First get your connective thoughts down; then go back and worry about grammar. Don't let grammar get in your way while you are trying to say what you mean. Grammar is a skill that makes it easier for your reader; so do it later. Try *not* to write more than the following lines allow. QUALITY not QUANTITY: Remember, show the fits and the non-fits."

"The student writes:

" 'All parts of a car are like the individuals in a democracy. When they are all in good shape they are free and the car runs well. The way each part was made was its education. God gave men the right to be free and God gave the car's engine the right to run—how the gases explode in the engine is God's gift. If democracy is neglected, then no freedom. If the car runs out of gas then no freedom.' "

"...one further small phase is necessary to make sure the students realize that analogues are not exact parallels...The student is told: 'on the lines below explain where your analogue doesn't fit.' "

A sample response follows:

" 'In a democracy, all the people must neglect the country. In a car it is the owner who neglects when he forgets to fill her up. Also I tried to find "profit" in a car—and couldn't. Any competition is a race in a car—not like competition in a democracy. Also, there are so many freedom laws in a democracy and the only law I can think of for a car is the science law that makes the engine run.' "

The Strategy of Exploring the Unfamiliar is decidedly analytical. That is, the original objective of increasing understanding is met by comparing and contrasting analogies. In the next strategy, which we call Creating Something New, the analogies are used to create conceptual distance rather than the closeness produced from comparison. Except for the final step in which the student returns to the original problem or task, he does not make comparisons. In this strategy the analogues are generated and explored for their own sake not for comparative purposes.

## CREATING SOMETHING NEW

The objective of this second strategy is to create something new, that is, to see familiar things in unfamiliar ways. Depending on the original tasks, this might include a new understanding, i.e., more empathetic view of a showoff or bully; a new design for a doorway or a city; new ideas for solutions to many social or interpersonal problems such as improving relations between the police and the community and fighting between two students, or dealing with a personal problem regarding How Can I Get Myself to Do My Math Lesson.

The format for Strategy Two consists of first, describing the present conditions ("If you were to design a city, how would you go about it? What might it look like?") and second, stating the problem or task ("All right, we have some ideas. Our job now is to design a city. Let's see if we can do this in a way that makes us go beyond some of the suggestions here"). Next the teacher rotates the discussion through a series of analogies, first direct, personal, compressed conflict, etc. ("Can anyone think of an animal?" Let's use the example of the jellyfish. How would you feel if you were a jellyfish? Now, you mentioned many things about the jellyfish and how it felt to be a jellyfish. Here are some of them. "Can you pick two words that fight with each other?") The teacher continues rotating the analogue until the students have moved far enough along in conceptual distance from the original problem. Then, she gets them to move back into the original task. ("Using the ideas we talked about in our analogies, how would we go about designing our city now?") Following is a transcript of a class in which the teacher is using Synectics procedures to get the students to develop unique characterization reflecting empathetic thought. We have annotated the transcript to illustrate some of the points we have mentioned.

> It is very important to understand the purpose of the following class discussion. . . . The goal was for each student to develop a sense of a process for going beyond stereotypes. The verbal descriptions produced in class acted as conceptual jump-off points for written work that expanded on these descriptions.

> Teacher: Do you have any ideas? Whom should we pump our life into?
> Student: Charlie Brown! (Groans from the class.)
> Student: Prince Valiant! (Groans from the class.)
> Student: How about a hood? A male hood? (Class likes the idea.)

Teacher: Where?

Student: Cincinnati.

1. Teacher: Now the problem is how to present this hood so that he's the hoodiest of hoods; but also a special, individualized person.

   Student: He robs the Rabbinical School.

   Student: Let's name him.

   Student: Trog.

   Student: Al.

   Student: Slash.

   Student: Eric.

   Teacher: His names don't matter all that much. Let's call him Eric. What can we say about Eric?

   Student: Black, greasy hair. They all have black, greasy hair.

   Student: Long, blonde hair—bleached—peroxided—With baby-blues. Eyes, I mean.

   Student: Bitten finger nails.

   Student: He's short and muscular.

   Student: Maybe he should be scrawny.

   Student: Bow-legged and yellow teeth and white, tight levis.

1. Phase One: *Describing the Problem or Present Condition.*

2. Teacher: Is there anything here that's original? If you wrote that and backed off and read it, what would you think?

   Class: No! Stereotyped! Standard! No personality! Very general! Same old stuff!

   Teacher: I agree. Eric, so far, is like every other hood. Now we have a problem to attack!

   Teacher: We must define a personality for this hood, for Eric.

   Student: He's got to be individualized.

   Student: He has to have a way of getting money.

2. Phase Two: *Problem Statement and Task.* Teacher is getting students to state the problem . . .

   and define the task.

3. Teacher: That's still an over-general idea of Eric. Let's put some strain into this idea. Hold it. Suppose I ask you to give

3. Phase Three: *Direct Analogy.* Teacher moves the students into analogies. He asks for a direct analogy. He also speci-

me a Direct Analogy, something like Eric, but it's a machine. Tell me about a machine that has Eric's qualities as you see him. Not a human being, a machine.

Student: He's a washing machine. A dishwasher.

Student: An old beat-up car.

Student: I want him to be a rich hood.

Student: A beer factory.

Student: A pinball machine in a dive.

Student: Roulette.

4. Teacher: You're focusing on the kinds of machines that Eric plays with. What is the thing that has his qualities in it?

Student: An electric can opener.

Student: A vacuum cleaner.

Student: A neon sign.

Student: A jelly mold.

5. Teacher: What is the machine that would make the strangest comparison between it and Eric? Go ahead and vote.

(The class voted for the dishwasher.)

6. Teacher: First of all, how does a dishwasher work?

Student: People put in the dirty dishes and the water goes around and around and the dishes come out clean.

Student: There's a blower in the one that's in the common room.

Student: It's all steam inside. Hot!

Student: I was thinking that if you want to make an analogy between the washer and the boy...

7. Teacher: Hold it. Just stay with me. Don't look backward and make an analogical comparison too soon...and now is probably too soon.

fies the nature of the analogy, i.e., a machine, in order to assure getting one of some distance (organic-inorganic comparison).

4. Teacher reflects to students what they are doing so that they can be pushed to more creative analogies.

5. Teacher lets students select the analogy to go with, but he provides the criteria for selection, "strangest comparison."

6. Teacher moves students simply to *explore* (describe) the thing they selected before making comparisons to their original source.

7. Teacher controls responses to keep students from pushing to a comparison too soon. No comparisons to original source are made before moving on to another analogy.

8. Teacher: O.K. Now, try being the dishwasher. What does it feel like to be a dishwasher? Tell us. Make yourself the dishwasher.

Student: Well, all these things are given to me. Dishes are dirty. I want to get them clean. I'm trying. I throw off some steam and finally I get them clean. That's my duty.

8. Phase Four: *Personal Analogy.* Teacher asks for personal analogy.

9. Teacher: Come on now people! You've got to put yourself into the dishwasher and be it. All she's told us is what we already know about a dishwasher. There's none of her in it. It's hard, but try to *be* the dishwasher.

Student: It's very discouraging. You're washing all day long. I never get to know anybody. They keep throwing these dishes at me, and I just throw the steam at them. I see the same type of dishes.

Student: I get mad and get the dishes extra hot, and I burn people's fingers.

Student: I feel very repressed. They keep feeding me dishes. All I can do is shut myself off.

Student: I get so mad at everybody maybe I won't clean the dishes and then everybody will get sick.

Student: I just love garbage. I want more and more. The stuff that falls off the dishes is soft and mushy and good to eat.

9. Teacher reflects to students the fact that they are describing the dishwasher, not what it *feels* like to be a dishwasher.

10. Teacher: Let's look at the notes I've been making about your responses. Can you pick two words that argue with each other?

Student: "used" vs. "clean"

Student: "duty" vs. "what you want to do."

Teacher: How can we put that more poetically?

10. Phase Five: *Compressed Conflict.* Teacher asks for compressed conflict as outgrowth of the personal analogy: "Can you pick two words that argue with each other?"

Student: "duty" vs. "inclination."

Student: "duty" vs. "whim."

Student: "discouraging fun."

Student: "angry game."

11. Teacher: All right. What one do you like best? Which one has the truest ring of conflict?

Class: "Angry game."

11. Teacher ends enumeration of possible compressed conflicts and asks them to select one. The teacher furnishes the criteria, "Which has the truest ring of conflict?"

12. Teacher: All right. Can you think of a Direct Analogy, an example from the animal world, of "angry game?"

Student: A lion in the cage at the circus.

Student: Rattlesnake.

Student: A pig ready for slaughter.

Student: A bear when it's attacking.

Student: Bullfrog.

Student: A bird protecting its young.

Student: Bullfight.

Student: A fish being caught.

Student: A skunk.

Student: A horse.

Student: A charging elephant.

Student: A fox hunt on horseback.

Student: Rodeo.

Student: Porcupine.

Teacher: Does anyone know where we are?

Student: We're trying to put personality into Eric, trying to make him more original.

12. Phase Six: *Direct Analogy*. Recycling the analogies; compressed conflict is not explored in itself but serves as the basis of the next direct analogy, an example from the animal world of "angry game." There is no mention of the original.

13. Teacher: All right. Which of all the things you just thought of do you think would make the most exciting Direct Analogy? (Class chooses the bullfight.)

Teacher: Now we go back to Eric. How can we get the bullfight to describe Eric for us? Does anyone know what I mean by that?

14. (Class doesn't respond.)

13. Teacher ends the enumeration of direct analogies. Again he has the student select one but he gives the criteria, "Which of all the things you just thought of do you think would make the most *exciting* direct analogy?"

14. Students are not into the analogy of the bullfight yet.

15. Teacher: All right. What do we know about a bullfight?

Student: He'll have to be the bull or the matador. I say he's the bull.

Student: Bull runs into the ring and he's surrounded by strangeness.

Student: They stick things into him and goad him...

Student: ...from horses and from the ground.

Student: But sometimes he doesn't get killed.

Student: And every time the bull is downgraded the crowd yells.

16. Teacher: What happens at the end?

Student: They drag him off with horses.

Teacher: How do they finish him off?

Student: A short sword.

17. Teacher: How can we use this information to tell us something about Eric? How will you talk about Eric in terms of the material we've developed about a bullfight?

Student: He's the bull.

Student: He's the matador.

Student: If he's the bull, then the matador is society.

Teacher: Why don't you write something about Eric in terms of the bullfight? Talk about his personality and the outward signs of it. The reader opens your story about Eric, and he reads. It is your reader's first introduction to Eric.

(Three-minute pause for students to write.)

Teacher: All finished? All right, let's read your stuff, from left to right.

15. Teacher gets students to explore the characteristics of the bullfight, the analogy.

16. Teacher tries to obtain more information about the analogy.

17. Phase Seven: *Reexploration of the Task.* Getting students to make comparisons; return to the original problem or task.

(Here are a few examples of students' writing.)

Student: In rage, running against a red neon flag and blinded by its shadow, Eric threw himself down on the ground. As if they were going to

> fall off, blood throbbed in his ears. No use fighting anymore. The knife wound in his side; the metallic jeers that hurt worse than the knife; the flash of uniforms and the flushed faces of the crowd made him want to vomit all over their clean robes.

Student: He stood there in middle of the street staring defiantly at the crowd. Faces leered back at him. Scornful eyes, huge red mouths, twisted laughs; Eric looked back as the crowd approached and drew his hand up sharply as one man began to speak. "Pipe down kid. We don't want any of your nonsense."

Student: He was enclosed in a ring, people cheering all around for his enemy. He has been trained all his life to go out and take what he wanted and now there was an obstacle in his course. Society was bearing down and telling him he was all wrong. He must go to them and he was becoming confused. People should cheer at the matador.

Student: The matador hunts his prey. His claim to glory is raised by the approaching approval of the crowd. For although they brought all their holiday finery, the bull is goaded, and the matador smiles complacently. You are but my instrument and I hold the sword.[21]

The media for creative expression are numerous. The products of Synectics need not remain conceptual and verbal. Students can "build" the window, paint the picture, design the city (while actually manipulating their concrete analogues), redo the script, film or picture, re-enact the role-play, or change one's behavior. Creativity applies to feelings, actions, pictures, and concrete objects as well as words! It is important, however, for the learner and the teacher to have the student's initial conception on some identifiable form. That is, discussion, painting, role-playing, and/or writing should take place before and after the metaphoric experience. In this way, the individual's new insights or understanding are externalized for his recognition.

## MODEL

### SYNTAX

Synectics principles, as we have seen, can be used in several ways. In developing a Model of Teaching we have made some adaptations in the format by distinguishing two instructional strategies with differing objectives, each having its own syntax and principles of reactions. However, the heart of both strategies is still the metaphorical mechanism. Strategy One is referred to as Exploring the Unfamiliar. Its objective is to help the student better understand and internalize new information by comparing and contrasting a familiar analogy to the unfamiliar material. In this strategy, Phase One is the substantive input. In Phase Two the teacher or students suggest a direct analogy. Phase Three involves being the familiar analogy (personal analogy). In Phase Four the students make connections between

---

21 Gordon, *The Metaphorical Way of Learning and Knowing*, pp. 7–11.

the analogy and the substantive material and then explain the connections. That is, they identify and explain the points of similarity. Next, Phase Five, they examine the differences between analogies. As a measure of their understanding of the new information, the students can suggest and analyze their own familiar analogies.

Strategy Two is called Creating Something New. As its title suggests, the objective is to produce something newer, a more creative viewpoint, a new product, a solution to a social problem. Unlike Strategy One, the metaphorical mechanism is not used for analysis but for creating conceptual distance. In Phase One the students are asked to describe the condition or problem as they now see it. In Phase Two the teacher states the task. Phases Three through Five include the rotation of analogies through the cycle of direct analogy, personal analogy, and compressed conflict. This may be repeated as many times as necessary. In Phase Six the students move back into the original task; how is the original problem looked at now?

## Principles of Reaction

The training agent guides himself by noting the extent to which individuals seem to be tied to regularized channels or patterns of thinking and he manipulates among and within the operational mechanisms in order to induce psychological states more likely to generate a creative response. In addition, he must display a use of the non-rational himself to encourage the reluctant student to indulge in a play-of-fancy, the use of irrelevance, fantasy, symbolism, and other devices which are necessary in order to break out of his channels of thinking. The teacher as exemplar is probably an essential of the method. Consequently, he has to learn to accept the bizarre and the unusual. He must be acceptant of all student responses in order to ensure that students feel no external judgment on their creative expression. The more difficult the problem is to solve, or seems to be, the more it is necessary for him to accept far-fetched analogies in order to help individuals break sets, and develop fresh perspectives on problems.

In Strategy Two, the teacher guards against premature analyses. He also reflects the students' problem-solving behavior to them by clarifying and summarizing the progress of the learning activity.

## Social System

The model is moderately structured with the teacher initiating the sequence and guiding the use of the operational mechanisms. He also helps the students intellectualize their mental processes. The students, however, have a good deal of freedom in their open-ended discussions as they engage in the metaphorical problem-solving. Norms of cooperation, "play of fancy," and intellectual and emotional equality are essential to establishing the setting for creative problem-solving. The rewards are internal. They come from the students' satisfaction and pleasure with the learning activity.

## SUPPORT SYSTEM

The group needs most of all facilitation by a leader competent in Synectics procedures. It also needs, in the case of scientific problems, a laboratory in which it can build models and other devices to make problems concrete and to permit practical invention to take place. In general also, it needs a work space which it can regard as its own, and an environment in which creativity will be prized and utilized.

In a classroom, all of these solutions can probably be brought about, except that a classroom-sized group is probably somewhat large for many of the kinds of activity which are necessary. Hence, smaller groups would have to be created for the purpose of Synectics training.

## APPLICABILITY OF THE MODEL

The method of Synectics has been explicitly designed to improve the creativity of individuals and groups. However, the implicit learning from this model is equally vivid. Participation in a Synectics group invariably creates a unique shared experience that fosters interpersonal understanding and sense of community. Members learn a great deal about one another as each person reacts to the common event in his unique way. Individuals become acutely aware of their dependence on the various perceptions of each member of the group. Each thought, no matter how prosaic, is valued for its potential catalytic effect on one's own. Synectics procedures manifest a community of equals in which simply having a thought is the sole basis for status. This norm and that of playfulness quickly give support to even the most timid participant.

Synectics procedures may be used with students in all areas of the curriculum, the sciences as well as the arts. In addition, they are useful for gaining new insights into human behavior and social problems and for reaching deeper levels of understanding into the dynamics of personality and interpersonal relationships.

Synectics procedures can be implemented in both the interactive teaching situation and in materials-mediated learning experience. However, because Synectics is a process whose creative richness is often supported and produced from the emergent ideas of the group, the interactive teaching situation may be preferable. It permits the teacher to update the programming and feed-back to the students: "Come on; you are not putting yourself into this object. Let's talk about what it feels like to be a tractor, not how you look." Dynamic feedback and self-correction are not possible with Synectics materials.

Synectics principles have also been applied at the curricular level. They have governed the selection and sequence of the content. For instance, Gordon has developed a sixth-grade textbook integrating biology, history, arithmetic, and music. Particular units employing Synectics exercises were designed. One compares the settlement of American colonies with the musical development of Beethoven's "Fifth Symphony"; another gets the student to draw comparisons among volcanoes, the American Revolution, and the development of numbers.[22]

Our student-teachers have worked quite successfully and enthusiastically with Synectics procedures in the classroom. They have found it especially suited to creative writing. Strategy Two seems especially applicable to children of all age levels with one note of caution. Moving back into the original condition or problem requires analytical thinking, an activity which is beyond the capacity of very young children. Although the final product has always been more creative than the original (it is quite useful to both students and teachers to have a tangible basis for comparison), the magnitude of creativity probably varies with analytical ability. We have also found that most students are quite unused to "play-of-fancy." It is probably best to move into a Synectics model gradually, first spending a few days on stretching exercises.

## INSTRUCTIONAL AND NURTURANT VALUES

As shown in Figure 14-1, the Synectics Model contains strong elements of both types of values. Through his belief that creative process can be made clear and communicable and that it can be improved through direct training, Gordon is led to the development of specific instructional techniques (as contrasted to those who feel that creativity is mysterious, personal, and can only be taught indirectly). On the other hand, Gordon emphasizes a social environment which encourages creativity and uses group

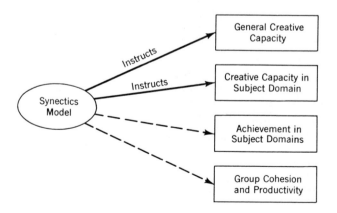

**Figure 14-1**

[22] William J. J. Gordon, *Making It Whole* (Boston: Synectics Incorporated, 1968).

cohesion to generate energy which enables the participants to function interdependently in a metaphoric world.

Synectics is applied not only to the development of general creative power but also to the development of creative responses over a variety of subject-matter domains. Gordon clearly believes that the creative energy will enhance learning in these areas.

**TABLE 14-1 Summary Chart: Synectics Model**

*Syntax:*

*Strategy One: Exploring the Unfamiliar*

| *Phase One* | *Phase Two* | *Phase Three* |
|---|---|---|
| Substantive Input. Teacher provides information on new topic. | Direct Analogy. Teacher suggests direct analogy and asks students to describe the analogy. | Personal Analogy. Teacher gets students to "be the direct analogy." |
| *Phase Four* | *Phase Five* | *Phase Six* |
| Comparing the Analogies. Student identifies and explains the points of similarity between the new material and the direct analogy. | Explaining the Differences. Student explains where the analogy doesn't fit. | Exploration. Students re-explore the original topic on its own terms. |
| *Phase Seven* | | |
| Generating Analogy. Students can provide their own direct analogy and explore the similarities and differences. | | |

*Strategy Two: Creating Something New*

| *Phase One* | *Phase Two* | *Phase Three* |
|---|---|---|
| Description of Present Condition. Teacher gets students' description of situation as they now see it. | Problem Statement and Task Definition. Teacher states problem and defines task. | Direct Analogy. Students suggest direct analogies, select one, and explore (describe) it further. |
| *Phase Four* | *Pha Five* | *Phase Six* |
| Personal Analogy. Students "be the analogy" they selected in Phase Three. | Compressed Conflict. Students take their descriptions from Phases Three and Four and make a compressed conflict. | Direct Analogy. Students generate and select another direct analogy based on the compressed conflict. |
| *Phase Seven* | | |
| Reconsider Original Task. Teacher gets students to move back to original task or problem utilizing last analogy and/or entire synectics experience. | | |

# 15

# AWARENESS TRAINING

## A Model to Increase Human Awareness

Recent years have seen an explosion of interest in freeing the human being to develop more fully, particularly in helping human beings to develop more possibilities for fulfillment in interpersonal relations. For many, this quest begins with a recognition that most of us are only shadows of what we could be, and that somehow we have surrounded ourselves with invisible chains which keep us from reaching out and becoming more than we are. While there has been much attention to physical development, emotional development, personal expression, and other forms of individual development, it is in the interpersonal realm that the movement has found its fullest expression. This may be because many of those interested in expanding personal awareness have used interpersonal training methods even when they are concerned with personal development, or it may simply be that the interpersonal realm is more clear than the other possibilities. In any event, we have chosen to focus on a model described by William Schutz, especially in *FIRO: A Three-Dimensional Theory of Interpersonal Behavior* and more recently in *Joy: Expanding Human Awareness,* which emphasizes interpersonal training as a means of increasing awareness or joy (defined as the feeling that one is fulfilling one's potential).[1]

Since many of the therapists and educators who have been concerned

---

[1] William Schutz, *FIRO: A Three-Dimensional Theory of Interpersonal Behavior* (New York: Holt, Rinehart & Winston, 1958); *Joy: Expanding Human Awareness* (New York: Grove Press, 1967).

with awareness training have not wished to commit themselves to writing and have described their methods in personal or vague terms, it is particularly pleasing to find the amount of specificity with which Schutz writes. His explicitness gives us an opportunity to attempt to describe his model with some completeness and to compare and contrast it with other models.

Schutz has acknowledged indebtedness to many colleagues for many of his approaches, particularly colleagues from the Esalen at Big Sur in California, including Fritz Perls, George B. Leonard, Frank Barron, and others.

## ORIENTATION OF THE MODEL

### RATIONALE

Schutz leaves no doubt about the mission of his work. "The theme of this book is Joy. The theories and methods presented here are aimed at achieving joy. Joy is the feeling that comes from the fulfillment of one's potential. Fulfillment brings to an individual the feeling that he can cope with his environment; the sense of confidence in himself as a significant, competent, loveable person who is capable of handling situations as they arise, able to use fully his own capacities, and free to express his feelings."[2] Schutz feels that there are four types of development necessary to the realization of an individual's full potential. One of these is bodily functioning. Another he calls personal functioning (including the acquisition of knowledge and experience, the development of logical thinking and creative thinking, and the integration of intellectual development). The third is interpersonal development and the fourth is the individual's relationships to societal organizations, social organizations, and culture. It is on the third of these, the personal awareness of interpersonal needs, that we will concentrate in this chapter.

Within the interpersonal arena there are three basic needs which "form the basis for exploring the realm of interpersonal relations and the methods whereby full human potential can be achieved between man and man."[3] These needs are *inclusion, control,* and *affection.* Inclusion refers to one's need to be perceived, attended to, and given reasonable attention by others. Part of this need is manifested by one's need for identity, to know that one is distinct from other persons, and to know that one has an identity and justification in his uniqueness and at the same time that others identify with him and empathize with him as a fellow human being.

Control is the second basic need: "The need for control varies along a continuum from the desire for power, authority and control over others

2 *Ibid.,* p. 15.
3 *Ibid.,* p. 117.

(and therefore over one's future) to the need to be controlled and have responsibility lifted from oneself."[4] There is no necessary relationship between one's desire to control and one's desire to be controlled. One may combine both or tend toward only one. Some of us need to control others and also to be controlled by others, while some of us want control or want to be controlled.

Affection, the third basic need, "...refers to close personal feelings between two people, especially love and hate in their various degrees."[5] All of us have a powerful need to feel affection and to express and receive it whenever we are with other people. Schutz's methods are designed to help individuals recognize their modes of behavior with respect to inclusion, control, and affection, and to help them cope with both their own state of development and their participation in groups in relation to these three basic needs.

## THE NATURE OF THE STRATEGY

Schutz does not describe any overall conceptualization of the types of strategies that are used. Nearly all of the many activities he describes are depicted specifically rather than in generic terms, and nearly all are group activities which emerge into various forms, depending on what happens in any specific group. Generally speaking, however, the activities begin with a move by the teacher (counselor, therapist, group leader) who poses a problem, or gives a task, or asks a question designed to get the group or individuals within the group involved so that they will explore the area in question and begin to generate means of coping. All of Schutz's methods are group activities, or at least involve two people. Each activity begins with an exercise or a problem to be explored, or a task such as role-playing to be done, which provides the individuals in the group and sometimes one student, or client, or subject in particular, to encounter the area in which growth is desired (inclusion, control, or affection).

Hence, we have the name *Encounter Group* which is the characteristic type of socially therapeutic activity used by Schutz and most others who are concerned with awareness training. All members of the group are expected to engage either in the activity or in the discussion of it, and to help one another come to grips with the area and begin to develop coping behavior. The group leader or therapist may play an especially important part in this activity, but there is a strong emphasis on group responsibility and on the obligation of each individual to open himself up before the group to the extent that he is able to do this.

4 *Ibid.*, p. 118.
5 *Ibid.*, p. 119.

Emotionality of the encounters can become very intense, and it is impera-
tive that the group members accept the potential utility of this intensive-
ness and that they be aware of the fact that they will be probing areas of
great sensitivity with and in front of other people, and that frequently this
will be painful.

Schutz's account of an encounter activity illustrates the importance of
social climate and also the potential intensity of some of the seemingly very
simple exercises which are included in the encounter group.

"First impression. Specifically focusing on another individual while using
many senses helps a person to make contact. Ordinarily we are either
oblivious to many cues the other person gives us or we are reacting to them
unconsciously rather than consciously. One way of exploring these cues is to
begin a new group by having each member stand in front of the whole
group. The group is instructed to give a first impression, perhaps a few
adjectives, based entirely on appearance, preferably even before the person
speaks. 'Watch the structure of the body, the way the body is held, look
carefully at the expression on the face, at the way he moves, at the tension
and relaxation reflected in movement and positioning. Then go up and
touch him, note the feel of the skin—the firmness or softness; the size, firmness and tension of the muscles; the quality of the hair. Now push him or
have him push you and see the resistance or compliance. Then add more
adjectives or reinforce or amend the first ones. Now smell him.' How rarely
we deliberately use smell, but it is often the repository of memories (who
can forget the Prom gardenia smell), and may affect or impress in a way
of which we are not aware.

"After this first contact, group members may be allowed some time
together, perhaps half an hour, and then be asked to continue giving their
first impressions. This time several new features are added. First, group
members are brought into direct interaction with each other. Each person
is asked to give his first impressions of each of the other group members,
not only verbally, but by standing directly in front of the person to get a
much more direct awareness of his presence, looking him straight in the
eye so that his attention is more easily directed to the person, and touching
him in whatever way best expresses the toucher's feelings while he describes
his impression. This procedure makes the reality of the other person much
greater.

"This experience is usually a very emotionally involving one for both the
teller and the told, and typically brings the group members much closer
together. Often there is resistance to the touching. This follows from the
meaning given to it in our society, which interprets touch as basically
aggressive or sexual. Such an interpretation, of course, need not be the
case, but it does prevent warmer direct expression of feeling. A group
context can frequently release people to feel more comfortable about touch-

ing. If the resistance to actual contact is too great, a person may give his impression without touching."[6]

Awareness training, particularly the encounter group model, is presently enjoying a considerable vogue especially on the West Coast of the United States. It links with the desire by many people today to create in the automated, urbanized, alienated culture new ways of contacting people and learning how to grow with them. In terms of public schools, the method has not been used very much. Many people are suspicious of it, and many who are sympathetic to the encounter group model are suspicious of the possible effect it might have on young children. Other types of awareness training have also been tried in public schools. Important among the attempts is the experiment which was supervised by George Brown in the Santa Barbara area and is reported in the following section, "Classroom Application."

The encounter group model varies from one leader or therapist to another and from one group to another. Most of the advocates of this kind of model would resent its being sterotyped or confined into any given formula, and despite our interest in clarifying and coding teaching models we would not want to subvert their interest in keeping the process open and flexible. However, there are many similarities in techniques among encounter group advocates, particularly in the posing of a task to a group which involves exploration of an area in a warm emotional way, and in the extensive use of discussion in which frankness and open expression of affect are encouraged. There is also a common emphasis on unlocking the potential of each individual and capitalizing on the unique possibilities of the group.

## CLASSROOM APPLICATION

In a recent project on Humanistic Education, George Brown of the University of California and Esalen Institute examined affective approaches to education and analyzed their potential for integration into the conventional curriculum.[7] In addition to inventorying suitable awareness experiences and encounter group techniques, Brown and his staff trained five elementary and secondary school teachers and assisted them in developing and trying out lessons and units based on these techniques. The project report is replete with their annotated accounts of classroom experiences spanning all subjects, grade levels, and special learning situations. We can illustrate only a few of these accounts here.

[6] *Ibid.*, pp. 126–27. Reprinted by permission of Grove Press, Inc. Copyright © 1967 by William C. Schutz.

[7] George Brown, *Humanistic Education, Report to the Ford Foundation on the Ford-Esalen Project,* "A Pilot Project to Explore Ways to Adapt Approaches in the Affective Domain to the School Curriculum," 1968.

The first two exercises actually take place with one of the five teachers acting as trainer for other inservice teachers unfamiliar with encounter group activities. However, in both instances the teacher-trainer describes how he has utilized this procedure with his own high-school English class.

Mr. Hillman asked the members of the group to get up and mill about in the center of the room and, without talking, end up in groups of exactly four people. If there were five, one had to leave; if three, someone had to be found to join the group. The participants then discussed the process by which the groups were formed—what caused them to choose the group they chose, etc. Mr. Hillman related this procedure to his English classes' discussion of Crane's *Red Badge of Courage.* The protagonist of the novel enters and leaves several groups during the course of the story, encountering both acceptance and rejection. The use of this technique enables students to get more in touch with the hero's feelings. It was used again in connection with the grouping of the boys in the novel *Lord of the Flies,* illustrating how grouping is often unconscious. Becoming aware of what causes us to choose certain groups can give us some insight into ourselves.

The group was asked to complete, in turn, the statement, "It takes courage for me to. . ." (". . . look people in the eyes"; ". . . to have anyone touch me.") Mr. Hillman related this to his classes' discussion of *Red Badge of Courage* as a means for helping students understand the meaning of courage, and to personalize and humanize the struggle going on in the mind of Henry Fleming, the hero of the novel.[8]

Mr. Hillman continued the session with a "touch conversation." Grouped in dyads, the participants closed their eyes and carried on a conversation with their hands. They said hello, got acquainted, took a walk together, danced, got into a fight, made up, and said good-bye. He then explained how he had used this technique in the discussion of the lack of communication between the members of the Loman family in *Death of a Salesman,* showing the class through experience, that people can communicate in other ways than talking, and often much more effectively.[9]

Another core-staff teacher describes an account of the blind walk with her first-grade class. "In the blind walk, one person closes his eyes and is led around by the other who tries to give the blind one many different kinds of sensory experiences. After about twenty minutes, the partners switch roles, the leader becoming blind and vice versa."[10] The teacher used the technique to build trust and to help students discover things other than through sight. Excerpts from her report follow.[11]

*Blind walk:* We're trying to get the children to the point of taking a meaningful blind walk. I'm beginning to think the experience itself won't be nearly as meaningful as all the learning that will build up to it. We may not even get that far.

[8] *Ibid.,* pp. 4–8.
[9] *Ibid.,* pp. 4–9.
[10] *Ibid.,* pp. 4–10.
[11] From George Brown, *Human Teaching for Human Learning,* pp. 143–45, 150–51. Copyright © 1971 by George Brown. All rights reserved. Reprinted by permission of The Viking Press, Inc.

Jan. 9: Step One: Introduce Blindfolds

After much consideration I made blindfolds for the whole class. We have discovered great difficulty in keeping eyes closed.

On the first day, Peggy instructed the class to put the blindfolds on and to explore first only the rug. There was a lot of chaos, bumping each other, much more fun to explore each other than the room. There was a lot of peeking. Many wore their blindfolds slightly too high so that they could see well enough to run around. We let them try to explore the whole room and then let them go outside to the grass by our room. I would say about 5 children seemed to be really exploring the world without sight. About half were running around (most of the boys). About five girls did not like to wear the blindfolds at all. These girls were mainly the ones who always had to be "right." In their words, "good students." They seemed very afraid of the uncertain experience without their eyes. After about 20 minutes of exploring, we called them back in and talked a while about the experience. It seemed that most of the children did not like it. Many found the blindfolds uncomfortable.

I feel that many negative responses were of a "me too" type—especially since verbal and physical response was very different in many cases. And the girls who really did not enjoy the experience are "stars" whose reactions are closely attended to by others in the class. I recommended more structure and a safer environment for the next lesson.

The following comes from that and again, Peggy is the teacher. I told the children to bring things the next day to "share and tell," things they could share while all of the class had on their blindfolds. That day we decided to start with a kind of structured experience before the sharing, which is usually first. I've forgotten exactly what I did; however, most of the kids did not like the experience. (I think I was trying to give them "mystery sounds.") Most of them peeked to see what I was doing rather than using their ears. By the time it was sharing time many of them did not want to wear their blindfolds any longer. I permitted them to take them off and not play if they didn't want to. About six started the sharing period with their blindfolds on. Some dropped out and others joined in as the period went on. After about 10 minutes the disorganization was too much for me to bear, so I collected all of the blindfolds and we went on with sharing without the blindfolds.

Insights: First of all, we're having trouble timing this new—maybe fearful—experience. I feel much was lost today on two counts. First, the period should have started out with them feeling, smelling and listening to the sharing objects, and then gone into mystery sounds if they were still with it. Second, the items shared should have been handled in a structured way—such as sitting in a circle and passing items from hand to hand, rather than one child doing it. Some of the problems were those of control. Perhaps items should be teacher-chosen at first. Another insight in regard to children bringing things: be sure to include a teacher preview of the items so that they really do have a tactile quality to them.

I would like to try this: Have the children sit in the circle blindfolded. Give each child an item. Set up a sound signal. When they hear the sound, they are to pass the object to the next child. Do this only for about 5 minutes.

After the first two days, we just let the blindfolds sit. We left them out so the kids could play with them if they wanted. All during this time I saw evidence that they had been used during indoor recesses on rainy days.

Jan. 15

Today Peggy used the blindfolds again in a lesson. Most of the children wanted to take them. Only about three said they didn't want to use them. These three were easily persuaded to try them. I had the kids find their own space, lie down on their backs on the lawn, and put on their blindfolds and listen to the sounds around them. Except for about five or six who had difficulty, most of the classes enjoyed the experience.

Insights: Steps still needed. More experience with wearing the blindfolds and taking directions at the same time. More trust in moving without using their eyes. Perhaps instruction about how to move when you can't see. Finding and practicing a way of selecting a partner—someone you really trust. Demonstrating and practicing how to be a leader in a blind walk, how to protect and guide and show your partner what you want him to attend to.

. . .

Jan. 23. Blindfolds

We're still trying to get the children used to wearing the blindfolds long enough to experience feeling more intently.

I sat all the children around in a circle wearing blindfolds. I gave each child an item from the classroom—scissors, brushes, ball, pencil, chalk, eraser, etc. I asked them to feel each object. Try not to worry about what it is. Try to experience the feel of each thing. I clicked sticks when they were to pass the object to their right. (A good lesson in directions.) I continued to do it until each object was passed all the way around.

I was very impressed at how quiet the children were. The lesson was about twenty-five minutes, and they were interested and in good control the whole time. I whispered any direct statements to individual children. At first a few could not resist saying out loud what they had. This stopped after about the fifth object.

I stayed pretty busy picking up "lost" items. I was happy that the children waited until I could get them back to them rather than taking off their blindfolds to find them themselves. After that we discussed how some of the items felt, rather than how they look.

Jan. 24: Red Letter Day! Accidental Blind Walk

Since Monday several children have asked if they could do what Kathy and I had done. I sat, she was blindfolded, and I took her hand exploring.

Today we took the children out on the grass after asking them to choose someone they could trust. They went out in groups of two or three. Peggy instructed us to sit close to our partners. One put on the blindfold, the other directed his hand. I was working with two girls. They both put on blindfolds. I began moving their hands on things around us. Out of the corner of my eye I saw some movement. Upon looking up, I saw one girl begin to lead another on a blind walk. Others, who were sitting on the grass with "blind" partners, saw this, got up, and led their partners around. The area we were in was rather confined and not at all the area I would have chosen for this experience, and yet here it was happening. My mind raced through all the "little steps" I had thought to be prerequisites before we could do this, and yet here they were, leading each other all around—to the fence, to the pillars, walls, trees, drinking fountains, even back into the room and out again. I couldn't believe it. After about 10 minutes, Peggy instructed the children to change—those wearing blindfolds were to give them to their partners.

Away they went again.....

In another effort this teacher combined a literature lesson with body awareness exercises. She made the following reports of the lesson.

Oct. 24: Literature and Self-Awareness (Body)

1. Read *Somebody's Slippers, Somebody's Shoes*.
2. Talk about being barefooted. Take off shoes and socks.
3. Go outside and walk on:
    a. dewy grass (cold, wet)
    b. blacktop (dry, warm, rough)
    c. concrete (dry, cool, smooth)
    d. sand (rough, warm, stuck to wet feet)
    e. climb on Jungle Gym
4. Come inside and feel:
    a. rubber mat
    b. vinyl floor
    c. rug
5. Put on shoes while talking about feet.
6. Write stories—watch for drawings of feet.

While putting on his shoes, Mark yelled out, "Wow! I can really feel my feet inside my shoes now. I know right where they are."

I said, "Go draw a picture of your feet and show how they feel if you want to."

Reflections: Some boys, not necessarily the same as before, were very uncomfortable with this. They balked at removing their shoes and then refused to go in all the areas.[12]

An inventory of affective techniques and additional examples of sample lessons and units can be found in George Brown's recent work, *Human Teaching for Human Learning*.[13]

## Syntax

While there is seldom a clear structure or a clear phasing to encounter group sessions, they generally consist of two phases, the first is the posing of the task and its completion, the second is a discussion or an analysis of what has gone on. For example, with respect to the area of inclusion, Schutz describes the following activity. "All members of the group are asked to gather close together, either sitting on the floor, (which is preferable) or sitting in chairs. Then they are asked to close their eyes and stretch out their hands, 'feel their space'—all space in front of them, over their heads, behind their backs, below them—and then be aware of their

12 Brown, *Humanistic Education,* pp. A4–1–2.
13 Brown, *Human Teaching for Human Learning.*

THE PERSONAL SOURCES

contact with others as they overlap and begin to touch each other. This procedure is allowed to continue for about five minutes.

"Usually there are a variety of clear reactions. Some people prefer to stay in their own space and resent as an intrusion anyone coming into it. Others feel very chary about intruding themselves into another's space for fear that they are not wanted. Still others seek out people and enjoy the touch contact. Where one person is inviting, another may be forbidding and simply touch and run. Discussion following this activity is usually very valuable in opening up the whole area of feelings about aloneness and contact."[14] The activity, in short, begins with the arrangement of the people, and the instructions to them. Then they engage in the activity, generating experience and the variety of reactions that is anticipated. Next, discussion identifies the different types of reactions, and the participants are encouraged to analyze their reactions and those of others and to begin to probe into the area under concern and generate some ideas about their development in that area.

The leader presents the task, of course, but does not attempt to influence what the group members do with the task. He then participates in the discussion but more than likely in a nondirective role, attempting to get others to explore their reactions, and noticing their reactions as they compare and contrast with others. The activities from this point emerge from the encounter and are controlled largely by the interactions of the group, rather than being imposed by the moves of the leader.

### PRINCIPLES OF REACTION

The leader guards against over-intensity or over-exposure to any member of the group who he feels does not have the stability to "take" the action. However, in general he acts in such a way as to help the individuals obtain insights into their own behavior and to develop conceptual tools for describing their behavior, and thinking about it, so that they can manipulate it if they choose. The leader works to maintain openness at all times, both with respect to his own acceptance of feelings and ideas from others and the other group members' acceptance of feelings and ideas from their fellows. He attempts to communicate a climate of directness and honesty and of an uninhibited exploration of one's feelings and reactions.

### SOCIAL SYSTEM

The encounter group is really a social encounter which is all-dependent on the social climate that is generated—a willingness to explore oneself; a sense of responsibility in assisting others to explore themselves; an open-

14 Schutz, *Joy: Expanding Human Awareness*, p. 123. Reprinted by permission of Grove Press, Inc. Copyright © 1967 by William C. Schutz.

ness for interaction over issues, however intimate they may turn out to be; a considerateness of one's own need for growth and others' need for growth; and, above all, a recognition of the shared need for men to work together to improve their possibilities as individuals and as groups.

## APPLICABILITY OF THE MODEL

Awareness training is specifically designed to help people realize themselves more fully. The type of group encounter model which has been described here bears similarities to laboratory method or T-group work, and some practitioners of both use methods from each more or less interchangeably. However, the primary purpose of awareness training is to open up to the individual his possibilities for development, for increasing his awareness of the universe and his possibilities in it, his awareness of the possibilities of interpersonal relations he might have with people. It is designed to begin to enable him to cope with dimensions of his behavior which can open up potential to him. In the examples we have given here, the styles of behavior which are to be opened up relate to interpersonal relations and focus on inclusiveness, control, and affection.

Very few awareness trainers would want to employ their models to teach school subjects. Nearly all of them, however, would admit that awareness training, through improving the functioning of the individual, would probably lead to increased school learning among its other beneficial effects. However, the model is to focus on opening people up for greater personal development and the subject-matter agenda would subvert this purpose. An organization characterized by awareness training activities would be likely to be a more effective organization, as well as a more humane one, for the individuals in it would be able to work out their problems more fully. Awareness trainers on the whole are frankly Messianic. As Schutz says in the closing of *Joy,* "More and more we can enjoy other people, learn to work and play with them, to love and fight with them, to touch them, to give and take with them, to be with them contentedly or to be happily alone, to lead or to follow them, to create with them. In our institutions, our organizations, the establishment—even these we are learning to use for our own joy. Our institutions can be improved, can be used to enhance and support individual growth, can be reexamined and redesigned to achieve the fullest measure of human realization. All these things are coming. None are here, but they are closer. Closer than ever before."[15]

### INSTRUCTIONAL AND NURTURANT VALUES

The awareness trainer does not avoid direct instruction deliberately, but he uses training devices that are extremely nondirective. As illustrated in

[15] *Ibid.,* p. 223. Reprinted by permission of Grove Press, Inc. Copyright © 1967 by William C. Schutz.

Figure 15-1, encounters open up to the "student" the possibility of development, but they do not lead him precisely toward pre-selected goals—he grows as he can in directions greatly determined by his readiness and his wishes.

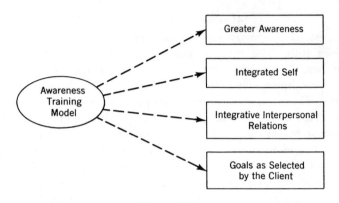

**Figure 15-1**

**TABLE 15-1 Summary Chart: Awareness Training Model**

| *Syntax:* | *Phase One* | *Phase Two* |
|---|---|---|
| | Posing and completing task. | Discussion or analysis of Phase One. |
| *Principles of Reaction:* | Instructor: 1. Guards against over-intensity. 2. Helps individuals gain insight into their own behavior and develop conceptual tools. 3. Attempts to maintain openness and honesty at all times with respect to himself and group-member feelings. | |
| *Social System:* | Characterized by norms of mutuality, trust, and openness. How to moderate external structure is provided by the task sequences. | |
| *Support System:* | Teacher who is characterized by personal openness and who has the requisite interpersonal and intrapersonal skills. | |

# SUMMARY

## The Personal Sources

One of the distinctive characteristics of the personal sources is that educational output is emergent—it is not specified for the student but takes shape as he selects goals or forms his own personality. Thus, the teacher creates an environment designed to help the student actualize himself instead of an environment that shapes the student in specified ways.

The personal sources are quite demanding of teachers because each of them provides for a complex environment—one in which the interpersonal or conceptual structure is constantly being negotiated by teacher and student—and each source has a definite view about the conditions facilitating personal growth. Because of this, reactions to the personal models are often polarized. Perhaps no family, except the behavior modification group, results in such acrimonious debate between advocates and detractors. The emphasis on a facilitative, idiosyncratic environment appeals greatly to some and annoys others to distraction.

As we have attempted to help young teachers understand and to work within the personal sources models, we have been particularly interested in the relationship between the preferred teaching styles and value orientations of teachers, and their appreciation for and ability to learn the personal models. Especially because our recent research has indicated that teaching styles are becoming more individualized, it seemed likely that personality would be an important factor in appreciating and learning these models.[1]

[1] For examples, see David Hunt and Bruce Joyce, "Teacher Trainee Personality and Initial Teaching Style," *American Educational Research Journal,* 1967, 4, 253–59; and P. D. Murphy and M. M. Brown, "Conceptual Systems and Teaching Styles," *American Educational Research Journal,* 1970, 7, 529–40.

Our evidence thus far is mixed. One group of students who preferred the Awareness Training Model explored it deeply, and experimented widely with children. This group was composed largely of persons with a preference for low structure in general and strong leanings toward affective development.

On the other hand, the Synectics Model with its moderate structure, more so than any other model described here, has proved to be enormously popular with a wide range of students and they have found many applications for it. It appears to be a good model to help teachers who ordinarily would not select the personal models, to begin to explore them.

The most difficult technical aspect of learning the personal models is that they require great restraint and great sensitivity to the students. In all these approaches one explores his student, observing him, and listening to him, and then moves to help him explore himself and reach out toward growth. The models are nurturant and their effects are gradual, depending less on specific instructional effects than on slow but basic changes in the student. The teacher "feels" the texture of the students' life, modulating his behavior so that the environment gently facilitates the students' development. This is extremely difficult under normal classroom conditions. Yet entire schools have operated for years on personal models (The Bank Street School, for example) and these models have probably had their widest application with the most difficult population to teach—very young children.

Confusion often occurs among teachers trying personal models for the first time. The confusion comes from too shallow an understanding of the belief that helping the learner to find his own direction will result in greater learning than if he is directed toward goals and activities selected by others. The confusion manifests itself when the teacher, operating under that belief, is disappointed when students do not choose the directions or activities which he would have chosen. The personal models nurture personal capacity and independence and they depend on a low degree of control over specific objectives and activities.

# IV

# Behavior Modification

## as a

## Source

# INTRODUCTION

## *The External Environment*

Behavior modification had its major origin in the work of B. F. Skinner and other "behavior shaping" or S-R psychologists.[1] The work of these men is historically related to the early psychological studies into conditioning and the other mechanisms by which animal and human behavior becomes shaped into certain patterns. These psychologists conceptualized the conditioning process primarily in terms of stimulus and reinforcement, hence the term S-R psychology. They studied the variable of reinforcement asking such questions as: What is it that increases the probability of certain responses? Can reinforcement be scheduled? Are certain schedules more effective than others for certain purposes? They looked at the nature of the stimulus and wondered if the stimulus could be controlled and in conjunction with appropriate reinforcement could shape behavior systematically. They also looked at the function of feedback or knowledge of correct or incorrect results, in reinforcing behavior. Does a person who knows what he has learned, for example, reinforce himself? Is feedback a sufficient reinforcer or are additional reinforcers needed to elicit particular behavior? These psychologists have also studied the role of practice—how much and what kind.

Behavior modification theorists seek to establish a science of behavior. This aim proceeds from the assumption that human behavior is lawful and is subject to external variables, variables that lie outside the organism

[1] B. F. Skinner, *Verbal Behavior* (New York: Appleton-Century-Crofts, 1957).

in its immediate environment and personal history. The attention to external variables possesses distinct advantages, particularly for the educator. One does not have to imagine an inner agent or process (i.e., thinking, understanding) inaccessible to observation and manipulation, yet responsible for human behavior, and one can concentrate instead on visible learner behavior and manipulable environmental variables. The task of the psychologist is to discover what kinds of environmental variables affect behavior in which ways. The educator can apply the findings directly to his work— changing variables in order to change behavior. The leverage of external control can also be given to the individual; if the teacher can by appropriate techniques control the external variables, so can the student. In this sense, a deterministic formulation can free human beings by increasing the possibilities for self-control.

Implicit in Skinner's analysis is the notion that behavior is an observable, identifiable phenomenon, functionally related to external variables. In more scientific terms, behavior is the dependent variable; the external causes of behavior are the independent variables. Thus, one can account for behavior in terms of the manipulable, external conditions of which it is a function. If these conditions can be changed, then behavior can be changed. In educational terminology, learning acquires a new meaning. Rather than speaking of the acquisition of subject matter, one now refers to the bringing of behavior under environmental control. For example, learning to play the piano (the behavior) is under the control of the printed music (the subject matter). In the case of learning to drive an automobile, the behavior of driving is under the control of the road signs, the stop lights, other automobiles, etc. The teacher's task, then, is one of "establishing a complex class of behaviors and of bringing the class of behaviors under the control of particular features of the environment."[2]

The instructional model drawn from Learning Theory and the one we present here is the Operant Conditioning Model. The basic model is widely used for Programmed Instruction materials and can be used in the face-to-face interactive teaching situation for what we call Behavior Modification. (In the broad and learning-theory sense, both exemplify modification of behavior, but behavior has the more common usage in the latter.) In the model we focus on both of these applications.

---

2 Edward J. Green, *The Learning Process and Programmed Instruction* (New York: Holt, Rinehart & Winston, 1962), p. 1.

# 16

# OPERANT CONDITIONING

The person most responsible for applying behavioral principles to education is B. F. Skinner, whose Theory of Operant Conditioning provided the basis for programmed instruction.[1]

The Theory of Operant Conditioning represents the process by which human behavior becomes shaped into certain patterns by external forces. The theory assumes that any process or activity has observable manifestations and can be behaviorally defined, that is, defined in terms of observable behavior. Either or both of the theory's two major operations, reinforcement and stimulus-control, are emphasized in the educational applications of operant conditioning theory.

After describing and defining the basic elements of the theory, we will examine those operations by which behavior is changed. To complete the transition from laboratory to classroom, we will recast common learning activities in behavioral terms and then examine two classroom illustrations of the model. Finally, we will present the model in terms of our descriptive framework and then discuss its applicability and related issues.

## ORIENTATION OF THE MODEL

### THEORETICAL BACKGROUND

Conditioning refers to the process of increasing the probability of occurrence of existing or new behavior in an individual by means of reinforce-

[1] B. F. Skinner, *Verbal Behavior* (New York: Appleton-Century-Crofts, 1957).

ment. In *operant* conditioning the response (behavior) *operates* upon the environment to generate consequences. The consequences are contingent upon the emission of a response, and they are reinforcing. For example, the response "Pass the butter" operates upon the environment, another person, to obtain the butter. The response is reinforced by the receipt of the butter. In other words, the probability that a future desire for butter will elicit the same response is increased by its initial success. The introduction of an appropriate stimulus will also increase response probability. When a parent throws a small ball to a young child after he says "ball," the probability of the word "ball" being emitted is increased. In this case the physical object serves as a prior stimulus to the response "ball" which is reinforced by a mother's smile, nod or "That's right," and receiving the ball itself. These examples of operant conditioning may be represented by the following paradigm:

$$\text{Stimulus} \longrightarrow \text{Response} \longrightarrow \text{Reinforcement}$$

or

Reinforcing Stimuli

The stimulus and reinforcement are independent variables upon which the response is dependent. As Skinner phrases it "...the stimulus acting prior to the emission of the response, sets the occasion upon which the response is likely to be reinforced."[2] A stimulus is "any condition, event or change in the environment of an individual which produces a change in behavior."[3] It may be verbal (oral and written) or physical. A response may be defined as a unit of behavior. It is the basic unit upon which complex performances or response repertoires are built. Response repertoires consist of many kinds of responses which are functionally related (as in the solution of a long division problem).[4] The response is an ever changing, somewhat artificial unit of behavior. In a classroom the condition upon which reinforcement will occur depends upon the standard set by the teacher. With skill development, for instance, a poor writing performance is acceptable for the beginner. However, with increasing practice the teacher expects greater accuracy. In mathematics the teacher may on one occasion accept the response "Triangle" and later accept only "Isosceles triangle" as a response to the same stimulus. Obviously, the behavior which is ultimately desired does not come forth in the first stages but is the result of a continuous shaping process executed by changing the contingencies of reinforcement. The initial response must exist in some strength in the individual repertoire; the task of the instructor is to build more complex patterns of responses from this initial response by changing the contingencies of reinforcement. Since

---

[2] *Ibid.,* p. 81.

[3] Julian Taber, Robert Glaser, and H. Schaeffer Halmuth, *Learning and Programmed Instruction* (Reading, Mass.: Addison-Wesley, 1965), p. 16.

[4] *Ibid.,* p. 18.

behavior is a continuous activity, its breakdown into identifiable units to facilitate analysis is necessarily somewhat artificial, but is useful, especially when simple responses must be built into more complex ones.

According to Skinner, reinforcement must immediately follow a response if it is to be effective. Delayed reinforcement is much less effective in modifying behavior. This contrasts sharply with the current educational practice of testing students and returning the papers several days later. It also underscores a difficulty in the teacher-centered classroom. (How, for instance, can one person reflectively reinforce 30 different patterns of behavior?)

## THEORETICAL OPERATIONS

We must now examine the paradigm in action, the operations related to the two variables within the teacher's management—reinforcement and stimulus control.

### Reinforcement

Reinforcement lies at the heart of Operant Conditioning, for without it behavior cannot be brought under stimulus control. Four important aspects of reinforcement are relevant to training: (1) its general nature, (2) the kinds of reinforcement which can be employed, (3) possible schedules of reinforcement, and (4) the effects of lack of reinforcement.

THE NATURE OF REINFORCEMENT. Unlike primary reinforcement (as reinforcing the value of food for hunger), most reinforcement used in education or training is secondary or learned. Money, affection, approval, and attention are appropriate examples. Another major secondary reinforcer within the educator's control is *confirmation* or knowledge of results. Knowing that you have behaved correctly or adequately is highly reinforcing. Self-instructional programmed material is sequenced by such small steps as to virtually ensure correct responses and the subsequent reinforcement the learner derives from knowledge of his correctness.

Often merely controlling the environment, such as turning a page after reading its contents, stimulates continued activity. (Part of the attraction of teaching machines as disseminators of programmed material is the reinforcement quality of mechanical manipulation. One can design a teaching machine to encourage many satisfying actions.)

REINFORCEMENT MAY BE EITHER POSITIVE OR NEGATIVE. Both kinds increase response probability though they differ in their mode of operation. Positive reinforcement entails an addition to the situation (approval for instance); negative reinforcement removes something from the situation (possibly by adding something disagreeable). Punishment which decreases response probability presents a negative reinforcer (aversive stimuli), or removes a prior positive reinforcer. The present-day school system is built upon aversive control—students are threatened with reprisals if they do not learn. Years ago it was the birch rod; today the aversive stimuli are more subtle (poor grades, disapproval) but no less present.[5] Punishment suffers from several drawbacks. First, since its effects are temporary, punished behavior is likely to reoccur. Second, the aversive stimuli used in punishment may generate unwanted emotions such as predispositions to escape or retaliate and disabling anxieties.[6]

REINFORCEMENT SCHEDULES. The effectiveness of reinforcement programs is determined not only by establishing close temporal relation between reinforcement and behavior and by the type of reinforcement selected, but also by the scheduling or frequency of reinforcement. In Skinner's opinion, reinforcement should be as continuous as possible, occurring after every response. Research on reinforcement schedules shows that continuous reinforcement contributes to the most rapid *acquisition* of behavior but does not engender the most retention strength. A variable ratio schedule in which reinforcement is contingent on the number of responses and is administered irregularly creates the most durable response levels.

We may ask what happens when a response goes unreinforced? Should this occur, the response will become less and less frequent until it is extinguished. Extinction differs from forgetting in that with forgetting the effect of conditioning is passively lost through the passage of time rather than actively through the non-reinforcement of an emitted response.

*Stimulus Control*

Stimulus control is particularly important in a classroom in which the primary instructional objective is to bring the students' behavior under the control of the subject-matter stimulus. Stimulus discrimination is perhaps the most fundamental process in the learning situation. When we respond differently to different stimuli, we are distinguishing or discriminating between the properties of the various stimuli. Most subject matter is brought to control behavior through discrimination training. For example, we have previously conditioned the response "ball" to the round object, ball. To ensure that the new response "ring" is not called forth in the presence of a ball, we must present the similar but slightly different stimulus and extinguish the response "ring" if it is made. In this manner, the control of the response "ring" to the appropriate stimulus is sharpened. Or a child may have learned to respond to the letter "d" and may then need to distinguish "d" from "b" and learn not to give the "d" response when "b" is the stimulus.

5 B. F. Skinner, "Teaching Machines," *The Technology of Teaching* (Des Moines, Iowa: Meredith, 1968), p. 57.
6 B. F. Skinner, *The Science of Human Behavior* (New York: Macmillan, 1956), p. 183.

A related process is known as stimulus generalization or extension of discriminative stimulus control. In this case, several stimuli possessing similar properties share the response control. The response "animal" is shared with many discriminative stimuli. The child learns to apply it to a few animals, then more, then all. In this way concepts are acquired that refer to classes of objects and events.

The apparent simplicity of the three-term contingency (stimulus, response, reinforcement) in operant conditioning is marred by the fact that "All sustained verbal behavior is multiply determined."[7] Multiple causation can be utilized, however, to promote stimulus control. By supplying supplemental stimulation in the form of prompts, response probability can be increased. Prompting in the theatre, in which the prompt is in the same form as the response, exemplifies formal prompting. In reciting poetry, the rhyme of the previous line thematically prompts the following line. Graphs or charts can be used as visual thematic prompts. Clever use of prompts can be invaluable in establishing verbal behavior. However, the terminal behavior cannot be considered established until all prompts have been withdrawn and the response follows the stimulus unaided.

## CLASSROOM APPLICATION

Unobservable mental processes with which so many instructional endeavors concern themselves are rejected in behavioral analysis. Behaviorally-defined processes are substituted for the unobservable processes. The behaviorist does not speak of "thinking"—he speaks of processes like discrimination and stimulus generalization. Like thinking, problem-solving may be broken down into its component parts, which then lend themselves to behavioral analysis. These include surveying the problem situation, stating a problem in its clearest terms, and learning "how to try." Problem-solving may be defined as ". . . any behavior which, through the manipulation of variables makes the appearance of a solution more probable. This definition seems to embrace the activities most commonly described as problem-solving."[8] When we have lost something, we may manipulate the environment by mentally retracing that day's activities or by physically looking in different places.

Finally, to the dismay of many idealists, creative thinking or original ideas normally associated with spontaneity or absence of lawfulness are submitted to behavioral analysis. "Original" ideas are simply responses which are not imitative or controlled by explicit verbal stimuli. In the case of metaphor, the connection between the response and the evoking stimulus is a tenuous one. "We reserve the term 'original' for those ideas

---

7 *Ibid.,* p. 211.
8 *Ibid.,* p. 247.

which result from manipulation of variables which have not followed a rigid formula and in which the ideas have other sources of strength."[9] The stimuli for such responses may be found in the personal history of the individual or may spring from manipulation of the material in the world about us. Creativity, behaviorally-defined, loses its mystery and is couched in terms of defined behaviors. Accepting the longstanding philosophical and psychological controversy over the validity of this interpretation of some educational objectives and this view of human behavior, let us pragmatically examine two classroom applications of operant conditioning.

## Programmed Instruction

Programmed instruction stands to date as the most extensive application of Operant Conditioning to human learning, and perhaps as the most highly developed application of learning theory in the typical school situation. Although Skinner's initial programmed instruction format has undergone many transformations, most adaptations retain three essential features: (1) an ordered sequence of items, either questions or statements to which the student is asked to respond; (2) the student's response which may be in the form of filling in a blank, recalling the answer to a question, selecting from among a series of answers, or solving a problem; and (3) provision for immediate response confirmation sometimes within the program frame itself, but usually in a different location as on the next page in a programmed textbook or in a separate window in the teaching machine. Examples of programmed material appear on the following pages.

Recent research on programmed instruction shows that considerable deviation from these essentials can be made with no significant difference in the amount of learning that takes place. Programmed lectures with no overt student response is one example. The original linear self-instructional programs in which each student is submitted to the same material though at his own pace were not sufficiently individualized for some educators. Hence, "branching" programs were developed. The idea in branching is that slower students, unable to correctly respond to a particular frame or sequence of frames, may need not only more time but also additional information or review of background information. The more advanced student could benefit by additional and more difficult material. At various points the branching program directs students to the appropriate material depending upon their answer to a particular frame or the number of correct responses within a particular frame sequence. Branching programs, like linear ones, have their variations. Some multiple-choice programs will automatically direct the student to a special section depending upon his

---

[9] *Ibid.*, p. 254.

choice. If he selected any of the wrong responses, his particular mistake in reasoning is pointed out; if he chose the correct response a more difficult example may appear.

Programmed instruction has been successfully employed by a variety of subject matters of which English, math, statistics, geography, and science are just a few. It has been used at every school level from preschool through college. Programmed instructional techniques have been applied to a very great variety of behaviors. Concept formation, rote learning, creativity, and problem-solving have all been the subjects of programs. Programs have even taught by discovery (leading the student to discover, which superficially is often thought to be incompatible with conditioning). How is programmed instruction different from the traditional workbook approach? Workbooks have been used by classroom teachers for years with no startling effect. Their emphasis, however, has been on practice (response maintenance) rather than behavioral acquisition through carefully sequenced material. Workbooks provided endless "frames" of review material. Obviously, review is of little value unless the behavior has first been successfully established, and the traditional workbook was not designed to do this. Second, the reinforcing effect of continuous review is bound to suffer diminishing returns. (The learner only goes over material already mastered.) Lastly, most workbooks made no provision for immediate feedback, supplying the answer only in the teacher's copy!

On the following pages we have included two examples of programmed materials. The first is an excerpt from a high school English grammar course and the second is from an elementary school arithmetic book.

## PROGRAMMED ENGLISH[10]

### M. W. SULLIVAN

1. Words are divided into classes. We call the
largest class nouns.
Nouns are a class of _____ .          words

2. In English the class of words called *nouns* is
larger than all the other _____ of words    classes
combined.

3. We call the largest class of English words
_____ .                                      nouns

4. You will learn a number of ways to recognize
and to use the class of _____ called        words
nouns.

[10] Reprinted with permission of The Macmillan Company from *Programmed English: A Modern Grammar for High School and College Students* by M. W. Sullivan, pp. 1–4. © M. W. Sullivan, 1963.

5. The words in a class are all alike in some way. All the members of the _____ of words called nouns have characteristics in common.  

class

6. You will see that nouns occur in special positions in English sentences. Any word that occurs in a noun position must be a _____.  

noun

7. Any word which fits the blank in the sentence
    "I saw the _____."
occurs in a noun position.
Can the word DOG occur in a noun position?  

yes

8. Any position which is occupied by a noun in English is part of a NOUN PATTERN.
    "I saw the (*noun*)."
This entire sentence is a _____ pattern.  

noun

9. When a word occurs in the noun position in a noun pattern, we say that it fits the _____ pattern.  

noun

10. When a word fits a noun pattern, we say that it FUNCTIONS as a noun.
A word which does not fit a noun pattern cannot _____ as a noun.  

function

11. When a word functions as a noun, we say it belongs to the class of words called _____.  

nouns

12. But a word may function as a member of several classes.
We classify it as a noun only when it _____ as a noun.  

functions

A word functions as a noun only when it occurs in the _____ position in a noun pattern.  

noun

13. A word which fits the blank in the following sentence occurs in a *noun* position:
    "I saw the _____."
We say that a word which occurs in a noun _____ in a noun pattern functions as a noun.  

position

Any word which fits the blank in the above pattern _____ as a noun.  

functions

Therefore we will use the above pattern as one test for _____.  

nouns

14.         "I saw the *book*."
In this pattern, the word BOOK is in a _____ position.  

noun

We therefore say that the word _ _____ functions as a noun.  

book

15.             "I saw the *airplane*."

Here the word _____ is in a noun posi-    airplane
tion.

16. Test the following words in the noun pattern
    to see whether or not they can function as
    nouns:
                              desk
        "I saw the _____." cat
                              stone
    Can these three words function as nouns?      yes

17. We use the pattern "I saw the _____ "
    to decide whether or not a word functions as a

    _____.                                 noun

18. Can the word BOAT function as a noun?         yes
    We know that BOAT functions as a noun
    because we can say "_____ _____ _____      "*I saw the* boat."
    boat."
    From now on, when several words are to be
    filled in, we will often indicate this with a
    series of dots. For example, instead of writing
    "_____ _____ _____ boat," we will write
    "............. boat."

19. Give the pattern which we use to test for
    nouns.                                        "I saw the _____."

20.          "I saw the _____."
    If a word fits this blank, we say that it can

    _____ as a noun.                       function

21. Which of these words can function as a noun?
                chair
                cautiously                         chair

22. CAUTIOUSLY does not function as a noun
    because we do not say "..................."    "I saw the cautiously."

23. Which of these words can function as a noun?
                hat
                usually                            hat

## BEHAVIOR MODIFICATION

Programmed instruction is an illustration of the Operant Conditioning
Model in which the emphasis is on stimulus control. With programmed
instruction the learning environment is fairly simple in that the stimulus
and reinforcement properties are limited and easily identified; the main
stimulus comes from the curriculum and the reinforcement comes from
knowledge of the correct or incorrect status of the response. When the
behavior-shaping paradigm is transferred to the more complex environment
of the everyday classroom, we find that numerous stimuli and known and

## INTRODUCTION TO SETS

Some children like to collect stamps.     1

Charles collects records. John likes to collect pic-   2
tures of baseball players.

Roger has a collection of model airplanes.     3

col *lec* tion        Roger collects model planes. He has a plane    4
col_____tion.

collec*tion*        Dick collects coins. He has a coin collec_____    5

collection        A bunch of flowers is a _____    6
of flowers.

set        Another word for collection is set. A collection of    7
stamps is a _____ of stamps.

11 From *Programmed Modern Arithmetic: Introduction to Sets,* by Jack Starr, pp. 1–3. Reprinted by permission of the publishers, D. C. Heath and Company, copyright 1965.

A collection of butterflies is a _____ of butter- 8
flies.

set

Set and_____ have the same mean- 9
ing.

collection

A collection of things is a_____ of things. 10

set

Each thing in a set is called an element of the set. 11
Jim has a stamp collection.

His World's Fair stamp is a thing or e_____
in his collection.

*element*

Each roller skate in a set of roller skates is an 12
e_____t of that set.

*element*

In John's set of train cars a flat car is an e_____. 13

*element*

In a set of cars, an element of this set would be a 14
(car/thing) _____. Choose the better answer.

car

| | | |
|---|---|---|
| dog | An element of the set of dogs is a(n) _____ | 15 |
| element | A cat is a (n) _____ of the set of cats. | 16 |
| element<br>set | A funny face is a(n) _____ of the _____ of funny faces. | 17 |

Here is a set of kittens. Pick out an element of this set 18
by drawing a circle around this element.

| | | |
|---|---|---|
| element | A cup is a(n) _____ in the set of cups. | 19 |
| books | A book is an element in the set of _____. | 20 |
| set | An element is one of the things in a(n) _____. | 21 |

282

unknown reinforcers operate to shape the behavior of the student. In this context, it is one thing to espouse a behavior modification strategy and and quite another to apply it! Operant conditioning in the face to face interactive situation usually entails greater emphasis on reinforcement and reinforcement schedules than on stimulus control, though elaborate situations have been created to effect both. It is possible, theoretically, to "program" in an interactive learning situation, but in practice it is difficult to establish careful sequencing on an extemporaneous basis and it does present some problems in terms of reinforcement. (How do all 35 students in a class differentially respond and get differential reinforcement?) For this reason, most interactive applications utilize reinforcement as a disciplinary tool rather than as a stimulus control for instruction as such.

In a recent study Michael Orme and Richard Purnell, with the assistance of two inner-city teachers, successfully employed these procedures to modify the out-of-control behavior of 18 students in a combined third and fourth grade classroom. The pupil behavior prior to the experimental procedures was described as follows:

> ...pupil behavior in the classroom was, for the most part, impulsive, aggressive and destructive. Neither T1 nor T2 was able to prevent pupils from taking apart their slatted wooden desks, tearing up classmate's papers, throwing books, yelling and singing. The noise level in the room was such one could frequently hear the class from any one of the rooms in the three story building.
>
> Aggressive pupil behavior was of central concern. In one twenty minute period T2 recorded aggressive acts in the classroom. She found that while not every child had acted as an aggressor, every child in the room had been struck by another one or more times during that period....
>
> Finally, the teachers were not able to stop pupils from running out of the classroom, through the halls, into other classes and offices, or outside of the school....[12]

Two of the objectives of the study were to reduce the kind of aggressive behavior described earlier, substituting more acceptable responses, and to increase the percentage of time the students spent on educationally related tasks. To accomplish these objectives, the researchers proposed to institute "total milieu control," that is, to apply teaching techniques which manipulate *multiple* aspects of both the stimulus conditions and the reinforcement program. The stimulus properties they identified included the surrounding conditions of the room, the curriculum, and the teachers' verbal and non-verbal behavior. The reinforcement program included the teachers'

[12] Michael Orme and Richard Purnell, "Behavior Modification and Transfer in an Out-of-Control Classroom," Paper delivered at the 1968 AERA Convention, Chicago, p. 4.

verbal and non-verbal responses to student behavior as well as a specially designed, elaborate token (tangible) reinforcement program. It is useful to have these various aspects identified but more important is how they were translated into instructional procedures. We can use the framework of the Stimulus-Response-Reinforcement Model to examine the specific instructional procedures used by the teachers.

*Stimulus Properties*

Surrounding Conditions:

Physical changes in the room were made to 1) encourage teacher movement, 2) facilitate teacher control, and 3) reduce extraneous stimulation. For example, the desks were joined together to form a U-shaped table which was strategically located to enable the teacher to control the door and also to encourage her to move from the blackboard into the U and over to the work table. All books and child art were removed from the room. They were replaced by content-relevant posters that were changed as the curriculum changed.

Teachers' Verbal and Non-Verbal Behavior:

The teachers were acquainted with the stimulus determinants of attention and were taught a variety of verbal and non-verbal techniques designed to elicit attention and curiosity, desirable behaviors that could then be reinforced. Some examples of these techniques are: presenting the content as a problem rather than a statement, rapidly shifting class focus, asking heuristic questions, enforced debates, non-verbal patterns such as silence or decisive movement patterns when shifting from one activity to another.

Curriculum:

The teachers selected their content with an eye to its "control" potential. For instance, choral reading and drama were used to teach English literature. This required a relatively high level of cooperative verbal behavior by the students and provided opportunities for teacher reinforcement. Another teacher selected a math workbook which lent itself easily to the token reinforcement for work completed. In another instance, a game was played with reading flashcards. This set up a quasi-competitive situation which assists in capturing student interest.

*Reinforcement System*

Token Reinforcement:

An excellent description of this system is provided in the study. Unusual problems usually require unusual solutions. To be sure token reinforcement systems are not a new idea; they are, however, perceived as unusual by a substantial majority of educators. Like other systems, the one in this study was set up in such a way that pupils could "earn" points by emitting certain specified behaviors. The points or tokens earned could then be used to purchase preferred back-up reinforcers from the "store." Thus, tangible reinforcers were manipulated in such a way that children's responses become contingent upon their prior behavior. The token system described here differs from those outlined in the previous literature in that the pupils shared actively in the determination of backup reinforcers. In addition, the range of store items available went considerably beyond the usual variety of consumables and manipulables to include educationally relevant reinforcers.

In view of the strength and frequency of disruptive pupil behavior, and the teachers' lack of reinforcement value in the classroom, the store included tangible items such as candy and gum. We could not be sure that the children would find more esoteric "reinforcers" reinforcing. Indeed, there was little or no evidence to indicate that they would be capable of delaying gratification long enough to accumulate any points. In anticipation of this T2 provided herself with a liberal quantity of small candies (they were not needed, as the children immediately set their sights on items requiring fairly large numbers of points).

In addition to several kinds of candy, gum, balloons, baseball cards, and the like, the store also included items such as: comics, selected novels and math puzzles, the opportunity to write poetry, a "conversation" with a computer (feed in disease symptoms for diagnoses), a short series of art lessons from a *real* artist, a model airplane together with instruction on aerodynamics, a ship building project, science projects and puzzles, field trips to several types of museums and art institutions, and finally an opportunity to attend a *real* lecture at a major university. Apart from the last (for which there were no final takers), each of the "items" above were designed to provide further in-school opportunities for individual or small group study. Thus, the student was given the opportunity to earn the right to select his own curriculum for a part of the school day.

All items were displayed on a table and a large white sheet of cardboard immediately above it. Trips, lessons, and projects were illustrated on colorful cards, together with their prices. Small suckers and taffy twists were priced at 15 points (the cheapest items). From there, point prices rose, with the highest priced items being the field trips and projects leading to preferred study. The latter ranged from 450 to 1000 points.

Upon initial exposure to the room all the pupils were given 25 points to spend immediately. This was done to impress upon them the reinforcement value of the points. Items were priced in such a way that if they purchased an item, they would still have 10 points left over. This meant they had only a few more points to earn before they could purchase another item. This was done to avoid short-term satiation effects, and to maintain a high incentive level.

Each pupil's name was listed on the front board. The recording and decision to give points was controlled by the teacher at all times. As the children came into the room, T2 began selectively dispensing points and continued to do this throughout the experimental period.

The system was explained briefly, and the point-getting rules were outlined on the side blackboard. They were: *Keep Busy All the Time, Have Good Manners,* and *Don't Bother Your Neighbor.* The teacher pointed out that these were very general rules, and that the next few minutes would be devoted to allowing the pupils to suggest specific things that they thought should get points. The teacher then proceeded to list the *do* and *don't* behaviors suggested by pupils. Throughout this discussion hand-raising, questioning (defining terms) and volunteered comments were reinforced verbally, non-verbally and with points.

Both teachers were trained to emit verbal and non-verbal "reinforcement" along with points on the assumption that the teachers' reinforcement value would increase through contiguous association with the point system. At the same time they were told to reinforce only when they really felt that the behavior in question was desirable or approximated some desired terminal pupil response.[13]

Teachers' Verbal and Non-Verbal Reinforcement:

The teachers were given training in 1) discriminating the pupil behaviors that would be reinforced (task behavior, silence, hand-raising, pupil attending to another pupil discussing lesson content, pupil-pupil cooperation); 2) providing positive and negative verbal and non-verbal gestures, teacher change in position reinforcement. The teachers were directed to ignore disruptive behavior by focusing on an adjacent pupil who modeled desirable behavior; 3) manipulating schedules of reinforcement.

The results of the study were very encouraging. The disruptive behavior so prevalent before the behavior-shaping procedures were instituted virtually disappeared, and the pupil time spent on educationally-related tasks increased from 50% to 80%.

The Orme study attempted to effect both stimulus-control and reinforcement properties. It is possible to use the paradigm in interactive situations, say to reduce deviant behavior by manipulating reinforcement and reinforcement schedules. That is, when students emit undesirable responses, the teacher can be aware of the reinforcing or non-reinforcing qualities of his own behavior and choose not to reinforce certain kinds of student behaviors when they arise and to reinforce others. The key is to make sure of the reinforcing or non-reinforcing quality of the teacher's behavior. Often

[13] Orme and Purnell, "Behavior Modification and Transfer," pp. 12–15. Reprinted by permission of the authors.

receiving any kind of attention from the teacher, though it may be of a chastizing sort, is a positive reinforcer in terms of the culture of the class.

## MODEL

The Theory of Operant Conditioning has extensive possibilities for application in interactive classroom teaching as well as in the construction of instructional materials. It can be used to extinguish objectionable behavior as well as to establish complex behavior repertoires under subject matter (stimulus) control. In either case the basic model remains the same. What differs is the number of units or frames necessary to establish the desired terminal behavior.

### SYNTAX

The first phase of the model consists of presenting the stimulus either verbally or physically to the learner. Thematic or formal prompts may be used in the initial stimulus presentation. They should gradually be withdrawn in subsequent instructional frames or units if behavior is to be considered established. In subject-matter control the Phase One content of one instructional frame should overlap with the content in Phase One of succeeding frames so that the response to one frame prompts or cues the response to another. The amount of overlap (size of step) must be individually determined depending on the background and abilities of the learner or learners. Presentation of the stimuli should also specify the form of the response, such as blanks indicating the number of words in the response. Possible responses could be presented along with the stimuli and the student could select the response from among several choices.

Phase Two is composed of the learner's response to the stimuli presented by the instructor or instructional material in the preceding phase. In a strictly Skinnerian program, the response must be constructed by the learner rather than provided in the first phase simply to be repeated or read by the learner in Phase Two. Active learning and recall, as opposed to recognition and reading, are essential characteristics of the learner's response in Skinner's original formulation. The constructed response may be either oral or written. The "correctness" of the response is determined by the instructor, particularly in skill development in which succeeding trials call forth the expectation of greater accuracy. Although subject-matter control presumes *a* correct response to a particular stimuli, there may be acceptable variations in wording.

In Phase Three the learner's correct response is reinforced or confirmed by the instructor or by the student's knowledge of results. For Skinner this would be immediate and continuous in order to maximize the efficiency of behavioral acquisition. As previously discussed, however, schedules of reinforcement vary depending upon one's objective, and maximization of retention is best obtained by a schedule which varies reinforcement. In applying the model to a disciplinary situation, the instructor may choose not to reinforce a behavior or to substitute a competing stimulus-response unit such as "Why don't you collect the papers, John?" (instead of talking to Charles).

## SOCIAL SYSTEM

Although the social system is cooperative and, ideally, most aversive stimuli have been removed from the educational environment, the instructor is the initiator and controller of the instructional process. Most of the reinforcement is intrinsic in the instructional model in the form of active learning and confirmation.

## PRINCIPLES OF REACTION

The teacher's principles for reacting and responding are carefully determined by the principles of operant conditioning and the selected schedules of reinforcement. The learning situation is optimally directed—each student response is teacher initiated and calls forth a confirmatory instructor response. In short, the teacher controls the student rather than supporting student-directed behavior.

## SUPPORT SYSTEM

In applying the model to the construction of instructional materials, the most difficult and most critical aspect is the design of the programmed material into an organized, logical sequence. Much preliminary work is required by the instructor prior to the presentation of a program. Fortunately, several fine references are available to assist the neophyte programmer with the details. At this time we will simply enumerate the various stages in program development.

1. Identify the terminal repertoire in terms of what the student must be able *to do*. Be specific, eliminating ambiguous terms such as "to know." Does "to know" mean "to recite," "to memorize," "to spell," etc.?
2. Identify the learner(s) and his (their) entering repertoire upon which to establish the new behavior.
3. Formulate criterion achievement measures.
4. Specify the content subtopics and component examples.
5. Identify subtopic relationships, i.e., overlap, similarities, differences, generalizations, abstractions, applications.
6. Sequence the component repertoire into small, overlapping steps (frames).
7. Design the terminal frame.

Prior knowledge of the student's initial behavior and command of the subject-matter stimulus is crucial for successful programming.

In the interactive situation, the optimal support is a teacher who is aware of the reinforcing and non-reinforcing properties of his behavior and who can modulate his behavior on the basis of this knowledge.

## MODEL APPLICABILITY AND RELATED ISSUES

The Operant Conditioning Model, despite the negative reaction to it in many quarters, has a record of successful performance in many fields. As one authority points out, "...programs do teach regardless of the kind of program or kind of learning."[14] The model's limitations lie not so much with the model as with the human beings who employ it or with the subject-matter which feeds it. It may well be that many subjects and many behavioral objectives require lengthy or complex programs too taxing for most instructors to design and/or deliver. Highly abstract subjects may be too costly to program, even commercially; highly subjective materials may be unsuitable for programming. To some critics the condition of controlled, externally directed behavior outweighs the instructional advantages. Subject-matter competence may be acquired at the expense of self-direction. In the realities of the classroom, conditioning and discovery are not mutually exclusive. Short programmed sequences especially suitable for concept formation, basic skills, and memory work can be designed by the teacher to supplement other instructional strategies. If these are self-instructional units, the teacher frees himself to handle the more difficult learning objectives.

Programming can be interpreted in several ways in the contemporary climate of individual choice and freedom. Some see the controlling instructional paradigm as antithetical to personal freedom. However, programmed instruction may provide for individual choices—situations in which the student can freely choose from among several programs. Programmed instruction is student-oriented in the sense that he controls his own pace. If the student does not learn (the terminal behavior is not established), the fault lies not with the student but with the program design. The program must then be revised to resequence the material, to allow for shorter steps, or to include more prompts. In traditional educational strategies, the teacher grades student; he is at fault; in programmed instruction the student grades the teacher.

Philosophical issues aside, an important but unanswered technical question in the application of the interactive instructional model to the classroom is, "In a classroom of 35 students, who responds?" This is a fundamental question because one of the primary advantages of mechanically

---

[14] Wilbur Schramm, *Programmed Instruction: Today and Tomorrow* (New York: The Fund for the Advancement of Education, 1962), pp. 11–12.

programmed materials is individualization. A student is free to work through the material at his own pace, going back to certain items if necessary. If a student no longer has the option, and, in fact, he only actively responds to one out of every 35 items, or if he proceeds at the pace of the others, how much value is left? Although programmers contend that the reinforcing quality in the design of the material itself eliminates traditional attention problems and research shows that covert response can be effective, classroom-administered operant procedures are not as neat and clearly useful as are those embedded in instructional material. Nevertheless, the Operant Conditioning Model seems to be highly durable and versatile. The enduring quality of its performance apparently withstands radical variation in its form.

Applicable to any subject-matter areas and a variety of behaviors, operant conditioning principles are equally appropriate for live instruction, curriculum planning, and materials design. Before leaving the model, we will look at some principles for interactive applicability simply to underline this process with concrete principles because so many of us teaching have difficulty seeing how the model is applied to our own behavior.

## APPLICABILITY: SPECIFIC

As in the Orme study, the teacher can design a behavior modification program manipulating both stimulus conditions and reinforcement. Following is an outline of the suggested steps for developing such a program.

### SUGGESTED STEPS FOR DEVELOPING A BEHAVIOR MODIFICATION PROGRAM[15]

*Preliminary Activities*

1. Directly observe the behavioral setting noting those things you want to take into account in the behavior modification (age, socioeconomic status, peer relationships, etc.).
2. Decide what behaviors you are going to deal with, i.e., academic or non-academic.
3. Label for yourself the specific inappropriate behaviors. The child or class can help you decide this.
4. Identify the behavior(s) you want to foster. If the behavior is complex and you plan to use shaping techniques, delimit the successive steps that will be reinforced as successive approximations, i.e., making a vowel sound, repeating the whole syllable, saying the word.

[15] We are grateful to Diane Cole of the Preservice Staff who provided us with this helpful outline. Other useful sources for designing a behavior modification program are John R. Neisworth, Stanley L. Deno, and Joseph R. Jenkins, *Student Motivation and Classroom Management: A Behavioristic Approach* (Newark, Del.: Behavior Technics, Inc., 1969); Charles H. Hadsen, Jr., and Clifford K. Madsen, *Teaching/Discipline* (Boston: Allyn and Bacon, 1970).

5. Decide if you are going to use an individualized program or total class involvement.
6. Choose the type and schedule of reinforcement. The kids can help decide the type of reinforcement.

### Phase One of the Model

Make the contingency announcement. That is, tell students what behaviors you are working on and indicate how they can attain reinforcement.

### Phase Three of the Model

Institute the modification program—reinforcing the learner's response (Phase Two).

### Evaluating Your Behavior Modification Program

Have the inappropriate behaviors decreased substantially?
Have the appropriate behaviors increased substantially?

## INSTRUCTIONAL AND NURTURANT VALUES

Behavior modification theorists explain nurturing *as* the shaping of behavior. The individual learns by interacting with an environment which shapes him by facilitating and rewarding some activities and ignoring or punishing others. When behavior modification theory is employed deliberately, however, it would not be consistent with our previous analyses to say that there are any nurturant effects since the theory provides for the deliberate arrangement of the environment to produce pre-selected effects. Hence, strictly speaking, we have to describe behavior modification as entirely instructional. When possible, goals are specified and are directly planned for.

**TABLE 16-1 Summary Chart: Operant Conditioning Model**

| *Syntax:* | *Phase One* | *Phase Two* | *Phase Three* |
|---|---|---|---|
| | Present the stimulus if terminal behavior is to be brought under stimulus control. Specify form of the response. Gradually reduce prompts in succeeding Phase One's. | Response emission. | Reinforcement of response depending upon selection schedule of reinforcement. |
| *Principles of Reaction:* | Optimally *directive.* The principles for reacting and responding are carefully determined by the principles of operant conditioning and the selected schedules of reinforcement. | | |
| *Social System:* | Highly *structured.* Teacher controls the action. No open-ended dialogue. | | |
| *Support System:* | Development of organized, sequenced material is crucial for stimulus control. | | |

The model (Figure 16-1) is extremely versatile. It can be directed toward goals in every domain and can be employed by teachers or used to guide the development of instructional materials.

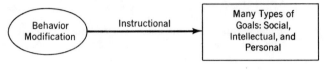

Figure 16-1

# SUMMARY

## *Teaching Behavior Modification*

The essence of behavior modification lies in its formulation of the learner's relationships to the external environment. According to the theory, human behavior is a function of conditions outside of the organism. Learning, therefore, is observable behavior that is modified by the environment; the learner is either reinforced by natural environmental processes or by someone else who manipulates the environment. In one sense, all teaching is a manipulation of environmental conditions, however unsystematic or inaccurately done. Behavior modification offers guidelines for increasing our efficiency in arranging the conditions for learning.

Ironically, the primary obstacle we have found is in getting teachers to be comfortable with the philosophical basis of behavior modification. There seems to be no problem in their using programmed materials. Many teachers could not get along without programmed reading and math materials. Yet, they feel it is something different to be the direct and conscious source of behavior modification techniques.

Behavior modification is often associated with non-academic or "behavior problems." The charge is frequently leveled that behavior modification obscures or ignores the underlying, emotional causes of deviant behavior. We have tried to stress that manipulating reinforcement to reduce these behaviors so that individual or class learning can take place does not eliminate further probing into the other "behavioral contingencies," emotional causes, if you will. To some teachers we suggest developing their initial behavior modification program for an academic behavior until they are more comfortable with the theoretical viewpoint and the feel of the model.

There is also the social criticism that we are, once again, fostering a genre of "other-directed" human beings. In our language this might be construed as a nurturant function of the model. To this the behavior modification theorist might respond that "human behavior operates that way anyway, we are simply harnessing the principles. Besides, might one not 'condition' independent, self-directed learning or creative thinking?" Our positive is less positivistic; we believe there are alternative modes of teaching for differing objectives and we do give credence to the notion that the "message is the medium."

# V

## Using Models

## of

## Teaching

# 17

# A MODEL FOR MATCHING

# ENVIRONMENTS TO PEOPLE

Where does the student fit into the equations of the models of teaching? How can we approach the models so that they facilitate the development of the student and help him achieve increasing control over his own growth?

For some of the approaches described here, at least partial answers to these questions can be found in the models themselves. The person-oriented family, especially the non-directive representative, centers entirely on the student and imposes no direction that he does not initiate himself. Behavior modification, although highly structured, requires that instruction be closely matched to the achievement of the student, and instructional sequences based on it are usually structured to minimize student error by adjusting pacing to student progress or designing so that the student can pace himself. The interaction-oriented models also relate to the individual student although the process takes place in the matrix of the group interaction process. The Group Investigation Model, in fact, capitalizes on individual differences and uses the differences to generate the energy of the model.

In addition, several of the information-processing models are designed to adjust to the individual. The models developed from Piaget adjust instruction to the cognitive development of the child, and Kohlberg's adaptation of Piaget provides for an "optimal mismatch." That is, the moral development of the student is assessed and instruction is aimed slightly above his development. Even the Advance Organizer Model, although it is intended to facilitate the teaching of new structures to the student, provides a way of adjusting organizers to relate to the cognitive structure of the student.

In this chapter we will examine a theory which can be used for tailoring social environments to individuals and for judging the appropriateness of environments to facilitate individuals. Our purpose is twofold. First, we believe that the Conceptual Systems Model is interesting in its own right. Second and more compelling we want to stand back from the models of teaching and consider whether, despite their provisions for individual differences, it is possible to say anything about the *general* appropriateness of the models for particular individuals.

We feel that such a framework is extremely important if the models are to be considered together in a coherent decision-making framework. For example, granting that non-directive teaching is designed to focus on personal development, we still need to ask the questions, "Does it provide the best environment for everyone?" "Is it possible that some people need more structure than non-direction provides?" Similarly, we may grant the efficiency of operant conditioning but we may ask, "Are there some people who need less external control?" "Do some people need a mixture of externally-controlling environments and situations which give them responsibility for directing their activities?"

To help us look at these questions, we will examine the work of David Hunt and his associates. They have developed a comprehensive theory of personality development focused on how human beings process information about objects, events, and people. The result of their study of personality is a general theory called Conceptual Systems Theory.[1] The theory describes human development in terms of increasingly complex levels of behavior and sees growth as "an interactive function of the persons level of personality development (or stage) and the environmetal conditions he encountered."[2] Optimal development is assumed to occur when the environmental conditions facilitate the "conceptual work necessary for the person's conceptual growth. When environmental conditions are not optimal, then some form of arrestation is assumed to occur."[3] In other words, the learning environment is a critical aspect of growth and the environment most capable of producing optimal growth differs for *each* "level" of personality development. This assumption led to Hunt's second major focus—how environments can be shaped so that they help individuals of different characteristics

---

[1] See O. J. Harvey, David E. Hunt, and Harold M. Schroder, *Conceptual Systems and Personality Organization* (New York: Wiley, 1961); Harold M. Schroder, Michael J. Driver, and Siegried Streufert, *Human Information Processing* (New York: Holt, Rinehart & Winston, 1967).

[2] David E. Hunt, "A Conceptual Level Matching Model for Coordinating Learner Characteristics with Educational Approaches," *Interchange: A Journal of Educational Studies*, Vol. 1, No. 2 (1970), 4.

[3] *Ibid.*

develop. At its simplest, this concern can be stated, "Given this kind of person, which of these approaches is more effective for a given objective?"[4] A more complex version of the same focus is, "How can we build a model for optimal growth which enables teachers and others to match the learning environment to the characteristics of the individuals?" Hunt is, therefore, less concerned with developing one particular model of teaching than he is in developing a framework for identifying and describing learner characteristics and developing procedures for matching the appropriate instructional strategy with learners of different characteristics. This is the essence of a differential approach to education.

But what are the learner characteristics we should differentiate and to which we can match the environment? As mentioned earlier, the original focus was on Conceptual Systems Theory which focused primarily on the learner's cognitive complexity (the complexity of his information-processing system). Since the original work, Hunt and his associates refined the notion of conceptual system and added concern with other learner characteristics which affect his information-processing capacities, such as his motivational orientation (what turns him on), his value orientation (his preferred beliefs), and his sensory orientation (does he learn better through some senses than he does through others?).[5] Because the work on Conceptual Level (Cognitive Orientation) is by far the most developed aspect of Conceptual Systems Theory, we will concentrate our description of the Conceptual Systems Model on it, bearing in mind the need to consider the other learner characteristics and their interrelationships at some later point.

Our first task is to examine the construct of Conceptual Level (CL). Then we will explore the implications of Conceptual Level for the description of Optimal Training Environments and, finally, specifications for creating environments by using the models of teaching.

## ORIENTATION OF THE WORK

Many developmental theories describe personality in terms of attitudes, needs, norms, and the like. An information-processing view of personality development focuses on the structures, that is, the programs or sets of rules, by which individuals relate to their environment. For example, whereas many developmental theorists are concerned with the *content* of personality development—(with how a child feels about himself) or the content of a person's political or social beliefs (his preferences in political and social values), the Conceptual Systems theorist concerns himself with the structure of the system.

[4] *Ibid.,* p. 2.
[5] *Ibid.*

Harvey, Hunt, and Schroder focus on the integrative complexity of the conceptual structure. Some individuals, for example, relate to the environment through relatively few dimensions, and those few dimensions are not very well integrated with one another. At the opposite end of the continuum are individuals who view the environment through many dimensions and manifest a high level of integrative complexity in their relationships to the environment. The number of dimensions with which a person relates is not necessarily correlated with the degree of integrative complexity in his system (relationships among the dimensions), but there probably is some relationship. That is, the more dimensions one has, the more likely integration is present. Highly integrated information-processing systems have many more conceptual connections between rules, that is, "they have more schemata for forming new hierarchies, which are generated as alternative perceptions, or further rules for comparing outcomes. High integration structures contain more degrees of freedom, and are more subject to change as complex changes occur in the environment."[6]

By the conceptual systems view, therefore, we can discriminate individuals in terms of the number of dimensions they use for relating to the environment and the interrelationships of these dimensions. For example, Figure 17-1, illustrates the relationships among rules in situations of low and high integration.[7]

Individual (A) obtains information through three dimensions but reduces

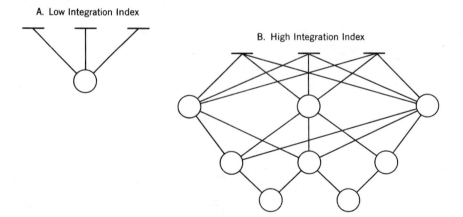

A. Low Integration Index

B. High Integration Index

**Figure 17-1** Variation in Level of Conceptual Structure.
*Source:* From Schroder, Driver, and Streufert, *Human Information Processing.*
© 1967 by Holt, Rinehart, and Winston. Reprinted by permission of the publisher.

[6] Schroder, Driver, and Streufert, *Human Information Processing*, p. 7.
[7] *Ibid.*, p. 8.

them to one integrated dimension. Individual (B) also uses three dimensions but processes the data he receives in complex ways.

To illustrate concretely, let us consider an interpersonal relations situation. Person (A) would tend to respond to ideas which conflict with his either by incorporating them into his own as if there were no differences, or by rejecting them completely. Person (B) would dissect the ideas, balancing them against his own, perhaps rejecting portions and accepting others, perhaps modifying his own.

### Four Levels of Integrative Complexity

Particular behavior patterns are characteristic of different levels of integrative complexity. Shroeder, Driver, and Streufert identify and describe · levels: low complexity, moderate complexity, moderately high complexity, and high complexity.

### Low Complexity

Let us look at the behavioral characteristics of individuals of low complexity.

### Low Complexity

These characteristics of behavior include:

1. Categorical, black-white thinking. The discrimination of stimuli along dimensions is minimally graduated; for example, if a person holds an extremely concrete attitude toward Negroes, and "Negroes" are categorized in a single way, it follows that all Negroes will tend to be lumped into one category (for example, "bad") and contrasted with others. A structure that depends upon a single fixed rule of integration reduces the individual's ability to think in terms of relativeness, of "grays" and "degrees."

2. Minimizing of conflict. Stimuli either fit into a category or are excluded from consideration. There is no conceptual apparatus that can generate alternatives; the result is fast "closure" in choice or conflict situations. . . .[8]

### Moderate Complexity

Now, let us look at the characteristics of individuals of moderate complexity.

The major characteristics of this second structural level are:

1. The presence of a conceptual apparatus that is able to generate alternate organizations of dimensions. That is, if there are three dimensions, such a structure would provide at least two possible rules for combining these dimensions.

This moderately low level of organization is characterized by the delineation of several alternative ways of structuring the world. Although such conceptual properties are not effective for relating or organizing differentiated

[8] *Ibid.,* pp. 16, 17.

sets of rules for decision-making processes, they do usher in the problem of choice and probability.

Some of the consequences of moderately low structural properties include:

1. A movement away from absolutism. Because of the availability of alternate schemata, "right" and "wrong" are not fixed as they were in structures with low integration index.[9]

A good deal of negativism is also present because the individual is struggling against his old rules and, hence against those who expose them. He especially resents parents and authority figures or any other controlling figures.

### Moderately High Complexity

Moderately high complexity is described as follows:

1. The system is less deterministic. Combining and using two alternate systems of interpretation greatly increase the number of alternative resolutions that can be generated. Even when the individual closes on a particular decision, he is still open to a number of alternative pressures. At this level, abstractness (that is, lack of fixity) becomes a formal rule of the system....

The environment can be tracked in many more ways. While moderately low integration index structure permits different ways of tracking or interpreting an environment at different times, moderately high integration index structure can vary combinations of alternate schemata. A person who is functioning at this level may view a social situation in terms of two points of view, see one in relationship to the other, perceive the effects of one upon the other. He is able to generate strategic adjustment processes, in which the effects of behavior from one standpoint are seen as influencing the situation viewed from another vantage point. This implies, for example, that a person can observe the effects of his own behavior from several points of view; he can simultaneously weigh the effects of taking different views. The adaptive utilization of alternate schemata here is much less compartmentalized than at moderately low levels.[10]

### High Complexity

To complete the picture, let us look at the characteristics associated with high complexity.

High level structure includes additional and more complex potentialities for organizing additional schemata in alternate ways. At the fourth level, comparison rules can be further integrated. Alternate complex combinations provide the potential for relating and comparing different systems of interacting variables. As with other system differences, the difference between the moderately high and the high levels is one of degree. In the latter, the potential to organize different structures of interacting schemata opens up the possibility of highly abstract function (see Figure 17-2)....

[9] *Ibid.*, p. 19.
[10] *Ibid.*, pp. 21, 23.

This very abstract orientation should be highly effective in adapting to a complex, changing situation. It is certainly much more effective than a structure that is dependent upon external conditions for building rules and upon past experiences for predicting events. . . .[11]

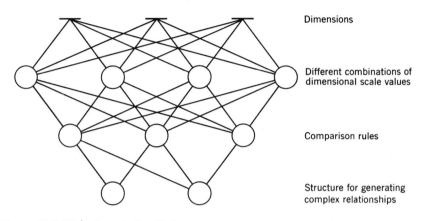

Dimensions

Different combinations of dimensional scale values

Comparison rules

Structure for generating complex relationships

**Figure 17-2** High Integration Index.
*Source:* From Schroder, Driver, and Streufert, *Human Information Processing.*
© 1967 by Holt, Rinehart and Winston. Reprinted by permission of the publisher.

### OPTIMAL TRAINING ENVIRONMENTS

According to the developmental theory of Harvey, Hunt, and Schroder the best procedure for inducing individuals to progress towards complexity and flexibility is to match their present stage of personality development to the training environment tailored to the characteristics of that stage, but in such a way as to pull the individual toward the next stage of development.[12] The following chart summarizes the conceptual levels described earlier and indicates in general terms the matching training environment:

| CHARACTERISTICS OF STAGE | OPTIMAL TRAINING ENVIRONMENT |
|---|---|
| I. This stage is characterized by extremely fixed patterns of response. The individual tends to see things evaluatively, that is, in terms of rights and wrongs, and he tends to categorize the world in terms of stereotypes. He prefers unilateral social relationships, that is, those which are hierarchical and in which some people are on top and others on the bottom. He tends to reject in- | In order to produce development from this stage, the training environment needs to be reasonably well-structured, because this kind of person will become even more concrete and rigid under an overly open social system. At the same time, however, the environment has to stress delineation of the personality in such a way that the individual begins to see himself as dis- |

[11] *Ibid.,* pp. 22, 23.
[12] Harvey, Hunt, and Schroder, *Conceptual Systems and Personality Organization.*

formation which does not fit in with his present belief system or to distort the information in order to store it in his existing categories.

II. In this stage the individual is characterized by a breaking away from the rigid rules and beliefs which characterized his former stage. He is in a state of active resistance to authority and tends to resist control from all sources, even non-authoritative ones. He still tends to dichotomize the environment. He has difficulty seeing the points of view of others, and difficulty in maintaining a balance between task orientation and interpersonal relations.

III. At this stage, the individual is beginning to re-establish easy ties with other people, beginning to take on the point of view of the other, and in his new-found relationships with other people has some difficulty maintaining a task orientation because of his concern with the development of interpersonal relations. He is, however, beginning to balance alternatives and to build concepts which bridge differing points of view and ideas which apparently contradict each other.

IV. The individual is able to maintain a balanced perspective with respect to task orientation and the maintenance of interpersonal relations. He can build new constructs and beliefs, or belief systems, as these are necessary in order to accommodate to changing situations and new information. In addition, he is able to negotiate with others the

tinct from his beliefs and begins to recognize that different people, including himself, have different vantages from which they look at the world, and that the rights and wrongs in a situation, and the rules in a situation, can be negotiated. In summary, the optimal environment for him is supportive, structured, fairly controlling, but with a stress on self-delineation and negotiation.

The delineation of self which is suggested above is now taking place, and the individual needs to begin to reestablish ties with others, and to begin to take on the points of view of others, and to see how they operate in situations. Consequently, the training environment needs to emphasize negotiation in interpersonal relations and divergence in the development of rules and concepts.

The training environment at this point should strengthen the re-established interpersonal relations, but an emphasis should also be placed on tasks in which the individual as a member of the group has to proceed toward a goal as well as maintaining himself with other individuals. If the environment is too protective at this point, the individual could be arrested at this stage and, while he might continue to develop skill in interpersonal relations, would be unlikely to develop further skill in conceptualization or to maintain himself in task-oriented situations.

While this individual is adaptable, he no doubt operates best in an interdependent, information-oriented, complex environment.

rules or conventions that will govern behavior under certain situations, and can work with others to set out programs of action and to negotiate with them conceptual systems for approaching abstract problems.

The learning environments described above are broader than that created on the basis of Cognitive Orientation alone. As previously mentioned Conceptual Level (CL) is thought to represent cognitive complexity as well as additional learner characteristics of value, motivational, and sensory orientation.[13] Hence, a description of Optimal Training Environments has matching implications beyond those just for conceptual (or cognitive) complexity.

## CONCEPTUAL DEVELOPMENT
## AND THE MODELS OF TEACHING

One basis for classifying the Models of Teaching in this book has been the degree of structure. This should facilitate matching for conceptual com-

**TABLE 17-1 Classification of Models by Amount of Structure**

| *Name of Model* | *Amount of Structure* | *Appropriate Conceptual Level* |
|---|---|---|
| 1. Inductive (Taba) | Moderate | Moderate |
| 2. Inquiry Training (Suchman) | High | Low |
| 3. Science Inquiry Model (Schwab) | Moderate | Moderate |
| 4. Jurisprudential Teaching (Oliver and Shaver) | High | Low |
| 5. Concept Attainment (Bruner) | Moderate | Moderate |
| 6. Developmental (Piaget) | Can vary from low to high (usually high) | Low |
| 7. Advance Organizer (Ausubel) | High | Low |
| 8. Group Investigation (Thelen) | Low | High |
| 9. Social Inquiry (Massialas and Cox) | Moderate | Moderate |
| 10. Laboratory Method (National Training Laboratory) | The T-Group is exceedingly *low* structure while the exercises can be *moderately* structured | High |
| 11. Non-Directive Teaching (Rogers) | Low | High |
| 12. Classroom Meeting (Glasser) | Moderate | Moderate-High |
| 13. Synectics (Gordon) | Moderate | Moderate-High |
| 14. Awareness Training (Shutz) | Moderate to Low | High |
| 15. Conceptual Systems (Hunt) | Varies from Low to High | —— |
| 16. Operant Conditioning (Skinner) | High | Low |

[13] Hunt, "A Conceptual Level Matching Model," *Interchange,* 19.

plexity, for the more highly structured models should be most appropriate for individuals of *low* complexity and vice versa. The preceding chart (Table 17-1) characterizes each of the models in terms of its degree of structure.

Hunt hypothesizes the following. "Given the characteristics of low CL learners—categorical, dependent on external standards, and not capable of generating their own concepts—the prediction follows they will profit more from educational approaches providing a high degree of structure. Given the characteristics of high CL learners—capable of generating new concepts, having a greater degree of internal standards, and being capable of taking on different perspectives—they should profit more from approaches which are low in structure, or degree of structure may not affect their performance. Thus, the heart of the CL matching model is a generally inverse relation between CL and degree of structure: *Low CL learners profiting more* from high structure and high CL learners profiting more from low structure, or in some cases being less affected by variations in structure."[14]

## CLASSROOM APPLICATION

There are three important tasks that a teacher can have in relation to the conceptual system of the child. First, he can learn to discriminate children according to these particular levels of development. For example, in Syracuse, New York, Hunt asked trained teachers to discriminate culturally disadvantaged junior high school youngsters in terms of levels of integrative complexity. Second, inasmuch as individuals of varying levels of integrative complexity perform very differently in different environments, the teacher must create an environment which is *matched* to the complexity of the student. Third, environmental prescriptions can be made to *increase* the integrative complexity of the individual, that is, the optimal environments for *growth* in personality can be identified.

Let us look closely at each of these three tasks. Discriminating the conceptual level of individuals is extremely important because of the effect of conceptual level on the individual's real world. The real world of a person of low complexity (who regards his environment as fixed, who prefers hierarchical relationships, is evaluative and becomes rigid under even moderate stress) is very different from the real world of a person of high complexity (who can generate many alternative avenues for dealing with stress and opposition, who accepts the responsibility for creating rules in new situations, and who can easily build conceptual bridges between himself and problem situations). The first individual is not likely to be adaptive, or flexible, whereas the latter individual is likely to have the capacity to generate new solutions to problems and to adapt to changing conditions. This would be true whether the individual is young or old.

[14] *Ibid.,* p. 22.

For example, mature physicists of about equal knowledge who differ greatly in integrative complexity could be expected to face problem situations very differently. Similarly, an elementary school youngster of very low complexity would be expected to perceive civil disorder differently from an individual of high complexity.[15]

The very different performance of individuals who differ in conceptual complexity under different conditions makes the second task—creating an environment matched to the student's complexity—an interesting challenge for the teacher. For example, when Hunt divided groups of culturally deprived youngsters in Syracuse according to their level of integrative complexity, teachers found that the groups of low complexity had extremely grave difficulty in carrying on discussion. A discussion technique simply was not appropriate for individuals who view the world as fixed and rules as unchanging and permanent. On the other hand, individuals of moderate structure who were engaged in delineating themselves sharply from authority were very easy to engage in debate, although the debate was terribly vigorous and difficult to control.

In other words, for optimal growth in complexity, the student needs to be exposed to an environment which is matched to the characteristics of his world. An environment in which a complex individual will flourish would create unbearable stress for a person of low complexity. There are considerable implications here for educational theory and practice. Many theorists, for example, advocate democratic-process teaching and even Rogerian methods of teaching for all learners.[16] Under conceptual systems theory, however, we would postulate that Rogerian teaching methods could even be threatening, stressful, and possibly even destructive if they are applied to individuals of very low complexity, although they might be optimal for individuals of moderate to high complexity.

Hunt's research on the Upward Bound programs in the United States validated the position that personality and training environment should be related. Hunt examined a sample of Upward programs and found that where environment and trainee personality were matched (high structure with low complexity and vice versa) the greatest growth took place.[17]

The third task is to provide environments that will help individuals become more complex, and the hypothesis that makes the most sense at this time is to attempt to lead the person's present state of development slightly; that is, when an individual is at a low level of complexity, one would want to have a moderate amount of complexity in the environment,

[15] David E. Hunt and Robert H. Hardt, "The Role of Conceptual Level and Program Structure in Summer Upward Bound Programs." Paper presented at the meeting of the Eastern Psychological Association, Boston, 1967.

[16] Carl R. Rogers, *Client-Centered Therapy* (Boston: Houghton Mifflin, 1951). Italics added.

[17] Hunt and Hardt, "The Role of Conceptual Level and Program Structure."

but not too much. The tasks presented to the individual, for example, should be done in such a way that there is some negotiating about rules, but not total negotiation, as for example under Rogerian conditions.

## MODEL

### SYNTAX

Hunt's model is really a plan for changing social systems in order to match the complexity of the learner. As such, none of the stage-prescribed environments really has a syntax in the sense that we have been speaking of it; that is, it suggests principles for behaving in relation to the student, depending on the kind of person that he is. For students of low conceptual level, tasks or educational approaches of low complexity, with high sequence, and a clear establishment of the rules would be indicated. For students of high complexity, a very emergent structure with higher task complexity and an interdependent social system would be indicated.

In addition to the basic dimension of structure, we may wish to take into consideration conceptual complexity as it relates to feedback preference, value orientation, or sensory orientation.

### PRINCIPLES FOR REACTION

The teacher is seen as the agent responsible for developing the training environment which is appropriate to the student. He is to radiate a variety of environments, depending on the students he is dealing with. For students of low conceptual level, he is to be fairly controlling, clear in his directions, supportive, but fairly direct. When dealing with students of high conceptual level, he needs to be much more interdependent and mutual, placing much more of the burden for learning on the students and helping them develop their own structure.

### SOCIAL SYSTEM

The social system has been described in detail in the earlier description of the training environment. Although other environmental factors are discussed, the social system is the critical factor in the entire conceptual systems matching model—an extremely high structured, clearly differentiated environment being appropriate for students of low conceptual level, and interdependent and emergent environment for those of a higher conceptual level.

### SUPPORT SYSTEM

The model is content-free. It can be used in nearly any curriculum areas. The training agent or teacher is the critical element; he must be able to radiate several teaching styles as necessary and appropriate to the learner's conceptual level. A teacher with only one strategy would be unable to execute the Hunt model at all.

## APPLICABILITY

Hunt's paradigm has been developed in order to produce changes in the personality dimension of the individual's general information-processing capacity. It represents a frontal approach to personality development. This contrasts with approaches which aimed at specific behaviors, rather than at the generic behavior of individuals. For instance, Margarite Warren has applied Hunt's work in counseling delinquents in San Francisco.[18] She has attempted to change the ways in which the delinquent processes information from his environment—the very ways he relates to the environment—and has tried to produce training environments which are likely to do this. A probation officer, on the other hand, is likely to simply try to keep track of a delinquent, making sure that he observes the rules and does not engage in any delinquent behaviors. As Walters would apply the Hunt model, however, the probation officer's task becomes one of attempting to create an environment which will be likely to change the way the delinquent relates to his social environment. The attempt is to change his general behavior rather than to suppress specific undesirable behaviors. Applied to mathematics teaching, an analogy would hold. The teacher applying Hunt's model would attempt to match the environment to the student in such a way as to improve his general capacity for handling information. This would be regarded as much the task of teaching as would be the task of teaching specific mathematical devices to process information.

The differential training model, as expressed by Hunt, is directly applicable to personality change. However, it is more widely applicable in the sense that a teacher should gain by placing students in environments which are optimal for their performance. Thus, a social studies teacher who can match her students and environments should be more effective at teaching the social studies and have a more comfortable time in managing the students than a teacher who does not make such a match. For example, students with a high preference for structure could be very uncomfortable under conditions of low structure, and might not learn as much as they would in highly structured environments. This notion is especially brought out in Hunt's work in the evaluation of Upward Bound, where the students who appear to be making the most progress are those who seem to be matched with the kind of training program which was best suited to them.

[18] Margarite Warren, "The Classification of Offenders as an Aide to Efficient Management and Effective Treatment," Community Treatment Project, Prepared for the President's Commission on Law Enforcement and the Administration of Justice, Task Force on Corrections, 1966.

No one type of training program appeared to be more effective than any other, but when students were matched with the appropriate program, greater growth seemed to occur. Presumably, if there is validity to this type of theory, the same should be true in any classroom situation.

There are a great many other theoretical positions from which matching models have been developed. We will shortly consider Piaget's views of cognitive development, and the kinds of models which are developed to match learning with the cognitive development of the learner. Thelen has emphasized the compatibility of both student types and teacher types in schools, recommending that a teachable group be composed of students who bear similarities of certain types, and work with a teacher who is well-suited to respond to students who share their characteristic.[19]

In the area of moral development, Kohlberg has recommended that moral education must take into account the kind of approach used by the teacher and the stage of development of the student. "There is also an important problem of match between the teacher's level and the child involved in affective moral communication. Conventional moral education never has had much influence on children's moral judgment because it has disregarded this problem of development match."[20]

A differential training model can actually be used as a blueprint for describing a wide variety of teaching strategies as they are appropriate to given individuals.

Looking over the models of teaching which are included in this book, it is possible that some of them will have great effectiveness with some learners, and very little with others. Possibly any science of behavior that ultimately emerges will require us to learn about the differentiation among human beings as well as the regularities to which we are all subject.

[19] Herbert Thelen, *Classroom Grouping for Teachability* (New York: Wiley, 1967).

[20] Larry Kohlberg, "Moral Education in the Schools," *School Review,* 74 (1966), 1–30.

# 18

# THE MODELS

# WAY OF THINKING

*An Operational Language*

We believe that to qualify as a model of teaching which should be taken seriously in the educational profession, a theory or program of education should be describable in terms of operational categories such as those we have been using. It should specify a discernible and characteristic environment, whether that environment is human or otherwise, and whether it is described in terms of human behavior or artifacts. It should specify the way the teacher, and other aspects of the environment, should react and respond to the learner as he engages in activity. It should also deal with the social relations which make up the model's interpersonal matrix. Finally, the theory or program should tell us quite specifically what technical support system will facilitate the implementation of the model, including the kind of teacher supports, student supports, and management supports which are necessary parts of the environment.

To be theoretically adequate, a model should also be accompanied by a description of its applicability, and the rationale for believing that the model will produce certain kinds of educational outcomes and avoid undesirable side effects.

## USING THE MODELS AS A TOOL FOR ANALYSIS

To assemble the models described in this book, we observed many school programs and classrooms and studied a large number of theorists whose work seemed applicable to the educational enterprise. In the course of our analysis, we identified a great many more viable models than the ones described here. Those which we selected either seemed representative of others or seemed to be more widely applicable or of more general interest than the ones that were not selected for description.

It was striking, however, that many of the programs and theories we examined proved to be undescribable in operational terms. There were two reasons for this; one applied when we were observing live programs in schools and looking at instructional materials, and the other occurred when we were examining theoretical written works about education.

### Analyzing Ongoing Programs

The most usual reason that we were unable to describe ongoing programs and instructional materials in terms of a model of teaching was that the program or materials seemed to be chaotically organized.

For instance, we visited one experimental school which is widely known for its innovative approach to teaching. The written materials describing the school curriculum were devoted mostly to criticism of what traditional schools do with and to children, and to a statement of desirable goals of education. There was very little indication of what kinds of curriculums are better than the "traditional ones," or what kind of model or curriculum plan one might use to achieve the goals. When we observed in the classrooms of the school a great variety of things seemed to be happening, many of them quite "traditional" in the sense that they were activities that normally take place in many schools, and subject to the very criticisms that the literature of that school subjected them to. In addition, many of the children's activities seemed to be planned more or less intuitively by either the staff or the children. The overall learning situation was in some ways very ordinary, and in other ways very charming and vigorous. But as we questioned the staff and talked about the program, it became clear that it was very difficult for the staff to articulate what they were doing. While they were using many words such as "inquiry" and "self-directed learning," the teachers often meant different things by these, and often were unable to explain what they meant or to pick out which activities represented "inquiry." In other words, we were unable to find any teaching models in that school, either in its literature or in its practice, except some rather traditional patterns of behavior.

In another "innovative" school, the superficial impression seemed to be very much the same. The brochures were full of clichés about desirable educational goals and how the traditional schools fail to achieve them, and again there were very few cues as to just what our innovative school did which was different or that might reasonably effect those goals. However, as we wandered around the school and observed the interaction between the teachers and the students, the students with the students, and the teachers and the teachers, it became apparent that there were several ways in which the environment was deliberately shaped in order to have certain effects on the students. The school had a characteristic social climate which emphasized student responsibility, with teachers helping students to look at their behavior and find ways of selecting their own goals and means. In addition, there were two or three other characteristic kinds of student-teacher interactions and the teachers could point to these and could talk about them to some extent, and they trained their new teachers how to use them. These activities were describable as models of teaching which were common to the whole staff of the school, although with very broad stylistic variations by teachers and students.

When we sat down with the staff, we talked about the activities we had observed, asked them about activities that went on when we were not there, and asked them to comment on our observations. At length, we were able to describe what we thought they were doing in terms of several models of teaching. One or two of the models are very similar to ones we have described in this book and belong to well-known educational theorists; the others were more unusual and characteristic of the activity of that school and a very few others that we have seen.

The staff corrected us to some extent, modifying our description of the models, but then agreed that we had described them fairly accurately. As a result of our encounter, they would be able to use the described models to orient and train new teachers as they came into the school, to analyze one another's teaching, and (very important to them) to describe what they were doing as a school so that other people would be able to understand the unique character of their program, and their reasons for believing that the models they were using would have a positive effect on children.

In other words, we used the "models of teaching" way of thinking to analyze the activities of both of these schools, each of which claimed to have about the same educational goals and each of which criticized traditional schools on about the same basis. At one school we found the teachers unable to articulate their means, and we were unable to determine any specific unique features characterizing that work. In the other school, however, we were able to help the teachers develop an understanding of the models they were using. They were then able to make use of that understanding in communicating among themselves what they were doing, and in articulating their program to other people. The first program may or may not have a positive effect on children (although there are many more traditional elements than they realize), but it certainly can not be disseminated to other people at this juncture. The second program consists of models which, because they are describable, are also teachable, and the program of the second school can be, and probably *will be,* disseminated to many other places.

If the teaching profession is to become able to examine alternative kinds of educational approaches and various ways of achieving them, it seems essential that approaches to education be described in operational terms and that languages be developed which can be used to compare and contrast them. It is very easy for educators to declare what they are *against*. Who is *not* against depersonalization, destructive competition among students, routine and dull lessons, and irrelevance? It is also easy to describe our goals in vague and general terms ("to foster each individual's growth") and our means in generalities ("individualization," "inquiry").

To develop a clarity and communicability so that teachers can work together toward agreed-on ends is a task which requires operational clarity and the development of specific and meaningful language.

## ANALYZING EDUCATIONAL THEORY

The same sort of situation exists in respect to educational theory. As we read the theoreticians, including some very well-known critics of the present schools and advocates of sweeping reforms, we found that they divided themselves into three groups—those who had articulated a pattern of teaching that was describable in operational terms and therefore could be used for a basis of action, and others in whose work we were unable to detect an operational model for action. There was a third category of critics whose writings consisted of loud rhetoric proclaiming ideal goals of education and criticizing present educational methods but whose means, although they were clearly articulated, appeared to be just exactly those that were being criticized. In other words, those critics had added nothing new to our repertoire.

This finding gave us a new appreciation of the problems of translating theory into practice in educational terms. Some theoretical or abstract positions were very easily operationalizable, and others on good examination were not operational. We began to see what can happen in a course on, say, theories of learning, when some of the theories turn out to be operational ones, and others turn out to be only apparent ones, which one cannot act on. We also began to feel that the use of operational terms for describing models of teaching could be useful not only as means for discriminating the potentially useful theories from those that are not (an important activity in itself), but also as criteria that a theoretician might use to determine whether or not he has the base on which he can construct a model. Educational theorists who wish to be useful in an operational sense will be concerned that their work can be acted on. To ensure this, they need to articulate it in terms of a model after which teachers can pattern their behavior, curriculums can be built, or instructional materials can be prepared. We do not feel that ours is the only operational language, however, and many theories and practices may turn out to need their own language and categories of operation.

### Applying the Operational Language

To illustrate the possibility of the models for describing a school and for comparing it to another school or to existing theoretical models, let us look at the operations of a series of support centers which are used to build the educational program for a large group of students who work with a team of teachers. In another work[1] we have described a team of teachers surrounded by the following support centers: (1) a self-instructional center in which students teach themselves, using sequenced, virtually self-administering instructional materials. (2) An inquiry center, in which students have access to varieties of instructional materials which provide for depth inquiry. (3) A human relations center, staffed by personnel who can help teachers and students alike work together more effectively within the community of the school. (4) A materials creation center which develops instructional materials to order as they are needed. (5) An evaluation center which develops assessment instruments, helps individuals track their progress, and promotes teacher-student communication concerning various types of achievement and development. (6) A computer-assisted instruction center in which technological devices are used, especially simulation, to help students experience processes which they are unable to experience within the ordinary school.

The personnel of these centers could operate on a wide variety of teaching models. In the self-instruction center, for example, materials might be developed using Systems Analysis (Chapter 19) and operate on Behavior Modification principles (Chapter 16). The student might have available to him a very wide variety of short courses built on behavior modification principles which he could apply in order to achieve various kinds of educational objectives.

In the human relations center, the Laboratory Method (Chapter 5), Synectics (Chapter 14), and Awareness Training methods (Chapter 15) might be applied. In the inquiry center, teachers might be trained to work in Rogerian fashion (Chapter 12), helping students to identify their own purposes and find the means for achieving them. In the materials creation center, teachers might use task analysis (Chapter 19), inductive models (Chapter 7), and many others in order to structure the materials they are building, or they could use support system requirements of the models which are being used by the direct instructional team. In other words, the

[1] Bruce R. Joyce, *Man, Media and Machines,* National Commission on Teacher Education and Professional Standards and Center for the Study of Instruction (Washington, D.C.: National Education Association, 1967).

life of a student might be made up of a wide variety of types of behavior; a whole set of teaching models might be employed to bring him a balanced type of education.

To those who suggest that there is one paramount teaching model, we offer a counter suggestion that in support centers like the ones we are mentioning here, it would be more appropriate for each of them to have their appropriate models which can be used to train personnel, order activities, and to create a balanced and effective education for children.

## DEVELOPING
## MODELS OF TEACHING

The invention of models of teaching is only in its infancy. We know very little still about how to help youngsters grow in myriad kinds of ways, and we may know even less about developing teaching models that will reach youngsters who have hitherto been unreachable by our educational processes. In addition, it may be that in order to be most effective, a teacher must develop his own particular models which blend with his particular style or his natural behavior patterns in such a way that he is able to engage in a kind of unique magic of his own making. Even more intriguing is the notion that students might develop their own models for teaching themselves. The ultimate educational activity, in fact, may turn out to be to help a student learn to build his own ways of teaching himself.

But how do we begin? Where do we turn when we wish to develop a model for teaching? In this book, we have seen models which illustrate a fairly large variety of ways for generating teaching approaches. Some of the models have been developed from therapeutic stances, others from models of society, disciplines, and sociological theory, yet others from developmental psychology, some from the application of task analysis, or cybernetic analogy to human functioning and learning. Resources of models are really very many. One place to look then, when one wishes to develop approaches to teaching, is in the kinds of sources that we have seen here. There are quite a variety of schools of therapy, for example, which one might draw on to develop models. There are many ways of looking at human development. For example, Louise Tyler of the University of California at Los Angeles has been developing teaching models based on the developmental psychology of Eric Erikson, the psychotherapist.[2] Erikson describes human development in terms of a growing unified identity.

Within developmental psychology, there are a number of other views of development that could be used to generate models in the same way

[2] Louise Tyler, "A Case History: Formulation of Objectives from a Psychoanalytic Framework," AERA Monograph No. 3, *Instructional Objectives* (Washington, D.C.: National Education Association, 1969).

they have been extrapolated from the work of Piaget, Hunt, and others.[3] For example, Kohlberg has conducted much research on moral development, using Piaget's constructs, and has generated approaches to teaching built around the developmental psychology which relates potentially to classroom practice and the development of curriculum materials.[4] Sociological theory has only begun to be mined. We use the example of Reference Group theory.[5] Theorists such as Bandura and Walters have developed and empirically verified theories describing the processes by which human beings learn through imitating others, and these have only begun to be elaborated.[6] Despite all the work of the Academic Reform movement, models of teaching derived from disciplines have only begun to tap the disciplines which are available. Oliver and Shaver's intriguing idea of constructing a discipline when one was not there to serve the purpose opens up a further array of possibilities.[7]

Similarly, models of society have only begun to be exploited for educational purposes. We have seen some outstanding examples, such as the development of the kibbutz in Israel and the creation of youth organizations designed to induce students in the U.S.S.R. It may well be that if we are to improve our social relations, we shall have to depend on educational institutions which are modeled around conceptions of human interaction.

Finally, the family of systems analysis and training psychology and the behavior modification approaches have within them the capacity for embracing an enormous variety of educational models. A recent experience of the United States Office of Education, which funded ten institutions to develop models of teacher education using systematic program analysis and the basic technique, resulted in ten models which bear some resemblance to each other, but which also manifest a wide variety of approaches to teacher education. If any of the several approaches described in this family, the cybernetic approach, the systems approach, the task analysis approach, or the behavior modification approach, were put to work on any given educational problem, we would probably see a great variety of approaches resulting therefrom.

There are those who hope that educational research will identify even-

---

[3] See Jean Piaget, *The Origins of Intelligence in Children* (New York: International Universities Press, 1952); David E. Hunt, "Matching Models to Moral Training," *Moral Education,* C. Beck, B. Crittenden, and E. V. Sullivan, eds. (Toronto: University of Toronto Press, 1970).

[4] Larry Kohlberg, "Moral Education in the Schools," *School Review,* 74 (1966) 1–30.

[5] Muzager and Carolyn Sherif, *Reference Groups: Exploration into Conformity and Deviation of Adolescents* (New York: Harper & Row, 1964).

[6] Albert Bandura and Richard H. Walters, *Social Learning and Personality Development* (New York: Holt, Rinehart & Winston, 1963).

[7] Donald W. Oliver and James P. Shaver, *Teaching Public Issues in the High School* (Boston: Houghton Mifflin, 1966).

tually those few models of teaching which are most efficient and effective. We certainly hope that the relative efficiency of models for various purposes will be investigated seriously, and that the results will be more conclusive than they have been in the past. However, it is extremely important that we continue to invent ways of diversifying our culture and bringing greater richness to the lives of individuals. The most efficient way of teaching the elementary child to read may not turn out to be the most desirable way of educating him for reasons quite separate from the efficiency with which they lead to one's goal. A model of teaching is likely to have a number of effects on a student. In a very important way, it does model his society for him. A Rogerian model, for example, tells the student not only how he might go about learning something, but also how certain people feel about him, and the kind of relationship they think he should have with others while he is learning. This knowledge may be more valuable to him and to the society than the efficiency with which any given set of goals is achieved.

Also, it is very difficult to compare many kinds of models because they approach goals so differently. If one uses a model, for example, which induces students to help to develop their own objectives, then it is very difficult to find a logical basis for comparing that model with one which specifies objectives for the student in advance of his coming to the learning situation. For example, to compare programmed instruction with group investigation is virtually meaningless. In programmed instruction the goals are specified, whether or not they match those of the learner. In group investigation, students develop the goals as they go along, and thus the things they achieve may not be comparable to those which are specified in a program model.

It may also be important for schools and teachers to develop their own characteristic models. Through this activity, they may get a greater vitality to improve their program than they would get from adopting the work of others. A vital, interested staff, trying to find ways of educating children, may create a more lively and moving atmosphere than a staff which simply uses models which are handed to it. On the other hand, however, as we point out elsewhere, teachers behave in strikingly homogeneous ways, all around the country and with all kinds of kids, even when they are teaching persons of different ages and teaching different subjects.

There is no need for us to have such cultural homogeneity in teaching. If more teachers used a variety of approaches of the kind which are identified in this book, and generated a still wider variety as they worked with other faculty members in their own schools, the world would probably be a richer and more interesting place for children, and for adults as well.

# 19

# MODELS

# AND CURRICULUM DEVELOPMENT

A curriculum is an educational program. It is designed to accomplish certain educational goals and to use specific educational means to accomplish those goals. It consists of the broader environment within which interactive teaching takes place and includes overall content and approaches to it (Figure 19-1).

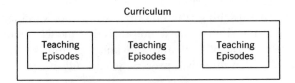

Curriculum

| Teaching Episodes | Teaching Episodes | Teaching Episodes |

**Figure 19-1**

When curriculum and teaching are in harmony, the effect of the environment can be considerable. A mathematics curriculum, for example, which is characterized by the inductive exploration of mathematical problems and concepts, will be strongest if the curriculum framework emphasizes really important and interesting problems and concepts and if the teaching brings the inductive process alive. If curriculum and teaching are not in harmony, the environment is likely to be ineffectual in meeting its goals (as when the teaching is not inductive or the curriculum framework does not organize concepts to facilitate inductive processes).

Put another way, the curricular design furnishes the broad design specifications and interactive teaching is the process by which the environment is actualized and given human energy.

The study of curriculum and teaching has often been separated and linkages between the two have often been missing. Curriculum plans have spelled out sequences of content—topics to be covered and concepts to be learned—while teachers and students have made instructional decisions and created environments unrelated to the curricular specifications. Thus, frequently curriculum has dealt with the *content* and teaching the *process* of instruction but without sufficient relationships between the two.

In an effort to overcome the separation between curriculum and teaching, the ideas of curricular *strategy* and teaching *strategy* have come into recent use. These provide a means to relate content and process to each other in an operational way so that curricular design and teaching process can be interdependent.

The models of teaching, applied to both curricular and instructional planning, provide a unifying way of looking at curriculum and teaching. Suppose, for example, that one wishes to develop a curriculum on international affairs and selects the Jurisprudential Model as the curricular strategy. The model suggests devices for curricular organization (case studies of public controversy in the international domain) and also provides specifications for the interactive teaching environment in the form of the stages and group process of the jurisprudential framework. Thus curriculum and teaching can be thought of in a unified fashion. A teacher, examining such a curricular design, could tell at once how teaching should be carried on to create the desired environment.

It is possible to plan a curriculum in which content is entirely emergent from the interactive teaching situation and is thus not specified. For example, a guidance curriculum using a non-directive model might suggest the kind of guidance to be offered and the kinds of topics which might be explored, but the non-directive process would fill in the content as it emerged.

There are so many possible educational goals, so many models of teaching available, and so many kinds of content to explore that curriculum planning and its relation to teaching is a very complex field of study. We will break the subject down into the following areas:

1. Kinds of curriculums and functions of curricular design.
2. Selecting educational missions and relating them to models of teaching.
3. Using the models of teaching to select educational means.
4. Proposals for curricular reorganization: multiple curricular models.

## Kinds of Curriculums

The educational programs that can legitimately be called curriculums are many and vary enormously in their characteristics. Some are very comprehensive designs for the entire educational program for a child; others are designs for education within a particular curriculum area, such as science or mathematics. Even very short courses, designed to achieve specific and narrow purposes (for example, a crash program to achieve minimal verbal competence in a foreign language), can be called curriculums. Curriculums vary also in the instructional technology they call for. Some depend on teachers, others on instructional materials. Some of them are managed by comprehensive systems which use computers to diagnose pupil needs, prescribe instructional remedies, evaluate the effectiveness of the curriculum, even revise the program as it goes along. Curriculums also vary in the media they use. Some depend on written materials or films while others depend on news accounts of international relations, on the data generated by students and teachers as the primary informational source. Finally, different curriculums provide children with many kinds of learning experiences. Some are built around social problems; others around the creative expression of students themselves or around the analysis of social dynamics.

Curriculum design in all cases should serve to identify the purposes of the curriculum area and the overall environmental characteristics likely to achieve those purposes.

## CURRICULUM DESIGN
## AND THE MODELS OF TEACHING

What relationship do the Models of Teaching bear to curriculum design? We feel they can serve this function in two primary ways: (1) to clarify and identify educational ends, and (2) to objectify and guide the selection of appropriate means for achieving those ends. In the first instance, the models lay out the panorama of objectives and articulate the many possibilities and facets of a given objective. Rogers' work, for example, can help us clarify ends and means having to do with certain aspects of the self; Glasser and Gordon dwell on other aspects of personal development. Taba's work (Inductive Thinking) can help us clarify what we mean by inductive reasoning and what specific goals we can aim toward. The Models of Teaching, then, help us to refine and specify such highly generalized, non-operational objectives as personal development or inductive thinking and alert us to the multiplicity of objectives a curriculum can have and the means which can be used to achieve them.

The Models of Teaching probably make their greatest contribution to curriculum design, however, when they are used to generate the specifications for the means of the curriculum. When broadly conceived, the teaching models represent models of curriculum, a repertoire which we can use to design educational environment. Continuing our earlier discussion on the relationship between curriculum and instruction, for years many curriculums have been designed without specified instructional strategy. Not surprisingly, the content that followed from these designs was conveyed to the learner with no particular strategy. This state of affairs was perfectly acceptable as long as the educational objective was primarily the intake of predigested bodies of information (though we know that there are models which presumably do even this more efficiently or effectively than others). In that case, the educational objective, the curriculum, and the instruction were in balance, so to speak. Today, however, when educators are reaching toward new educational ends, particularly those related to the so-called "process" goals (i.e., inductive thinking, creativity, inquiry), curriculum specialists might imbed these processes into their design, much as they did when content was the primary objective. In other words, today when there is a diversity of educational objectives, there must also be a supply of compatible curriculum and instructional means, all of which must be optimally matched in the learning situation.

The lopsided growth of the curriculum and instructional theory fields probably reflects an attempt to accommodate this diversity and to provide the necessary coordination. Some theorists quickly became aware of the validity of Marshall McLuhan's "the medium is the message" as an analogy for curriculum and instruction. Together, the curriculum and instructional means are the learning medium, which, after all, is the message. Creative thinking is not induced or developed by didactic presentation of "concluded" information!

## An Optimal Relationship

We may think of the optimal relationship among (1) educational objectives, (2) curriculum design, and (3) instructional strategy as a "one-to-one-to-one" relationship. They are in balance when they support the same educational ends. In the past these three facets of educational design have been out-of-joint with one another. More recently, instructional strategies have been developed which attempt to match the educational objectives. Some curriculums have been designed with this match in mind though they often fall short of this goal, placing the burden for the match on the individual teacher and the instructional strategy if she has one. "Why," some teachers wonder with frustration, "doesn't the proclaimed 'inquiry' take place when I use this curriculum and these materials from this New Social Studies project?" It is probably because, in spite of the project's educational goals, the appropriate strategy was never incorporated into the curriculum design in the first place! The models of teaching can help clarify and objectify the means of the curriculum and ensure the optimal match among the educational objectives, curriculum design, and instructional strategy. Implicit in the Balance Theory of educational design is the assumption that there is a common denominator against which we can compare the three facets for compatibility and optimality. The Models of Teaching provide the backdrop for coordinating and operationalizing these three components.

We have discussed the Models of Teaching largely in terms of teaching in the first parts of the book. The task for this chapter is to relate them to curriculum ends and means. Having selected educational objectives, one needs to ask these questions: What educational experiences are likely to lead to achievement of those objectives? What environment is likely to give us those experiences? Another way to pose these questions is to say, "What models for curriculum are most likely to achieve those objectives?"

## THE MODELS
## AND EDUCATIONAL ENDS[1]

Educational ends or objectives focus the curriculum. From the enormous range of possibilities, the objectives represent the few things of importance we will determinedly try to teach. It is essential that the objectives, in fact, should be few enough that the faculty can remember and discuss them. These major objectives can, of course, be analyzed into subsidiary objectives—if one is developing a sequenced instructional "program." They can also be assigned to various age levels. Some objectives may be for younger children, others for older students. Or, *parts* of some objectives may be appropriate for certain levels.

Generally, objectives are drawn from three sources—the person, the society, the disciplines and other information-processing systems. In the next pages we will try to indicate how the sources can be used to generate objectives.

### THE PERSON AS A SOURCE OF OBJECTIVES

When we make objectives on behalf of the student, what shall we want for him? How can we speak for his interests when we are shaping the curriculum? Let us examine a few possibilities.[2]

1. *Capacity for Self-Instruction*

We can choose to help him teach himself by selecting objectives that build the capacity for self-instruction. Objectives like these include:

a. Skill in selecting personal learning goals.
b. Motivation to teach oneself.
c. Willingness to organize one's own learning program.
d. Active curiosity about the social world.
e. Understanding of the use of sources of information and ideas.
f. Skill in using learning resources.

[1] Some of these ideas, in somewhat different form, have appeared in several books and articles. See especially: Bruce R. Joyce, *Alternative Models for Elementary Education* (Boston: Blaisdell, 1969); Bruce R. Joyce, *New Strategies for Elementary Social Studies* (Chicago: Science Research Association, 1971).

[2] From: *Unit Two: Developing New Curricula, Social Studies Extension Service* by Bruce R. Joyce, pp. 12–16. Copyright © 1967 by Science Research Associates.

(Note that we are using the current behavioristic form for starting objectives. Each objective begins with a word that denotes a behavior: understanding, skill, etc. The remainder of the objective describes the area in which the behavior is to be practiced. Hence, in *b* above, "motivation" refers to the student behavior to be developed, and "to teach oneself" is the area in which motivation is to be developed. It is extremely important that objectives have both the *behavioral* and *area* or *content* aspects.)

It is possible to devote major parts of the curriculum to teaching the individual to teach himself. A curriculum that will achieve these objectives must provide considerable opportunity for the student to teach himself many things, including things he has selected for himself.

## 2. *Self-Exploration*

We can focus the curriculum to help the student explore himself: who he is, his problems, his attempt to achieve identity, his social relations. Our objectives can both provide him with the knowledge and skill that is useful for self-exploration and provide him with the opportunity to seek for himself. Sample objectives in this area include:

a. Willingness to examine himself, his humanity, the forces that are shaping him.
b. Understanding of the factors that shape human behavior.
c. Skill in analyzing his personal concerns.
d. Awareness of the ego-concerns of those about him.
e. Confidence in his dignity and worth.
f. Belief in the dignity and worth of others.

Curricular objectives in this domain obligate us, when we choose to emphasize them, to study the maturation of self, and to develop teaching techniques that facilitate the slow process of self-discovery.

## 3. *Development of Creative Capacities*

A third type of emphasis is found in the attempt to help the student become a creative, productive thinker. Such an emphasis encourages his creativity, his flexibility, his ability to generate alternative solutions to problems. For example:

a. Openmindedness with respect to new ideas and situations of conflict.
b. Flexibility in ideas.
c. Confidence in advancing new syntheses.
d. Tolerance of ambiguous situations where final solutions must be delayed.
e. Fluency in creating alternatives.
f. Receptivity to unfamiliar experience.
g. Willingness to test hunches.
h. Ability to stand vigorous analysis and learn from it.

It may be that qualities like these come about as much by the way students are handled as by what they are taught. However, objectives like these would undoubtedly require considerable departure in content and teaching strategies from what is common now.

These three types of emphasis have been identified so that we can see some of the range of possibilities in curriculum goals when one considers just one source of curriculum goals—concern for the student as a person.

## CURRICULUM OBJECTIVES FROM SOCIETAL CHARACTERISTICS

When we take the point of view of the society, what purposes will we select? Again, the possibilities are legion. We will examine focuses on the development of productive citizens, national and international, on citizens steeped in the history and lore of the nations, and on the production of persons of superior interpersonal skills.

### 1. *Development of an Active Involved Citizen*

Some theorists favor objectives that develop an involved, active citizen whose outlook is intelligently national, but who has a well-developed world view as well. This approach leads to objectives like these:

a. Knowledge of the political and social history of the United States.
b. Commitment to participation in the political and social life of the nation and community.
c. Appreciation of the social history of African, Eastern, and Latin American peoples.
d. Commitment to the fulfillment of humanitarian ideas everywhere.
e. Skill in participating in political process.
f. Skill in democratic social process.

This orientation results in a curriculum whose goals are about equally divided among knowledge, values, and interpersonal skills.

### 2. *Development of an Historically Informed Citizen*

Some people feel that the special role of the school should be to impart the history and lore of the nation. Objectives like these result:

a. Knowledge of the political history of the United States.
b. Awareness of the values that have been expressed through the founding and development of the United States.
c. Acquaintance with the people and events that have shaped the present society.
d. Commitment to the core values of United States society.
e. Skill in participating in the American political and social process.

This point of view, resulting in objectives that lead to citizen capacity, can be directed either toward participation in the existing social order or toward reconstruction and improvement of the existing order. Generally speaking, American schools have favored teaching participation more than revision, but this has not been universally true.

### 3. Development of Interpersonal and Social Skills

A third point of view that arises from the societal source involves concern with the development of persons who are socially effective—whose interpersonal skills are highly developed. This point of view results in objectives like the following:

a. Skill in communicating effectively in groups.
b. Skill in analyzing and improving group processes.
c. Ability to assume different roles in functioning groups.
d. Understanding of the factors that affect social behavior.
e. Commitment to the development of interdependent interpersonal situations.
f. Skill in organizing and maintaining democratic, inquiring groups.
g. Self-control in interpersonal situations.

While this emphasis includes many skills, it is by no means non-intellectual, for many of these analytic and interpersonal skills require a high level of conceptualization.

### THE ACADEMIC DISCIPLINES AS A SOURCE

As in the cases of the learner and the society, there are many aspects of the disciplines. Thus, disciplines-oriented objectives can be very different, depending on the point of view that is taken. Once again, we will illustrate with three orientations from which objectives can be generated.

### 1. Methods of Inquiry

First, the "sciencing" aspects of the disciplines can be stressed. The objectives can be shaped to teach how the sciences operate, to acquaint the learner with what have come to be known as scientific processes, hence the term, "process goals."

a. Knowledge of the making of observations, inferences, value judgments.
b. Skill in engaging in the processes of observing, inferring, valuing.
c. Acquaintance with the development of scientific method and major theories.
d. Awareness of the tentativeness and continual reconstruction of knowledge.
e. Commitment to the inductive and deductive methods of verifying knowledge and testing values.

Many believe that it is in this domain that we find the learning most likely to be of long-term value to our students. Current concepts in the social sciences will become obsolete, it is reasoned; but the analytic method will persist and, in addition, is applicable to many problems in personal life.

## 2. *Major Concepts*

Second, the structural character of the disciplines can be stressed. One can attempt to teach the important concepts from one or more of the social sciences. Whether one tries to teach a single discipline, as in the case of some of the projects described in Part I, or several, does not affect the *kinds* of things one teaches; but the results, obviously, can be quite different.

    a. Knowledge of the unifying concepts of the discipline(s). (These have to be enumerated precisely as "scarcity," "division of labor," "marketing," in economics and "cultural universals" and "cultural change" in anthropology.)

    b. Skill in applying the unifying concepts of the disciplines to the understanding of the society and social life.

    c. Skill in using reference materials in the social process.

A curriculum emphasizing the "structure" of the discipline can be organized around a few concepts that are repeated or around many that are arranged sequentially. It is attractive partly because of the relative stability of its organizing elements.

## 3. *Frames of Reference*

A third approach to the disciplines is to try to teach the frame of reference of each as they help one gain insight into social processes. Hence, one teaches a few concepts of each social science, but mostly those· that define its point of view.

    a. Understanding of the frame of reference of the disciplines.

    b. Skill in applying these frames of reference to the study of human life and its environment.

    c. Skill in analyzing conceptual schemes within the disciplines.

    d. Ability to see alternative points of view and their rationale.

Actually, this approach can combine some features of the first two, with methods of the disciplines and their major frames of reference being selected.

Thus, the first task of the curriculum designer is to select and refine goals. The three domains provide the alternatives from within which he can select or within which he may create new objectives (Figure 19-2).

## MATCHING STRATEGIES TO OBJECTIVES

What models for curriculum are most likely to achieve the objectives which arise from the three sources?

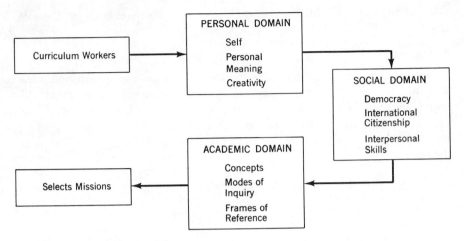

**Figure 19-2**

It is very unlikely that one will obtain a definitive answer to that question that will satisfy all parties, even given agreement on specific educational goals. More than one model is available for most types of objectives. Within the comparatively few models described in this book, we can identify several which have been used extensively in such a seemingly specialized area as human relations training. For instance, the Non-Directive Model (Rogers), Reality Therapy (Glasser), Awareness Training (Shutz), Laboratory Methods, Group Investigation (Thelen), and Behavior Modification strategies have been employed to that end in programs with which the authors have been involved.

The availability of several strategies for many objectives is due partly to the fact that some strategies have been designed to achieve a very wide range of educational objectives. For example, Behavior Modification models are used to approach objectives as widely separated as motor skills, problem-solving methods, and even to treat neuroses. Other models are believed to be widely applicable because either their philosophical or psychological underpinnings are very broad or persuasive. Rogerian teaching strategies have been used to teach content subjects, to improve interpersonal relations, and to develop problem-solving skills. If you accept Rogers' basic stance, both his orientation toward self-actualization as a goal and his rationale for non-directive, facilitative methods for therapy and teaching, then facilitating personal capacity for growth and fulfillment becomes paramount and considerations such as "efficiency" become less important. Hence, for example, one teaches skills non-directively because of the general benefits which are likely to accrue to the client.

Some models for teaching, however, have been created to serve specific purposes, or it can be reasoned that they are more likely to achieve some ends than others. Synectics, for example, is specifically designed to develop creative problem-solving groups. While Synectics might be used within any given curriculum area to promote creative thinking or to provide variety and interest, it would be unlikely that one would argue that an entire arithmetic program should be built around Synectic techniques. Its clear purpose is creativity and no general claims are made for efficiency in promoting other ends. T-group methods (Laboratory Methods) are specifically designed to teach interpersonal skills, and to help individuals grow in sensitivity to themselves and others. While T-group methods might be included as one of a variety of models within a curriculum area, they were not designed with the idea that they would be applicable to all kinds of educational ends: Laboratory Method, by itself, would not very likely suffice for the teaching of a complex academic discipline.

The chart appearing in Chapter 1 (page 11) lists the teaching strategies which have been described in this book, according to the kinds of educational ends for which they are likely to be appropriate on purely logical grounds.

## THE MODELS AND CURRICULUM MEANS

Earlier in this chapter, we mentioned that curriculums provide the design specifications for the learning environment and we explored some of the dimensions of curriculum design. From this we identified six dimensions involved in constructing or comparing design specifications:

1. The scope, substance, and specificity of their purposes (educational objectives);
2. Their comprehensiveness in terms of providing for the total educational program and environment of the child;
3. The units of construction (their organizing principles, format, specificity, etc.);
4. Nature of learning experience or curriculum strategy (their orientation toward social problems, creative expression, inquiry, etc.);
5. Instructional technology (Depending upon the goals and requirements in the design specifications, the educational designer might call upon the computer, the television, the text materials, or the individual teacher or student as the main source of instruction);
6. Learning medium (Different educational goals call for different learning media, that is, different media through which instruction is filtered. In some cases, the group is the essential medium and provides quite a different learning experience from that when the same subject is approached through a different educational medium, such as the tutorial.)

In a design the elements of its construction must be not only compatible, but also mutually supportive so that the final set of specifications is internally consistent. In addition to providing the tools for distinguishing compatibility between curriculum and instruction, the teaching models can assist in the development of internal coherence and strength within the curriculum design itself. The models as we have presented them have much to tell us about the relationships among some of the components of the curriculum design. Let us examine the Models concept as it has been applied to curriculum development.

One might build a curriculum around a single teaching strategy or around a combination of them. Single-model curriculums are fairly common, but more complex approaches are also used. The Contra Costa County, California social studies curriculum designed by Hilda Taba used the inductive teaching strategies described in Chapter 7 as the models for most of the curriculum activities.[3] Units of instruction were constructed around the inductive paradigm and specific lessons within the units were built on the inductive teaching models as well. Through the collection of data and its analysis, it was assumed that many facts would be learned and that, at the same time, inductive skills would be taught. In addition, the community of students working together in induction would develop the interpersonal skills appropriate for democratic society and for vigorous scholarly analysis.

The Contra Costa curriculum relies primarily on the teacher-administered inductive strategy. Sources of data are conventional media (books, film strips, films, etc.) and the units within the program, the suggested learning activities, build upon one another to develop sophisticated inductive thinking. An excerpt from the Contra Costa curriculum follows. It shows how the expressed curriculum strategy of induction is built into the curricular level by its organizational principles (sequencing for induction), activities, and the nature and specificity of unit of construction (the suggested learning activity). The careful sequencing of certain types of activities ensures that earlier lessons lay the informational groundwork for inductive learning activities, and the nature and size of the unit of instruction, corresponding to the phases of the inductive strategy, safeguard the inductive progression. The sources of raw data provide the technical support necessary to carry out inductive learning. These curriculum design dimensions seem to provide the optimal environment for inductive learning and for natural adoption of an inductive instructional strategy. One can only speculate as to the fate of this objective were the appropriate instructional strategy not employed (i.e., if the teacher developed expository lessons that predigested the data or did not encourage the students to draw their own inferences) or if the technical support system were not appropriate (if the data base were of a different sort).

---

3 Hilda Taba, *Teachers' Handbook for Elementary Social Studies* (Reading, Mass.: Addison-Wesley, 1967).

CHART 5[4]

SEQUENTIAL STEPS WITHIN A STRATEGY FOR
INTERPRETING DATA AND GENERALIZING
(EXCERPT FROM SIXTH GRADE UNIT ON LATIN AMERICA)

12. Organize the class into three groups. Each group will have responsibility for securing information about *one* culture. The study questions are meant to structure the reading in this first independent reading assignment so the groups will have parallel information that can be compared and contrasted in later discussions. (Note: These three groups will be much too large to act as committees. The grouping is meant to condense a lengthy study of Indians and to set a pattern for securing information and organizing it.)

Questions:
a) What is the land and the climate like where the (Mayans/Aztecs) lived?
b) How did these people secure their food, clothing, and shelter? (Farming, hunting, trading, etc.)
c) What tools did these people have?
d) What evidence of trade is seen? (Market places? Laws? Barter or money?)
e) How were these people governed? (By whom? Rules and laws?)
f) What language did the people speak?
g) How did these people educate their children?
h) If there were schools, who attended?
i) What kinds of things did these people invent?

13. Note: It is suggested the groups not make separate reports on the Indians studied. By putting information in some visible form discussion can center on topics that cut across the three cultures. Let the students plan a common way of organizing information gathered by all groups to facilitate comparison of the three societies. In planning, the students should consider:

a) What information about a people is most important if you wish to understand their way of life;
b) That the chart will be more effective if information is sampled; it is not necessary to chart all information gathered;
c) What is the most effective or efficient way for a particular class to present information.

Note: As an example of both the organization and content, see Chart 6 (Retrieval Chart).

14. Using the chart as a point of reference, discuss the similarities and differences among the three civilizations and their significances.

Suggested question sequence:
a) What differences do you notice among these different civilizations?
b) How do you account for these differences?
c) What might be the consequences of these differences?
d) How were these civilizations alike?

4 *Ibid.,* pp. 68–69.

e) In the light of what you know about any one culture, are there items that seem to be related to each other? For example, no domestic animals—use of human labor; large empire—well organized government; different elevations—different crops.

*Making Inferences.* Throughout the unit when information is organized so that certain points can be compared and contrasted, the students should be encouraged to draw inferences from this information. For this purpose the sequence of questions used should draw out the "whats" to be considered, uncover the "whys," and draw out relationships.

Quite a number of educational programs have been designed using behavior modification strategies. A very good example of these is the Individually Prescribed Instruction curriculums developed at the Research and Development Center at the University of Pittsburgh, and at Research for Better Schools, the United States Office of Education Regional Laboratory in Philadelphia, described in Chapter 20. Such a curriculum employs "ladders" of behavioral objectives, short modules of activity specifically related to objectives and, sequentially, to each other. Programmed instruction and other carefully sequenced approaches are prominent, with materials bearing a significant portion of the load, with the teacher working as diagnostician, prescriber, counselor, trouble-shooter, and tutor.

Comprehensive Systems Planning, (Chapter 20) using behavior modification strategies also has been recently applied to the development of teacher education curriculums. Michigan State University, for example, developed a curriculum for the preparation of teachers with 2,300 objectives, each one of which is accompanied by an instructional module of a particular kind, and all of these have been summarized and are stored in a computer retrieval system.[5] This system is joined to a general management system which operates very much like the IPI system. Each student is tested and a developmental profile is created for him, on the basis of which he is placed on certain developmental paths within the curriculum. As the student proceeds through the curriculum, further evaluation is made, on the basis of which he is either recycled through segments of the program or exits into higher levels of the program. Gradually, he builds up the sets of behaviors that make up the expected competencies of the teacher as specified in the program.

Models drawn from the disciplines have been used in recent years to structure quite a number of curriculums. The Science Inquiry Model was used to structure the Biological Sciences Curriculum Study (BSCS) whose construction was described in Chapter 9. The authors of the BSCS set out to induce the students to practice the methods of the discipline. The

---

[5] G. Wesley Sowards, Project Manager, *Behavioral Science Elementary Teacher Education Program,* Michigan State University, Washington, D.C., U.S. Office of Education. ED-027-205, 6, 7, 1968.

curriculum, through the selection of its major themes, its curricular strategy, and the design of its units, masterfully accomplishes its goal of providing an inquiry approach into the structure and methodology of the discipline. Despite the artfulness of its construction, the accomplishment of inquiry often rests with the instructional posture of the teacher. Joseph Schwab, in his "guidelines," carefully warns against the destructive effects of assuming an expository strategy and a norm of evaluation rather than tentativeness.[6] Similar models have been used to structure curriculums in such diverse areas as social psychology for elementary school children, anthropology for secondary school students, and in many other academic areas. For example, Lippitt and Fox have developed a three-year elementary school curriculum structured into units of approximately one month's duration, each of which teaches an aspect of social science methods for inquiring into human relations.[7] The materials are very rich, but the essence of the curriculum finds the teacher helping the students inquire into their own social life.

Group Investigation (Chapter 2) has been used to structure a good many curriculums. Theoreticians have recommended that courses in social studies be structured around Group Investigation because of its promise to provide practice in democratic life and to promote the development of social skills, societal knowledge, and democratic values at the same time. John U. Michaelis, whose book, *Social Studies for Children in a Democracy,* is by far the most widely used method textbook in the social studies for the elementary school, advocates a democratic process method not unlike Thelen's model.[8] He recommends that the teacher organize the students into a miniature democracy, and that this democracy inquire into the society, attacking problems which puzzle the children, and probing those problems, acquiring knowledge about the society, problem-solving skill, democratic process skills, and commitment to democracy more or less simultaneously. In this case, the essence of the strategy is probably found in the learning media of the group and their interaction.

We have seen a social studies curriculum developed on Synectics principles, particularly the use of metaphor.[9] In this curriculum, the United States Constitution was studied by analogizing it to magnets (science) and place value (arithmetic). The point was to discover by analogy why and how people, states, magnets, and numbers work together. This strategy rests primarily on the analogous nature of its content. The other curriculum design dimensions do not appear crucial.

[6] BSCS, Joseph J. Schwab, *Biology Teachers Handbook* (New York: Wiley, 1966), pp. 50–51.

[7] Ronald Lippitt and Robert Fox, *Michigan Social Science Project* (Chicago: Science Research Associates, 1969).

[8] John U. Michaelis, *Social Studies for Children in a Democracy* (Englewood Cliffs, N.J.: Prentice-Hall, 1963).

[9] William J. J. Gordon, *Making It Whole* (Boston: Synectics Incorporated, 1968).

The programs we have discussed here have been built primarily upon one model. A balanced, comprehensive educational program can be constructed using various teaching models to structure various aspects of education. In the following sections we will present such a comprehensive plan.

## A PROPOSAL
## FOR CURRICULAR REORGANIZATION

The following is a proposal for an elementary school organization that includes several actual schools or institutions, each employing a particular teaching model or combination of models designed to further certain aspects of the student's education.

### DIFFERENT KINDS OF EDUCATION

The recreation of the institution begins with the recognition that we have been trying to make one institution stretch over a variety of educational tasks that really require a large number of institutional forms. To get at this problem, let us begin by identifying several of the kinds of education that are critical for today's children and then see if we can determine the types of institutions and models that best serve those kinds of education.

First, children need to learn the basic skills and historical and geographic knowledge that will enable them to sort out today's world and teach themselves throughout the rest of life. Time-honored reading, writing, and arithmetic are essential, but also needed is a knowledge of contemporary technology. Children need to learn to use printed media, especially to learn to read and write, and to communicate through other media (as through dramatics, film, and television), as consumers of those media (and for some children, as creators). They need a knowledge of the workings of our governing body and of our economic system. They need to be able to compare and contrast our culture with other major world cultures, in terms of politics, economics, art, and social dynamics. They need to comprehend the world and the kinds of economic, racial, and political problems that beset the nations the world over. We can refer to this need for skills and knowledge as the basic skills and knowledge education of the child. The goals of this education are set outside of him. We want him to acquire this education and feel it is necessary for his development. We want to induce him to learn these things because they are the storehouse of our common culture that he will have to stand on as he builds his individual way in society, and they are the skills and knowledge that he will need in order to relate to the rest of us. Although children differ in the amount of basic education they will absorb, it is a shared education that gives them more in common.

A second kind of education begins with the child. We can think of it as personalized education or education for idiosyncrasy. It is designed to help him develop on his own terms and to become as unique as he can. A personalized education begins with the person's own particular talents and special interests and helps him develop these on his own terms. At certain times in his life, a personalized education will simply help him explore his interests. He may read through favorite authors or learn to play a musical instrument or design and build his own rocket. At other times, it may help him build a new career or a depth of knowledge in a certain area. In any case, however. it is desirable that everyone, and not simply the academically talented, have a part of their education devoted to their personal development.

A third kind of education has as its goal to help youngsters learn how scholars work or what we might call academic inquiry. It teaches them how social scientists analyze human culture, and how scientists build and test theories. It helps them try on the ideas of mathematicians and to learn how literature can be analyzed. This kind of education introduces the student to the most sophisticated ideas of his time, and helps him to learn how the academic community continues the struggle for knowledge. It is the kind of education that has been the object of the Academic Reform movement which has been going on in education since the middle 1950s and has resulted in the curricular changes known as the "New Math," the "New Science," and so on. As presently practiced in the schools, academic inquiry is sometimes dull and sometimes exciting. When it is carried on in the right way, it is always exciting, for it involves powerful ideas and systems of ideas. Like basic education, academic inquiry begins outside the child.

Yet a fourth kind of education introduces the students to a dialogue on the nature and the future of our society. This kind of education focuses on the critical issues and values of our culture. It deals in controversies and helps the student to sort out the issues in controversies, the kinds of values over which we are struggling, and to debate alternative solutions to our collective problems. At the present time, this kind of education would focus on the problems of alienation that divide us, on the problems of urbanization and mass society that are confounding us, on the domestic and international political issues on which we are joined as we attempt to forge the future of our society. This education is critical not only for the "radicalized" youth who are demanding that at least part of their education be built around the reconstruction of their society, but also for the apathetic youth who uncritically conform to the society without questioning it or engaging in the struggle to improve it. It helps the student learn to engage in the democratic process, to participate in the sharpening of issues and the development of alternative solutions to problems which confront us.

We could include many other kinds of education—aesthetic education, human relations training, creativity seminars, awareness training—the possibilities are many. However, for illustrative purposes only, let us look more closely at these four and design a set of institutions to accomplish them.

## A BASIC EDUCATION

The proper teaching of skills and basic knowledge requires great individualization. Children learn to read at vastly different rates, and both good readers and poor readers have characteristic problems that require individual attention. Some poor readers are such because they have general language problems, others because they have a specific problem of some sort. Some good readers have problems, such as in the application of phonics or in the development of their vocabulary, and these too require individual attention. An institution that asks a teacher to keep track of the range of individual differences that occur in reading, writing, arithmetic, basic skills and knowledge in the social studies, and basic skills and knowledge in the sciences, is simply overburdening the individual teacher with information to process. Teachers simply cannot do it. If they can diagnose adequately the individual problems in the basic skills and knowledge area, a teacher who is asked to teach one subject to a hundred students, or five or six subjects to thirty students, simply cannot find the solutions he needs to the panorama of individual differences that confronts him.

However, in the last few years, we have begun to experiment with institutional arrangements that show great promise for this kind of education. For example, researchers at the University of Pittsburgh Research and Development Center and the Philadelphia Regional Laboratory Research for Better Schools are developing and testing general systems for instructing individuals in the basic skills and knowledge area which accommodate the pattern of individual differences. Such a system consists of a diagnostic program in which an individual is tested and otherwise examined, and his pattern of individual development in an area such as arithmetic is assessed. On the basis of that assessment, the teacher makes a prescription for the youngster. The youngster takes his prescription to a storage center of self-instructional materials. He is provided with materials that match the prescription and he works on those materials, which may be tapes, programmed material, workbooks, or books with instructions. As he completes each section of work, an embedded test provides an indication of whether he has learned the things which those materials were designed to teach. On the basis of that assessment, the prescription is modified, and he continues in the same manner. Similar systems are being built using films, television tapes, and other media, and combining them with teacher-administered instruction.

Another promising program, sponsored by the United States Office of Education, is developing teacher-education programs on the same basis, with television being used to provide a diagnosis of the teacher's capabilities and instructional systems being provided to give the teacher practice in the skills that he needs help in, to teach him how to use television tape to view himself and make further diagnoses, and to track his own progress. At the Far West Laboratory in Berkeley, a series of self-instructional courses for teachers called Mini-Courses have been developed using a similar approach.

The kind of school that is good for basic skills and knowledge education is one that provides for elaborate diagnosis in the areas concerned, prescriptions based on the diagnosis, and then treatment or instruction closely tuned to the developmental pattern of the individual. Under such a system, some individuals complete the course of study in a very short time, others can take a very long time over the same material. Some will complete some kinds of development very quickly, and linger over others, but in any case, instruction is tuned to the individual.

### Personalized Education

Systems like the preceding ones, however, cannot very well provide an education which helps each person to do his own thing, to explore his own capacity for creativity and his own personal interests. For *that,* we need an institution which enables the student to meet with his teacher on a one-to-one tutorial basis so that the teacher can explore his interests and capabilities, and help the student develop a program which fits those needs and desires. The tutor, in addition to being able to help the student find his interests and develop his own educational program, has to be backed up by the kinds of instructional resources that can be shaped to an individual need. Some of these resources need to be other teachers, who might work at the school on a full or part-time basis, as artists, musicians, and writers. Good libraries are essential, and can include banks of motion pictures that the student can use to teach himself, television courses, particularly short courses that he can draw on when he needs them, laboratory materials, shops, and so on.

The institutional arrangements that make for good personalized education are the tutorial relationship and the battery of open-ended resources backing it up. The existing school as an institution is very poor for this kind of education, perhaps even worse than it is in basic skills and knowledge education. The teacher, meeting with large numbers of students and teaching large numbers of subjects, simply cannot provide the tutorial time necessary. Imagine, for example, an English teacher with only a hundred students (and that is very few students for an English teacher) trying to instruct students in grammatical skills, help them learn to read and analyze literature better, trying to provide them with creative writing opportunities, analyzing the products of those opportunities and providing feedback; *who in addition to that would be able to meet with interested students on a regular basis to provide tutorial help?* It is safe to say that the only kind of tutorial help provided in such an institution is built around the skills problems of individuals or is given to the highly talented. The average student simply cannot be catered to in such a situation.

### Learning What the Scholar Does

The third education is to learn how scholars analyze human society, how they engage in scientific activity, and how they analyze literature and art. The institutional arrangements which are appropriate for this education enable small groups of students to get together to analyze critical problems, applying tools of the social sciences and the other sciences as they are appropriate. They need the advice and counsel of skilled teachers who themselves enjoy engaging in scientific inquiry and who enjoy doing so with young students. In addition, they need to be backed up by library equipment and by instructional materials prepared by scholars which introduce students to the modes of analysis that the scholar uses.

In the present institution, we are beginning to have instructional materials which can be used for this purpose. They are materials that have been developed by anthropologists, political scientists, physicists, chemists, mathematicians, and others, which can help youngsters explore the scientific disciplines and apply these to the study of their society. Even in areas like Black Studies, which are relatively new in the schools, the paperback book has brought much material to junior and senior high school students, although the area is still lacking. What we do not have is an adequate supply of trained teachers who are themselves competent to do academic inquiry and who enjoy doing it. Nor do we have an institutional arrangement which provides the opportunity for small groups of students to work together with such teachers with relative leisure. Physics classes, poured in four or five a day on the science teacher 25 or 30 students strong, simply cannot engage in the vigorous, leisurely analysis of significant problems long enough to acquire the modes of inquiry of the discipline. The present institution, in other words, has shortcomings on two fronts—one is the proportion of teachers who are prepared to give this kind of education, and the second is a kind of institutional arrangement that does not permit the time-consuming cooperative inquiry characteristic of this kind of study.

### Engaging in a Dialogue on the Critical Problems of Society

There may have been a time when it would not have been critical for education to induct the student into the long dialogue over the nature of human society and ways of improving it, although we doubt it. But it is clear that today we cannot turn away from this kind of education as an important component of the student's life. Even if we were not aware of the society's serious problems, and even if the adult community were not engaged in serious debate over alternative ways of coming to grips with the problems of the internation, the cities, our relationships one another, our need to achieve broader representation, our need for aesthetic improvement, the students would be insisting that we include important issues, values, and alternative solutions in their education.

Until quite recently, there was much less of this kind of education in the schools than there should have been because so many people felt that the schools should steer clear of controversy, that the study of critical values were matters for the home and not for the schools. That day is gone, thank goodness, but the institution still has severe difficulties in this area for two or three quite obvious reasons. One of the most important is that there is a conflict between instruction and the carrying on of dialogue. A teacher who is preoccupied with teaching skills to his students is inhibited from engaging them in the slow processes of debate and analyses of social issues. The teacher often feels that when he gives time to the study of society he is robbing the student of important skills and basic information that will enable him to get on later. Second, many teachers have little experience or taste for this kind of education (while a few enjoy it greatly and regard it as of paramount importance). Third, many of the instructional materials that have been prepared for the consumption of school children have been deliberately bland and have avoided the issues. Partly this was from good motives, although they seem questionable today, or at least are questioned today, in that many educators did not feel that children are able to deal with the deep problems of the cities and the international arena. The responsibility does not lie in the hands of the textbook publishers alone, for the kinds of materials that were produced no doubt reflected the kind of market that existed. At any rate, the supply of materials is slowly changing and some honest efforts are being made to provide the schools with the kind of information sources that children need if they are to debate the serious and interesting issues of the society.

If we are to have genuine dialogue in our schools, however, the institution of the school itself must change in a number of ways. The school has always been organized so that it tended to isolate the students from the society. Education is not *inherently* irrelevant, but it is if it is carried on in a child's world. The problems of the mayor's office and the problems of the Congress take place a long way from the local public school. Also, the public is in general very nervous about the school's role in inducting the students into the hurly-burly of political and social debate. (Parents and other citizens are afraid that the school might induct the students to a point of view which conflicts with their own.) The present controversy over sex education illustrates this. The public is not afraid that the students will not eventually learn about sex, but it is afraid that the sexual attitudes that will be developed by the students will not correspond with their own. Many people would prefer to see the school leave sex and politics and many social issues alone, rather than risk the development of a different point of view from the prevailing one, or the one held by the parent or concerned community members.

The conditions for dialogue include an immersion in controversy, an openness of discourse, and an intention to act. These require an institution which is staffed by teachers who enjoy dialogue and where students are helped to engage themselves in deep issues and to see them through.

## Putting It All Together

We have outlined four kinds of education, and now we must talk about the possibilities for accommodating them. To break with our ways of looking at the school, let us dream a bit into a future in which we don't have one *kind* of school trying to serve all our diverse kinds of children or fulfilling all the possible kinds of education we want for children. *Instead of one school, let us imagine several kinds of education, each one to help our children in a particular way.* Let us begin our dream by reiterating our objective of providing four kinds of education for our children: basic education, education for idiosyncrasy, academic inquiry, and education for dialogue.

We have chosen these four kinds of education because they are very different in terms of goals, and yet all of them will seem important to most people. They are all necessary for a humane, contemporary education. They will not, by any means, satisfy every man's desire for an education for his children (or kids' desires, certainly!). Nor are they the only way of describing desirable education. But they can get us started on the way to thinking through a new kind of schooling and schools.

For the schools which we have inherited from our past generation were designed only for the first kind of education—basic skills and information. Worse, perhaps, they were designed better for elementary skills in reading and writing than for solid engagement with information about a contemporary world. We have stretched them and pushed them. We have changed their shape, building them in round shapes, in clusters of cottages, in television studios, and in great libraries. For all its failings in basic education, however, it is that kind of education that the present does best. Helping students develop on their own terms, helping them engage in academic inquiry, and helping them participate in a dialogue on the nature of society are things that our school does much less well than it does basic education, whatever may be its faults in that direction. In short, we have a one-purpose school, which does none too well at that one purpose, trying to do many jobs!

Suppose we dream of a kind of educational system that encompasses the four kinds of education and which provides them all to our children with equal efficiency. What would that educational system (school?) look like? Let us take each of the four kinds of education in turn and see what each one needs.

Would we put all these four kinds of education under one roof anywhere? We think not. We can have self-instructional centers scattered throughout our city which can accomplish basic education. Individualized self-instructional systems together with tutors in the basic subjects can work in neighborhoods for the young children and in large library-type complexes for the older children. A diagnostic system needs to be developed so that one can determine the stage of each youngster's knowledge and skills, and develop the kind of learning situation appropriate for him. If he cannot learn using self-instructional material, experts in basic education may teach him to read by having him write stories that he reads himself, or by having him select material that he can relate to easily (adventure stories for some, biographies for others, even "Dick and Jane" for some).

The second kind of education requires a lot of open-ended resources and requires that the student meet his tutor regularly. For the younger children, this also could occur in the neighborhood, and for the older children library-like complexes will be appropriate. In these complexes, we can have banks of television courses, films, self-instructional materials of various kinds, libraries, laboratory equipment, and the other kinds of things that young people need in order to develop on their own terms and follow their own interests. In our large cities we have artists, musicians, artisans, and many others who could work part-time in such centers offering their services. In neighborhoods and in city centers, art centers, music centers, literature centers, film studios, and the like can attract a substantial clientele of children.

Academic inquiry in the sciences and mathematics can be carried on in in laboratory centers equipped for the purpose. Some of the scientific inquiry might be centered around the traditional academic areas, other parts should be directly related to our current problems. The study of human ecology could be carried on right in the environment—our waters are there to be studied, as is our air, our earth, and the other things that fill our space. In the social sciences, the whole human environment is the laboratory: our industries, our armed forces, our government, and our international relations. Our local government is here to be studied. Our problems of overcrowding, transportation, and poverty and of our search for love and joy are everywhere around us and can be studied. Centers for the study of these things can be established throughout the city. Some should be in every neighborhood so that the younger children can have ready access to the center. Others, for the older children, can be located where it makes the most sense from the point of view of study. Around our transportation facilities, for example, are the possibilities for a myriad of centers and they will not lack for problems. Our ghettos, our money markets, our banks, our churches, our theaters, our industries, and our commercial world are all places in which there should be centers where children gather to study and reflect on their social world.

And where shall we carry on a dialogue with the children? Partly, of course, we should use our mass media for this purpose. Our political parties can present programs beamed to the young identifying problems from their point of view. But most of all, they need to be brought together in groups with the kind of adult that likes to engage in a dialogue with the young. These places will not look like schools with children sitting in rows learning dead languages. These groups would go to our theaters, visit our government officials, interview delegates to the United Nations, and the other things that should happen when groups of ten or twelve or fifteen children meeting two or three times a week with a wise adult really pursue their inquiry.

## THE FOUR KINDS OF EDUCATION
### AND THE MODELS FOR TEACHING

We have spoken at length about different kinds of education and different types of dwellings to house them, but if each of the various educations is not transmitted in a manner or manners compatible with its aims, then it cannot be realized. Thinking of the models as the learning medium, we may ask ourselves: What models of teaching could be used by such a "school"? Let us look at the available alternatives for just the four kinds of education we have been discussing.

*Basic Education.* In the previous discussion, we suggested a variety of *behavior modification* models (Chapter 16), but these are not the only possibilities. Group Investigation (Chapter 2) is a possibility. The modes of inquiry approach (Chapter 9) could be recommended (as by those who feel that arithmetic is best learned in terms of academic inquiry into mathematics, or those who feel that reading and "language arts" should be approached through linguistic inquiry). Non-directive approaches have been used in the basic skills and information areas (Chapter 12). Ausubel's Theory of Meaningful Verbal Learning and his Advance Organizer strategy was constructed expressly for the purpose. Taba's Concept Formation (Chapter 7) and Bruner's Concept Attainment (Chapter 6) are particularly appropriate for basic skills and information. Perhaps a combination of models would be most appropriate because they would accommodate a variety of learning styles. Systems planning might create a self-administering modular curriculum using behavior modification techniques (a la IPI) and modules structured around advance organizers or inductive strategies. Teachers called academic counselors might stand ready to assist the children and might use personalized teaching strategies modeled after Rogers or Hunt (Chapter 16) to help the children for whom the cybernetic system was not sufficient or appropriate to modify it for them.

PERSONAL EDUCATION. Non-directive models (Chapter 12) appear superficially to be sufficient for this area. The non-directive model would certainly make much sense as the basic pattern for the tutor's behavior, as does Hunt's Conceptual Systems Model (Chapter 16). However, short courses built on Training Principles (Chapter 20) could be available in a kind of educational smorgasbord from which the students could select. In addition, courses built on Synectics principles (Chapter 15) could be offered for those wishing to try to develop their creativity. Inquiry Training exercises might be made available for training in scientific inquiry.

ACADEMIC INQUIRY. The academic inquiry models, such as the Science Inquiry Model (Chapter 9), would appear to be ideal in this area. Groups of students could work together, trying on the modes of the disciplines and developing conceptions of the major ideas of the academic areas.

However, academic inquiry is not, by any means, the only possibility. The Advance Organizer Model (Chapter 10) was developed to teach the structure of the disciplines and could be used as the major model in this area. The Inductive Model (Chapter 7) is also used to structure academic inquiry, as are Inquiry Training models (Chapter 8), Group Investigation (Chapter 2), and Social Inquiry (Chapter 4). Models developed from developmental psychologies like Piaget's (Chapter 11) provide paradigms on which we could approach academic inquiry.

It could be reasoned that several models should be combined for this kind of education. For example, Group Investigation of Academic Inquiry might be employed part of the time and a more highly structured approach used for direct instruction of essential academic ideas. Simulations (Chapter 20) could be used to teach principles relating to real-life situations, as in internation simulation.

DIALOGUE. Oliver and Shaver's Jurisprudential Teaching Model (Chapter 3) was created for this purpose, but the Group Investigation, and Social Inquiry models are all appropriate. T-Group (Chapter 5) theorists could make a good case for human relations training as essential for an authentic dialogue.

## ALTERNATIVES FOR CURRICULUM

The available models are rich and varied and they can serve as a very diversified and coherent education. Whether to use one model or several is probably a moot point. A school or institute employing a single model well and enthusiastically could be a fine and defensible place. A school using a skilled blend of alternative approaches could provide an exciting education, well modulated for differences among children.

Imagine the world of alternatives which can be developed if we construct the world for the child so that it presents to him a pluralistic face— a diversity of ways he can educate himself. Figure 19-3 diagrams one such possible world by representing the student as relating to a variety of educational environments, each one of which might be developed around one or more models as indicated.

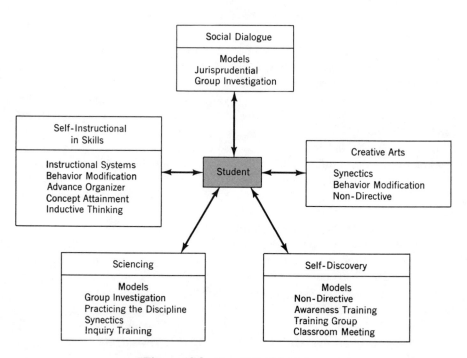

**Figure 19-3** Pluralistic Education

This variety of environments might be brought about by a number of organizational forms within a school:

1. Teams of teachers might provide the environments for a given group of children with the team assuming general responsibility for the education of that group of students (Figure 19-4).

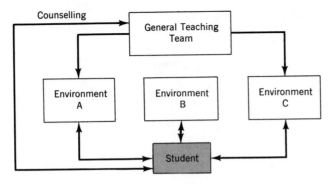

**Figure 19-4** Pluralistic Education Through a Team Teaching Structure

2. Teams of teachers (nurturing teams) might be responsible for the general education of the child, taking responsibility for preparing some of the environments for the child and working with support teams to provide other environments (Figure 19-5).

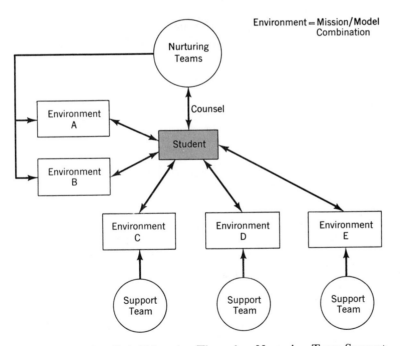

**Figure 19-5** Pluralistic Education Through a Nurturing Team-Support Team Structure

3. Teams could be responsible for the development of specific sets of environments with the student, aided by a counselor, relating himself to the environments (Figure 19-6).

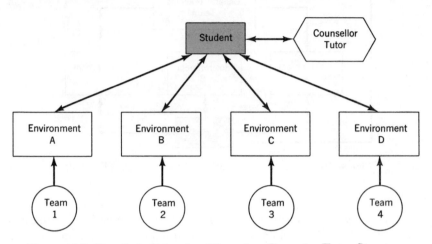

**Figure 19-6** Pluralistic Education Through a Counselor-Tutor Structure

4. The fourth type of organization occurs when a school elects to pursue one or two central missions with one or two preferred models (Figure 19-7). A "school for creativity" might be such an institution, seeking creative behavior as the mission and using appropriate models.

**Figure 19-7** A Central Mission Structure

5. Last, it is possible to imagine a school consisting of student-created environments, with faculty serving solely in counseling roles (Figure 19-8).

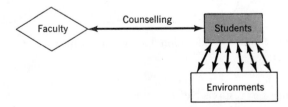

**Figure 19-8** Student Created Environments

## THE STUDENT'S ROLE IN THE CREATION OF
## HIS OWN LEARNING ENVIRONMENTS

Models differ enormously in the extent to which they enable the student—even *require* him—to share in the creation of his own learning environment. Highly structured, prescriptive models place the burden on the teacher and the systems designer. Models of low structure which also depend on nurturing rather than instructing, help the student take great responsibility for his own educational life.

A common fallacy, we believe, is to present to students *either* too little *or* too much responsibility for his own direction. The more self-directing an environment is, the greater also is its complexity, for it requires decision-making, self-awareness, and negotiation to a greater extent. Students vary greatly in their capacity to cope with complexity, hence the need for the "model of models" which can help us cope with the problem of matching students to environments of appropriate complexity.

# 20

# THE DESIGN

# OF INSTRUCTIONAL SYSTEMS

*Three Models*

Teaching, in a broad sense, includes the design of instructional materials, for students learn from media as well as from teachers with whom they interact.

In the last few years a new type of educational engineering has begun to take shape—an almost-science which consists of procedures and knowledge for designing and implementing instructional systems. These systems are composed of training tasks, multiple instructional media and complex teaching machines, and management systems which lead the student from task to task, recording his progress, feeding it back to him and his instructors, and shunting him to appropriate components and further tasks.

In this chapter we will examine three closely related streams of thought for designing instructional systems and indicate how they are being applied to educational problems. We will then relate the design of these instructional systems and their accompanying media or instructional materials to the Models of Teaching.

THREE APPROACHES TO THE CREATION<br>OF SYSTEMS FOR TEACHING

A number of complementary streams of thought have begun to come together since late 1950, making up a distinctive category of approaches toward educational, organizational, or training problems. The three streams of thought are: training psychology, cybernetic psychology, and systems analysis. All three subscribe to the notion that we can describe an organism only in terms of its *manifest* behavior and all three streams attempt to change the visible behavior of the organism in respect to a particular domain of functioning, i.e., reading, flying an airplane, mathematics, sailing, teaching. (They share this orientation with behavior modification psychologists.)

Though the three overlap in many respects, essentially they approach the task of designing training programs from different starting points and carry it through to different "way stations" en route. In other words, they focus on different aspects of the training process and emphasize different features of the change problem. Inasmuch as the magnitude and nature of training problems differs from situation to situation, (that is, each problem has its own requirements and starting point), one strategy or one emphasis may be more appropriate than another for any given training task.

The first stream of thought, training psychology, has come from research on complex training (learning) situations developed at least partly in reaction to the limitations of learning theory. Training psychology focuses on activities in which men perform functions that need to be executed with considerable precision and whose performance has to be meshed precisely with those of others. Much of training psychology developed in response to military needs. A typical example is to design the training of the members of a crew, as of a submarine, or of a bomber. The time for training the members of a crew is generally relatively short, and yet it is extremely critical that they all function with a high degree of coordination with each other, and a high degree of precision within their own tasks. If they do not perform at a high level, the consequences to themselves, the other members of the crew, and perhaps an entire military operation can be jeopardized. Psychologists found that the available knowledge of human learning from the simplified stimulus-response-reinforcement exercises of the learning laboratories was inadequate to permit the *design* of training components for more complex behaviors. Consequently, they gave birth to an entirely new type of psychology, which we can loosely call "training psychology."

Training psychology focuses on designing performance goals or tasks, breaking those tasks down into component tasks, developing training components to ensure the achievement of each of the subcomponents, and arranging the entire learning situation into sequences which ensure that there will be adequate transfer from one component to another and that prerequisite learnings would be achieved before more advanced ones. Like the behavior modification psychologists, the training psychologists are concerned with breakdown and sequencing of behaviors and with shaping behavior to an ultimate performance, but the behaviors within the components are complex and the component sequences add up to an even more complex final behavior. As do the behavior-shaping psychologists, training psychologists manipulate variables like reinforcement and feedback, but they also manipulate task definition and task analysis.

The second stream of work, which developed during World War II and is so very close to training research that it can be considered a branch of it, is based on the conceptualization of the human being in engineering terms. The human is likened to an electric machine or "cybernetic system" which uses the processes of *sensory* feedback to control and modify its own behavior. "Cybernetic theory views the individual as a feedback system which generates its own activities in order to detect and control specific stimulus characteristics of the environment. In keeping with this point of view, cybernetic research analyzes the intrinsic mechanisms by means of which control is established and maintained—that is, the closed-loop, sensory-feedback mechanisms that define the interactions between the individual and his environment. In contrast, conventional learning research conducts open-loop analyses of the relationships between extrinsic events—stimuli and reinforcements—and observed responses."[1] In other words, the cybernetic psychologist conceptualizes the learner as an electronic system, a kind of machine capable of self-regulatory activity by means of obtaining and using information which he gets from his environment.

Cybernetic psychologists frequently use devices such as simulators to study human behavior and as part of training systems. For example, a pilot in a flight simulator will receive a simulated buffeting of winds. The psychologist may be interested not only in how this stimulus effects his behavior, but also in how he goes about obtaining further evidence about the buffeting, the effect that his corrective action has on the attitude of his aircraft, and so on. Thus, a cybernetic psychologist conceptualizes the learner as a system which seeks continually to correct himself by obtaining feedback and processing it. They study the processes by which he obtains and uses various forms of feedback as well as the processes by which his behavior is shaped by external stimuli and events. For the most part, the feedback referred to by cybernetic psychologists is a dynamic or complex sort from which the learner must discriminate the relevant aspects and decide what modifications in his behavior are appropriate to make. In other words, the environmental feedback in Cybernetic Theory does not come with evaluation built in. (You're wrong! Turn left!) These decisions must be made by the trainee. The feedback will provide data in the trainee (the airplane may keel over sharply) but not furnish the "correct" answer or action.

The advent of training design made it possible to design training programs for complex behavior before psychology could account for the multi-stimulus and self-corrective characteristics of these behaviors in task situations. Hence, the design principles outran the psychological principles. The cybernetic concepts of dynamic feedback and self-regulation were essential additions in accounting for and substantiating the design of training programs for complex behaviors.

1 Karl U. Smith and Margaret Foltz Smith, *Cybernetic Principles of Learning and Educational Design* (New York: Holt, Rinehart & Winston, 1966).

The third stream of thought, closely related to both training psychology and cybernetics, has been called "systems development." Increasingly, training psychologists, military, industrial and educational planners, and designers of equipment have become aware of the fact that every human behavior operates as part of an organizational system. This system includes not only the human being who is behaving, but the organization of which he is a part, the machinery and communications systems that make up that organization, the ways personnel are deployed and the kinds of training that are utilized. Increasingly, designers are reluctant to develop a piece of equipment without conceptualizing it as part of a man-machine system, and seeing how it fits in with other pieces of machinery, with human operators, with communication, and so on. Similarly with respect to personnel, it is difficult to imagine training a functionary, such as a radio announcer, without conceptualizing the communication networks of which he will be a part, the types of equipment with which he shall work, the kinds of information that his environment is likely to bring to him, the kinds of personnel by whom he is likely to be surrounded, and the kinds of information with which he will be likely to deal. The other side of the coin to conceptualizing the components of the systems is the implicit concern for managing or orchestrating these components. Once one admits to a multiplicity of interdependent parts, the necessity for smooth coordination becomes paramount. Systems analysis aids us in this endeavor by identifying the pieces and in doing so, providing the outlines of management system requirements. While the "science" of developing man-machine systems is still in its infancy, it is an exceedingly robust infancy, and the systems designer is already beginning to speak to educational problems. Whereas advances in the area of cybernetic psychology make it possible to train the complex behaviors involved in man-machine endeavors, this possibility necessitated additional design techniques which can account for all the pieces and management dimensions of these behaviors.

As mentioned earlier, these three streams of thought and research are by no means unrelated, and individuals who have contributed to one have often contributed to another. For example, Robert Gagne has written extensively about systems development, about training psychology (task analysis), and about cybernetic principles of learning.[2] Many other psychologists have given more emphasis to one of these than to the others, but most have worked in all of them.

The three streams of work can be applied simultaneously. We can find a systems design process which includes conceptions of trainees as "cyborgs," and which uses training psychology principles. Despite the overlap and resemblance, however, we can differentiate the primary emphasis of each

[2] Robert Gagne *et al., Psychological Principles in System Development* (New York: Holt, Rinehart & Winston, 1962).

stream as it concerns itself with a training task: Cybernetic Psychology focuses on dynamic feedback and self-regulation; Training Psychology emphasizes task analysis and design of interrelated training components; and Systems Development focuses on systems analysis and the development of management systems.

## DESIGNING TRAINING SYSTEMS

We have taken some time to distinguish the three fields from one another. It is important now to explore their common elements which are important both in their history and in their implications for education. The first is that they arise primarily from concern with a training goal or with design as such, rather than from a philosophical or psychological conception of the totality of the human being or his society. The cybernetic psychologists, the training psychologists, and the systems designers build their work upon the study of design and of human behavior in the training situation. The social philosopher, for example, comes to education with certain predispositions about how people should learn and how they should be treated. These predispositions come from his conception of the human being as a social animal and from a particular kind of society which he is trying to bring into existence. He imposes that conception on the training situation and develops his instructional theory from it. Similarly, the therapist comes to education with conceptions of therapy and of how human beings develop mental health. They apply their knowledge of therapy to the educational scene and derive procedures therefrom. The training psychologist, the cybernetic analyst, and the systems design psychologist by contrast would ask, "What is the goal we are trying to achieve?" Once the goal has been specified, they tend to set to work to devise a training program to achieve that goal. The nature of the training program is derived from an analysis of the behavioral goal and an attempt to produce training conditions which will shape the behavior of the trainee into the desired patterns. This approach is nicely straightforward or linear, and it is sometimes criticized as being without theory. Sometimes this allegation is denied, sometimes it is accepted. But in any case, what the designers are after is the achievement of the goal by an efficient and humane route which is not preconceived from a "theoretical" educational stance about the nature of man, his society, or how he grows and develops.

This group of educational designers is generally willing to attack a very wide range of training problems, those involving psychomotor skills, complex problem-solving skills, and even at times therapeutic and interpersonal training. Hence, they have derived models which have extremely wide applicability in education and training.

In the next sections we will examine the application of these three approaches to the design of instructional systems. Generally speaking, however, none of the approaches provides straightforward guidelines to the behavior of the classroom teacher. Each is really an approach to educational design, or the development of organization, training programs, instruments of training, and communication networks which can monitor training programs. As a result, all have their widest applicability in design, rather than in teaching. However, teachers who will use instructional systems need to understand how they are developed. Further, in a very real sense, the teacher is a designer of a many-faceted educational system, and systematic design procedures may have many ideas for a teacher who is attuned to and wishes to master them. As guidelines for educational design, each of the three approaches can be highly compatible and interrelated with the other two or can be considered on its own terms, depending on the design task and the teacher's personal choice.

## SYSTEMS ANALYSIS
## AND INSTRUCTIONAL DESIGN

The essence of systems analysis is the making of a model describing an entire organization which fulfills a certain kind of goal in society or accomplishes a particular kind of goal within an organization.

In systems planning, one first develops a general identification of systems functions, and then builds details of the systems, including the specifications for particular kinds of man-machine systems and functions within the larger system. The book by Robert Gagne and others, entitled *Psychological Principles in System Development,* is comprised of a series of essays which describe particular aspects of systems design.[3] One essay, for example, suggests that in order to develop a strategic missiles system, we would need a high level of systems planning. The chart in Figure 20-1 shows the types of systems and departments which might be related within the systems organization.[4] At the first level, one identifies the categories of functioning which are required if the system is to fulfill the purposes for which it is designed.

At the second level, specific content and functions are identified. For example, if one looks at the chart, particular operations, such as preparing missiles for firing, would be specified as would particular maintenance operations, such as fueling and maintaining supplies of spare parts within logistics, mission planning, ground control, communications, personnel, and so on. Functions would be defined for operations, maintenance, and logistics.

At level three, one begins to specify the particular task descriptions which add up to a smoothly functioning system. For example, there are certain tasks which are necessary in order to prepare a missile for launching.

[3] *Ibid.*
[4] *Ibid.,* p. 196.

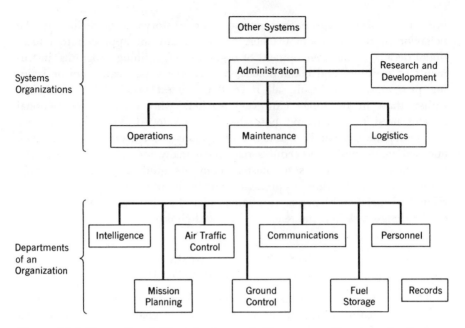

**Figure 20-1** Examples of Organization and Department Structure in Systems. *Source:* From Robert Gagne *et al., Psychological Principles in System Development.* © 1962 by Holt, Rinehart & Winston. Reprinted by permission of the publisher.

There are many kinds of tasks to be specified in the communication system, and so on. A full system design requires literally thousands, perhaps tens of thousands, of task descriptions coordinated with each other in an organized way.

Systems planning of this sort can be applied to the design of an educational program just as well as to the design of an organization which is to achieve functions other than education. For example, recently the U.S. Office of Education let contracts for the design of ten systems for the preparation of teachers. Each of these systems was designed by going through the three general levels described above. The functions of teachers in schools in the society were broadly defined, (Level One), and the more specific aspects of the functioning of a teacher were spelled out (Level Two). This resulted in a model of a teacher as he functions in schools, in this case ten sets of models of teachers. These models were used as objectives of training programs.

The most prominent example of an application of systems planning to elementary and secondary school instruction is the Individually Prescribed Instructional Program (IPI).

Individually Prescribed Instruction (IPI) is an individualized instructional system developed by the Learning Research and Development Center of the University of Pittsburgh, in collaboration with the Baldwin-Whitehall

School District. The system, originally designed for the Oakleaf School in suburban Pittsburgh, now operates in more than a hundred schools across the country, and includes instructional materials in five curriculum areas: mathematics, reading, science, handwriting, and spelling. A student receiving IPI instruction usually works independently on the materials which are prescribed daily (or every few days) for him, depending on his demonstrated level of competence, learning style, and particular learning needs.

IPI illustrates a modular curriculum developed by applying systems analysis procedures to curriculum materials development. It is a particularly useful case study because the available information readily demonstrates the steps the IPI planners took in creating the system. Let's walk through these steps, stopping briefly to show how each reflects the inner workings of the performance model.

First, the planners in conceptualizing a performance model operate with a set of goals and assumptions about the learner, the learning process, and the learner vis-à-vis the system in which he will work. The goals with respect to the learner are:

1. To enable each pupil to work at his own rate through units of study in a learning sequence.
2. To develop in each pupil a demonstrable degree of mastery.
3. To develop self-initiation and self-direction of learning.
4. To foster the development of problem-solving thought processes.
5. To encourage self-evaluation and motivation for learning.[5]

The assumptions regarding the learning process and the related learning environment are as follows:

1. One obvious way in which pupils differ is in the amount of time and practice that it takes to master given instructional objectives.
2. One important aspect of providing for individual differences is to arrange conditions so that each student can work through the sequence of instructional units at his own pace and with the amount of practice he needs.
3. If a school has the proper types of study materials, elementary school pupils, working in a tutorial environment that emphasizes self-learning, can with a minimum amount of direct teacher instruction, learn.
4. In working through a sequence of instructional units, no pupil should be permitted to start work on a new unit until he has acquired a specified minimum degree of mastery of the material in the units identified as prerequisite to it.
5. If pupils are to be permitted and encouraged to proceed at individual rates, it is important for both the individual pupil and the teacher that the program provide for frequent evaluations of pupil progress which can provide a basis for the development of individual instructional prescriptions.

[5] *Individually Prescribed Instruction,* Research for Better Schools (Philadelphia, 1966), p. 5.

6. Professionally trained teachers are employing themselves most productively when they are performing such tasks as instructing individual pupils or small groups, diagnosing pupil needs, and planning instructional programs rather than carrying out such clerical duties as keeping records, scoring tests, and so on. The efficiency and economy of a school program can be increased by employing clerical help to relieve teachers of many non-teaching duties.

7. Each pupil can assume more responsibility for planning and carrying out his own program of study than is permitted in most classrooms.

8. Learning can be enhanced, both for the tutor and the one being tutored, if pupils are permitted to help one another in certain ways.[6]

The second step was to analyze the performance model into a set of sequentially organized behavioral objectives. IPI planners believe that such a listing is fundamental to other aspects of the program and must have the following characteristics.

(a) Each objective should tell exactly what a pupil should be able to do to exhibit his mastery of the given content and skill. This should typically be something the average student can master in such a relatively short period as one class period. Objectives should involve such action verbs as solve, state, explain, list, describe, etc., rather than general terms such as understand, appreciate, know and comprehend.

(b) Objectives should be grouped in meaningful streams of content. For example, in arithmetic the objectives will be grouped (typically) into such areas as numeration, place, value, addition, subtraction, etc. Such grouping aids in the meaningful development of instructional materials and in the diagnosis of pupil achievement. At the same time, this grouping does not preclude the possibility of having objectives that cut across areas.

(c) Within each stream or area the objectives should to the extent possible, be sequenced in such an order that each one will build on those that precede it, and, in turn, be a prerequisite to those that follow. The goal here is to let the objectives constitute a "scale" of abilities.

(d) Within the sequence of objectives in each area the objectives should be grouped into meaningful subsequences or units. Such units can be designated as representing different levels in progress and provide break-points so that when a student finishes a unit in that area, he may either go on to the next unit in that area or may switch to a unit in another area. (For example, upon completing Level B Addition the pupil may either go on to Level C Addition or move on to Level B Subtraction.)[7]

Over 400 specific behavioral objectives are included in the 13 topics of the Mathematics Curriculum. The following excerpt is one small series from the sequence and illustrates the minute detail of the plan:[8]

6 C. M. Lindvall and John O. Bolvin, "The Project for Individually Prescribed Instruction," Oakleaf Project, unpublished manuscript, Learning Research and Development Center, University of Pittsburgh, Pittsburgh, 1966, pp. 3–4.

7 *Individually Prescribed Instruction,* Research for Better Schools (Philadelphia, 1966), p. 3.

|  | LEVEL E | LEVEL F |
|---|---|---|
| ADDITION SUBTRACTION | 1. Given any two whole numbers, the student adds or subtracts using the short algorithm.<br><br>2. Given an addition problem with ≤ 5 addends, the student solves using the short algorithm.<br><br>3. Given multiple step word problems requiring addition and subtraction skills mastered to this point, the student solves them. | 1. Given any two numbers ≤ 9,999.99 and an operation of addition or subtraction, the student solves. LIMIT: Answers must be positive numbers.<br><br>2. Given ≤ 5 addends which are mixed decimals with ≤ 7 digits, the student adds. LIMIT: Decimals to millionths.<br><br>3. Given two mixed decimals, the student subtracts. LIMIT: ≤ 7 digits, decimals to millionths.<br><br>4. Solves multiple step word problems using addition and subtraction skills mastered to this point. |
| MULTIPLICA-TION | 1. Given a two digit number and a one digit number, the student multiplies in horizontal form by using the distributive principle.<br><br>2. Given a problem with a three digit multiplicand and a one digit multiplier, the student solves using partial products.<br><br>3. Given a multiplication problem whose multipliers and multiplicands are whole numbers ≤ 10 times a multiple of ten, the student solves. LIMIT: Factors 9,000.<br><br>4. Given a multiplication problem whose multipliers are whole numbers < 10 times a power of ten, and whose multiplicand 3 digits, the student solves. LIMIT: Multipliers ≤ 9,000.<br><br>5. Given a multiplication problem with a two digit number times a two digit number, the student solves using partial products.<br><br>6. Given a two digit number and a one digit number, the student solves by using the multiplication algorithm.<br><br>7. Given a multiplication problem for skills to this point, the student checks the multiplication by commuting the factors and solving again.<br><br>8. Given a number ≤ 100, the student finds the complete factorization for the number. | 1. Given a two digit number times a two digit number, the student multiplies using the standard algorithm.<br><br>2. Given a three digit number times a two digit number, the student multiplies using the standard algorithm.<br><br>3. Given a whole number and a mixed decimal to hundredths as factors, the student multiplies. LIMIT: Whole number part ≤ 100.<br><br>4. Given two pure decimals ≤ .99, the student multiplies and shows the equivalent problem in fractional form and converts product to decimal notation, compares answers for check.<br><br>5. Given a multiple step word problem requiring multiplication skills mastered to this point, the student solves. |

8 From *Individually Prescribed Instruction: Mathematics Continuum,* Learning Research and Development Center, University of Pittsburgh, Pittsburgh, 1968. Used by permission.

Each of the 13 areas has 9 levels of difficulty, A through I. Within each level for a given topic area, several behavioral objectives are identified and sequentially organized. The breakdown of the 13 topics into levels creates certain options for the student and teacher. The student can cover one area in depth before moving to the next or can go from Addition level E to Subtraction level E. We can see that the content for the IPI math program was spelled out in great detail, ordered sequentially, and inter-related well in advance of the time the teachers and students would come together.

The third step in the program was to develop the materials that the students could use to achieve each objective. These were mostly self-study materials, that is, materials that a student could pursue by himself with minimal assistance from the teacher: in the mathematics curriculum, work-sheets, individual pages, or lesson groups of pages. In addition to the self-instruction, the program calls upon the teacher to offer some of her own instruction to small or large groups and to individuals. For instance, if several students are having difficulty successfully completing a particular objective, the teacher may bring them together for small-group instruction. The mathematics program makes the additional assumption that not all students learn equally well by the same approach. Some students may need more practice in the use of the concept while others learn the concept more effectively by being given examples in which they must decide what is and what is not an instance of the concept. Still others have difficulty transferring behavior from one situation to another and need experience with a variety of formats for using the concept. For example, students can add two digit numbers using a number line, an abacus, or memorized addi-tion tables with rulers for carrying! To accommodate this additional assump-tion, the mathematics materials for a given behavioral objective include a variety of approaches and formats.

The fourth step for the system planner is to bring together the compo-nents of the system—the student, the teacher, the materials—so that the behavioral objectives are achieved. To bring the students together with the appropriate learning materials, one program devoted a portion of the school day at the beginning of the academic year to testing.

> It was essential to find out exactly what abilities each pupil had in each of the many areas in reading, arithmetic and science. In arithmetic for exam-ple, sequenced materials had been developed for each topic, such as numera-tion, measurement, addition, and subtraction. Because so many topics were involved and because it was necessary to know where a pupil should start in each of them, several days had to be devoted to diagnosis of pupil abilities.
>
> On the basis of this diagnosis, a "prescription" was developed for each pupil in each subject. This prescription listed the materials that the pupil was to start with, which might be enough for one day, several days, or a week, depending on the ability of the student, and the difficulty of the unit.

Evaluation and feedback, then, were built into the ongoing curricular activities. This is in contrast to many educational programs which depend heavily on periods of examination and the like that are separated from other curricular activities.

The faculty also developed a system for guiding the students as they worked. A student was to begin working on his prescribed materials, usually by himself at a desk in a study area with eighty or ninety other pupils. In this room there were also two or three teachers to provide instructional assistance and three or four clerks to distribute materials and grade papers. Most pupils were able to proceed through their study materials with a minimum of help from the teachers. If a teacher found a pupil who needed more help than she could give in this large-group situation, she directed him to a small side room where another teacher gave him more extensive individual help or involved him in small-group instruction.[9]

Lastly comes the creation of a management system for monitoring the student's progress and adjusting prescriptions so that carefully tailored feedback, the heart of the cybernetic approach, can be given.

The materials prescribed for a student at any given time typically would include, as a final exercise, a "check test" or "curriculum embedded" test. This exercise, which the student viewed as just another worksheet, would play a large part in determining what the pupil did next. When a pupil completed his prescribed unit of work, he took it to a clerk for checking and then to the teacher who was developing the prescriptions. This teacher held a brief conference with the pupil, and examined the work he had just completed, developed his next prescription. As we can see, the learner role variables are carefully defined and provision is made for developing them under this system.[10]

In this case the management system for tracking a pupil's progress and specifying the role of functionaries is embedded in the instructional system. The management function is more comparable to that found in business. That is, the teacher-manager has the responsibility for bettering the system and adjusting it to the needs of the individual student. The teacher's role in IPI is a crucial one. She serves as a "diagnostician (analyzing the IPI diagnostic data about each student in order to tailor a program to meet the individual learning needs), a selector (drawing upon the bank of both human and material resources available to the IPI instructional situation), and a tutor (building meaningful and appropriate learning experiences that lead a student to a more independent and responsible role in his IPI learning setting.")[11] This represents an organizational approach to teaching

[9] Bruce R. Joyce and Berj Harootunian, *The Structure of Teaching* (Chicago: Science Research Associates, 1967), pp. 83–84.

[10] *Ibid.,* p. 84.

[11] Robert Scanlon and Mary Brown, "In-Service Education for Individualized Instruction" (unpublished manuscript, Research for Better Schools, Philadelphia) p. 1.

which is quite different from the concept of the self-contained classroom teacher working with the groups of children he sees everyday and for whose education he maintains total responsibility.

Another prominent example of an instructional system, one in which the machine components paved the way for an entirely different and more effective learning environment, is the Language Laboratory. The development of the Language Laboratory represents vivid application of the combined properties of systems analysis, task analysis, and cybernetic principles in the educational setting. Before the language laboratory became commonplace, the classroom teacher served as the model for foreign speech along with the classroom of 25 to 35 students who were more or less accurately reproducing sounds of speech. The individual in such a situation might have a maximum of one minute of speech practice per classroom session, hardly enough to produce fluency or accuracy.

Today the typical classroom laboratory is a classroom where learners use electrical equipment to hear, record, and play back spoken materials. The general physical equipment includes student stations and an instructor's control panel. Through the instructor's control panel, the teacher has the ability to broadcast a variety of content materials, new and remedial programs and instruction to individuals, selected groups, or the entire class. He can also monitor the student's performance. The students' stations are often a series of individual accoustically treated carrells. They are usually equipped with headphones, a microphone, and a tape recorder. The student listens through the headphones to live or recorded directions from the instructor to repeat, answer questions, or make other appropriate responses to the lesson. The instructor may also choose to use the chalk board, textbook, or other visual stimuli to supplement audio inputs. Modern technology has made it possible for near instantaneous situations where the student might:

1. Hear his own voice more clearly through earphones than he could otherwise.
2. Directly compare his speech with a model.
3. Provide himself immediate feedback.
4. Isolate items for study.
5. Permit pacing for specific drill.
6. Permit more finely sequenced instructional content.

Learning a foreign language requires the student to repeatedly hear vocabulary and speech patterns. These exercises are carefully sequenced and are followed by new combinations at various levels of complexity. The ultimate goal is to have the student readily comprehend what he hears and make immediate and appropriate responses. From the student's viewpoint the language laboratory serves as a base for tireless practice of finely sequenced behavior, matching audial models and the development of fluency of speech; from the instructor's viewpoint the language laboratory provides the facilities (hardware and software) for a more effective design of the language learning situation.

In systems analysis terminology the language laboratory represents the development of a man-machine system based on the performance objectives and requirements of foreign language proficiency. Prior to the language laboratory, it was possible to provide reasonably sequenced visual materials. But the critical elements of language training, the individualized audial practice and dynamic feedback, far outran the human management capacities and support facilities of the self-contained classroom teacher with 25 students. With the electronic hardware and software support sub-systems, the instructor can now divide his time more effectively between monitoring (management), diagnosis, and instruction. The student is provided immediate direct sensory feedback so that he can compare his performance with the desired performance and make the necessary self-corrective adjustments.

Meeting the requirements for effective language learning required the systems analyst perspective. Put another way, it required the ability to step outside the confines and capacities of the existing classroom in order to specify the additional components and perceive the interdependent functions of a total system that could meet the educational goal. It required the adherence to cybernetic learning principles and task analysis to develop appropriately sequenced learning activities content modules.

## PRINCIPLES OF TRAINING
## AND INSTRUCTIONAL DESIGN

To create the individual instructional modules of a systems' curriculum based on training research, one can utilize training principles or cybernetic principles, or a combination of the two.

As indicated earlier, when military psychologists were faced with massive training problems which they had to solve in a relatively short period of time, they were disappointed with the yield that was available from S-R learning psychology. They turned, for the most part, to a very straightforward analytic stance toward the development of training components. Robert Gagne has summarized these components in his article, "Military Training and Principles of Learning."

1. Any human task may be analyzed into a set of component tasks which are quite distinct from each other in terms of the experimental operations needed to produce them.

2. These task components are mediators of the final task performance; that is, their presence insures positive transfer to a final performance, and their absence reduces such transfer to near zero.

3. The basic principles of training design consist of: (a) identifying the component tasks of a final performance; (b) insuring that each of these component tasks is fully achieved; and (c) arranging the total learning situation in a sequence which will insure optimal mediational effects from one component to another.

These statements certainly imply a set of principles which have very different names from those we are now most familiar with. They are concerned with such things as task analysis, intra task transfer, component task achievement, and sequencing as important variables in learning, and consequently in training. These principles are not set in opposition to the traditional principles of learning, such as reinforcement, differentiation or task elements, familiarity, and so on, and do not deny their relevance, only their relative importance.[12]

These principles are embodied in the design procedure broadly known as task analysis. For example, if we were to ask students to learn a set of paired associates, we could by task analysis create an optimal learning situation. When we analyzed the learning task, we would find there were two components. One is the learning of the paired associates themselves and the other is the learning of their serial order. Research studies have shown that this is a more efficient sequence than learning units serially first—a practice which combines both subtasks rather than sequencing them until their mastery.[13]

In order to apply these principles to a training problem, let us turn to an example from teacher training which is different from the IPI system though it uses very similar principles. A team at the University of Georgia illustrates the training research principles within the development of their model of teacher education.[14]

The Georgia team began their development of a training program by preparing a job analysis of the elementary school teacher; all their preliminary activities were organized to this end.

The requirements of society and knowledge from various resources and materials contributed to the determination of the goals of the elementary school. These goals in turn serve as bases for determining the objectives. Yet, the selection of the objectives was also affected by the recommendations of professional societies and what was known of the effectiveness of educational

---

[12] Robert Gagne, "Military Training and Principles of Learning," *American Psychologist,* 17 (1962), p. 88. Reprinted by permission of the American Psychological Association.

[13] *Ibid.*

[14] Charles E. Johnson, Gilbert F. Shearron, and A. Joan Stauffer, *Georgia Educational Model Specifications for the Preparation of Elementary Teachers,* ED-025-491, 2. University of Georgia, U.S. Office of Education, Washington, D.C., 1968.

technology. Once the elementary school objectives were determined, pupil learning behaviors which would guide children in acquiring characteristics represented by these objectives could be identified. From these teacher teaching behaviors, the core for the job analysis, could be formulated. However, the task of job analysis was not complete until consideration was given to that which could be gleaned from observations of the teacher on-the-job, and knowledge from professional education focused at teacher performance. Throughout the entire flow, but especially in relation to the primary focus of this project in its initial stages (the job analysis), knowledge of the individual child as a learner was a constant factor for consideration.[15]

They provided an information flow chart for this job analysis of the elementary teacher. This information flow chart follows as Figure 20-2.[16]

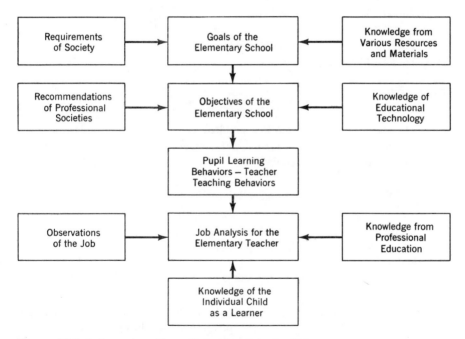

**Figure 20-2** Information Flow Chart for Job Analysis.
*Source:* From Johnson, Shearron, and Stauffer, *Georgia Educational Model Specifications for the Preparation of Elementary Teachers* (U.S. Office of Education, 1968).

The application of this process resulted in the development of the performance specifications and the competency requirements which a teacher would need in order to operate effectively in a teaching-learning situation. It proceeded from desirable pupil behavior to what a pupil would have

[15]Johnson, Shearron, and Stauffer, *Georgia Educational Model Specifications,* p. 8.
[16] *Ibid.,* p. 9.

to do in order to achieve those behaviors, to the kinds of behaviors that a teacher would have to manifest in order to enable the pupil to engage in those learning behaviors, and from those to the specifications of competence which would be the goals of the teacher education program. An example of this process is provided below.

*Objective*

To learn to solve problems.

*Pupil Learning Behaviors*

1. The child identifies problems.
2. The child formulates hypotheses.
3. The child gathers information.
4. The child analyzes data.
5. The child evaluates alternate solutions.
6. The child generalizes solutions.

*Teaching Behaviors*

1. The teacher organizes problem situations.
2. The teacher interests pupils in a problem and observes its formulation.
3. The teacher observes information gathering and processing.
4. The teacher assists, as required, in developing a solution to a problem.

*Suggested Specifications for a Teacher Education Program*

A teacher education program will provide the student with:
1. Knowledge of and skill in developing problem situations.
2. Knowledge of and skill in techniques of presenting problem solutions methods.
3. Knowledge of and skill in critiquing problem solutions.[17]

Since the teacher was conceptualized as being a member of a team, it was thought that he could have the position of teaching assistant, teacher, or specialist on a team. Figure 20-3 shows performance specifications for each of those three types of teaching functionaries.[18] The performance specifications list the necessary teacher behaviors and indicate the differential performance level for each of the three teaching functionaries with respect to any given behavior. In this case the performance specifications indicate not only the desired level of development but also the type of development. Each behavior is specified in terms of its cognitive and/or affective components. Cognitive, in this case, refers to the behavioral dimen-

17 *Ibid.*, p. 37.
18 *Ibid.*, pp. 42–43.

| Characteristic | Cognitive | | | Affective | | |
|---|---|---|---|---|---|---|
| | Teaching Assistant | Teacher | Specialist | Teaching Assistant | Teacher | Specialist |
| 3.01.01 Creativity as problem solving. | | 3 | 5 | | 4 | 5 |
| 3.01.02 Conditions where the creative process flourishes. | | 3 | 6 | | 2 | 4 |
| 3.01.03 Activities for the development of creativity in pupils. | 1 | 3 | 5 | 1 | 3 | 4 |
| 3.01.04 Development of curiosity. | | 3 | 5 | | 3 | 5 |
| 3.01.05 Techniques for discovering relationships (e.g., inquiry training). | 1 | 3 | 4 | 1 | 2 | 3 |
| 3.01.06 Techniques for problem solving. | 1 | 3 | 5 | 1 | 2 | 3 |
| 3.01.07 Application of principles from the disciplines to phenomena. | | 3 | 4 | | 2 | 3 |
| 3.01.08 Techniques for predicting cause and effect. | | 3 | 4 | | 3 | 4 |
| 3.01.09 Interpreting the results of change. | | 3 | 6 | | 3 | 5 |
| 3.01.10 Techniques for observing one's environment. | 1 | 3 | 4 | 1 | 2 | 3 |
| 3.01.11 Techniques for describing one's environment. | 1 | 3 | 4 | 1 | 2 | 3 |
| 3.01.12 Techniques for extracting information from one's environment. | 1 | 3 | 4 | 1 | 2 | 3 |
| 3.01.13 Relationships within the environment. | 1 | 3 | 4 | 1 | 2 | 3 |
| 3.01.14 Measurements and standards. | 1 | 3 | 4 | 1 | 2 | 3 |
| 3.01.15 Techniques for classifying and identifying items in the environment. | 1 | 3 | 4 | 1 | 2 | 3 |
| 3.01.16 Identification of basic types of personality. | 1 | 2 | 6 | 1 | 2 | 3 |
| 3.01.17 Acceptance of basic types of personality. | 1 | 2 | 4 | 2 | 5 | 5 |
| 3.01.18 Development of self-expression. | 1 | 3 | 4 | 1 | 2 | 3 |
| 3.01.19 Development of interpersonal communications | 1 | 3 | 6 | 1 | 3 | 4 |
| 3.01.20 Pupil feelings, attitudes, and interests. | 1 | 3 | 6 | 1 | 4 | 5 |
| 3.01.21 Techniques for acceptable pupil expression of their feelings. | | 3 | 5 | | 4 | 5 |

**Figure 20-3** Performance Specifications.
*Source:* From Johnson, Shearron, and Stauffer, *Georgia Educational Model* (U.S. Office of Education, 1968).

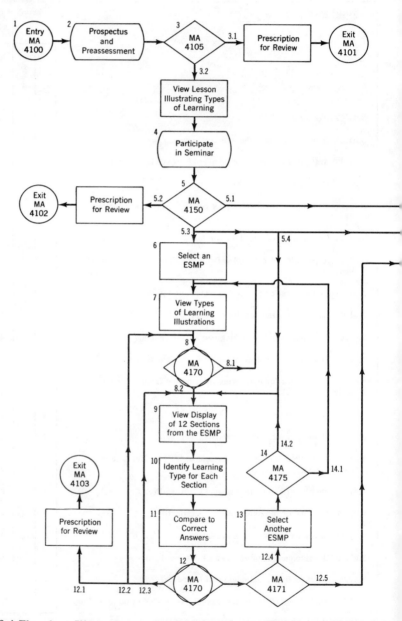

**Figure 20-4** Flowchart Illustrating an Implementation of a Mathematics Education Element Objective.
*Source:* From M. Vere De Vault, Wisconsin Elementary Teacher Education Program (U.S. Office of Education).

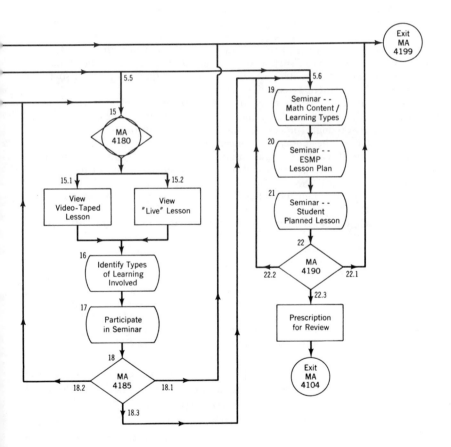

sion having to do with knowing. The affective domain has to do with the feeling, valuing, and other emotional aspects of a particular behavior.

## Linking the Objectives to Instructional Modules

From the specifications of training objectives via systems design, the Georgia Elementary Model staff developed the concept of a *proficiency module*. A proficiency module is a set of specifications of teacher performances and a series of learning tasks which are prepared to achieve those objectives.

> A proficiency module (PM) is defined as a published guide which is designed to direct individual student learning behavior in studying particular subjects or topics or in undertaking particular activities in laboratory situations. PMs are not correspondence courses; they are not programmed instruction guides; they are not void of provision for humanistic qualities; and they are neither workbooks nor textbooks. They are a means of organizing modules of content for instruction in such a manner that it is assured that the student either has acquired the content of that module, or that he will do so by carrying out the instructions contained in it.
>
> The content for any PM is a selected cluster of related teacher performance behaviors (see Specifications 3.00) including not only definitions, facts, and concepts, but also thought processes, motor skills, and attitudes. The core of the PM, insofar as the student is concerned, is a series of learning tasks prepared by specialists. These tasks are carefully designed and arranged in such a manner that they are regarded as the most effective known means of guiding students toward the acquisition of the performance behaviors. These tasks provide multiple sequences for the attainment of the desired end in such a manner as to make them adaptable to individual differences among students in such characteristics as rate of learning, sensory sensitivity, and cognitive styles.
>
> When properly constructed, PMs avoid duplication of content among offerings and permit the student to move through the program at a pace which is both comfortable and challenging to him. A qualified student may move as rapidly as he is capable of moving or as slowly as is necessary for him to move in meeting the specific requirements. However, unless PMs are constructed in accordance with the specifications contained in this report, they may become a weak substitute for the still weaker, current system of education which permeates traditional programs of teacher education today.[19]

Task analysis (training design) procedures were used to develop the performance modules, which consist of a series of learning activities designed to achieve the specific performance criteria specified in the performance model. For illustration, let us turn to the University of Wisconsin model shown in Figure 20-4.[20] It is organized very similarly to the Georgia one

---

19 *Ibid.,* p. 190.
20 M. Vere DeVault, Wisconsin Elementary Teacher Education Program, OE-58025, 6, 7, University of Wisconsin, U.S. Office of Education, Washington, D.C., pp. 183–87.

in the sense that the performance model of the teacher was developed, and then instructional modules were prepared to achieve each of the clusters of behaviors within the performance model.

GUIDE TO FIGURE 20-4

*EDUCATIONAL OBJECTIVE:* "CAN ANALYZE SECTIONS OF AN ESMP THAT ILLUSTRATE DIFFERENT KINDS OF MATHEMATICAL LEARNING."

(1) Enter Module. Go to (2)
(2) Comprehensive introduction to module, including:
    (2.1) Preview of nature and objectives (as listed in bold print, below) of module.
    (2.2) Pre-test covering characteristics or features of the eight types of learning identified by Gagne (*The Conditions of Learning,* 1965). Go to (3).
(3) Decision point:
    (3.1) Exit from module for review work on Gagne's eight types of learning. May re-enter at (2).
    (3.2) Viewing of video-taped or filmed mathematics lesson in which numerous types of learning are illustrated but not identified. Go to (4).

*INSTRUCTIONAL OBJECTIVE:* THE STUDENT IS ABLE TO IDENTIFY VARIOUS EXEMPLARS OF GAGNE'S LEARNING TYPES IN A SEMINAR DISCUSSION LED BY INSTRUCTOR (FOLLOWING THE VIEWING OF A TAPED OR FILMED MATHEMATICS LESSON).
*CRITERION:* IN CONFERENCE WITH INSTRUCTOR, FOLLOWING SEMINAR, THEY DECIDE THE STUDENT'S PROFICIENCY IN IDENTIFYING MATH EXEMPLARS OF LEARNING TYPES.

(4) Participate in seminar discussion of (3.2). Go on to (5).
(5) Decision point; in consultation with instructor and based on results of (2.2) and (3):
    (5.1) Exit: essential objective of module for student already achieved.
    (5.2) Exit: remedial prescriptions in educational psychology or mathematics, with later re-entry at (2).
    (5.3) Go to (6).
    (5.4) Go to (9).
    (5.5) Go to (15).
    (5.6) Go to (19).

*INSTRUCTIONAL OBJECTIVE 2:* THE STUDENT IS ABLE TO IDENTIFY LEARNING TYPES OF GAGNE AS ILLUSTRATED BY "DISPLAYS" USING CONTENT OF A PARTICULAR ESMP. (A DISPLAY MIGHT BE A SET OF PAGES FROM A TEACHER'S EDITION OF A BOOK, TAPED OR WRITTEN CLASSROOM DIALOGUE BETWEEN TEACHER AND PUPILS, ETC.)

*CRITERION:* STUDENT COMPLETES AN EXAM AND CORRECTLY IDENTIFIES AT LEAST 10 OUT OF 12 LEARNING TYPES.

(6) One of five ESMPs is assigned (selected at random). Go to (7).

(7) Call for display which, for the ESMP designated in (6), shows one illustration of each of Gagne's eight types of learning (to the extent that they are exemplified in the particular ESMP). Go to (8).

(8) Self-decision point:

    (8.1) Call for display of additional illustration(s) of any of the eight types of learning as exemplified in the ESMP assigned (designated) in (6). Then go to (9).

    (8.2) Go to (9).

(9) Call for display of 12 sections from the ESMP designated in (6),—no one of the displays to duplicate any shown earlier in (7). Go to (10).

(10) Identify the learning type(s) associated with each section of (9). Go to (11).

(11) Call for an "answer key" to provide (immediate) reinforcement. Go to (12).

(12) Self-decision point:

    (12.1) Exit from module for remedial suggestions pertaining either to mathematics or to educational psychology; may re-enter later at (6).

    (12.2) Loop back to (8.1) and proceed without duplication of displays.

    (12.3) Loop back to (9) and proceed without duplication of displays.

    (12.4) Go to (13) if not there before.

    (12.5) Go to (15) if already through (13).

(13) Select an ESMP from the four remaining after (6). Go to (14).

(14) Self-decision point:

    (14.1) Loop back to (7) and proceed with the ESMP selected in (13).

    (14.2) Loop back to (9) and proceed with the ESMP selected in (13).

*INSTRUCTIONAL OBJECTIVE 3:* THE STUDENT IS ABLE TO INDEPENDENTLY IDENTIFY LEARNING TYPES OF GAGNE VIEWED IN A LIVE OR FILMED MATH LESSON (CONTENT FROM A PARTICULAR ESMP).

*CRITERION:* THE STUDENT LISTS ALL THE LEARNING TYPES AND THE MATH CONTENT WHICH HE SEES INVOLVED IN EACH EXEMPLAR. THE STUDENT CHECKS HIS LIST IN SEMINAR.

(15) Self-decision point:

    (15.1) View a video-taped or filmed lesson. Go to (16).

    (15.2) Observe a "live" lesson. Go to (16).

(16) Identify which of the eight types of learning were involved in opted (15). Go to (17).

(17) Participate in seminar to discuss (15) and (16). Go to (18).

(18) Decision point (in consultation with seminar instructor):
    (18.1) Exit from module; optional portion accomplished.
    (18.2) Loop back to (15) for additional study.
    (18.3) Go to (19).

*INSTRUCTIONAL OBJECTIVE 4:* THE STUDENT IS ABLE TO ANALYZE, IN A GROUP SEMINAR (WITH INSTRUCTOR), THE RELATIONSHIPS OF LEARNING TYPES TO PARTICULAR MATH CONTENT IN AN ESMP.
*CRITERION:* IN CONFERENCE, FOLLOWING SEMINAR, THE STUDENT DECIDES ABILITY TO IDENTIFY LEARNING TYPES WHICH CAN BE USED WITH PARTICULAR MATH CONTENT IN A PARTICULAR ESMP.

(19) The student participates in a group seminar to analyze and relate math content and learning types. Go to (20).

*INSTRUCTIONAL OBJECTIVE 5:* THE STUDENT IS ABLE TO PLAN A MATH LESSON TO ILLUSTRATE SPECIFIC TYPES OF LEARNING.
*CRITERION:* INSTRUCTOR AND STUDENTS, IN SEMINAR, DETERMINE IF THE PLANNED LESSON ACCOMPLISHES THE OBJECTIVE.

(20) The student participates in a seminar to present and discuss a planned math lesson from a particular ESMP which contains exemplars of learning types. Go to (21).

*INSTRUCTIONAL OBJECTIVE 6:* THE STUDENT IS ABLE TO "IMPLEMENT" A PLANNED MATH LESSON WHICH ILLUSTRATES PARTICULAR TYPES OF LEARNING FOR A SPECIFIED ESMP.
*CRITERION:* INSTRUCTOR AND STUDENTS, IN SEMINAR, DETERMINE IF THE LESSON, AS TAUGHT, FULFILLS THE OBJECTIVE.

(21) The student participates in a seminar to present and discuss his lesson. Go to (22).

(22) Decision point. The student consults with instructor:
    (22.1) Student exits from module.
    (22.2) Loop back to (19) for further work.
    (22.3) Student exits with advice to retake portions of module at a later time.

The student is led through a sequence of activities shown in Figure 20-5 to achieve several instructional objectives. There are activities related to each objective and they have been sequenced in order to develop elements of the desired behavior sequentially. Decision points (diamond-shaped figures on the flowchart) permit the student to exit from the module to return back to an earlier stage for additional study or to go on to a further

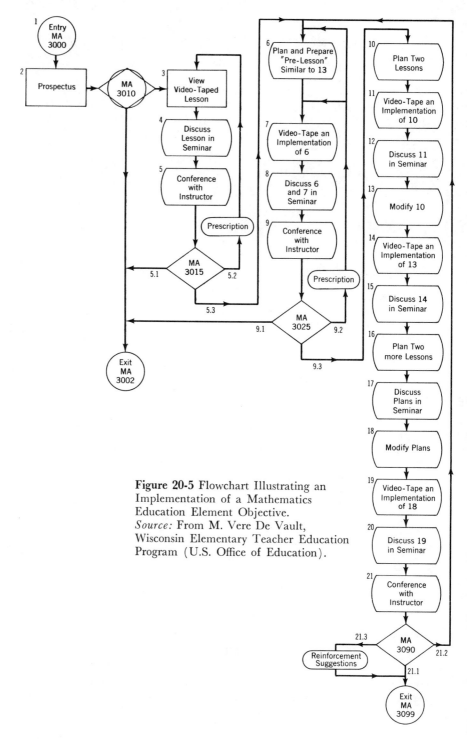

**Figure 20-5** Flowchart Illustrating an Implementation of a Mathematics Education Element Objective.
*Source:* From M. Vere De Vault, Wisconsin Elementary Teacher Education Program (U.S. Office of Education).

set of activities. The instructional module illustrates this even more graphically.[21]

This short intra-module instructional unit involves a sequence of four related lessons:

1. showing representations of rectangles that have specified perimeters;
2. showing representations of rectangular regions that have specified areas;
3. studying the perimeters of different rectangles which bound surfaces having a constant area; and
4. studying the areas of different regions which are bounded by rectangles having a constant perimeter.

(1) Enter. (MA 3000)

(2) Preview of the objective(s) and nature of the unit.
Decision point (MA 3010)
Exit (MA 3002), or
Go to (13).

(3) View a video-taped "terminal lesson" in which pupils demonstrate their ability to find (a) perimeters of rectangles and boundaries of rectangular regions, and (b) areas of rectangular regions and surfaces bounded by rectangles, in which a variety of representations are used:

1. geoboards with outlines of rectangles,
2. cross-section paper with outlines of rectangles,
3. sticks or dowel rods for outlines of rectangles,
4. square tiles for outlines of rectangular regions,
5. cardboard or oaktag rectangular regions,
6. drawings of rectangles on plain paper, etc.

(4) Discuss in a small-group seminar the lesson viewed in (3), from the standpoint of its mathematical content, the materials used, and the appropriateness of particular materials for particular pupils, with implications regarding pupils' levels of ability to find perimeters and areas.

(5) In conference with the instructor involved in (4), decide (MA 3015) to:

(5.1) Exit, or
(5.2) Follow suggestions to strengthen one or more aspects of background and then loop back to (3), or
(5.3) Go on to (6).

(6) Plan and prepare materials for a "pre-lesson" similar to (3).

(7) Have video-taped an implementation of (6) with a small group of pupils.

(8) Discuss (6) and (7), and implications, in a small-group seminar.

(9) In conference with the instructor involved in (8), decide (MA 3025) to:

---

[21] M. Vere DeVault, *Wisconsin Elementary Teacher Education Program*, pp. 188–91.

(9.1) Exit, or

(9.2) Follow suggestions for strengthening (6) or (7) and loop back to (6) or (7) with a different small group of pupils, or

(9.3) Go on to (10).

(10) Based on (6) thru (9), plan a sequence of two lessons involving the same pupils used for (7):

(a) a lesson in which pupils use a variety of materials (as in [3]) to show different rectangles (having integral sides) whose perimeters are constant. (Exclude perimeters of 18 and 24 from the examples.)

(b) a lesson in which pupils use a variety of materials (as in [3]) to show different rectangular regions (with integral bounding sides) whose areas are constant. (Exclude areas of 24 and 36 from the examples.)

(11) With the same pupils used for (7), have video-taped an implementation of (a) of (10).

(12) Discuss (11) in a small-group seminar, with particular attention to any modifications that should be made in (b) of (10).

(13) Based on (12), modify (b) of (10).

(14) Have video-taped an implementation of (13), using the same pupils as for (11).

(15) Discuss (14) in a small-group seminar, with particular attention to implications for (16).

(16) Plan a sequence of two more lessons involving the same pupils used for (7), (11) and (14):

(c) a lesson in which pupils use a variety of materials (as in (3)) to determine the areas of all rectangular regions (with integral bounding sides) having constant perimeters of 18 and 24, leading to conclusions about changes in area for specified perimeters, and

(d) a lesson in which pupils use a variety of materials (as in (3)) to determine the perimeters (integral sides) of all rectangles which bound surfaces having constant areas of 24 and 36, leading to conclusions about changes in perimeter for specified areas.

(17) Review plans with small-group seminar and instructor.

(18) Based on (17), modify (16).

(19) Using the same pupils as for (7), (11) and (14), have video-taped an implementation of (18).

(20) Discuss (19) in small-group seminar.

(21) Based on (20) in consultation with instructor, decide (MA 3090) to:

(21.1) Exit: objective attained (MA 3099), or

(21.2) Loop back to (6) and repeat with another small group of pupils, or

(21.3) Exit and reinforce objective by entering a unit which deals with a sequence of lessons on using different materials to develop ideas of decimal base and place value associated with our familiar numeration system.

This is a typical type of module which results when training procedures are applied to the development of a particular instructional module. An analysis has been made of the terminal behavior which is desired, sets of activities have been sequenced to achieve aspects or components of the terminal behavior, and the components within the module have been related to each other to ensure transfer from one aspect of the module to another.

### Systems Design and Training Psychology

These examples of systems design to specify training objectives and of training design to develop the components of the performance modules show the very close relationship between systems planning and the principles of training psychology. The examples given above are quite typical in that frequently systems design principles are used in conjunction with the application of training psychology principles, in order to build instructional programs. The former identifies system functions and objectives and the latter aids in the development of training activities or performance modules which establish a particular training objective specified earlier by systems design procedure.

### CYBERNETIC PRINCIPLES
### AND INSTRUCTIONAL DESIGN

From one perspective, cybernetic psychology represents the machine's contribution to the humanization of man, for in making an analogy between humans and machines, the cybernetic psychologist comes up with the conceptualization of the learner as a self-regulating feedback system.

Cybernetics as a discipline "has been described as the comparative study of the human (or biological) control mechanism, and electromechanical systems such as computers."[22] The central focus of the analysis is the apparent similarity between the feedback control mechanisms of electromechanical systems and human systems. "A feedback control system incorporates three primary functions: it generates movement of the system toward a target of defined path; it compares the effects of this action with the true path and detects error; and it utilizes this error signal to redirect the system."[23] For example, the automatic pilot for a boat continually corrects the helm of the ship, depending on the readings of the compass. When the ship begins to swing in a certain direction, and the compass moves off the desired heading more than a certain amount, a motor is switched on, the helm is moved over. When the ship returns to course, the helm is straightened out again, and thus the ship continues on its way. As we have seen, steering a boat operates on essentially the same principle as does a human being. In both cases, they watch the compass, and in

---

[22] Smith and Smith, *Cybernetic Principles of Learning*, p. 202.
[23] *Ibid.*, p. 203.

both cases, they move the wheel to the left or right depending on what is going on. In both cases, action is initiated in terms of a specified criterion ("Let's go north"). And, depending on the feedback or error signal, the initial action is redirected. Very complex self-regulating mechanical systems have been developed to control devices such as guided missiles, ocean liners, and satellites.

The cybernetic psychologist interprets the human being as a control system, which generates a course of action and then redirects or corrects the action by means of feedback which is received. This can be a very complicated process, as when the Secretary of State of the nation reevaluates the foreign policy base, or a very simple one, as when we notice that our sailboat is coming up into the wind too much and we ease off just a little bit. In applying the analysis of mechanical systems as a frame of reference for looking at human beings, psychologists came up with the central idea "...that performance and learning must be analyzed in terms of the control relationships between a human operator and an instrumental situation. That is, learning was understood to be determined by the nature of the individual, as well as by the design of the learning situation. Further, human engineering analysis called attention to the concept of the behaving individual as a closed-loop or cybernetic system, utilizing the processes of sensory feedback in continuous control of behavior."[24]

In any learning situation, we must be able to identify and characterize the pertinent human factors and the instrumental and symbolic features which make up the learning environment. More important, we have to specify the relationships between the capacities of the learner and the instrumentalities of the learning situation. The basis for this analysis is the sensory-motor capabilities of the learner. From this information the learning situation can be designed to fit the feedback capabilities of the learner.

All human behavior, according to cybernetic psychology, involves a perceptible pattern of motion. This includes both overt and covert behavior, such as thinking and symbolic behavior. In any given situation, an individual modifies his behavior depending on the feedback he is getting from the environment. He organizes his movements and his response patterns in relation to the feedback he receives. Thus, his own sensory-motor capabilities form the basis of his feedback system and his ability to receive feedback constitutes the human system's mechanism for receiving and sending information. As the human being develops greater symbolic capability, he is able to utilize indirect as well as direct feedback, therefore expanding his control over his physical and social environment. He is less dependent on the concrete realities of the environment because he can utilize the symbolic representations. The essence, then, of cybernetic psychology rests on its principle of sensory-oriented feedback which is intrinsic to the indi-

[24] *Ibid.,* p. vii.

vidual (he "feels" the effects of his decisions) and is the basis for self-corrective choices. The individual can "feel" the effects of his decisions because the environment responds in full rather than, "You're right" or "Wrong! Try again." That is, the environmental consequences of one's choices are played back to him. Learning in cybernetic terms is sensorially experiencing the natural environmental consequences of one's behavior and engaging in self-corrective behavior; instruction concerns itself with creating for the learner an environment in which this full feedback takes place.

The application of cybernetic principles to educational procedures is perhaps most dramatically and clearly seen in the development of simulators as training devices. A simulator is a training device which represents reality very closely, but in which the complexity of events can be controlled. For example, a simulated automobile has been constructed in which a driver sees a road (through a motion picture film), has a wheel to turn, a clutch and brake to operate, a gear shift lever, turn signal indicator, and all the other devices of a contemporary automobile. He can start this simulated automobile and when he turns the key, he hears the noise of the motor running. When he presses the accelerator, the noise increases in volume, so that he has the sensation of having actually increased the flow of gas to a real engine. As he drives, the film can show him curves in the road, and as he turns the wheel, he can have the illusion that his automobile is turning. The system of the automobile on the road has been reproduced in a simulation. In the simulator, the student can be presented with learning tasks to which he can respond, but his responses do not have the same consequences that they would have in a real-life situation, that is, the student's simulated automobile does not crash into anything, although it looks like it is crashing from his point of view. Also, he can be presented with tasks (in the manner of training psychology) which are less complex than those he would have to execute in the real world, in order to help him acquire the skills he would later need for real world operation. For example, in a driver-simulator, the student can simply practice shifting from one gear to another, until he has the feel of that and has it down pat. He can also practice putting the brake on, and turning the wheel, and get some sense of how the automobile responds when he does those things.

The advantages of a simulator are several for certain kinds of training. One is that things can be made much less complex than in the real world to provide the student with the opportunity to master tasks that are extremely difficult when all the factors of real-world operation impinge upon him. A very good example of this is the flying of an airplane. To learn how to fly a complex airplane without the aid of a simulator leaves very little room for error. A student pilot has to do everything adequately the first time, or the plane is in difficulty. By the use of a simulator, training can be staged. The trainee can be introduced to simple tasks, and then more complex ones until he builds up a repertoire adequate for piloting the ship. Also, difficulties of various kinds can be simulated, as storms, mechanical difficulties and so on, and he can learn how to cope with those kinds of things. Thus, when he comes to the real-world situation, he has built up the repertoire necessary for his operation. In the second case, the use of a simulator permits the student to learn from self-generated feedback which he experiences himself. As he turns the wheel of the great plane to the right, for example, he can feel the plane bank; he can feel the loss of speed in some respects and he can learn what needs to be done in order to trim the craft during the turn. In other words, he can learn through his own senses, rather than simply through verbal descriptions, the corrective behaviors which are necessary. If in the driver simulation, he heads towards curves too rapidly, and then has to jerk the wheel in order to avoid going off the simulated road, this feedback permits him to adjust his behavior, so that when he is on a real road, he will be more gingerly as he approaches sharp turns. The cybernetic psychologist designs simulators in this way—so that by receiving feedback about the consequences of his behavior, the learner is able to modify his own responses, and develop a repertoire of appropriate behaviors.

Some very eleborate applications of cybernetic psychology have been made in military training. For example, there is a submarine simulator in which several members of the crew are connected by the radio and other communication devices that are used. They are able to take their "submarine" under water, to maneuver against enemy ships, to put their periscope up, to site ships through the periscope, to fire torpedoes. The simulator is constructed so that they can then be attacked by enemy destroyers, and they can emerge and engage in evasive action, hearing their enemy only over sonar and other undersea listening devices.

Thus far, the applications within normal elementary and secondary education are somewhat less spectacular, although the Metropolitan Studies Center of Washington, D.C. has developed an urban simulator with which they are experimenting with children from the upper elementary grades.[25] Omar Khayyam Moore's famous talking typewriter really simulates a human being who talks back to the student as he presses typewriter keys representing particular words or letters. However, most applications to education up to this point are fairly simple. If we look at a number of them, the cybernetic principles will be made more explicit than we can make them didactically.

## The Life Career Game

The Life Career Game was developed to assist guidance counselors and students in their mutual task of planning for the future, a task which requires the student to take into account many factors such as job oppor-

[25] Washington Center for Metropolitan Studies, 1717 Massachusetts Ave., Washington, D.C.

tunities, labor market demands, social trends and educational requirements.[26] Vocational and educational guidance attempts to assist students in becoming aware of these multiple factors, to evaluate their significance, and to generate alternative decisions.

In the Life Career Game the student is able to *interact* with these various components of the environment. He makes decisions about jobs, further education or training, family life, and the use of leisure time and receives feedback on the probable consequences of these decisions. The environment in this case is represented by other persons or organizations. That is, the responses from the environment are determined by the probability of the responses from persons in the actual roles of teachers, college admissions officers, employers, and marriage partners. As the player moves through the different environments of school, work, family, and leisure, he is able to see the interrelationships among his decisions and among the components of his life. The game is played as follows:

> The Life Career Game can be played by any number of teams, each consisting of two to four players. Each team works with a profile or case history of a fictitious person (a student about the age of the players).
>
> The game is organized into rounds or decision periods, each of which represents one year in the life of this person. During each decision period, players plan their person's schedule of activities for a typical week, allocating his time among school, studying, job, family responsibilities, and leisure time activities. Most activities require certain investments of time, training, money and so on (for example, a full-time job takes a certain amount of time and often has some educational or experience prerequisites as well; similarly having a child requires considerable expenditure of time, in addition to financial expenses), and a person clearly cannot engage in all the available activities. Thus, the players' problem is to choose the combination of activities which they think will maximize their person's present satisfaction and his chances for a good life in the future....
>
> When players have made their decisions for a given year, scores are computed in four areas—education, occupation, family life, and leisure. Calculations use a set of tables and spinners—based upon U.S. Census and other national survey data which indicate the probability of certain things happening in a person's life, given his personal characteristics, past experiences, and present efforts. A chance or luck factor is built into the game by the use of spinners and dice.
>
> A game usually runs for a designated number of rounds (usually ten to twelve) and the team with the highest total score at the end is the winner.[27]

The variations of the Life Career Game serve to illustrate the educational features of a simulation game as well as the enormous potential of simulation for incorporating several educational objectives into the basic simulation

---

[26] Barbarba B. Varenhorst, "The Life Career Game: Practice in Decision-Making," *Simulating Games in Learning,* Sarane Boocock and E. O. Schild, eds. (Beverly Hills, Calif.: Sage Publications, Inc., 1968).

[27] Sarane S. Boocock, "An Experimental Study of the Learning Effects of Two Games with Simulated Environments," *Simulating Games in Learning,* p. 108.

game design. For instance, every simulation implies a theory about behavior in the area of life being simulated. This is represented in the goal-achievement rules (the objectives of the game), and the rules governing the environmental responses.

One version of the Life Career Game assumes that every person receives a different amount of satisfaction from each of the several areas of life. Put another way, each person attaches a different amount of importance to the various areas of life. Following this assumption, each player determines his own goals by weighing these areas in terms of importance to him. At the end of the game, the objective achievements in those areas are converted to subjective satisfaction according to the weighted conversion ratios selected by the player. Alternately, if one of the processes being simulated is the selection and modification of goals contingent upon the consequences of one's actions, the player may be asked to weigh these areas at various times during the course of play. In both cases, the student is "playing against" the environment according to a personal criteria rather than an externally determined goal (i.e., Do I have more points than someone else?).

The game may also be played to include certain requisite skills such as actually making formal applications for jobs and interviews, selecting courses, setting up interviews, selecting courses from the college catalog. It can also be conducted to allow group discussion at the end of rounds, analyzing and challenging each other's decisions and identifying the values underlying them.

## A Computer-Based Economic Game

Two computer-based economics games for sixth graders were recently developed by the Center for Educational Services and Research of the Board of Cooperative Educational Services (BOCES) in Northern Westchester County, New York.[28] The use of the computer adds the possibility of individualizing the simulation in learning pace, scope, sequence, and difficulties of material. Aside from this feature, the properties of the simulation remain the same as in other non-computer-based simulation games.

One game, the Sumerian Game, is intended to instruct the student in the basic principles of economics as applied to three stages of a primitive economy, an agricultural period, the development of crafts, and the introduction of trade and other changes. The game is set during the time of the Neolithic revolution is Mesopatamia about 3500 B.C. The student is asked to take the role of the ruler of the city-state of Lagash, who must make certain agricultural decisions for his kingdom at each six-month harvest.

[28] Center for Educational Services and Research, Board of Cooperative Educational Services, 42 Triangle Center, Yorktown Heights, N.Y. 10598.

For example, he is presented with the following problematic situation: "We have harvested 5,000 bushels of grain to take care of 500 people. How much of this grain will be set aside for next season's planting and how much will be stored in the warehouse?"[29] The student is asked to decide how much grain to allocate for consumption, for production, and for inventory.

These situations become more complex as the game continues, for the student must take into account such circumstances as changes in population, the acquisition of new land, and irrigation. Periodically, technological innovations and disasters alter the outcome of his decisions. The effect of each decision upon the economic condition of the kingdom is shown in an immediate progress report. Students are apprised of certain quantitative changes, i.e., in population, in the amount of harvested grain, and in inventory, and are furnished with some substantive analyses of their decisions, "The quantity of food the people received last season was far too little."[30] In Phase Two of the Sumerian Game, the student can apply his surplus grain to the development of crafts.

## INTER-NATION SIMULATION

Harold Guetzkow and his associates developed a very complex and interesting simulation for use at the high school and upper secondary levels for teaching students principles of international relations.[31] The inter-nation simulation consists of five "nation" units, and the participants are grouped into these nations as the decision-makers and "aspiring decision-makers" within the countries. The development of the relations among the nations has been derived from the characteristics of nations and from principles which have been observed to operate among nations in the past. Each of the decision-making teams have available to them information about the country. This information has to do with the national economic systems' basic capability, the consumer capability, what is called "force" capability, or the ability of the nation to develop military goods and services, and trade and aid information. The nations play together an international relations game which involves trading and the development of agreements of various kinds. International organizations can be established, for example, or mutual aid agreements, or trade agreements. The nations can even make war on one another, or go to war, the outcome being determined by the relative force capability of one group of allies against another group. The

---

29 Richard L. Wing, "Two Computer-Based Economic Games for Sixth Graders," *Simulation Games in Learning*, Sarane Boocock and E. O. Schild, eds., p. 156.

30 *Ibid.*, p. 164.

31 Harold Guetzkow *et al.*, *Simulation in International Relations* (Englewood Cliffs, N.J.: Prentice-Hall, 1963).

simulation enables students to play the roles of decision-makers in nations, to be required to make realistic negotiations of the kinds diplomats and other representatives of nations have to make as nations interact with one another, and to refer to the economic conditions of one another as they do so. In the course of this game-type simulation, the student learns ways in which economic restraints operate on a country. For example, if he is the member of the decision-making team of a small country and he tries to engage in a trade agreement, he finds that he has to give something in order to get something. If his country has a largely agricultural economy, and he is dealing with an industrialized nation, he finds that is in a disadvantageous position unless that nation badly needs the product which he has to sell. By receiving feedback about the consequences of his decisions, therefore, the student and his fellow participants come to an understanding of the kinds of principles which actually operate in international relations.

### Cybernetic Psychology
### and the Classroom Teacher

The cybernetic psychologist attempts to study human beings by making analogies to electronic feedback systems, and he attempts to apply those analogies to the development of training devices. Simulators are only one of the kinds of training devices that have been made by the application of cybernetic principles, but they are an interesting one and show the possibilities in the area. Teachers can use cybernetic principles in two ways. First, of course, they can use game-type simulations, or other simulations, in their own teaching. Social studies teachers can use games prepared by the High School Geography Project,[32] or the urban simulator developed by the Urban Studies Council of Washington, D.C., or inter-nation or any of a wide number of games which have been prepared in that area. In driver training and other areas, simulation is frequently used as an aid to instruction—not really simply as an aid, but as a primary vehicle for instruction. In addition, however, the principle of simulation, that is, that people learn from the dynamic consequences of their own action, can be employed by any teacher who will help students engage in realistic activity, help them apprehend the results of their behavior, and learn to modify their behavior by understanding what they are doing and what they are about. For example, teacher-trainers now frequently use television tape as an aid to the teacher in training. The young teacher, as he teaches, is taped, and the tape is played back to him. As he analyzes the tape, he begins to see more clearly the consequences of his own behavior, and can engage in attempts to modify the behavior. Some young teachers find that the types and amounts of

---

[32] High School Geography Project (New York: Macmillan, 1970).

questions that they ask affect the responses of their students. If they ask questions requiring their students to think, the students are more likely to respond with thinking than if they ask questions which permit the student simply to recall information or follow directions. Learning this about his students' behavior, the teacher can begin to modify his own behavior—learning to ask questions which will pull more thinking from the student and which will challenge him more completely.

## INSTRUCTIONAL SYSTEMS, MATERIALS, AND MODELS OF TEACHING

In this chapter we have discussed at some length the development of instructional systems and throughout the book we have talked about the technical support systems need to implement a particular instructional model. Often this technical support has been of a material sort. Let us turn now to the interrelationships among instructional systems, materials, and the models of teaching. Although we are already familiar with the individual functions of the models for teaching and the instructional systems, we have not explicitly considered all the possible roles of instructional materials. In addition to providing the critical technical support needed to carry out teacher- or student-led instruction, instructional materials can, as in the case of the IPI instructional system, carry the major instructional responsibility. In either case, many models of teaching can be used to structure instructional systems and materials.

When the materials themselves carry the major instructional responsibility, they may be designed to actually embody one or more of the models. The model in this case is used to provide the specifications for the development of the materials. Some models for teaching stand out as being highly amenable as models for instructional materials. A clear example is the Behavior Modification Model (Chapter 16) which has probably been used much more as a model for instructional materials than for any other use. Programmed instruction is an example of one kind of material built according to the specifications of the Behavior Modification Model. The Advance Organizer Model (Chapter 10) is another model which is probably more suitable for instructional materials than for personal interaction. One can imagine developing materials using an advance organizer with student worksheets. In this case the model is being embodied in the material even when the material is functioning as a technical support.

Some of the other models are shaped in such a way that it is difficult to imagine building instructional materials around their structure, although instructional materials might be used to support them. An example is the Jurisprudential Teaching Model described in Chapter 3. This strategy was developed according to a view of dialogue about controversial public issues, and can be carried on only by a group of people in interaction with each other. It is not impossible to imagine programming a computer to accomplish some of the functions of dialogue specified by the Jurisprudential Teaching Model. However, it is more likely that one would build support systems of original documents, (as Oliver and Shaver have done to some extent) dealing with significant controversial issues and use these to support teacher-led inquiry, rather than trying to design a machine or a set of other materials to do the job.

Group Investigation (Chapter 2) is another strategy which is built around the interaction of a group and uses instructional materials, such as original source materials and documents, to *support* it. This model could be used to derive the specifications of those materials, but the materials themselves would not embody the phases, the emergent face-to-face interaction of the model, of the group investigation itself.

Procedures such as Synectics, Laboratory Method, and Awareness Training are designed around emergent interaction. While there are manuals which groups could follow in order to carry on appropriate activities or exercises, to build direct instructional materials around those models would not seem appropriate.

If instructional materials can be arranged so that they induce the learner to follow the phases of activity specified by a model, if the materials can provide some measure of the environmental responses that are necessary to help the learner on his way, if the materials can be made compatible with the social system requirements of the model, and if the technical supports can be built into the materials, then we can say that a model can serve as a structure around which instructional materials can be validly built. Clearly, it is possible to build a system of instructional materials which utilizes more than one model for its implementation. For example, one might use a program built on behavior modification principles to provide information to the student. A computer might then operate on an inductive model to induce the students to group the data and analyze the grouping. A simulation might then draw on this background in order to train students in the problem-solving skills relative to the domain involved. For example, in international relations one might begin with input of information about several nations, then proceed with the inductive analysis of that information, and finally engage in an inter-nation simulation game to teach students how nations with those characteristics might interact,* and the principles that would be likely to govern their involvements with one another.

To give some idea of the range of possibilities, we include here the bare outline of a design for a television-mediated instructional system structured around the Group Investigation Model (Chapter 2). It consists of the specifications for a television series trying to lead students to explore and attack the phenomenon of alienation in modern life.

# A TELEVISION-MEDIATED INSTRUCTIONAL SYSTEM DESIGNED TO EXPLORE THE PROBLEM OF ALIENATION

## THE MISSION:
## A WAR AGAINST ALIENATION

Our mission is to bring together the young people of America against the alienation that divides men in a mass society.

The term alienation has been rather loosely used in the popular press, although generally it refers to the sense of aloneness and disaffiliation among men in a mass technological society.

Kenneth Kenniston has become a spokesman for the factors which compound youth's dilemma against this general background of cultural alienation. He has pointed out that American society makes extraordinary demands on its members. In the first place they are asked to adapt to chronic social change. Ideas come in and out of fashion at a dizzying rate. The insatiable and pervasive media transmit these as fast as they are discovered. Under such conditions, a sense of the past which is so important to the achievement of an identity is virtually impossible. Second, Americans are asked to achieve a sense of personal wholeness and social integration in a complex and fragmented society. On the personal level, a man's specific work is but a fraction performed by the organization. In addition, his work is unrelated to other aspects of his life. In his public life, he is expected to be rational and cognitive while at home, in his private life, he is expected to be loving, passionate, and idealistic. On a social level, America is like a collection of minority groups rather than a main stream with variations. Caste and class combine with ethnic stratification to separate Americans from each other. In a societal matrix, there is a great sense of fragmentation and separation both from oneself and from others, conditions which prevent a sense of personal wholeness and identity. Third, there is an extraordinary discontinuity between childhood and adulthood. The adolescent is required to negotiate his way toward adulthood in a situation of extreme competitiveness (which itself increases alienation) and great uncertainty. The adolescent is required to make decisions which will affect his entire life during a period in which he is very young and while faced with an almost impossibly complex economic and social matrix through which he must find his way. To achieve participation in the culture he has to accomplish many years of an education that often seems irrelevant to his growing up. (In fact, it has been tailored to his later education and work rather than to his needs as a growing individual.) Last, the adolescent has to make this negotiation in an intellectual climate which makes the development of positive values very difficult. As Friedenberg has pointed out, in an open technological society, the pressures to conform are fantastic, because by conforming and by becoming impersonally and technologically capable, great economic reward is possible. Also, there exists in American society sets of spoken values which conflict with behaviors that are actually carried on. For many years a prime example of this has been the belief that all citizens are equal and are treated equally by official agencies. Recently, of course, there has become general verbal recognition that this is not so. To the young person, such a conflict between spoken values and behavior by adults appears to be extremely cynical and it disrupts the dialogue which might otherwise take place between the young and the old, making it difficult for the young to receive the help they might otherwise receive from older persons.

The purpose of the instructional system which we propose will be to reduce the sense of alienation and to decrease the fact of alienation by enabling young people to make life more personal and more filled with the dialogue in which they and their elders examine this aspect of society and attempt to do something about it.

## The General Behavioral Objectives

It is not possible in a document of reasonable length to provide the detailed behavioral objectives which are necessary to develop a complete curricular approach. However, it is necessary to provide enough behavioral objectives to give the reader a clear idea of the direction that we are recommending. The first objectives that we will mention are positive in nature and are behaviors to be acquired. The second set of behaviors we will mention are negative in the sense that they are behaviors to be reduced. For one of the goals of the effort is to reduce alienation.

1. *Knowledge of and ability to apply Keniston's conceptual framework for analyzing alienation in contemporary society.* The achievement of this objective would be demonstrated by the student's ability to use Kenniston's concepts to describe behavior in the contemporary society, including exemplars from his own behavior and those of his associates, and the ability to point out or demonstrate exemplars of alienated and non-alienated behavior.

2. *Knowledge of and ability to apply conceptual systems for analyzing bureaucratic behavior in contemporary society.* The achievement of this objective could be demonstrated as in the case immediately above.

3. The willingness to engage in a dialogue with peers and elders over the problem of alienation and affiliation in the society.

4. The willingness and ability to study alienated and non-alienated behavior in the individual's local situation. Implied is the ability to carry on surveys of behavior and to interpret the results of those surveys.

5. The ability to carry on interpersonal relations in such a way that impersonal and personal contact is established. This implies the ability of the student to control his own behavior so that he achieves the ability to personalize his behavior as well as to depersonalize it.

6. The formulation of a plan for reducing alienation in a situation in which the student has involvement. This includes working together with others in the school situation to create a less alienated and more authentic and affiliated mode of behavior within that institution.

7. The ability and willingness to formulate and defend a plan for reducing alienation in this nation. This again implies the ability to work together with others, for very few individuals could formulate such a plan alone, and the willingness to debate the plan with those who might help one to put it into effect.

## Negative Objectives

The following objectives describe the manifestations of a reduction in alienation.

8. A decrease in withdrawal from social contact or avoidance of dialogue with peers and elders. This implies that, given the opportunity, students

would be more likely to engage in attempts to interact with others, particularly in warm and authentic ways.

9. A decrease in hostile acts including criminal behavior, a willingness to face problems openly and directly and to try to work out mutual solutions.

10. A reduction in feelings of aloneness and fear of contact with others.

11. A reduction in feelings of futility with respect to the "system" and with respect to making contact with other individuals. This objective derives from the fact that alienated individuals frequently feel that it is impossible to cope with the existing order of things either with respect to large organizations and routines or with respect to making personal contact with other individuals who can interact openly.

These are really very general objectives which are only designed to give the flavor of the specificity with which our mission should be approached.

## THE TEACHING STRATEGY

Our strategy is designed to capitalize on the unique advantages of television to enable people all over the country to engage in a simultaneous study of matters of concern to all. The strategy is to introduce the curriculum to the largest number of students possible, including secondary school and junior high school students from all over the nation if that can be arranged. (However, there would be considerable benefits from a curriculum directed only to the entirety of a metropolitan area or a state.) The strategy hinges on the possibilities of using open-circuit television plus television tapes to induce the students from all over the area concerned (we will speak of the nation for illustrative purposes) to engage in the simultaneous study of alienation. This nation-wide student body would develop ways of attacking and defeating alienation and replacing bureaucratic contact with authentic personal contact and meaningful interpersonal relationships. The key idea is the radical one of trying to induce a national group investigation into the problem area—to apply the Thelenesque strategy to what would result in cooperative groups all over the nation being related to each other by means of television, working in the same area. Let's see how this might work—group investigation on a nationwide scale.

### Phase One

The strategy begins with televised confrontations with the problem situation. These confrontations can be in the form of dramatizations or puzzling incidents which are related to alienation. An example would be the Kitty Genovese incident in which apartment dwellers in New York heard and at times watched a young woman being stabbed to death in the courtyard of the apartment house and declined to get involved even to the extent of calling the police. But alienation comes in many forms less dramatic, and a good many of the confrontations should deal with the less dramatic but equally important incidents of human behavior which exemplify the alienated condition. Alienation is so widespread in the contemporary human scene that the task of generating the dramatization should be discouragingly easy. Driver behavior, for example, or commuter behavior in subways, behavior in large organizations, competitive situations, all abound.

Our suggestion is that the sequence begin with the presentation of a number of dramatizations in which various types of alienated behavior are illustrated. These should include routine behavior toward others, the failure to respond or get involved in social situations, withdrawal, criminal behavior of various kinds, interpersonal situations in which individuals do not respond to one another with warmth and authenticity, and others.

## Phase Two

In the second stage, following the Thelen sequence, students should begin to make clear their reactions to the situations. For this purpose classes of youngsters in high schools and junior high schools throughout the country could react to the incidents and groups of them could be brought together to make television tapes or to have discussions which would be broadcast live in which they would share their various reactions. A dramatization should stimulate a wide variety of reactions and the variety itself should be puzzling to the student. Some students will not see the alienating effects of competition, or cliques, etc., whereas others will feel them keenly.

Ideally, classrooms all over the country would discuss their reactions to the confrontation dramatizations and then representatives from various regions of the country would appear on television to describe their reactions. This would set the stage for the next phase of the work, planning inquiry into the problem area.

## Phase Three

At this point, using a nationwide hookup, social scientists could meet with the students in the studio and help them to formulate inquiry into their reactions to the situations that they had observed. Some of the scholars could introduce them to frameworks for analyzing various phenomena in the alienation complex. Television tapes could be prepared also and distributed to local classrooms to provide suggestions for lines of study into the phenomena.

This phase could be shaped so as to induce groups of local students in classrooms all over the country not only to study the confrontation dramatizations and the questions they raise, but also to expand their range of study into their community life and to begin to study the same phenomena in daily life that they are studying by means of their analysis of the confrontation dramatization.

As the study proceeded, classrooms could communicate problems and progress by television. Again the nationwide hookup could be used to provide consultation with social scientists over the study problems as they developed. For example, if a group of students in New York, Los Angeles, and New Orleans were studying bureaucratic behavior in large organizations, the social scientist might appear on the television hookup and present to them ways to go about their study. Simultaneously, television tapes could be made and distributed to the local schools providing further and perhaps more detailed advice.

As the studies proceeded, students could begin to share their findings with students in other parts of the United States. Other students could comment on the findings and the social scientists could have their commentary as well. The results of the students' study could be compared with the results of scholarly study. Keniston, for example, could compare the findings of his analysis with those that are being turned up by students in various parts of the United States.

As soon as the studies were developed considerably and had been discussed and analyzed thoroughly, it would be time for the next phase.

## Phase Four

In phase four the television medium would be used to challenge the students to two kinds of efforts. One would be to formulate plans to reduce alienation in some aspects of their lives. A second would be to formulate plans which could be applied on a nationwide scale to reduce alienation.

Over the nationwide network students and experts could present their plans as they were formulated, criticize the plans, and discuss their implementation. Groups in various parts of the United States which were formulating similar plans could be addressed over the nationwide network or through specially prepared television tapes to provide consultation from experts. (During all the phases up to this point, quite a number of programs would continue to introduce theoretical and student-generated ways of looking at the allienation problem so that in the course of the phases a rather complete coverage of the area would be ensured.) Considerable time would be taken with this phase so that alternative approaches to the reduction of alienation could be well aired and analyzed.

## Phase Five

In this phase local groups would begin to put into effect their plans for alleviating some aspect of alienation within the orbit of their competence. As the plans were put into action, they would be reported over the nationwide network and particular local groups would prepare television tapes which would be sent to other local groups reporting their progress and problems. As the progress and problems were reported, experts would address the local group over the nationwide network and also use the medium of video-tape.

Simultaneous with the local activity, a nationwide organization of children would be started using the nationwide network and representatives of the local groups throughout the country would be put together to select some aspect of alienation for a nationwide frontal attack.

## Phase Six

In this phase the local efforts would continue and more nationwide effort would be inaugurated. The nationwide network would be used to coordinate the efforts, to keep the students from various aspects of the country in contact with one another, and to develop and refine further plans. Using the nationwide network, aspects of the plan could be put into effect simultaneously all over the country. For example, let us suppose that one aspect of the plan was to increase warmth in hitherto impersonal relations such as the way that one related to restaurants, waiters, and waitresses. Over the nationwide network, ways of doing this could be discussed and the students could set a target date for implementing the new form of behavior. Then, simultaneously all over the United States, restaurant employees would find that young people were acting differently toward them. The students would know the plan was being implemented throughout the United States, they would have the reinforcement of the nationwide community, and the obligation of holding up their end of the game.

## Phase Seven

Phase Seven would consist of reports from local activities and the preparation for further national action. In addition, students would be taught how to engage in evaluation of their efforts, that is, how to determine whether or not they would be becoming less alienated in interpersonal relations and in inducing less alienation in other people.

Though the essence of Group Investigation is found chiefly in the emergent face-to-face interaction of the participants (a highly appropriate model given the nature of the problem of alienation), the instructional materials, in this case, television tapes, are critical supports in several phases of the model. As mentioned earlier in this chapter, the materials themselves, while not embodying the Group Investigation Model, derive their specification from it. For instance, Phase One of the model calls for confronting incidents. Television tapes showing dramatizations of puzzling incidents would be prepared. Instructional materials again play a critical role in Phase Three as students are introduced to frameworks for analyzing phenomena related to alienation and other sources on the problem itself. We might imagine these instructional sequences (tapes) constructed along other models from the academic disciplines. We could also forsee instructional sequences built around a Taba's Concept Formation strategy (Chapter 7) or Bruner's Concept Attainment Model (Chapter 6) as students attempt to formulate or apply their understanding of the concept of alienation. The models could also be used for informational sequences showing alienation in the particular communities. In Phase Five tapes built around simulation strategy could "play-out" some of the consequences of plans to reduce alienation.

# 21

# FOR AN IMPROVED BASIS

# FOR DIALOGUE

We have repeatedly voiced our hope that the 1970s would see a renewal of vigorous and humble dialogue on approaches to education. There is much quackery abroad in educationland—much selling of models as panaceas with little evidence that they can achieve even limited goals. No more fruitful is the assertion that action in education is not justified until there is proof of the superiority of whatever is tried. There is as yet so little certain evidence available to us that to wait for evidence would require us to cease most educational activity for a generation or more.

What is needed is a proper recognition of our ignorance combined with acceptance of the stance that we have many hypothetical bases for action—bases which we can use for present action. In fact, so many and different ones are available that the likelihood that any one of us has opened the way to all the truth is ridiculously unlikely. Vigorous experimentation and lively debate appear very much in order.

## DIMENSIONS FOR DEBATE

Any debate in education should be directed toward action, for educational theory is the theory of action in education. To analyze, debate, and experiment with models of teaching requires that we identify classes of activity to which the models can be related. We postulate that there are three dimensions to the educational environment to which models of teaching can be related. These are: the personal dimension, involving the individual's quest for meaning and development; the social dimension, involving both the interpersonal aspects of teaching and the obligation to the larger society, and the need to improve it and find meaning in relation to it; and the intellective dimension, relating to sources for improved problem-solving strategies.

We can discuss models for teaching in terms of their relevance to each of these. In the first place, some of the models emphasize one or more of the dimensions. In Group Investigation, for example, the social system is specified in detail and dominates the others. Similarly, Non-Directive Teaching and Laboratory Method are primarily social models also. The information-based models, on the other hand, are generally curricular in nature, for they specify type and nature of learning activities. The Conceptual Systems Model is designed to generate differential systems which relate environments and students. If an educational environment is designed solely in terms of one of these models, then one system or dimension of the environment is likely to be emphasized and the others to be deemphasized.

Another and not entirely different way to analyze models for teaching is in terms of the specifications which they yield for each of the dimensions. We can ask, for example, what the Developmental Model says for the specification of each of the dimensions, and we find that it is fairly clear with respect to curricular and social systems and less clear but still applicable to the derivation of others. Hunt's differential model begins with differentiation, for the individual has much to say about the social system, and speaks to aspects of curricular structure and complexity. Behavior modification is quite versatile, speaking to all dimensions, but assuming the learner is dependent on the social environment.

Thus, we find that models differ with respect to the dimensions they emphasize and can provide specifications for (Figure 21-1). There are two implications of this finding; one is that some models need to be augmented to be fully implementable (all three dimensions need to be filled in); the other that in the creation of environments models will have varying utility, some providing help in some areas, others in different ones.

As a comparison of models proceeds on this basis, dialogue should emerge on the philosophical implications of differences in the shape of environments derived from the models. Part of the debate can center around learning output and involve questions about what different models are good for and how efficient they are. For example, some will debate that some of the *less* efficient models in terms of skill and knowledge outcomes are preferable because of desirable social effects. (There will be two sides to that debate!)

Probably a more significant set of questions concerns the implication of "living" a model. What are the relatively permanent effects on students of living in a client-centered environment, an environment steeped in group

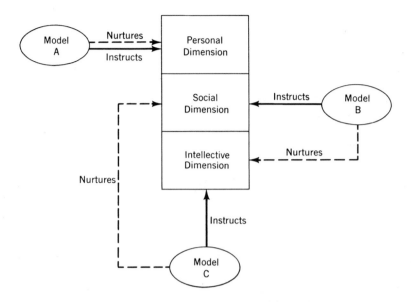

**Figure 21-1** Relationship of Three Hypothetical Models to Three Dimensions of Teaching

analysis, one centered on academic debate? Does a student gradually come to construct reality in a way that reflects his educational environment? In an environment characterized by instructional systems would a student gradually become production-oriented and utilitarian, whereas in an awareness-training environment would he gradually become more humanistic and personal? In short, does living a model produce replicas of it in the form of student personality, aside from intended outcomes, as skills developed, knowledge acquired, and attitudes formed?

We believe the answer to these last questions is resoundingly "yes," and we offer the following propositions for discussion:

1. That the major significant differences between models are less in their efficiency for achieving particular instructional goals than in the effects of their internalization by the student. Educationally speaking, one becomes what he lives. It is the differences in nurturant effects that make the real differences.

2. That there are significant differences between models. Exposed to a particular environment for a reasonable time, one begins to construct reality in ways similar to that environment.

3. That every environment has a ceiling of growth. Thus a pluralistic environment, one reflecting several models, is necessary if the student is to go beyond the limits of his mentors and create new syntheses. (See Chapter 20.)

Thus, the students will benefit most from teachers and schools which manifest multiple ways of educating, not because educational pluralism offers something for everyone but because the exposure to several vigorous ways of living will induce greater complexity of growth and ward off those great subverters of education—dogmatism and boredom!

We *could* extend this discussion into a long exhortation, but the issues should be worked out in dialogue, not in one-sided exposition—so we close with the hope that teachers and other educational workers will continue the dialogue through word and, far more important, through action. The glassy homogeneity of our schools at present simply cries out for more models which are actualized, schools with vigorously developed, unique characters.

## NEEDS FOR RESEARCH

There is great need for research which examines the dimensions of the instructional and nurturant effects of the various models or various individuals. There has been much research on various models but most of it has taken place within the framework of one model rather than in a cross-disciplinary framework. There are some notable exceptions, such as Almy's study of the effect of teaching the structures of the disciplines on the logical thinking of young children.[1] Shaver and Oliver examined recitative and dialogue-based approaches to the teaching of the jurisprudential framework.[2] Roberts examined the use of laboratory method in social studies teaching.[3] Sohuck studied the use of forms of organizers on learning within the BSCS framework.[4] Romberg and Wilson examined a variety of forms of organizers with respect to various learning outcomes.[5] Hawkes studied the effects of operant conditioning on student's inductive activity in studying important social problems.[6]

[1] Mildred Almy, *Logical Thinking in Second Grade* (New York: Teachers College Press, 1970).

[2] Donald W. Oliver and James P. Shaver, "The Effect of Student Characteristics and Teaching Method Interactions on Learning to Think Critically." Unpublished paper presented to the American Educational Research Association, February 1968.

[3] Julian Roberts, *Human Relations Training and Its Effect on the Teaching-Learning Process in Social Studies.* Final Report, New York State Education Department, Division of Research, Albany, New York, August 1969.

[4] Robert F. Sohunk, "An Assessment of the Impact of Set Induction Upon Student Achievement and Retention." Unpublished paper, University of Southern California School of Medicine.

[5] Thomas A. Romberg and James Wilson, "The Effect of an Advanced Organizer, Cognitive Set, and Post Organizer on the Learning and Retention of Written Materials." Unpublished paper presented at the Annual Meeting of the American Educational Research Association, Minneapolis, March 1970.

[6] Ellen Hawkes, "The Effects of an Instruction Strategy on Approaches to Problem-Solving." Unpublished Doctoral dissertation, Teachers College, Columbia University, 1971.

All of these studies represent the type of cross-disciplinary framework which is necessary if the nurturant and instructional effects of the models are to be studied in productive relationship with one another.

## CODA

Our final word is one of caution and hope intermingled. Models of teaching are often deliberate and theoretical. Those are the kinds we have emphasized in this book. Others are patterns which emerge from intuition. Some of the latter are very attractive. Others are not so pleasant. By analyzing practice, using a framework for describing and clarifying its meaning, we can see more clearly what the teacher is up to. For example, let us look at an educational practice which is truly horrifying but which has elements which are not uncommon in real schools.

## A MODEL NOBODY WILL LOVE

The following is partly comic, partly serious, and intended to be provocative of the value issues in teaching.

### BASIC ORIENTATION

The model is designed to make the student docile. He is to be alienated from his fellow man and then provided with an ideology which will direct his behavior.

If he learns his lessons well, he is rewarded with privilege and responsibility. If he does not, he is subjected to scorn and subjected to deprivation, physically and socially. Then, when he begs for surcease, he is given the opportunity to practice his ideology until he is ready for responsibility.

This process is repeated until he loses a sense of any egoistic self and is ready to submerge himself in the discovery of the true way to fulfillment.

The family of the model is, of course, the anti-person, anti-social, anti-informational family, a category especially created for this illustration.

### *Structure or Phasing*

In the first phase, the subject is quartered with a group of fellow subjects in a hut on a campus which is removed from ordinary social activities. Any in the group who show signs of leadership are removed from the group until only the apathetic remain. "Group members" are interviewed daily and asked to relate defects in the character or behavior of the others. The interviewer lets each individual know what he has heard about them and once a day the information gleaned about each is publicly narrated to all in a group meeting. If this phase is successful, members of the group become increasingly suspicious of one another, interact less, and members become unable to respond to initiative from their peers.

*Phase Two*

Contact with the outside world is discontinued. No letters or telephone calls or mass media are permitted. The members receive tranquilizing drugs at breakfast and at night. Rote lessons on the evils of old social systems and advantages of the new social ideology are begun. If any members resist, all are punished by deprivation of food, warmth, and clothing.

In addition, each member publicly states his own defects at group meetings. All members correct him if he falters or defends himself in any way.

*Phase Three*

The conditions of Phase Two are maintained. Rote lessons now concentrate on the defects of the United States imperialist system and remedies proposed by the International Committee on World Social Improvement.

Lessons learned well are rewarded with food, clothing, or shelter. These are removed if resistance or inadequate learning occurs. The group is encouraged to deal with any members who cause deprivation in this way.

*Phase Four*

The conditions of Phase Three are maintained. Interviews are initiated with individuals, who are offered the opportunity to serve the New Ideology in a number of ways. They may make radio broadcasts or write news stories denouncing the old ideology and praising the new. They can defect from the old country to the new. They can return to the old country to initiate revolutionary activity or to carry on espionage activities.

When judged ready, they can leave the campus and rejoin society in these roles.

## PRINCIPLES OF REACTION BY TRAINING AGENTS

Trainers are to be alert for leadership and to remove leadership when it is found. In the early stages they are to humiliate the students and drive them from each other. In the later phases, they should encourage individuals who have become completely docile or who eagerly seize the new ideology and wish to serve it. They should punish severely those who wish personal profit or privilege, however, by depriving his group of clothing and shelter until he confesses his egoism and recants his personal desires.

## SOCIAL SYSTEM

Leadership is to be entirely with the trainers. Social control is to be punitive and mass punishment, with consequent retaliation by group members on the offender, is to be employed.

Members are to become alienated from one another until they become totally dependent on the mediators of the New Ideology. They are to become completely subservient to the ideology.

## CLASSROOM IMPLEMENTATION

Generally, the model is not designed for use in the classroom and its use in American classrooms will be left to the reader's imagination.

## GENERAL APPLICABILITY

The most famous application was, of course, in prison camps in Korea during the period 1950 to 1953, in the so-called "brainwashing" of the Americans imprisoned by the Chinese People's Republic. The direct purpose was to produce turncoats who would provide propaganda for the Communists' public relations arm. The latent effects, of course, were to destroy ego-mediation and produce individuals incapable of acting as individuals or of relating warmly with their fellow men.[7]

**TABLE 21-1 Summary Chart: Brainwashing Model**

| *Syntax:* | *Phase One* | *Phase Two* |
|---|---|---|
| The phases can be identified as follows: | Deprivation of privacy and dignity. Establishment of physical punishment. | Development of group pressure and alienation. Introduction of ideology. |
| | *Phase Three* | *Phase Four* |
| | Indoctrination to New Ideology. | Preparation for subversion of Old Order. |

The instructional and nurturant effects can be diagramed as follows (Figure 21-2):

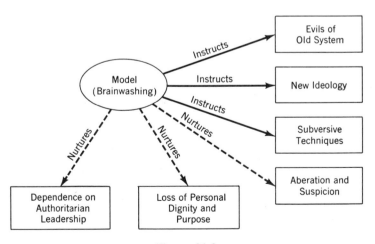

**Figure 21-2**

[7] See Eugene Kincaid, *In Every War But One* (New York: Norton, 1959).

## WARNING!

The frightening thing is the similarity of elements of the Brainwashing Model to common educational practices. For example, competition is common in some schools. It tends to isolate students from each other and to alienate them from themselves. Public self-criticism is not uncommon in circumstances less harsh than described above. Repetition of doctrine is by no means rare in schools and adherence to particular ideologies is certainly not unexpected (nor should it be, considering the function of the schools in the society). Many opinions, if expressed, are punished in many schools.

To live with truth and dignity as educators we have to teach so that our models have moral validity. When we select practices we nurture not only short-term growth but the testing of our students and our society. Deciding what to instruct and what to nurture and how to instruct and how to nurture are humble decisions made by each of us in our classrooms and in curricular and learning-material laboratories. These humble decisions, each affecting just a few students, operate to shape the reality of humanity, for all of us are created in some part by our teachers and by the models they use.

## INDEX